Brill's Studies in Intellectual History

General Editor

Han van Ruler (*Erasmus University, Rotterdam*)

Founded by

Arjo Vanderjagt

Editorial Board

C.S. Celenza (*Johns Hopkins University, Baltimore*)
M. Colish (*Yale University, New Haven*) – J.I. Israel (*Institute for Advanced Study, Princeton*) – A. Koba (*University of Tokyo*) – M. Mugnai (*Scuola Normale Superiore, Pisa*) – W. Otten (*University of Chicago*)

VOLUME 324

Brill's Texts and Sources in Intellectual History

General Editor

Leen Spruit (*Radboud University, Nijmegen*)

Editorial Board

J. Lagrée (*Université de Rennes 1*)
U. Renz (*Universität Klagenfurt*)
A. Uhlmann (*University of Western Sydney*)

VOLUME 23/3

The titles published in this series are listed at *brill.com/btsi*

Early Modern Prophecies in Transnational, National and Regional Contexts

Volume 3: The British Isles

Edited by

Lionel Laborie
Ariel Hessayon

BRILL

LEIDEN | BOSTON

Cover illustration: William Blake, 'Europe a Prophecy' (1794), plate 01.

Library of Congress Cataloging-in-Publication Data

Names: Laborie, Lionel, editor. | Hessayon, Ariel, editor.
Title: Early modern prophecies in transnational, national and regional contexts / edited by Lionel Laborie, Ariel Hessayon.
Description: Leiden ; Boston : Brill, 2020. | Series: Brill's studies in intellectual history, 0920-8607 ; volume 324/1- | "This edited collection of primary sources originates from a major international conference on early modern prophecies, which we organised at Goldsmiths,University of London, in June 2014"–ECIP acknowledgements. | Includes bibliographical references and index. | Contents: v. 1. Continental Europe – v. 2. The Mediterranean world – v. 3. The British Isles.
Identifiers: LCCN 2020040926 (print) | LCCN 2020040927 (ebook) | ISBN 9789004442658 (v. 1 ; hardback) | ISBN 9789004442634 (v. 2 ; hardback) | ISBN 9789004442641 (v. 3 ; hardback) | ISBN 9789004342668 (hardback) | ISBN 9789004443631 (ebook)
Subjects: LCSH: Prophecy–Christianity–History–Sources.
Classification: LCC BR115.P8 E27 2020 (print) | LCC BR115.P8 (ebook) | DDC 231.7/4509015–dc23
LC record available at https://lccn.loc.gov/2020040926
LC ebook record available at https://lccn.loc.gov/2020040927

Typeface for the Latin, Greek, and Cyrillic scripts: "Brill". See and download: brill.com/brill-typeface.

ISSN 0920-8607
ISBN 978-90-04-34266-8 (hardback, set)
ISBN 978-90-04-44265-8 (hardback, vol. 1)
ISBN 978-90-04-44263-4 (hardback, vol. 2)
ISBN 978-90-04-44264-1 (hardback, vol. 3)
ISBN 978-90-04-44363-1 (e-book)

Copyright 2021 by Koninklijke Brill NV, Leiden, The Netherlands.
Koninklijke Brill NV incorporates the imprints Brill, Brill Hes & De Graaf, Brill Nijhoff, Brill Rodopi, Brill Sense, Hotei Publishing, mentis Verlag, Verlag Ferdinand Schöningh and Wilhelm Fink Verlag.
All rights reserved. No part of this publication may be reproduced, translated, stored in a retrieval system, or transmitted in any form or by any means, electronic, mechanical, photocopying, recording or otherwise, without prior written permission from the publisher. Requests for re-use and/or translations must be addressed to Koninklijke Brill NV via brill.com or copyright.com.

This book is printed on acid-free paper and produced in a sustainable manner.

Printed by Printforce, the Netherlands

Contents

Abbreviations   VII
Notes on Contributors   VIII

Millenarianism and Prophecy in Eighteenth-Century Britain   1
   William Gibson

10 Jane Lead and the Philadelphians   31
   Ariel Hessayon

11 The French Prophets and the Scottish Mystics: Prophecies and Letters   158
   Michael B. Riordan

12 Thanksgiving and the Apocalypse: Two Eighteenth-Century Sermons   207
   Warren Johnston

Bibliography   269
Index   282

Abbreviations

AUL	Aberdeen University Library, Aberdeen, Scotland
AFSt	Archiv der Franckeschen Stiftungen zu Halle, Germany
Bodl.	Bodleian Library, Oxford, England
DWL	Dr Williams's Library, London, England
EUL	Edinburgh University Library, Edinburgh, Scotland
G & C	Gonville and Caius College, Cambridge, England
GCA	Glasgow City Archives and Special Collections, Mitchell Library, Glasgow, Scotland
LPL	Lambeth Palace Library, London, England
NLS	National Library of Scotland, Edinburgh, Scotland
NLW	National Library of Wales, Aberystwyth, Wales
NRS	National Records of Scotland, Edinburgh, Scotland

Notes on Contributors

William Gibson
is Professor of Ecclesiastical History at Oxford Brookes University and director of the Oxford Centre for Methodism and Church History. He specialises in the history of religion and politics in the period 1660–1900. He is the editor of the *Oxford Handbook of the British Sermon, 1689–1901* (Oxford: 2012) and author, with Joanne Begiato, of *Sex and the Church in the Long Eighteenth Century* (IB Tauris: 2017).

Ariel Hessayon
is a Reader in the Department of History at Goldsmiths, University of London. He is the author of one monograph and co-editor / editor of several collections of essays and primary sources. He has also written extensively on a variety of early modern topics: antiscripturism, antitrinitarianism, book burning, communism, environmentalism, esotericism, extra-canonical texts, heresy, crypto-Jews, Judaizing, millenarianism, mysticism, prophecy, and religious radicalism.

Warren Johnston
is an Associate Professor of History at Algoma University in Ontario, Canada. He specialises in the history of ideas in early modern Britain, and has published articles and books on apocalyptic thought and sermon literature in early modern Britain, including *Revelation Restored: The Apocalypse in Later Seventeenth-Century England* (Boydell: 2011) and *National Thanksgivings and Ideas of Britain, 1689–1816* Boydell: 2020).

Michael B. Riordan
(PhD, Cambridge) is an independent scholar based in Edinburgh. He has written widely about the French Prophets, Scottish mysticism and the religious culture of Scottish Episcopacy. His book, *The Moral Reformation in Scotland 1660–1730*, will shortly be published by Oxford University Press.

Millenarianism and Prophecy in Eighteenth-Century Britain

William Gibson

Introduction[1]

One of the features of religion in Britain in the long eighteenth century was the survival of what might be thought of by some scholars as an out-dated and regressive form of Christian belief: millenarianism and prophecy.[2] The biblical teachings of the second coming of the Messiah in books of the Old Testament, such as Isaiah and Daniel, and in some New Testament books, particularly the Book of the Revelation of St John the Divine, are various and indistinct. But by the time of the Reformation in Europe, the teaching had come to include the belief that the return of Christ would be prophesied so that the world could prepare. It was based on a new-found biblicism that Christ's second coming to judge the world was imminent, and that faith and repentance were the only preparation for it This was largely as a result of identifying the Papacy as the Antichrist, whose fall was believed to be a sign of the approach of the second coming. The fierce resistance by the Papacy of the Protestant presentation of the Gospel reinforced an intense sense of spiritual battle, which would only be settled in the "Last Day". A particular focus of the expectation was the restoration of the body of Jews, who had rejected Christ as the Messiah, as a culmina-

---

1 I am grateful to Simon Lewis, John Harding and Jonathan Pike for their advice and comments on an earlier version of this paper.
2 Prophecy and millenarianism ought not to be conflated since they represented distinct strands of Christianity, nevertheless in the eighteenth century they were linked in a way that makes separation of them problematic. The "Reformed" theologians, sometimes at least, recognize Providence as the immanent working of an eternal, sovereign divine purpose through the course of ordinary events. The biblical sense of "prophecy" is often misunderstood. It does not mean soothsaying, or foreseeing future events. It means an inspired comment on human deeds and concerns, given as a special revelation to humanity. Often the comments referred to the future, and well as the present. I owe this to John Harding. In this essay, prophecy and millenarianism are treated as aspects of the same scriptural traditions and religious movement. Important sources on this subject are L.E. Froom, *The Prophetic Faith of Our Fathers, The Historical Development of* Prophetic Interpretation, 4 vols (Washington DC: 1946–1954); S.C. Orchard, "English Evangelical Eschatology, 1790–1850", PhD thesis (Cambridge University: 1969); J.A. Oddy, "Eschatological Prophecy in the English Theological Tradition, c.1700-c.1840", PhD thesis (London University: 1982); J.F.C. Harrison, *The Second Coming and Popular Millenarianism, 1780–1850* (London: 1993).

tion of events before the end of the world. The return of Christ would, in some schemes, usher in a Millennium, a thousand years of divine rule on earth. This triumph of good over evil was the Apocalypse that would conclude with the end of the temporal world. Prophesy and forewarning were integral to the idea that the faithful would be alerted to what was to happen, so signs and symbols were vitally important means of identifying what would follow.

The Intellectual Tradition of Prophecy

In Britain, prophecy and millenarianism had a long intellectual tradition. Joseph Mede (1586–1639), the polymath fellow of Christ's College, Cambridge, was enormously influential in pressing home the scholarly legitimacy of the imminence of the second coming.[3] He even prophesied that the end of the world would come in 1716.[4] Mede's polymath talents meant that his ideas spread among theologians, scientists, naturalists and linguists.[5] He was a strong influence on Thomas Goodwin, the leader of the Independents under the Commonwealth, and later on Isaac Newton.[6] Newton wrote that "Mr Mede layed the foundations and I have built upon it".[7] Subsequent adherents of the importance of prophecy, such as Bishops Thomas Newton and William Warburton, also acknowledged a debt to Mede.[8] Despite the scepticism and derision of Deists, like Matthew Tindal, millenarianism remained as stubbornly influential in eighteenth-century Britain as Arianism.[9] William Lloyd and William Whiston subscribed to the idea that the Apocalypse was about to happen and therefore religious endeavour had to focus on prophesy and preparation for it. Others, like Newton, concluded that the Millennium was likely to occur much later, some said as late as the year 2000.[10] All of this ignored Christ's warning in Acts 1.7 that the thing they would not know was the date of the second coming.

---

3   J. Mede, *Clavis Apocalyptica, or, A Prophetical Key by which the Great Mysteries in the Revelation of St. John and the Prophet Daniel are Opened* … (1627; repr. London: 1651).
4   J. Mede, *The Key of the Revelation, Searched and Demonstrated Out of the Naturall and Proper Charecters of the Visions* (London: 1643).
5   J.K. Jue, *Heaven Upon Earth: Joseph Mede (1586–1638) and the Legacy of Millenarianism* (Dordrecht: 2006).
6   F.C. Mather, *High Church Prophet, Bishop Samuel Horsley (1733–1806) and the Caroline Tradition in the Later Georgian Church* (Oxford: 1992), 263.
7   Quoted in F.E. Manuel, *The Religion of Isaac Newton* (Oxford: 1974), 121.
8   Oddy, "Eschatological Prophecy in the English Theological Tradition", 12.
9   Tindal poked fun at Millenarianism in his *Christianity as Old as Creation: or, the Gospel a Republication of the Religion of Nature* (London: 1732), 236.
10 M.C. Jacob, *The Newtonians and the English Revolution* (Ithaca, N.Y.: 1976), 116. In addi-

Isaac Newton had begun to study the Apocalypse in the 1670s; he temporarily set aside the *Principia Mathematica* to work on the Bible. Although he sustained a lifelong interest in mystical religion, he was to return to biblical study in the last two decades of his life with renewed intensity. Remarkably, Newton's initial scepticism about the Trinity, and later flat rejection of it, did not challenge his absolute faith in the Bible, indeed he claimed that it was Scripture that taught him that Trinitarianism was a corruption of true Christianity.[11] He spent much time organising the prophecies in the Bible into an ordered and logical sequence. From these he concluded that he was living in the end of days and that he would be one of the faithful to whom divine revelation would be made. He brought a scientific rigour to the language of the biblical prophets, and sought to establish accurate rules for understanding the signs and symbols often used in biblical books, like Revelation. These included his own system of interpretation of metaphysical language.

Newton was powerfully influenced by the "Great Apostasy" that seemed to him to condemn the current events, in which Catholic Europe was a threatening force. He wrote frequently of the "Whore" who represented the arrival of the false prophets who would try to lead the world astray—though his work was largely devoid the establishment of connections between Biblical and contemporary events. In some respects, Newton held that holding firmly to biblical prophecies would insulate Christians against the claims of false prophets that he felt circulated in his time. What Newton seems to have spent a good deal of time on were the connections between the Bible's theoretical or entirely abstract images and signs and those which had some empirical value to people in the seventeenth century.[12] There is an assumption that Newton's ideas remained locked in his manuscripts until rediscovery in the twentieth century. In fact, Newton's executors permitted publication of his *Observations upon the prophecies of Daniel, and the Apocalypse of St. John* in 1733. Consequently, his ideas on the meaning of the two most important biblical books of prophecy were revealed to the public.[13]

---

tion, see Scott Mandelbrote, "Becoming Heterodox in Seventeenth-Century Cambridge: The Case of Isaac Newton", in *Erudition and Confessionalisation in Early Modern Europe*, ed. D. Levitin and N. Hardy (Oxford: 2019), 300–394; and S. Mandelbrote, "Newton and Eighteenth-Century Christianity", in *The Cambridge Companion to Newton*, ed. R. Iliffe and G. Smith (Cambridge: 2016), 554–585; and S. Mandelbrote and H. Pulte (eds), *The Reception of Isaac Newton in Europe* (London: 2019), 3 vols.

11 M. Wiles, *Archetypal Heresy, Arianism Through the Centuries* (Oxford: 2001).
12 We are only beginning to accommodate Newton's religious thinking in the light of Rob Illife's *The Priest of Nature, The Religious Worlds of Isaac Newton* (Oxford: 2017).
13 For the impact of the publication of Newton's work see R.G. Ingram, *Reformation without*

At the same time as Newton was developing ideas about the Apocalypse, Thomas Burnet published his *Sacred Theory of the Earth*.[14] Much of Burnet's work sought to endorse the biblical narratives of the creation. Like Newton, Burnet discussed whether the days in the Old Testament were the same length as days in their time. Both scholars pointed to the end of time in their works, and Burnet's defence of the literal accounts of the creation included claims that prophecy was also to be taken seriously. Burnet's work was enormously influential with Cambridge academics and established a strong link between the biblical narratives of the Flood and of creation, which suffused Christianity in the eighteenth century, and the expectation of an end of the world that also conformed to biblical accounts. Burnet's book went through numerous editions in the eighteenth century, with major republications and substantive additions in 1726 and 1753.[15]

When Burnet considered the structure of the earth, he suggested that such phenomena as earthquakes and comets were likely to be the signs and symbols sent from heaven as a warning that the world was coming to an end. In the eighteenth century, the earthquakes in Lisbon and London in the 1750s were regarded in this light. So were the Great Comet of 1680 and the return of Halley's Comet in 1682. Significantly, such portents were in the forefront of the minds of some of the leading bishops, such as Sancroft and Lloyd during the last months of James II's reign since they had both read Burnet's book.[16]

For some time, modern scholars seemed to think that Newton's eschatology represented the end of a religious tradition. Margaret Jacob commented that "after 1714 Millenarianism appears to be in complete decline in church circles"—though she conceded that it was sustained by John Wesley in early Methodism. She argued that the social and religious stability after the Han-

---

    End: Religion, Politics and the Past in Post-Revolutionary England (Manchester: 2018), chapter 12.

14   First published in 1681, its full title was *The Sacred theory of the earth: containing an account of the original of the earth and of all the general changes which it hath already undergone, or is to undergo, till the consumation of all things*.

15   J.E. Force & R.H. Popkin (eds), *Millenarianism and Messianism in Early Modern European Culture: Volume III: The Millenarian Turn: Millenarian Contexts of Science, Politics and Everyday Life in Anglo-American Life in the Seventeenth and Eighteenth Centuries* (Dordrecht: 2001). See for Burnet especially James E Force's essay: "The Virgin, the Dynamo and Newton's Prophetic History", 67–94.

16   Jacob, *The Newtonians and the English Revolution, 1689–1720*, 120–121. W. Johnston, *Revelation Restored: The Apocalypse in Later Seventeenth-Century England* (Woodbridge: 2011). T. Claydon, "Latitudinarianism and Apocalyptic History in the Worldview of Gilbert Burnet, 1643–1715", *The Historical Journal* 51/03 (2008), 577–597.

overian succession in Britain made millenarian ideas politically dangerous and socially marginalised. Inside the Church of England, millenarianism—or at least predicting and focusing on the Millennium—was associated with radicalism that had no place in the eighteenth century. Ironically, she also offered the explanation that millenarianism was affected by the rise of Newtonian science.[17] Yet, as Jacob conceded, some thinkers like William Whiston unconsciously deployed their millenarianism in defence of the new Hanoverian order, by seeing in the War of Spanish Succession and subsequent conflicts a holy conflict designed to suppress the Great Apostasy.[18]

Whiston saw himself as standing in a long tradition of eschatological thinking, including Mede, whose views he regarded himself as refining.[19] Whiston's views on the Apocalypse were developed in his Boyle Lectures of 1707. He argued that the spread of the Gospel to all lands would hasten the conversion of the Jews which was a biblical precondition to the second coming of Christ.[20] He expected the second coming in his own lifetime and said so. In the end, after a number of mistakes in calculations, he concluded that the world would end in 1736.[21] It was these warnings that coincided with those prophets who proclaimed the second coming in the heyday of the French Prophets.[22]

Politics and the Millennium

Political events were especially likely to be viewed as harbingers or portents of the second coming, for these were often seen as the way in which St John the Divine's Revelation should be interpreted. Consequently, throughout the sixteenth and seventeenth centuries major political and military events were watched with care to ascertain whether they were signals for the faithful. The siege of Malta in 1565, the European wars of religion, the English Civil

---

17 Jacob, *The Newtonians and the English Revolution*, 129–130.
18 Jacob, *The Newtonians and the English Revolution*, 131.
19 W. Whiston, *An Essay on the Revelation of Saint John, so far as concerns the past and present times* (London: 1706).
20 W. Whiston, *The Accomplishment of the Scripture Prophecies* (London, 1708). There were of course Anglicans who rejected this interpretation of events, see W.J. Bulman, *Anglican Enlightenment, Orientalism, Religion and Politics in England and its Empire, 1648–1715* (Cambridge: 2015), 65.
21 He published this in the second edition of his *An Essay on the Revelation of Saint John*.
22 L. Laborie, *Enlightening Enthusiasm, Prophecy and Religious Experience in Early Eighteenth Century England* (Manchester: 2015).

Wars, the siege of Vienna in 1685, the Glorious Revolution in Britain and other events were seen by contemporaries as world events that might presage divine action.[23]

In Britain, this trend was given exceptional energy by the force of radical theology born during the upheavals of the Civil Wars between 1638 and 1660. John Milton, Roger Williams and Richard Overton linked religious freedom and political liberty to an expectation that the struggle for those principles were a sign of the coming Millennium.[24] Such ideas gave rise to a plethora of sects that embraced the radical theology of the Apocalypse: Anabaptists, Brownists, Muggletonians, Fifth Monarchists, and a number of others.[25] They shared one feature, which was a certainty that they were living in the last years of human reign on earth before the thousand years under divine ordinance. Many regarded 1665 or 1666 as the likely date of the end of the world.

The succession of the Catholic James II to the throne in 1685 caused considerable anxiety among Protestants. Cambridge millenarians, such as John Worthington, the master of Jesus College, Cambridge, and Simon Patrick, the dean of Peterborough and later a bishop, saw a clear sign in political events. Both believed that the prophecies regarding the collapse of the Papacy before the Millennium specifically referred to the events of the autumn of 1688. As Margaret Jacob pointed out, Patrick was an example of a Latitudinarian and a scientist who embraced millenarian thinking.[26] Among such churchmen was the belief that, as a prelude to the end of days, there would be the dissolution of Catholicism. In order to secure this, Latitudinarians held that Protestantism had to be strengthened and unified. Indeed the comprehension of Protestant Dissenters into the Church of England was one of the goals of Latitudinarians who saw it as a means to an eschatological end. International Protestantism would also unite to force the decline of the Papacy. Science, many Latitudinarian churchmen believed, gave an order and precision to their expectations for the end of the world.

The Revolution of 1688 was an especially potent event, and theologians could not help but see the flight of James II as both providential and prophetic.

---

23 T. Claydon, *Europe and the making of England, 1660–1760* (Cambridge: 2007) and T. Claydon, "Protestantism, universal monarchy and Christendom in the ideology of William's war, 1689–1697", in *Redefining William III: The Impact of the King-Stadholder in International Context*, ed. E. Mijers & D. Onnekink (Aldershot: 2007), 125–143.

24 A. Williamson, *Apocalypse Then: Prophecy and the Making of the Modern World* (Westport, C.T.: 2008), 141–145.

25 A. Hessayon, *"Gold Tried in the Fire": The Prophet TheaurauJohn Tany and the English Revolution* (Aldershot: 2007).

26 Jacob, *The Newtonians and the English Revolution*, 42–48.

The links between providentialism and prophecy have perhaps been underemphasised by scholars, but the word "providence" indicated not merely divine sanction—or intervention—but also foreknowledge and foresight. Some clergy, like Walter Garrett, rector of Titchfield, Hampshire and a fellow of Trinity College, Cambridge, identified the deliverance of the Church of England from James's Catholicising policies as part of the prophesies of the Book of Revelation.[27] In the wake of the Glorious Revolution, Protestants of all sorts believed they were under an obligation to warn people of the end of days. For dissenters like John Quick, pious Protestants were modern prophets who "stood in the gap and had power with God to keep off judgements from us". Quick claimed that when such men died they hastened the prospect of "the chariots of Israel and the horsemen thereof".[28]

In the few years after 1688, a scholarly interest developed in the prophet Elijah, led by Edward Pocock, Canon of Christ Church, Oxford and the author of a biblical commentary. Pocock was an Orientalist who had travelled widely in the middle east and had collected an important library. He published works in Arabic and a Polyglot Bible, but had dedicated the last decades of his life to producing studies of prophets.[29] Elijah seemed to represent the case of a man who intervened at a time of political crisis, and was assumed to endorse both the actions of those who resisted James II and also the prophetic nature of the events of 1688. "Elijah-mania" momentarily gripped the country when in 1695 Thomas Moor, a well-read Cambridge barber, claimed that he was Elijah who had returned to earth. Moor's identification with Elijah was based in part on his visions and ecstatic experiences which he recorded and published.[30] Moor's death two years later ended the debate, but the episode emphasised the strongly prophetic element in the way people viewed the Revolution.

It has been largely forgotten by scholars, that events in world and national history extending into the eighteenth century were viewed from this perspective of the anticipated second coming of Christ. Most of the participants in wars,

27 W. Garrett, *An Essay Upon the Fourth and Fifth Chapters of the Revelation Shewing that the Church of England is Particularly Described in Those Chapters* (London: 1690).
28 J. Quick, *The Dead Prophet Yet Speaking A Funeral Sermon* (London: 1691), iii–iv.
29 G.J. Toomer, "Edward Pococke, (1604–1691)", ODNB, online (www.oxforddnb.com/view/article/22430, accessed 7 April 2020). Pococke should be distinguished from his son, also Edward and also a Canon of Christ Church, Oxford.
30 T. Moor, *The Mystery of Iniquity laid open and the Doctrine of Freewill Fully Refuted: By Proving that Sin is an Infirmity* (London: 1695); and, *A Disputation whether Elijah in Malachi 4 Be any other Prophet then what hath Already Been in the World* (London: 1695). W.E. Burns, "London's Barber-Elijah: Thomas Moor and universal salvation in the 1690s", *Harvard Theological Review* 95 (2002), 277–290.

revolutions and political upheavals saw their actions as part of the conflicts that would usher in the end of time. Among those who regarded the evidence of the second coming as clear in the contest between Catholicism and Protestantism was Thomas Bray, founder of the Society for the Promotion of Christian Knowledge (S.P.C.K.) and Commissary for Maryland. Bray preferred not to be known as holding these views and asked friends not to reveal it—suggesting that they were not entirely respectable. Nevertheless, his sense that Rome was the Babylonian whore referred to in the Book of Revelation meant that his American activities were framed by an urgent belief that he was standing on the edge of a religious precipice. His desire to spread Christianity in North America was consciously driven by such views.[31] He was so haunted by this knowledge that he expressed the fear that he might be murdered and referred to the death of Sir Edmundberry Godfrey in 1678, which he thought was also occasioned by Catholic malice.[32] Like Bray, many evangelicals in North America regarded the colonies as part of a wider millenarian agenda.[33]

Modelling themselves on English sermons, later American preachers interpreted the War of Independence and the Revolution of 1688 as a millenarian moment in which political events were bringing the time of the end of the world nearer.[34] This feature had a long lineage stretching back past Cotton Mather's eschatological writings to the Puritans of seventeenth century England and New England.[35] It was not only in North America that millenarian concerns affected politicians. Though it rarely surfaced, some British political figures were deeply influenced by millenarian thinking, an example being Edward Harley and, later, Spencer Perceval.[36]

The mid eighteenth-century attempt to grant naturalisation to Jews in England has been viewed as emphasising the political and ecclesiastical expediency in both the passage and the repeal of the 1753 Act. But those who suppor-

---

31 C.T. Laugher, *Thomas Bray's Grand Design: Libraries of the Church of England in America, 1695–1785* (Chicago: 1973).

32 L.W. Cowie, *Henry Newman: An American in London, 1708–43* (London: 1956), 27.

33 C. Gribben, *Evangelical Millennialism in the Trans-Atlantic World, 1500–2000* (Basingstoke: 2011).

34 O.C. Edwards, Jnr, "Varieties of Sermons: A Survey", in *Preaching, Sermon and Cultural Change in the Long Eighteenth Century*, ed. J. van Eijnatten, Brill History of the Sermon, vol. 4 (Leiden: 2009), 38–39. See also James P. Byrd, *Sacred Scripture, Sacred War, The Bible and the American Revolution* (Oxford: 2013).

35 J. Stievermann, *Prophecy, Piety, and the Problem of Historicity. Interpreting the Hebrew Scriptures in Cotton Mather's Biblia Americana* (Tübingen: 2016).

36 A. McInnes, *Robert Harley, Puritan Politician* (London: 1970), 184. See also W.M. Lamont, *Richard Baxter and the Millennium: Protestant Imperialism and the English Revolution* (London: 1979).

ted Jewish naturalisation, and those who opposed it, drew on biblical prophecies of the Jews' return to Palestine. Opponents of Jewish naturalisation warned that it might imperil the process of the return and thereby frustrate the biblical prophecies. Supporters of naturalisation suggested that the Act offered Britain a unique opportunity to fulfil prophecy. They argued that the Act permitted Britain to contribute to the fulfilment of the apocalyptic role God had prepared for it as the nation that would "bless" the Jews. Both sides of the argument placed prophecy and millenarianism at the heart of political debates on the nature of Britain.[37]

By the end of the eighteenth century, the same political concerns saw a resurgence of millenarian anxieties. Napoleon's conquest of the Papal States and the entry of French troops to Rome in 1804 led to a sense that some of the prophetic writings in the Book of Revelation were coming to pass. In London, this led to a flurry of religious activity. The Avignon Society, formed in the 1770s, and the Church of the New Jerusalem, established in 1787, embraced the views of Emanuel Swedenborg who taught that the Millennium had started in 1747. Joseph Priestley declared in 1793 that the fall of the Papacy, the collapse of the Ottoman Empire, and the return of Jews to the Holy Land, meant that he would see the return of Christ in his lifetime.[38]

Some convinced Millenarians went beyond proclaiming the return of Christ: Richard Brothers, a naval officer, declared himself to be the nephew of God and king of the Hebrews. He prophesied that an earthquake would destroy London and pledged himself to lead the Jews back to Jerusalem.[39] He was quickly placed in an asylum. But others followed. Joanna Southcott claimed to be the "woman clothed in the sun" referred to in the Book of Revelation. She poured out prophecies and issued seals to believers, ensuring them a place in the imminent Kingdom of Heaven.[40] By 1814, she had sent out more than 20,000

---

37 A. Crome, "The 1753 'Jew Bill' Controversy: Jewish Restoration to Palestine, Biblical Prophecy, and English National Identity", *English Historical Review* 130/547 (2015), 1449–1478.

38 Stewart J. Brown, "Movements of Christian Awakening in revolutionary Europe, 1790–1815", in *The Cambridge History of Christianity. Vol. VII: Enlightenment, Reawakenings and Revolution, 1660–1815*, ed. Stewart J. Brown & Timothy Tackett (Cambridge: 2006), 582–583. For Priestley's millenarianism see C. Garrett, "Joseph Priestley, the Millennium and the French Revolution", *The Journal of the History of Ideas* 34 (1973); and C. Garrett, *Respectable Folly: Millenarians and the French Revolution in France and England* (Baltimore: 1975).

39 R. Brothers, *A Revealed Knowledge of the Prophecies and Times, Book the First, wrote [sic] under the direction of the Lord God and published by His Sacred Command, it being the first sign of Warning for the benefit of All Nations* (London: 1794).

40 Such seals were pieces of paper with the inscription: "The Sealed of the Lord—the Elect precious Mans Redemption, to Inherit thee Tree of Life. To be made Heirs of God—and

seals to her followers, all of whom anticipated the second coming.[41] There were also Southcott's successors, John "Zion" Ward, and John Nichols Tom.[42]

It would be easy to suggest that millenarian political views were held only by cranks and the marginalised. But mainstream Christians also embraced such views. Bishop Samuel Horsley of St Asaph certainly interpreted European events as bringing the world to the brink of the Apocalypse. By 1806, he seems to have reached the conclusion that Napoleon was the Anti-Christ.[43] The Prime Minister, Spencer Perceval, was also convinced that prophecies contained serious warnings for the world and poured over them in an attempt to grasp their meaning.

Anglican Prophecy

In May 1577 Queen Elizabeth I had written to her bishops asking them to suppress in sermons "the exercise called prophesying". It was a charge renewed under the Stuart kings in their "directions" since prophecy was regarded as suspect theologically and politically.[44] It was a rule that was more recognised in its breach than its observance.

Margaret Jacob commented in 1992 that "we have mistakenly assumed that such [millenarian] views were held only by radicals or fanatics, the understandable expression of their longing for justice and economic freedom".[45] She also pointed out that Anglican millenarianism was strong in the seventeenth century. Jacob's study, with an end date of 1720, failed to appreciate that millenarianism did not decline after that date but survived and flourished during the eighteenth century.

Important individuals in the Church of England regarded prophecy as a central feature of the Christian faith. Bishop William Lloyd (1627–1717) had been active in searching the Book of Daniel as a means of detecting the second

---

Joint heirs with Jesus Christ. [signed] Joanna Southcott" and dated. An example is in the British Museum, object number 1864,1210.496—they cost between twelve shillings and a guinea.

41   J. Shaw & P. Lockley (eds), *The History of a Modern Millennial Movement: The Southcottians* (London: 2017).
42   J.F.C. Harrison, *The Second Coming: Popular Millenarianism, 1780–1850* (London: 1979) 152.
43   Mather, *High Church Prophet*, 261–268. Mather rescues Horsley's millenarian views from the condemnation of R.A. Soloway who dismissed them as the ramblings of an old man.
44   "Appendix III: Preaching Regulated" in H. Adlington, P. McCullough & E. Rhatigan (eds), *The Oxford Handbook of the Early Modern Sermon* (Oxford: 2011), 552–553.
45   Jacob, *The Newtonians and the English Revolution*, 70.

coming; and in 1712 even warned the British government that the Papacy would be destroyed in four years.[46] It earned him the derision of some of his contemporaries, who nicknamed him "Old Mysterio", and ascribed his prophecies to his advanced age.[47] Yet it is clear that throughout his career he had relied heavily on prophecy and millenarianism; in 1685 he regarded the revocation of the Edict of Nantes as a prelude to the arrival of the Anti-Christ.[48] Moreover, Lloyd's sense of the mystical, and the imminence of divine intervention, shaped his response to the political events of the 1680s and especially his resistance to James II. After 1689, Lloyd's millenarian ideas were encouraged by Queen Mary II, who often arranged to meet him when he attended the court. Lloyd's position emphasised that millenarian thought was not the preserve of fifth monarchists or republicans and that moderate and conservative Anglicans could be as comfortable with expectations of the end of the world as republicans.

Thomas Sherlock (1678–1761), Bishop of London, preached two sermons in defence of prophecy and miracles and these published sermons became a "prized resource" for parish clergy in mounting their own defences.[49] Of course some mainstream Anglicans remained sceptical about whether miracles and prophecies were limited to the Apostolic Age or whether they had continued to occur into their own times. But even those who constrained prophecies to the past did not challenge their truth or authenticity.[50]

Between 1754 and 1757, Thomas Newton published his *Dissertation on the Prophecies which have remarkably been Fulfilled, and at this time are Fulfilling in the World*. It went through numerous editions and was reprinted well into the nineteenth century. When Newton was appointed to the see of Bristol in 1761 his episcopal status appeared on the title pages of subsequent editions and helped to make the prophetic enquiry respectable.[51] Newton had been encouraged to publish his thoughts following a conversation with the military road-builder, General George Wade. When Newton mentioned that he believed in the literal nature of biblical prophecy, Wade remarked that "if this point could be proved

---

46 A.T. Hart *William Lloyd 1627–1717* (London: 1952), 177.
47 W. Shippen, *Faction Display'd. A Poem* (London: 1709), 5–6.
48 Hart, *William Lloyd 1627–1717*, 245–246. It was a view that did not go unchallenged, Laurence Addison, Lloyd's dean at Worcester, challenged the Bishop in a work which explicitly attacked Lloyd's brand of millenarian thought. Bulman, *Anglican Enlightenment*, 261–262.
49 N. Aston, "Rationalism, The Enlightenment and Sermons" in *The Oxford Handbook to the British Sermon 1688–1901*, ed. K. Francis & W. Gibson (Oxford: 2012), 400.
50 J. Redwood, *Reason, Ridicule and Religion, The Age of Enlightenment in England 1660–1750* (London: 1976), 135–136.
51 D.M. Whitford, *The Curse of Ham in the Early Modern Era: The Bible and the Justifications for Slavery* (Farnham: 2009), 141.

to satisfaction, there would be no arguing against the plain matter of fact [of Christianity]".[52] This stimulated Newton to activity. He drew on Thomas Sherlock's sermon on prophesy and on Isaac Newton's published work on the Book of Daniel.[53]

Newton was joined in the study of prophesy by the Bishop of Gloucester, William Warburton, whose goal was to argue the case for divinely-revealed religion. Warburton preached a sermon on "The Rise of Antichrist", which was later published in his collected works.[54] His *Discourses* (1767) included a strong endorsement of prophecy, as did his widely-read *Divine Legation of Moses* (1738–1741), which argued that the expectations of an Anti-Christ were authentic. Warburton went on to establish a trust which sponsored a series of lectures on revealed religion; the first lectures were given by his friend Richard Hurd, Bishop of Worcester, defending miracles and prophecy.[55] Subsequent lecturers were Bishops Samuel Hallifax and Lewis Bagot.[56]

The historian Fred Mather suggested that interest in prophecy was an element in the High Churchmanship of clergymen like Samuel Horsley, who found mystical divinity to be a bridge between biblical scholarship and revealed faith. Horsley found himself increasingly attracted to the notion of a "Second Advent" and by 1799 published on the character of the Anti-Christ to be expected from the Book of Isaiah. He drew around him a circle of High Churchmen like William Jones and G.S. Faber, as well as like-minded scientists such as Edward King.[57] William Jones of Nayland identified the atheists of the French Revolution as "the Man of Sin" from the Book of Revelation. Yet this High Church millenarianism was at odds with evangelical millenarianism.[58]

Anglican millenarianism displayed a number of significant features, including lay involvement, social penetration and the use of print to propagate it.

---

52   Quoted in Oddy, "Eschatological Prophecy in the English Theological Tradition", 37.
53   Thomas Newton was not related to Isaac Newton.
54   It is not clear exactly when this sermon was preached but from internal evidence it was probably in the 1750s.
55   The Warburton Trust was endowed with £500 in 1768 and had as its goal "to prove the truth of revealed religion, in general, and of the Christian in particular, from the completion of the prophecies in the Old and New Testament, which relate to the Christian Church, especially to the apostasy of Papal Rome". This information was given in Hurd's lectures: R. Hurd, *An Introduction to the Study of the Prophecies concerning the Christian Church* ... (London: 1772), viii.
56   The lectures continued until 1846 and the lecturers included Edward Nares, Professor of Modern History at Oxford, Thomas Rennell, dean of Winchester and William Rowe Lyall, dean of Canterbury.
57   Mather, *High Church Prophet*, 263.
58   Williamson, *Apocalypse Now*, 256.

These features can be seen in the life of William Freke, a well-educated Dorset landowner, who in 1709 declared he was the second Elijah who had come to earth to proclaim the coming of Christ.[59] As noted earlier, Elijah-mania gripped England in the post-Revolutionary period. There were clerical and lay claimants to be the second Elijah.[60] Freke was not only a gentleman, he was also an Oxford educated lawyer and magistrate and seems to have combined his role as a justice of the peace with his millenarian views without difficulty. Freke also used the growth of printing to produce a series of books and tracts, which advanced his claims to be Elijah and contained his prophecies and declarations about the end of the world. A further, and intriguing, feature of his beliefs is that they seem to have arisen from his Arianism rather than other religious traditions. Scholars have tended to see Arianism as connected to Latitudinarianism and associated with the growth of rationalism and rational Christianity. If Freke came to millenarianism though his involvement with Arianism, rather than as a rejection of it, it suggests that historians have perhaps placed them at too great a theological distance from one another. Like other millenarians, Freke was in contact with like-minded prophets in the Philadelphian Society and among the French Prophets. Another landowner who certainly regarded prophecy as a practice of his own time was Sir John Philipps of Picton in Pembrokeshire. In the first decade of the eighteenth century, Philipps, who was also an MP, discussed with Bishop Lloyd of Worcester and William Whiston, their firm conviction that that Jews would regain Jerusalem in 1716 and would restore the Temple in fulfilment of prophecy.[61]

Beyond the Church of England, prophecy and millenarian thought was also alive and lively. But it showed considerable diversity. Richard Baxter, one of the most influential Protestant Dissenters of the late seventeenth century, believed that the Millennium had begun with the establishment of Christianity in the Roman Empire. He also anticipated the second coming, but held that to predict when that might happen was presumptuous.[62] Prophecy was also found in the Society of Friends, where the best-known prophet was Elizabeth Stirredge.

---

59   Freke's life can be best approached through Martin Greig's "Elijah in Dorset: William Freke and Enthusiasm in England and the Atlantic World at the Turn of the Eighteenth Century", *Church History* 87/2 (2018), 424–451.
60   Burns, "London's Barber-Elijah"; P. Korshin, "Queuing and Waiting: the Apocalypse in England, 1660–1750", in *The Apocalypse in English Renaissance Thought and Literature*, ed. C.A. Patrides and J. Wittreich (Manchester: 1984).
61   Aberystwyth, National Library of Wales (NLW), MS 584, Personal memorandum-book, Philipps family mss. I owe this reference to my doctoral student, John Harding.
62   F. Powicke, *The Reverend Richard Baxter, Under the Cross (1662–1691)* (London: 1927), 181.

Stirredge's prophesies were directed at giving women a role and voice in Quaker society, but they later became warnings of the danger the persecutors of the Quakers placed themselves in.[63] By 1689 she extended her warnings to the whole country and predicted the end of the world.[64]

Popular Millenarianism and Prophecy

Margaret Jacob claimed that popular millenarianism survived the Restoration Church's attempt "to destroy it".[65] In the claim that the Church sought to destroy millenarianism she was mistaken. Either way, popular millenarianism and prophecy were not eradicated. Evidence of the survival of prophecy in everyday life is not uncommon in the eighteenth century. In October 1716, Henry Prescott, the deputy registrar of the diocese of Chester, noted in his diary that the local population in North Wales was "in full expectation of the event of a bold pretender to prophecy his prediction who according to it, dy'd and was put in a coffin at 7 in the morning yesterday and was to rise at 9 tomorrow".[66] Some of this popular, or folk, prophecy was not confined to the ill-educated. An example is William Coe's note in the 1690s of a prophecy he heard "when our Lord falls on our Ladyes lapp, then let England beware of a clap"—which was in Suffolk popularly interpreted as when Easter Day fell on Lady Day. Coe, an affluent farmer, recorded in his diary that Easter Day would fall on Lady Day in 1722, 1733 and 1744. He wrote "I pray God prevent the like".[67]

It is clear that female prophecy was closely associated with other features that strengthened their claims to authority and authenticity. One example of this is the phenomenon of fasting women. Jane Shaw has shown that such women's fasting was evidence of a test for their spiritual authority and consequently made their prophetic pronouncements weightier. They were also, with rare exceptions, local phenomena, rather than episodes that caught the

---

63 E. Stirredge, *A Salutation of my Endeared Love in God's Holy Fear and Dread, and for the Clearing of my Conscience, Once More unto You of that City of Bristol* (London: 1683).
64 E. Stirredge, *A Faithful Warning to the Inhabitants of England, and Elsewhere, With An Invitation Of Love Unto All People, To Call Them To Repentance, And Amendment Of Life; For By So Doing, Many Have Escaped The Judgments That Have Been To Be Poured Down Upon Their Heads* (London: 1689).
65 Jacob, 251.
66 J. Addy & P. McNiven (eds), *The Diary of Henry Prescott, LLB, Deputy Registrar of Chester Diocese*, Record Society of Lancashire and Cheshire, vol. 2 (1994), 538.
67 M. Storey (ed.), *Two East Anglian Diaries, 1641–1729*, Suffolk Records Soc, vol. XXXVI (Woodbridge: 1994), 205.

attention of the nation and so were aimed at the religious experience of ordinary men and women in the provinces.[68]

Those who were well-versed in the Biblical evidence for the second coming, like William Whiston, were not immune from popular speculation. Whiston heard of the case of Mary Toft, the so-called "Rabbit Woman of Godalming" who claimed to have given birth to rabbits and who was, briefly, a sensation which even claimed gullible members of the court in London. Whiston's response was to claim that Toft might be a fulfilment of the animal prophecy of Esdras.[69]

One of the ways in which prophecy remained a potent force in eighteenth century society was in the most popular and accessible literary form: the chapbook. Chapbooks were the cheapest and most ephemeral forms of published work, and were sold to the poor by hawkers. Many were passed from hand to hand to be read and re-read. They were packed with romances and folk tales; but a recurring theme in them was the prevalence of prophecy. Mother Shipton, the Yorkshire prophetess (c.1488–1561), who was claimed to have foretold the Great Fire of London and many other events, was a hugely popular figure in chapbooks and repeatedly appeared in them. *Nixon's Cheshire Prophecies*, first published in 1714, was so popular that it reached its twenty-first edition in 1745. "Mother Bunch" and "the Wandering Jew" were two other very popular prophetic figures who often appeared in chapbooks. Sometime chapbooks included comparatively scholarly works of prophecy such as *A Gold Chain of Four Links* by J. Stephens, D.D., a contemporary of John and Charles Wesley at Oxford, which passed through numerous editions by 1760 and was still in print in 1820.[70] Nevertheless, Stephens's work was produced with crude woodcut illustrations and sold as a chapbook. Such works retained their traditional interest in the prodigious and sensational, and these things were thought to attract popular attention as a means of calling people's attention to the prospect of the end of the world.[71] One chapbook, entitled *A New Prophecy*,

---

68   J. Shaw, *Miracles in Enlightenment England* (London / New Haven: 2006), chapter 5.
69   L. Cody, "'The Doctor's in Labour'; or a new Whim Wham from Guildford", in *Gender and History* 4 (1992), 175–196. Shaw, *Miracles in Enlightenment England*, 177. J. Shaw, "Mary Toft, Religion and National Memory in Eighteenth-Century England", *Journal for Eighteenth-Century Studies* 32/3 (2009), 321–338. See also Alastair Hamilton, *The Apocryphal Apocalypse: The Reception of the Second Book of Esdras (4 Ezra) from the Renaissance to the Enlightenment* (Oxford: 1999), 277–278, and K. Harvey, *The Imposteress Rabbit Breeder, Mary Tofts and Eighteenth-Century England* (Oxford: 2020).
70   Its full title was *A Gold Chain of Four Links to Draw Poor Souls to Their Desired Habitation. Or, the Four Last Things Briefly Discoursed Of; Viz. Death, Judgment, Hell.*
71   D.M. Valenze, "Prophecy and Popular Literature in Eighteenth Century England", *Journal of Ecclesiastical History* 29/1 (1978), 75–92.

was an account of an eight year old girl who lay in a trance for two days and awoke with "an account of the strange and wonderful sight that she see [sic] in the other world". Her visions were a warning to "this last and worst age, agreeable to the Holy Scriptures and Divine Revelation".[72] In such works the insight of children was often cited, perhaps regarded as the most reliable because it came through those perceived to be the purest in society.

The most significant presence in Britain in the eighteenth century of millenarians was the community of French Prophets.[73] Lionel Laborie has shown that the traditional historical assumption that the French Prophets were small in number and active only in the first decade of the century is erroneous. In fact the Prophets were more numerous, diverse and enduring than historians have understood. In just two years after 1706, the French Prophets in London grew to more than five hundred followers. Laborie's analysis of their members shows the social diversity of the movement, which included many from the "middling sort": army officers, physicians, merchants, scholars as well as artisans and tradesmen and servants, apprentices and those at the bottom of the social pyramid.[74] The French Prophets were widely known and the subject of an extensive series of pamphlet campaigns of denunciation, principally for their behaviour rather than their beliefs. They were attacked by, among others, fellow millenarians Bishops William Lloyd and Edward Fowler, which suggests that the spectrum of millenarian opinion was broad and diverse. They attracted followers from other denominations, including Quakers, Anglicans, Baptists and other Protestant dissenters and were also a pan-European movement with over eight hundred followers in other countries.

The message of the French Prophets was unmistakably millenarian. The Camisards, from whom they were descended, had experienced brutal Catholic persecution in France and held that it presaged the fall of Rome and the second coming. Although they were not Huguenots, the French Prophets had experienced the effects of the revocation of the Edict of Nantes in 1685 and regarded it as the starting pistol for the preparation for the end of the world. They were radical French Calvinists: the Huguenots largely distanced themselves from the Camisards because of their use of violence and claims to prophecy. After they arrived in London and began attracting Philadelphians and Quakers, they

---

72 J. Ashton, *Chap-books of the Eighteenth Century* (London: 1882), 64.
73 The French Prophets were the direct link between the Philadelphians and the Scottish Quietists, which are respectively discussed by Ariel Hessayon and Michael B. Riordan in this volume. On the origins of the French Prophets in France, see Lionel Laborie's chapter in vol. 1 of this collection.
74 Laborie, *Enlightening Enthusiasm*, appendix.

strongly supported the idea of a New Jerusalem, as a utopian prelude to the second coming, and prepared to call the Jews to convert to Christianity as a means of hastening it. These were ideas that the Prophets shared with some Presbyterians, Philadelphians and even Moravians.[75]

Millenarianism and Evangelicalism

The evangelical movement in Britain in the eighteenth century was deeply imbued with millenarian thinking. Those from whom it inherited strands of spirituality were powerful advocates of millenarianism. Samuel Wesley, father of John and Charles and author of a verse rendition of the Bible, was deeply millenarian. The principal portrait of Samuel Wesley depicted him in the robes of an Old Testament prophet with pyramids in the background.[76] His poetic output included a contribution to the verse published in Oxford in 1688 to celebrate the birth of James Edward, son of James II. His poem was a piece of political prophecy:

> I feel, I rising feel the God within
> There, there I see the glorious Mystic scene
> In decent ranks each coming bliss appears
> And in their hands lead up the harness years.
> Here he defends his Father's mighty Throne
> And there he Conquers others of his own ...[77]

John Wesley was wary of ecstatic expressions of millenarianism, and Lionel Laborie has shown that his reputation as a "reasonable enthusiast" was derived from a concern about the behaviour and reputation of the French Prophets. His brother, Charles, was appalled when he saw the French Prophet, and former Baptist, Isaac Hollis fall into an agitated state and gobble like a turkey.[78] Yet John Wesley and the Methodist movement in the eighteenth century were committed to both enthusiastic experience of religious conversion and to divine revelation. Wesley claimed to follow in the line of the Old Testament prophets,

---

75 Laborie, *Enlightening Enthusiasm*, 80–83.
76 London, National Portrait Gallery (NPG) D9050, "Samuel Wesley the Elder", by George Vertue, after unknown artist, line engraving, circa 1732, 12 1/4 in. × 6 1/2 in. (310 mm × 164 mm) plate size.
77 W. Gibson, "Strenae Natalitia: Ambivalence and Equivocation in Oxford in 1688", *History of Universities*, vol. XXXI:1 (2018).
78 Laborie, *Enlightening Enthusiasm*, 100, 107, 152.

"Such as Nathan, Isaiah, Jeremiah, and many others, on whom the Holy Ghost came in an extraordinary manner ...".[79] A number of the French Prophets interacted with the Methodists and Moravians and in many respects the Prophets were antecedents of the Methodist movement.[80]

Wesley's own millenarian ideas were derived in part from his family tradition and partly from his wider experience.[81] In his *Explanatory Notes on the New Testament* (1755), John Wesley acknowledged a debt to Johannes Albrecht Bengel, a Lutheran pietist who had made a deep study of the Revelation of St John. In 1740 Bengel had written an exposition of the Apocalypse and Wesley indicated that his own views on the Book of Revelation in the *Explanatory Notes* largely followed those of Bengel.[82] Wesley even included in his book Bengel's timetable of the fulfilment of the Book of Revelation.[83] In 1764, Wesley thanked Thomas Hartley for his writings in anticipation of the second coming, which Wesley referred to as "comfortable doctrine".[84] Charles Wesley was equally committed to millenarianism, having calculated that the world would end in 1794.[85] Kenneth Newport has shown how detailed and obsessive this could become in the work of Joseph Sutcliffe. Sutcliffe's *Treatise on the Universal Spread of the Gospel, the Glorious Millennium and the Second Coming of Christ* of 1798 shows not just how powerfully the French Revolution affected Methodism but also the detailed analysis of the Old Testament that lay behind predictions of the end of the world.[86] One view suggests that "many first-generation evangelicals were sufficiently intoxicated with their own importance to suppose that their existence presaged the imminent return of Christ".[87]

---

79 Sermon 121, "Prophets and Priests", in *The Sermons of John Wesley: The Works of John Wesley*, ed. A.C. Outler, vol. 4 (Nashville, T.N.: 1984–1987), 77.
80 See Colin Podmore's chapter on the Fetter Lane Society in his book *The Moravian Church in England, 1728–1760* (Oxford: 1998).
81 Luke Tyerman, *The life and times of the Rev. John Wesley*, M.A., vol. 2 (London: 1870–1871), 523.
82 According to this chronology, the end of the world would happen some time after 1836.
83 Oddy, "Eschatological Prophecy in the English Theological Tradition", 105.
84 K. Newport, "Methodists and the Millennium: Eschatological Expectation and the Interpretation of Biblical Prophecy in Early Methodism", *Bulletin of the John Rylands Library* 7/1 (1996), 104.
85 K.G.C. Newport, "Charles Wesley's interpretation of some biblical prophecies according to a previously unpublished letter dated 24 April, 1754", *Bulletin of the John Rylands University Library of Manchester* 77 (1995), 31–52. John Fletcher seems to have believed that the world would end in 1754: Newport, "Methodists and the Millennium", 106.
86 Newport, "Methodists and the Millennium", 109.
87 D.C. Jones, *"A Glorious Work in the World". Welsh Methodism and the International Evangelical Revival, 1735–1750* (Cardiff: 2004), 6–7.

Nevertheless, the sort of millenarian thought that John Wesley espoused has been the source of debate and disagreement.[88] It is clear that Wesley did not regard prophecy as having the same authority as scripture.[89] He was also unconvinced by some of those men and women who claimed prophetic powers. In the case of George Bell, Wesley wrote: "from the time that I heard of George Bell's prophecy, I explicitly declared against it both in private, in the society, in preaching, over and over ...".[90] Even so, those who attacked Methodism, like George Lavington, did so in part because it seemed to be associated with forms of religion that were dangerous or not respectable. Prophesying was one of these.[91] The concern for Anglicans was not interpreting the Scriptures to calculate the second coming, but prophesying under the pretended influence of the Holy Spirit It was this claim to revelation that led to the association of prophecy with enthusiasm.

The leaders of early Methodism were not alone; millenarian thinking was common among their followers. John Wesley encountered such a case in Newcastle in 1742 when he came across a man called John Brown who loudly shouted of the coming of the kingdom of God and of God's assurance to him that he would be a king.[92] In some respects, the passion and force of early Methodism arose not just from the emotional experience of conversion but also from the urgency with which the converted exhorted their friends to share the experience because time was short and the world would end in their lifetimes and therefore delay risked damnation.[93] The popular sense that the world was on a precipice and that only precipitate action to embrace faith would save men and women was a common principle of evangelicals. Attacks on Methodists were in part rooted in their emphatic embrace of millennialism and their prophecies that the end of the world was imminent.[94] This was in some measure because early Methodist preachers were often powerful expo-

---

88 K.O. Brown, "John Wesley, Post or Premillennialist?", *Methodist History* 28 (1989), 33–41.
89 S. Juster, *Doomsayers: Anglo-American Prophecy in the Age of Revolution* (Philadelphia: 2003), 34.
90 A.C. Outler (ed.), *Works of John Wesley*, vol. 3 (Nashville T.N.: 1986) 13 (23 April 1763).
91 Lavington's anti-Methodist work was republished during the nineteenth century with a lengthy preface by Richard Polwhele to combat the rise of Southcottian "enthusiasm". I am grateful to Simon Lewis for this.
92 Quoted in Newport, "Methodists and the Millennium", 107.
93 Joseph Benson, *Four Sermons on the Second Coming of Christ and the Future Misery of the Wicked* (London: 1781).
94 Richard Hardy, *A Letter from a Clergyman to One of His Parishioners Who Was Inclined to Turn Methodist* (London: 1753).

nents of millenarianism. John Kershaw and Thomas Taylor are two examples, but there were many others who displayed "a distinct tendency towards premillennialism".[95] This was a source of disquiet for some, who occasionally wrote to John and Charles Wesley about ecstatic millenarian preaching that was disturbing.[96] There was also a strong association between the emotional component of evangelicalism and millenarianism, as evidenced in the dreams of some early evangelicals.[97]

Among Calvinistic Methodism, millenarian thinking was especially strong. In Wales, the combined preaching of Daniel Rowland, Howel Davies and William Williams was a forceful case for the imminence of the second coming.[98] George Whitefield also espoused millenarianism and supported preachers who advanced prophetic expectations. David Ceri Jones argues that 1739–1743 was a particular peak in preaching that the kingdom of God was not just at hand but likely to happen in very short time.[99] It was also a peak in political tensions in Britain and Europe. In such circumstances, the appearance of spirits and ghosts was associated with prophecy, and was promoted by the writing of Edmund Jones.[100]

Millenarianism formed part of the complex compound of evangelical social thinking in the eighteenth century. Millenarianism found a strong congruence with the campaigns for the abolition of slavery. In 1789 John Newton, a firm abolitionist, preached to his congregation at St Mary's Woolnoth of the imminence of the second coming and the voice of the archangels which would herald the rise of the dead. In such circumstances, the ownership of slaves placed men and women in a peril about which Newton warned.[101]

Missionary activity was also strengthened by the sense that the Millennium was at hand. Malachi was an especially important biblical text for sermons on mission activity since he prophesied the advancement of faith among heathens. The Society for the Propagation of the Gospel (S.P.G.) found that its preachers turned to Malachi time and time again. Rowan Strong identified

---

95   Newport, "Methodists and the Millennium", 122.
96   Erika Stalcup, "Sensing Salvation: Spiritual Experience in Early British Methodism, 1735–65", PhD thesis (Boston University: 2016), 146–147.
97   P. Mack, "Dreaming and Emotion in Early Evangelical Religion", in *Heart Religion: Evangelical Piety in England and Ireland, 1690–1850*, ed. J. Coffey (Oxford: 2016), 157–180.
98   Jones, *"A Glorious Work in the World"*, 103.
99   Jones, *"A Glorious Work in the World"*, 251–252.
100 J. Harvey (ed.), *The Appearance of Evil, Apparitions of Spirits in Wales by Edmund Jones* (Cardiff: 2003).
101 G.M. Ditchfield, "Sermons in the Age of the French and American Revolutions", in *Oxford Handbook of the British Sermon 1688–1901*, 285.

three important sermons in the eighteenth century that drew on Malachi to argue the case for prophetic missionary activity. In 1704 Bishop Gilbert Burnet of Salisbury used Malachi as a means of making a call to moral reform and as the basis of God choosing to make his teachings available to the Gentiles and then to the whole world.[102] Malachi showed that God intended Christianity should be spread over the whole world. But Burnet was also careful to distance Protestant missions from the corrupt and corrupting Catholic "cruelties and barbarities" that were inflicted on South America. In 1740 Bishop Martin Benson of Gloucester preached on the same text as Burnet (Malachi 1:11). He argued that prophecy needed human agency to enact it. The Old Testament prophecies of the spread of faith required men and women to do their part in taking the Gospel to the world. Benson argued that the right sort of Christian example was needed to convince heathens to convert. Slavery, said Benson, was not such a model and was therefore hindering the spread of the Gospel.[103] In 1791, Bishop Edward Smallwell of Oxford preached on the prophecies of Malachi on the kingdom of God. Smallwell was wary of the dangers of unfounded prophecies and speculations on the second coming, but he clearly saw missionary activity as a means to achieve the end of the Millennium.[104] Once converted, the world would be ready for Christ's second coming.[105]

Antiprophecy

It must be recognised that not all people regarded prophecy in the same light. There were some who treated it with caution and restraint. Among these was the Revd Abraham Campion, a former chaplain to Archbishop John Tillotson and later dean of Lincoln, who in 1694 delivered an assize sermon that challenged the notion of prophecy. He said: "God governs the world now in a spiritual manner, not by visible appearances of Angels or messages of Prophets; His

---

102   G. Burnet, *Of the Propagation of the Gospel in Foreign Parts. A Sermon Preach'd at St Mary-le-Bow, Feb 18 1704. Before the Society Incorporated for that Purpose* (London: 1704).

103   M. Benson, *A Sermon Preached before the Incorporated Society for the Propagation of the Gospel in Foreign Parts* (London: 1740).

104   E. Smallwell, *A Sermon Preached Before the Incorporated Society for the Propagation of the Gospel in Foreign Parts; at Their Anniversary Meeting in the Parish Church of St. Mary-le-Bow, on Friday February 18, 1791* (London: 1791).

105   R. Strong, "Eighteenth Century Mission Sermons", in *Oxford Handbook to the British Sermon*, 500–503. See also Travis Glasson, *Mastering Christianity Missionary Anglicanism and Slavery in the Atlantic World* (Oxford: 2011).

footsteps are only discerned by the eye of reason and faith".[106] For such rational Latitudinarians the age of miracles and prophecies was over—it had died with the Apostles. What God had left to humanity was faith and reason and these were the twin guides that were to be relied on. Even those who held that miracles were possible sometimes questioned whether they were a legitimate basis for people to rest their faith upon.[107] In this sense, Latitudinarianism was by no means homogenous in its response to millenarianism and prophecy.

There were moreover clergy who warned people from the pulpit of the dangers of prophecy of the second coming. In April 1694 Richard Lapthorne wrote to his friend Richard Coffin of an occasion on which he had heard a sermon on the text "wherefore walk circumspectly" [Ephesians, 5:15] in which a parson warned his congregation of a neighbouring clergyman who "pretended to visions and declared that it was revealed to him that at Whitsunday our Saviour would personally appear on the earth" and that this would lead to "a strange change". The prophet parson had urged people to arrange a "Judaical sacrifice of oxen" and had attracted a number of people from outside his parish to bring their "goods and treasure to this prophet".[108] There was no doubt that Lapthorne and Coffin were worried by such episodes and viewed them with alarm.

The Sources

Ariel Hessayon's edition of the letters and writings relating to Jane Lead is also a rich source of material for understanding the range of millenarian thought in the eighteenth century. Lead, in some respects acted as bridge between the seventeenth and nineteenth centuries, drawing on the ideas of Jacob Boehme and in turn influencing Joanna Southcott. She also embodied the sense that millenarianism—like other forms of experiential and speculative faith—was a form of faith in which women could legitimately play a significant role. Both Boehme and Lead clearly saw a female component in divine wisdom and spirituality as important. Hessayon's work, like that of others in this collection

---

106   A.B. Campion, *A Sermon Concerning National Providence Preached art the Assizes Held at Ailesbury in Buckinghamshire* (Oxford: 1694), 4.
107   W. Gibson, *Enlightenment Prelate: Benjamin Hoadly 1676–1761* (Cambridge: 2004), 73–74.
108   R.J. Kerr & I. Coffin Duncan (eds), *The Portledge Papers, being extracts from the letters of Richard Lapthorne, Gent., of Hatton Garden, London to Richard Coffin Esq, of Portledge, Bideford, Devon from December 10th 1687-August 7th 1697* (London: 1928), 175–176.

and in other works on enthusiastic Christianity, shows how socially differentiated adherence to revelatory religion was. It was perhaps as much as for the social influence of the Philadelphians as for their spirituality that they attracted the attention of churchmen like Archbishop Thomas Tenison. While the Philadelphians burnt brightly and briefly, compared to the "French Prophets", they nevertheless represented a form of Christianity that was both troubling and interesting for contemporaries. Hence, Tenison went to the trouble of keeping them under observation, intercepting their correspondence,[109] and annotating the contents.

The contents of the correspondence relating to Jane Lead is complex and suggests that the Philadelphians undertook a close reading of Scripture, and were searching it for signs and understanding. They were also seeking out other people, like Archdeacon Edward Waple of Taunton, who had, they thought, made discoveries in Christian antiquity. Their connections with, and attention to, English thinkers were broad. They included Henry Dodwell whose 1682 work *Dissertations upon St. Cyprian* they read and discussed. Richard Roach, a fellow of St John's College, Oxford and rector of St Augustine, Hackney, was a similarly significant figure.[110]

A feature of the writings is their interest in medicine and physic. This was—and remained—a long-standing interest of Puritans and evangelicals in Britain and in Europe.[111] The attention to medicine extended to the close observation of symptoms and even to a detailed account of the deathbed of Jane Lead. The focus on the body and healing was an expression of one of the signs of prophetic and miraculous behaviour.[112] The attitude and response of the patient to imminent death also suggested the state of their souls: a good death and bearing pain with fortitude and resolution were also seen as evidence of strong faith and assurance of salvation.

---

109   The interception of post was something of an Anglican monopoly, at least until the 1720s. W. Gibson, "An Eighteenth Century Paradox: The Career of the Decypherer-Bishop Edward Willes", *The British Journal for Eighteenth Century Studies* 12/1 (1989), 69–76. As Ric Berman has shown, in the years after 1720, there was a number of Huguenots into the decypherer's office. R. Berman, *Espionage, Diplomacy & the Lodge: Charles Delafaye and The Secret Department of the Post Office* (Goring Heath: 2017).

110   B.J. Gibbons, "Roach, Richard [*name in religion* Onesimus] (1662–1730)", ODNB, online (http://www.oxforddnb.com/view/article/23704, accessed 4 November 2019).

111   Randy Maddox and James G. Donat (eds), *The Works of John Wesley*, vol. 32 "Medical and Health Writings" (Nashville, T.N.: 2018), is dedicated to his medical writing and runs to almost 800 pages.

112   Richard Roach claimed to have cured a mad woman in 1711, which seemed to endorse his sanctity. Gibbons, "Roach, Richard".

The letters bear testimony to the importance of international networking and maintaining connections between supporters from Russia, the German states, the United Provinces and in Britain. Exchanging, and seeking, information on the marriages, concerns and writings of fellow millenarians suggests that they saw themselves as part of a continent-wide movement and community. They looked to people of national standing as evidence of the support they had. They mentioned the natural daughter of Charles II and even the Duke of Buckingham and the king himself as alchemists.

Signs and symbols were important for Lead's millennial supporters. The mention of a "fire ball" seen in London in July 1697 produced dread among its witnesses, and Loth Fisher in Utrecht asked Jane Lead for her views of its significance. Signs of this sort, like those of meteorology, were widely assumed to be messages from God; and the period 1694–1704 was a decade in which such events were especially prominent in popular thought. The deaths of Archbishop Tillotson and Queen Mary II in 1694 was interpreted as a sign of God's anger at the displacement of James II, and the "Great Storm" of 1703 was interpreted as a sign of God's fury that vice and immorality had not been eradicated. For those with a millenarian turn of thought, such warnings implied that God was reminding humanity to hasten to repent before the end of time.

The millenarians' theological ideas were also much preoccupied with issues such as "the commerce with spirits" and communion with saints. Keith Thomas argued that such ideas were a strong feature of Protestantism and there have been more recent views that they were especially associated with women's expressions of faith. But such communications were also affected by fears that some manifestations were inauthentic and others were demonic in origin.[113]

Michael B. Riordan's edition of the letters and prophecies of Lady Abden, Thomas Dutton and James Cunningham suggests something of both the mobility and diversity of the French Prophets in the early eighteenth century. Scotland in 1709 was a turbulent matrix from which the Scottish French Prophets arose. The Union with England was only two years old and already circumstances were not favouring the new settlement of the government. Poor weather in 1708 and 1709 led to low harvests and starvation in some places. The link between low calorific in-take and ecstatic religious activity has been observed elsewhere.[114] In addition, witchcraft remained a concern, Elspeth Rule having

---

113 K. Thomas, *Religion and the Decline of Magic, Studies in Popular Beliefs in Sixteenth and Seventeenth Century England* (Oxford: 1971), 5; See also L. Sangha, "The Social, Personal and Spiritual Dynamics of Ghost Stories in Early Modern England", *The Historical Journal* (2019), 1–21.
114 Linda A. Ryan, *John Wesley and the Education of Children: Gender, Class and Piety* (London:

been arrested and tried on the charge and sentences to branding and banishment from Scotland. The refusal of the Scottish Episcopalian bishops to swear the oaths to William and Mary led to their exclusion and to the formal establishment of the Presbyterian Church in Scotland. This led to years of political and religious tension in which religious identity was connected with political loyalty to the Hanoverian state. Episcopalians in Edinburgh, like James Greenshields, who used the Anglican liturgy, were seen as a threat to the establishment and although he was imprisoned, he was freed by the House of Lords in London, which included Anglican bishops. There were also fierce debates about innovations in worship among both Presbyterians and Episcopalians.[115] Equally, there were assertive acts by the Presbyterians. In 1709, Queen Anne granted a royal charter to the Society in Scotland for Propagating Christian Knowledge (S.S.P.C.K.), which created schools to spread the Kirk's program of education, and this involved the imposition of the English language and religious conversion.

In this context, it is important to recognise that there had been a generation of the Scottish Episcopalian mystics based at Sir Thomas Hope's estate at Craighall, near St Andrews. In addition, there was a congregation at Rosehearty under George Garden, who had been expelled from his parish for defending mysticism.[116] Before the arrival of the French Prophets, they had been issuing warnings and prophecies in Scotland and intensified their activities after 1709. It was therefore natural that the Yorkshire lawyer Thomas Dutton should come to Scotland to establish a base for his group of French Prophets in 1709. Their arrival was heralded as the cleansing of Creation in preparation for the Second Coming.[117] Among the Episcopalians who were converted by Dutton's group was Lady Abden, a twenty-seven-year-old widow whose daughter had been born after the death of her father, John. Lady Abden's tract *The Last Revelation that shall be putt in print to the sons and children of men* was widely circulated and enormously influential. Lady Abden claimed it came to her in person from the Holy Spirit and was a direct result of the religious turbulence in Scotland. What made the work especially significant were her statements in support of the French Prophets and the urgency that was needed as Christ was even then making his way to earth.

2017) chapter 5. See also http://ianchadwick.com/blog/bread-madness-and-christianity/ (accessed 18 March 2018).

115 A. Raffe, *The Culture of Controversy: Religious Arguments in Scotland, 1660–1714* (Woodbridge: 2012).

116 G.D. Henderson, *Mystics of the North-East* (Aberdeen: 1934).

117 M.B. Riordan, 'Mysticism and Prophecy in Early Eighteenth-Century Scotland', *Scottish Historical Review*, vol. 98, supplement (October 2019), pp. 333–360.

The essential question was whether Lady Abden's revelations were directly from the Holy Spirit. Mystics had tended to prefer to claim that their inspiration was a product of their inner holiness and drawn from their own divination. The claim that Lady Abden's words came from an external source, and one as irrefutable as the Holy Spirit, made her *Last Revelation* highly contentious. Even Thomas Dutton doubted the source of Lady Abden's prophecies and ordered that his followers should mark copies of her revelations as inspired by the devil. Nevertheless James Cunningham, one of the Scottish mystics from Craighall, found himself entirely inspired by Lady Abden's prophecies, which he felt were issued under a new divine dispensation and therefore were valid. He joined her campaign touring Scotland and urging men and women to heed her warnings and prophecies.

The documents edited by Michael B. Riordan demonstrate a number of important elements in our understanding of millenarianism in the eighteenth century in Britain. First they show the degree to which millenarianism and mysticism could penetrate the upper reaches of society. The Scottish mystics had obtained the protection of Lord Forbes and Sir Thomas Hope before Lady Abden's conversion. Thomas Dutton was a man of the "middling sort" a lawyer and London magistrate before he came to Edinburgh and James Cunningham came from the landed gentry. The significance of this is that men and women of this class were models for the lower classes. If they found mysticism and divine revelation convincing, how much more so would the ill-educated and those who were taught to emulate and defer to their "betters". The power of emulation lay at the heart of the eighteenth century commercial and economic revolutions, why should it not have been as strong a pull on the beliefs and faith of the poor?

Secondly, the evidence suggests that the moral reform movement in the early eighteenth century, what Dudley Bahlman called "the moral revolution of 1688", was one which was propelled in part by millenarian concerns.[118] This is an aspect of the rationale for the societies for the reformation of manners, the Society for the Promotion of Christian Knowledge and the Society for the Propagation of the Gospel in Foreign Parts which has not hitherto been explored. But it is clear that the campaigns against immorality and sexual misbehaviour were sustained with at least one eye on the salvation of the individual transgressor and the other on the imminence of the end of the world.[119]

---

118   D.W.R. Bahlman, *The Moral Revolution of 1688* (New Haven: 1957).
119   W. Gibson & J. Begiato, *Sex and the Church in the Long Eighteenth Century* (London: 2017), 59–69.

Moreover, the Scottish episode also indicates something of the theological variegation of millenarian and prophetic groups. It might have been expected that the Scottish mystics and French Prophets would have found themselves as allies and collaborators in God's work. This was perhaps one of the expectations of Dutton in moving to Edinburgh. But the issue of the origin of prophecy was not a minor one that could be overlooked or brushed aside; it lay at the core of prophetic and millenarian activity. If the revelations that issued from the prophets were not derived from an authentic source—or what was held to be an authentic source—they opened the followers to the accusation of being led astray by false prophets, and these had been as explicitly predicted as the end of the world. Thus false prophetic pronouncements, derived from untrue sources, were to be expected since they were as much a sign of the end of the world as the second coming of Christ himself. If anything, false prophecy was testimony to the truth of valid prophecy and endorsed the necessity of true endeavour. Thus the French Prophets were on their guard to reject prophecy of the wrong sort.

Warren Johnston's edition of the sermons of Joseph Jacob and Richard Dobbs illustrates the links between millenarianism and politics by connecting the Apocalypse to the military ventures of the eighteenth-century British state. In both the War of Spanish Succession, which occasioned Jacob's 1705 sermon, and the Seven Years War, which stimulated Dobbs's 1759 sermon, Britain was at war with the forces of Catholic Europe, which seems to fit easily into the prophecies of the end of times. The connection of millenarianism and the Protestant victory over Catholic forces was a theme that had been powerfully advanced in the seventeenth century and reached a climax in the period around the Exclusion Crisis and the Glorious Revolution.[120] But, as Johnston points out, there is an assumption that millenarian preaching disappeared from English pulpits thereafter.[121] Johnston's two sermons show, that this assumption is erroneous and clearly other recent evidence suggests that millenarian preaching was alive and well throughout the eighteenth century.[122]

---

120 For which see W. Johnston, *Revelation Restored*.
121 This is an assumption that could be drawn from older studies of the English sermon on the eighteenth century, see for example: J. Downey, *The Eighteenth Century Pulpit, A Study of the Sermons of Butler, Berkeley, Secker, Sterne, Whitefield and Wesley* (Oxford: 1969). R.P. Lessenich, *Elements of Pulpit Oratory in Eighteenth Century England (1660–1800)* (Vienna: 1972); B.F. Mitchell, *English Pulpit Oratory from Andrewes to Tillotson* (London: 1932).
122 See for example Francis & Gibson (eds), *The Oxford Handbook to the British Sermon 1688–1901*, 285–286, 377–387, 503.

What is interesting about the two sermons is that they suggest something of the ecclesiological and geographical span of millenarianism: Jacob was a Dissenter, of a stiff and unbending sort, and Dobbs was an Irish Anglican parson based in County Tyrone. Johnston shows how diverse their interpretations of the Millennium were. But what is also clear is that they both located their sermons in a commitment to the Revolutionary regime established in 1689. In other words, a religiously tolerant Protestant regime was a basis for the defence of Christianity against foreign Catholic apostasy. Jacob and Dobbs clearly elevated their sense of the significance of the victories of 1705 and 1759 from the military and political to global and apocalyptic forces and trends. By implication, local and parochial disputes between and within Protestant churches were a distraction in the face of events that presaged the end of the world. Nevertheless their denominational outlook meant that Jacob was more likely to decry ecclesiastical authority and Dobbs more prone to uphold the settled constitution of Church and State. It is instructive that Jacob's preface anticipated that he would be attacked by

> such, as most Cry up, and yet least of all practise Moderation, Peace, Unity and Charity; Matters of Great Worth, and chief Consequence, but so little understood, and so much less exercis'd, by many vain and unruly Talkers (in the front of which Let Occasional Conformists ever be plac'd) ...

These two groups were those at political loggerheads in Convocation and Parliament in 1705. Those who aimed to "cry up" Moderation were the High Church Tories, determined to exclude Dissenters from public office by shutting down their evasion of the Test Act allowed by occasional conformity. The "talkers" were those, usually Whig, Dissenters who practiced occasional conformity and thereby broke into the Anglican monopoly on public office. This fierce contest was threatening to shatter the Revolutionary settlement.[123] Jacob's anticipation that he would be attacked from both sides of this fierce contest, that eventually forced the Queen to call the 1705 election, suggests that he saw the disputes between Protestants as draining energy from the global apocalyptic struggle that was the real threat to Church and State.

Richard Dobbs's sermon is equally focused on both the immediate events of 1759 as well as on the time horizon that he believed was hurtling towards him. It was no chance that he chose as his text Revelation, chapter six, verse

---

123 See W. Gibson, "English Provincial Engagements in Religious Debates: The Salisbury Quarrel 1705–15", *The Huntington Library Quarterly* 80/1 (2017), 21–45.

two, which referred to a white horse. The white horse of Hanover was a well-known symbol for the Hanoverian regime—indeed the horse featured on the arms of the House of Hanover and from 1714 to 1837 was on the royal standard of the British monarchs.[124] The English white horse chalk hill figures at Uffington, Westbury and Cherhill were created, or renovated, to celebrate the Hanoverian succession and its cause against the Jacobite threat. But of course they also had other biblical resonances. Dobbs's use of the white horse, which in Revelation carried a bow and a crown and went forth to conquer, seemed to be a clear suggestion that the Hanoverian victories of 1759 were part of the signs that the end of the world was at hand.

Johnston's edited sermons are suggestive of two key themes in the consideration of eighteenth-century millenarianism. Firstly, it seems extremely likely that ideas about the Millennium and the second coming of Christ were much more widely heard from the pulpit than has hitherto been recognised. If this is so, it means that eighteenth century congregations experienced teaching in churches and chapels up and down the country that the Millennium was at hand, and that they should anticipate it imminently. Consequently, our view of the lives of men and women in the eighteenth century needs to be adjusted to accommodate this aspect of their experience. Secondly, it seems likely that people associated political and military events with the prophecies in the Bible and saw them as a direct message of the direction in which God had preordained that events would unfold. This also must have affected the experience of men and women in the eighteenth century—from the peasant to the field marshal.

Conclusion

The continuity of millenarian and prophetic thought in the eighteenth century enabled later generations to pick up the themes in their sermons and writing. In the nineteenth century, millenarianism was a strong theme in Protestant preaching in Britain of many denominations.[125] Historians and theologians

---

124 In 1837 Queen Victoria succeeded to the throne of Great Britain and Ireland but, due to Salic Law, could not inherit the throne of Hanover which her uncle the Duke of Cumberland inherited, so the white horse of Hanover disappeared from the arms of the British sovereign.

125 K. Francis & R. Surridge, "Sermons for the End Times: Evangelicalism, Romanticism and the Apocalypse in Britain", in *Oxford Handbook to the British Sermon*, 374–389. D. Hempton, "Evangelicalism and Eschatology", *Journal of Ecclesiastical History* 31/2 (1980), 179–194.

have not easily accommodated millenarianism into accounts of the eighteenth century in part because it runs counter to the prevailing discourse of Enlightenment determinism and secularisation. An Enlightenment model of the period has no place for what appears to be regressive and obsolete modes of thought. Yet prophecy and millenarian thinking were present, and in such strength as to make them important features of the period which are often overlooked. This presence calls for scholars to accommodate millenarian and prophetic thinking much more fully into the historical, theological and cultural account of the period. Without it, our knowledge and understanding of the eighteenth century will remain partial.

CHAPTER 10

Jane Lead and the Philadelphians

Ariel Hessayon

Introduction

Jane Lead (pronounced Leed or Leeds by contemporaries) and sometimes written with a final "e" (especially in printed German translations of her works) was among the most prolific published female authors of the long eighteenth century. More than a dozen different printed titles bearing Lead's name, with one consisting of multiple volumes, were originally issued in English between 1681 and 1702. Her final work "The Resurrection of Life" (1703) was issued posthumously in German translation and has recently been re-translated into English. Moreover, during Lead's lifetime four of her works appeared in a second edition, while from 1694 several writings were also published in translation at Amsterdam—primarily in German, with two rendered into Dutch as well. In addition to these languages one tract was translated into Swedish, most likely from the German version, although this remained in manuscript. Besides being the author of extensive spiritual diaries, theological treatises, epistles and some verse, during the last decade of her eighty-year life Lead became the centre of an extensive correspondence network stretching from Pennsylvania to the Electorate of Saxony. Yet as her son-in-law and amanuensis Francis Lee (1661–1719) conceded, outside a small community of believers Lead's writings were largely ignored in her own country. Instead they enjoyed a widespread if mixed continental reception among an audience of assorted Spiritualists, Behmenists and Pietists—not to mention occasional curious readers, such as Gottfried Wilhelm Leibniz.[1]

During the eighteenth century Lead initially attracted readers generally interested either in the German Lutheran mystic Jacob Boehme [Böhme] (c.1575–1624) or the doctrine of universal salvation. Afterwards she was read by several people attracted by the teachings of Emanuel Swedenborg (1688–1772) and subsequently by certain followers of Joanna Southcott (1750–1814). All the same, outside these small circles her prophetic pretensions and obscure style tended to be judged harshly. Thus the jeweller and goldsmith Christopher Wal-

---

1 Ariel Hessayon, "Introduction: Jane Lead's Legacy in Perspective", in *Jane Lead and her Transnational Legacy*, ed. Ariel Hessayon (Basingstoke: 2016), 1–2.

ton (1809–1887), a humourless Methodist who owned copies of several printed titles by Lead together with important manuscript accounts, complained that the "chief heroine" of the Philadelphian Society had buried her profound spiritual experiences in "a huge mass of parabolicalism and idiocratic deformity".[2]

Such criticism was not new. It went back to an early eighteenth-century life of Lead in Latin by Johann Wolfgang Jaeger, a German professor of theology hostile to mysticism and chiliasm.[3] But it meant that there was greater interest in Lead's writings among German rather than English speakers—at least until the mid-1970s. Since then, in the wake of Second Wave Feminism Lead's reputation has undergone a remarkable ascent from the depths of disdain to the peaks of veneration. So much so, that she is now lauded as an example of "female genius" and regarded—at least by one of her recent biographers—as the most important female religious leader in late seventeenth-century England.[4]

Jane Lead (1624–1704)

Jane was baptized on 9 March 1624 in the parish of Letheringsett, Norfolk. She was a younger daughter of Hamond Ward and his wife Mary. Essentially her life can be divided into three phases: (1) the period from her birth until she became a widow in 1670; (2) the period from 1670 to 1695, the year when she went blind; (3) the period from 1696 to 1704, which spans the public emergence of the Philadelphian Society to her death.

Concerning Lead's life before widowhood, I have suggested elsewhere that she was far more radical than has been supposed. Indeed, her religious beliefs were largely moulded by a militant puritanism that she may have shared with an elder brother, but which conflicted with her parents' more moderate attitude, reflected in their outward adherence to the Church of England. Making use of a great many archival discoveries, which formed the cornerstone of a painstaking reconstruction, I provided mainly circumstantial but nonetheless cumulatively overwhelming evidence that Lead's relatively well-known autobiography "Lebenslauff Der AVTORIN" (Amsterdam: 1696) conceals almost as much as it reveals. Constructed to reassure its intended audience of continental Spiritualists, Behmenists and Pietists of Lead's upright character, respectable

---

2 Christopher Walton, *Notes and Materials for an adequate Biography of the celebrated divine and theosopher, William Law* (London: 1854), 141, 148.
3 Johann Wolfgang Jaeger, *Dissertatio historico-theologica, de Johannæ Leadææ Anglo-Britan. Vita* (Tübingen: 1712).
4 Hessayon, "Introduction", in *Jane Lead*, 2–4.

social status and divinely bestowed gifts this so-called "Life of the Author" adopted a similar strategy to that observable in a number of Philadelphian publications which masked private heterodox beliefs and rituals with public professions of irenic conformity. Thus some key names have been omitted, while the activities and teachings of others have been passed over silently or treated superficially. Doubtless this was because some of these individuals, including one of Lead's older brothers and several relations by marriage, had been Parliamentarian stalwarts and functionaries during the English Civil Wars. This suggests that in the aftermath of the revocation of the Edict of Nantes (1685), the Glorious Revolution (1688–1689), William III's campaign in Ireland, Jacobite risings in Scotland, and a resurgence of apocalyptic exegesis more generally, the spectre of revolutionary radicalism still engendered fear within the British Isles and continental Europe at a moment when the Nine Years' War (1688–1697) had yet to be concluded. Consequently, detailing past associations would have damaged Lead's reputation among her heterogeneous readership.[5]

The period from 1670 to 1695—that is from the beginning of Lead's widowhood until she went blind—is much better documented than the preceding phase of her life because Lead now began keeping extensive spiritual diaries. Even so, Lead's memory began to deteriorate with age with the result that her recollection of certain dates is not always reliable. Added to this are some stylistic interventions introduced by Lead's first amanuensis to his manuscript transcripts of her earliest writings, not to mention subsequent minor editorial intervention on their publication. All of which means that when reading Lead's printed works we should not assume that every sentence is an exact copy of the original, even if we can be confident that the text accurately conveys her sense.

Here additional discoveries enabled me to reinforce my suggestion that Lead was more radical than has been supposed. My argument again relied somewhat on association, with the focus on extensive and overlapping domestic and continental networks. These consisted of assorted millenarians, prophets, theosophists and devotees of mystic and spiritualist authors generally including, among others, Dr John Pordage (1607–1681), Francis Pordage (1622–1692?), Thomas Bromley (1630–1691), Dr Edward Hooker (c.1614–c.1705), William Burman (*fl.*1688), Joseph Sabberton (*fl.*1680), Mary Pocock (*fl.*1649–*fl.*1691), Elizabeth Blagrave (*d.*1693), Helen Pight (1611–*fl.*1692), John Bathurst (*d.*1694?), John

---

5   Ariel Hessayon, "Lead's Life and Times (Part One): Before Widowhood", in *Jane Lead*, 13–37.

Coughen (c.1638–1717?), Tanneke Denijs (d.1702?), Friedrich Breckling (1629–1711),[6] Loth Fischer (d.1709), Johann Georg Gichtel (1638–1710), Johann Wilhelm Petersen (1649–1726), and his wife Johanna. What we see in this period is an evolution of Lead's thought as she came under successive influences and began to develop her own distinctive beliefs. It was a religious journey with staging posts: an initial Calvinist obsession with sin and predestination wedded to a conventional Protestant understanding of the coming apocalypse; then the introduction of Boehme's teachings and accompanying visions of a female personification of divine wisdom; finally the adoption, albeit with inconsistencies, of the doctrine of the universal restoration of all humanity. It was the last, together with Lead's apparent dependence upon visions and revelations, that repulsed certain former admirers of her writings, turning them into some of Lead's most vehment critics.[7]

The concluding phase from 1696 to 1704 spans the period from Lead's first published message to the Philadelphian Society until her death and burial. Taking their name from Philadelphia ('brotherly love'), the sixth of the seven churches in Asia Minor to whom John sent a book containing his revelation (Rev. 1:11, 3:7–13), Lead's little band of supporters intended to warn and prepare prospective believers of the coming Philadelphian age through a flurry of publications. Or to quote from the clergyman Richard Roach's poem "Solomon's Porch":

> When the fair Virgin Pilgrims Stage is done,
> Her Travails ended, and her Garland won;
> A Temple-Glory of Living Stones to rise;
> Whose Base shall fill the Earth; whose Head the Skies,
> *Love* yet can't triumph here, without its Mate,
> Till Light and Beauty too become Incorporate.[8]

Yet this co-ordinated publicity campaign abruptly fractured the Philadelphians' precursor society, which hitherto had negotiated a path between secrecy and openness, combining private prayer meetings and selective circulation of members' spiritual diaries through scribal publication with public preaching and print publication. Consequently only the minority who favoured a public

---

6 See Viktoria Franke's chapter in vol. 1 (*Continental Europe*) of this collection.
7 Ariel Hessayon, "Lead's Life and Times (Part Two): The Woman in the Wilderness", in *Jane Lead*, 39–69.
8 Onesimus [*pseud.* = Richard Roach], "Solomon's Porch: or the Beautiful Gate of Wisdom's Temple", in Jane Lead, *A Fountain of Gardens* (London: [1697]), sig. *E2.

testimony owned the Philadelphian name, with some clandestine "waiters for y^e kingdom" even accusing the Philadelphians of schism.[9] Wanting to expose her visions and teachings to public view, Lead was given the opportunity to do so through a succession of mainly male patrons and amanuenses—including Baron Dodo von Knyphausen (1641–1698), a privy councillor at the Brandenburg-Prussia court in Berlin who financed several publications.[10] Consequently when the first instalment of Lead's spiritual diaries appeared as *A Fountain of Gardens* together with Francis Lee's lengthy editorial preface dated 1 January 1697 Lead became synonymous with the Philadelphian Society. Lee and Roach, on the other hand, remained guarded: their printed contributions appeared anonymously or pseudonymously under the names Timotheus and Onesimus respectively.[11]

The Philadelphian Society

According to the various versions of Roach's manuscript history of this small religious community, the Philadelphians were not a "peculiar sect" or party.[12] Rather, while the term was a particularly appropriate description of certain "Spiritual People" in England, indeed of a blameless, weak community treated with contempt even by their fellow Christians, it signified more generally a belief in "ye Coming of Christ to his Glorious Kingdom".[13] Besides this strong millenarian aspect, Philadelphian teaching emphasised the fulfilment of prophecies and full completion of divine promises—including the conversion of the Jews (usually regarded as "Antecedent to the coming of Christ"), as well as the "call of the *Turks* and other Infidels";[14] the "deeply Mystical Work of the *Regeneration* and *Ascension* of Souls";[15] primitive Christianity as practised by the Apostles; peace, love and Protestant church unity; the Reformation of Manners; charity; and the "absolute necessity" of private and public revelation,[16]

---

9   Oxford, Bodleian Library (hereafter Bodl.), MS Rawlinson D 833, fol. 55^v.
10 Knyphausen had already supported the Flemish mystic Antoinette Bourignon (1616–1680). Hessayon, "Lead's Life and Times (Part Two)", 56. On Antoinette Bourignon, see Michael Riordan's chapter in the present volume.
11 Ariel Hessayon, "Lead's Life and Times (Part Three): The Philadelphian Society", in *Jane Lead*, 71–90.
12 Bodl., MS Rawlinson D 833, fols 54^r–66^r, 82^r–87^v.
13 Bodl., MS Rawlinson D 833, fol. 63^r.
14 [Francis Lee], *The State of the Philadelphian Society* (1697), 7.
15 [Lee], *State of Philadelphian Society*, 9.
16 Cambridge, Gonville and Caius College, MS 725/752, [Thomas Haywood], "An Essay

which superseded insufficient human learning, and on which subject Lee had written a very large but unfinished manuscript treatise.

From autumn 1695 a private week-day prayer meeting had been initiated at Lead's rented property in Hoxton Square, Shoreditch. It is unclear if this Hoxton gathering pre-dated what Roach called the "long Rooted & Mother meeting" of the Philadelphians at Baldwin's Gardens in St Andrew's, Holborn. All the same, he indicated that the Baldwin's Gardens meeting was held at Mrs Anne Bathurst's on Sundays for the "General resort of those who were of this way".[17] At some point Mrs Bathurst combined with Mrs Joanna Oxenbridge (d.1709), an impoverished widow. Both women were said to have received "great & wonderful experiences" and Roach considered them two of the "principle persons in carrying on ye Spiritual work".[18]

About the end of March 1697 there appeared the first volume of *Theosophical Transactions by the Philadelphian Society*. Edited by Lee and Roach, this short-lived journal consisted of "conferences, letters, dissertations, inquiries" and the like for the advancement of "Piety & Divine Philosophy".[19] While its title partly recalled the Royal Society's *Philosophical Transactions*, the sub-title "Acta Philadelphica" suggests a parallel with the Acts of the Apostles. Yet its publication caused a stir resulting in the Baldwin's Gardens meeting becoming overcrowded as "so many flocked" there.[20] This necessitated moving to a larger place, namely Hungerford Market. Situated near Charing Cross between the Strand and the Thames, this was also the site of a French church. Their first meeting was held there on Sunday, 18 July 1697. It was attended by Lead and her family as well as by Caleb Gilman (1670–*fl*.1708), who noted the fact in the fly-leaf to his copy of Boehme's *Aurora*. Evidently the Philadelphians hoped to attract a large gathering to the Hungerford meeting since they publicised it through the circulation of an announcement. Among the variety of curiosity seekers and scoffers who attended was the former Baptist-turned-Quaker Richard Claridge, who recorded his impressions of a meeting held on Sunday afternoon, 15 August 1697. Claridge noted that when he entered the men's hats were off and that an unnamed man was preaching in a "very careless and lazy posture". Another speaker was a woman called Cresilla, who to Claridge's annoyance was fashionably dressed. She talked much of "the

---

towards the Life or rather some account of the late Learned and pious Francis Lee, M.D." (1722), no foliation.
17   Bodl., MS Rawlinson D 833, fols 23^r, 82^v.
18   Bodl., MS Rawlinson D 833, fols 27^r–28^v, 65^r.
19   Bodl., MS Rawlinson D 833, fols 65^v, 82^v, 86^v.
20   Bodl., MS Rawlinson D 833, fols 65^v, 82^v.

spiritual flesh and blood of Christ, pretending it was a great mystery". Moreover, Claridge observed that:

> they held universal redemption, pretended to a special dispensation of the Spirit, were against water-baptism, and outward breaking of bread; but were for justification by Christ's imputed righteousness; and that though the guilt of sin was taken away in believers, and the power and dominion of sin much subdued, yet corruptions and imperfections remained during life.[21]

The Hungerford meeting endured about six months subjected to, on the one hand, "great Opposition" and violence from the "rude multitude" and, on the other, increasing internal divisions that eventually tore it apart. Beforehand, however, Lead and her family had absented themselves on the pretext that it was "inconvenient" to travel such a "great distance" from Hoxton.[22] Instead they obtained licence to gather at Westmoreland House, near Bartholomew Close (St. Bartholomew the Great); a site formerly occupied by a Presbyterian congregation. One Sunday, probably 29 August 1697, a "very great concourse of people" came. Among them were some boys and "rude fellows" who caused trouble, yet there was also a "sober sort of company very attentive and inquisitive". They outnumbered the Philadelphians, who could be counted on one hand: Lead, Francis and Barbarie Lee, a woman using the pseudonym Hephzibah (possibly Mary Sterrell), and "the good honest man" (perhaps Heinrich Johann Deichmann).[23] Although the audience at Westmoreland House was said to have been "more favourable & civilized" the volume of disturbances gradually increased. So Lead's group was driven to relocate, firstly to Twisters Alley near Bunhill Fields (St. Giles-without-Cripplegate); then after a "considerable time" to Loriners' Hall (which stood on the corner of Aldermanbury Postern and London Wall, facing the north end of Basinghall Street), and finally—sometime after Easter Sunday 1699—back to Hoxton.[24] Again, it is noteworthy that Loriners' Hall was an established venue for nonconformist

---

21 Manchester, Chetham's Library, 3.F.3.46 (a), endpaper; Joseph Besse (ed.), *The Life and Posthumous Works of Richard Claridge*, 3rd ed. (London: 1836), 31–33.
22 Bodl., MS Rawlinson D 833, fols 56^v, 66^r, 82^v.
23 Bodl., MS Rawlinson D 832 fols 53^{r-v}, 94^r–95^r.
24 Anon., *Propositions Extracted From the Reasons for the Foundation and Promotion of a Philadelphian Society* (London: 1697), 11; Anon., *The Declaration of the Philadelphian Society of England, Easter-Day, 1699* (1699), 6; Bodl., MS Rawlinson D 833, fols 56^{r-v}, 65^v–66^r, 82^v, 84^r; Richard Roach, *The Great Crisis: or, the Mystery of the Times and Seasons Unfolded* (London: 1725), 99.

preaching. It was used, for example, by a Particular Baptist congregation in 1699 and subsequently by an Independent congregation in 1704.

To recap, the Philadelphian Society emerged openly at a particular moment: after the revocation of the Edict of Nantes (1685), the Glorious Revolution (1688–1689), the Toleration Act (1689), and the lapse of the Licensing Act (1695). The Protestant Prince of Orange become William III of England had defeated the Catholic James II in Ireland and suppressed Jacobite risings in Scotland, while the Nine Years' War (1688–1697), which pitted a coalition lead by William known as the Grand Alliance against the territorial ambitions of Louis XIV, was shortly to be concluded with the Treaty of Rijswijk. More broadly, this period has been viewed by some scholars as the beginning of an English Enlightenment, a so-called "Age of Reason" brought into being by certain interconnected factors. Among them was the formal creation of a Royal Society, a body populated by experimental scientists who attempted to achieve public respectability through their apparent scepticism, empiricism, affected disinterest and use of non-sectarian language. Isaac Newton's *Principia Mathematica* had been published in 1687 forcing open-minded readers capable of understanding its contents to reconsider their views of the universe. Added to this was the contribution of Baruch Spinoza and his followers who, if Jonathan Israel is to be believed, provided the intellectual backbone of the European Radical Enlightenment. Another disputed strand of Enlightenment rationalism was anti-Trinitarian thought, which arguably contributed to the gradual development of an alternative, reasonable form of Protestantism through its hostility to Papal authority, Catholic dogma and superstition against a backdrop of growing anticlericalism and interest in the historical Jesus. Stripped of its mystery this naked Christianity meshed with an acceptance of the cessation of miracles while dismissing the pretensions of those tarnished with the brush of enthusiasm.[25]

At first glance the Philadelphians do not fit comfortably within this framework. Indeed, their belief in the continued communication of higher knowledge through visions and revelations, apocalyptic expectations, privileging of individual religious experiences, engagement with prophecy, theosophy and mysticism, not to mention their reverence for female figures and secret heterodox rituals, collectively positions them as an alternative to some scholarly conceptions of the Enlightenment. Yet it simultaneously situates them at the

---

25 For an excellent recent discussion of "enthusiasm", see Lionel Laborie, *Enlightening Enthusiasm. Prophecy and Religious Experience in Early Eighteenth-Century England* (Manchester: 2015).

heart of what Clarke Garrett dubbed the Mystical Enlightenment.[26] This is not a paradox given how elastic and comprehensive our understanding of the Enlightenment has become.

Another context was the proliferation of religious societies. Roach's associate the educator Charles Bridges estimated that there were about 50 in London. These were mainly concerned with eradicating "vice and debauchery", with some also instrumental in founding free schools for poor children. Significantly, the establishment of these Charity Schools fostered links with likeminded Pietists at Halle—a university Lee had visited on his travels. Indeed, Lee would anonymously translate and probably provide the preface to the English version of *Pietas Hallensis* (1705), an account of an orphanage and other charitable institutions in Saxony by the educator and social reformer August Hermann Francke (1663–1727).[27] Accordingly the Philadelphian Society was preceded by the Society for the Reformation of Manners (1690), but anticipated the Societies for Promoting Christian Knowledge (1698) and for Propagation of the Gospel in Foreign Parts (1701).

Then there is 1697. The year had been carefully selected since it was based on the extensive apocalyptic exegesis of two biblical commentators that can be connected with the Philadelphians—Thomas Beverley (d.1702) and Edward Waple (1647–1712). An Independent minister and prolific author, Beverley envisaged Philadelphia as partly arising out of a combination of Protestant sufferings in France and an undefiled remnant of Protestant churches. This would lead to a settlement "upon the pure Laws and Ordinances of Christ": the *"Philadelphian state"*.[28] The appointed time of "Christ's coming to judge the world" was Monday, 23 August 1697 and it is no coincidence that on that very day the Philadelphian Society finalised their constitutions at Westmoreland House.[29] Although Beverley was forced to issue a public apology when his prophecy failed, Roach recalled that Beverley had sought out and conferred with the Society when they openly declared and warned the world of the coming *"Kingdom of Christ"*.[30] And while it is difficult to determine the extent of

---

26 Clarke Garrett, "Swedenborg and the Mystical Enlightenment in Late Eighteenth-century England", *Journal of the History of Ideas*, 45 (1984), 67–81.
27 Berlin, Staatsbibliothek Preussischer Kulturbesitz Handschriftenabteilung, Nachlaß A.H. Francke, Kapsel 30—England betreffend, fol. 673; Bodl., MS Rawlinson D 832, fol. 45^r; G & C, MS 725/752.
28 Thomas Beverley, *An Exposition of the Divinely Prophetick Song of Songs* (1687), 47–50; Thomas Beverley, *The Prophetical history of the Reformation* (1689), sig. a2^{v-2}, 64–65, 72–73, 78.
29 Anon., *Propositions*, 11.
30 Richard Roach, *The Imperial Standard of Messiah Triumphant* (London: 1727), xix.

this collaboration, it should be noted that through their network of international correspondents the Philadelphians facilitated the publication of several of Beverley's treatises in German translation at Frankfurt.

Similarly, in his annotations on each chapter of Revelation, Waple predicted that about 1697 there would be "some more than ordinary appearance" of the *"Philadelphian* State". He too incorporated recent events such as the revocation of the Edict of Nantes and the capture of Savoy by a Waldensian force in 1690 within his apocalyptic chronology, reckoning that 1697 would mark both the end of *"the Beasts Months"* and the *"Days of the Witnesses"* (Rev. 11:3).[31]

∴

Just as Lead's autobiography of 1696 had been crafted to reassure readers of her respectability, so Lee and Roach were the principle movers in fashioning an image of irenic conformity and social standing for the Philadelphians at large. Thus in a later published account Roach portrayed a meeting of the Philadelphians' precursor society headed by Joseph Sabberton as an "Eminent" assembly frequented by "Gentry and Persons of *Quality*", including a number of women.[32] Besides this claim to social respectability, Philadelphians stressed how they differed from Quakers. Denying that they were a new sect or faction, they did not challenge the authenticity of the Bible and outwardly conformed by hearing the word preached in Protestant churches. In addition, they acknowledged the authority of civil government and did not have a reputation for disturbing church services. They were "not for *turning the World upside down*" as some had misrepresented them. Nor were they "so silly as to place Religion in *Thouing* and *Theeing*, in keeping on their Hats".[33]

Hostile observers, however, readily compared Philadelphians with Quakers. Some even incorporated them within a catalogue of innumerable sects or else grouped them with foreign Quietists and Pietists. More damaging still was the allegation that Lead envisaged herself as the woman clothed with the sun (Rev. 12:1), indeed as the grandmother of a new Christ. Evidence is partly supplied in Philadelphian correspondence intercepted by the Archbishop of Canterbury's agents. Together with other documents these reveal an extensive transnational correspondence network; the adoption of new spiritual names; the existence of a heterodox religious ritual known as the love feast; and association with

---

31 Edward Waple, *The Book of the Revelation Paraphrased; With Annotations on Each Chapter* (London: 1693), "The Argument", 54–55, 210, 236, 241–243.
32 Roach, *Great Crisis*, 99.
33 [Lee], *State of Philadelphian Society*, 2.

disreputable figures including an alchemist, confidence trickster, bigamist and murderer. That and previous connections with the Behmenist prophet and martyr Quirinus Kuhlmann (1651–1689). Even so, it should be emphasised that while the Philadelphians were maligned as enthusiasts, they were not the victims of religious persecution.

∴

The Philadelphians remained in public view for six years. On Sunday, 13 June 1703 they issued a protestation at Hoxton, London against the degeneracy and apostasy of the Christian churches in their day. Thereupon they retreated from the world in acknowledgement of their failure to bring about Christ's second coming. Almost immediately, satirists exulted. As for Lead, she died at Hoxton on 8 August 1704 aged 80, possibly of stomach cancer. Her body was interred in the nonconformist burial ground at Bunhill Fields. Thereafter Lead's followers claimed that they had received visions attesting to her sanctity. Besides this consolation, her authority was also invoked in the leadership struggle that ensued for control of the Philadelphians.

What happens to a small religious group on the death of a central charismatic figure is a well-worn question. Disappointment as prophecies come to naught, falling away from the faith, leadership struggles, schism, new personalities and fresh predictions, promoting certain doctrines at the expense of others—including adapting and usually softening the original message to suit changed political and religious contexts, as well as rewriting the movement's history so as to give greater prominence to the triumphant second generation of leaders are all occurrences familiar to students of the subject. We see all this in the Philadelphians with the added peculiarity that so many of their guiding spiritual lights, so many readers and indeed authors of their texts, had been women. There would be a second incarnation, as the movement was reborn, reinvigorated by the arrival of the Camisards at London in 1706. But as Lionel Laborie has recently shown, that too would ultimately end with personality clashes, dissension, fragmentation, disappointment, ridicule and failure.[34]

---

34   Lionel Laborie, "Philadelphia Resurrected: Celebrating the Union Act (1707) from Irenic to Scatological Eschatology", in *Jane Lead*, 213–239.

1   "Letters / To Various Persons Abroad; Written in 1697. With Notes of
     Abp. Tenisons Own Handwriting"[35]

Selected letters written between May and October 1697 concerning Jane Lead and the Philadelphians. These were intercepted by agents of the Archbishop of Canterbury, Thomas Tenison, and contain occasional notes in Tenison's own handwriting as well as a contemporary index.

20   July [28?]. Out Letters
     A monsieur monsieur Loth Fischer a Utrecht. June 29. subs. Timotheus.[36]
     Dominus tecum & vir belli ora, Labora, Pugna, vince, vale.[37]

     The Publication of ye Transactions does here excite a spirit of enquiry in very many,[38] they passing under all kind of censures, so y^t ye little meeting of our Society wch was before very private, is now hereupon exceeding throng'd. God
21   will bring light out of all this. Some have in vain endeavoured | to stifle w^t is now to break out. My learned friend who makes such considerable discoveries in ye X^{ian} Antiquity, is a person of a very slow & examining genius, & has a considerable power wth an Arch-deaconry in ye Regular Church of England, his name Waple.[39] He has always studied a most retired life, except where his duty obliges, & yet most exactly informs himself of all y^t passes: & will never give his assent to any thing, before he has examin'd all y^t can be found said on both sides. I have some knowledge of Ludolphi,[40] he is an easy man, & I believe has no ill will. May ye good spirit of our God direct all for y^e best, y^t there may be no occasion given for y^e enemy to triumph. 50*li* to be p[ai]d positively wthin a month.

     Wth one to Gideon, & one to Matthias subsc: J. Lead.[41] In y^e strain of Quietisme.[42]

---

35   London, Lambeth Palace Library [hereafter LPL], MS 1048a.
36   Timotheus = Francis Lee (1661–1719), to Loth Fischer (*d.*1709) at Utrecht, dated 29 June 1697.
37   "God be with you, and (you) man of war pray, work, fight, win. Goodbye".
38   *Theosophical Transactions by the Philadelphian Society, Consisting of Memoirs, Conferences, Letters, Dissertations, Inquiries, &c.* (London: 1697). These consisted of five numbers: the first dated March 1697; the last dated September, October and November 1697.
39   Edward Waple (1647–1712), Archdeacon of Taunton and vicar of St Sepulchre's, London.
40   Heinrich Wilhelm Ludolf (1655–1712), former secretary to Prince George of Denmark. A Pietist and correspondent of August Hermann Francke, Ludolf was familiar with Lee's translation of Johann Wilhelm Petersen's *A Letter to some Divines* (London: 1695).
41   Gideon = Loth Fischer; Matthias (*fl.*1701) = unidentified correspondent of Jane Lead [cf. Acts 1:23, 1:26].
42   For further references to Quietism, see Adelisa Malena's chapter in vol. 2 of this collection and Michael Riordan's in the present volume.

W^th another in a strange language, for ought I know Dutch, for I can hardly read one word of it, it is written so very badly.

Out Lett[ers] July 5.
A Monsieur Mon^sr Loth Fischer a Utrecht. July 2. Sub. Jane Lead.[43]

We have now receiv'd ye Baronesses second Bill for 25*li*, we are doing all we can to hasten ye Baron away.[44]

If ye Treasury of ye monastery y^t is mentioned could be safely received by ye Abbot, whereby ye monastery there demolished might be transplanted into England it might make room for you & your Family, wth other Families y^t are under ye same dispensation.[45]

Out Post July 9.
A Mon^sr Mon^sr Loth Fischer a Utrecht. July 9. Sub. Jane Lead.[46]

Dear & Beloved Gideon, whom methinks in spirit I am still conversing wth all, to uphold & strengthen you against ye many tumults & assaults commenced from ye Regions & Worlds y^t ly in disharmon[y] but let us fortify & comfort each other y^t we are ye children of Peace & unity, born from aboue, even from ye God of Love, of wch we shall not be ashamed, because this love is our joy as he [...]

[An undated letter from Jane Lead to an unknown recipient. Although the first two pages have been removed, a contemporary index indicates that Baron von Burkersroda (Bergastrode) is mentioned on page 45. The last few lines on page 47 are also extant]

I committ you & yours to y^e outspreading wing of y^e Dove, y^t breatheth flames of Love, resting yours
  In y^t linck of Unity wch never can be broken
  Jane Lead

---

43 Jane Lead to Loth Fischer at Utrecht, dated 2 July 1697.
44 Baroness = possibly Lucie Ölgard von Burkersroda (*d.*1705), sister of Christoph baron von Rantzau (*d.*1696) and widow of Frederik baron von Burkersroda (Bergastrode). Baron = possibly Augustin von Burkersroda (*fl.*1699), their son, who had matriculated at Halle University on 6 August 1694. The Baroness was also a correspondent of August Hermann Francke, financially supporting charitable initiatives in Halle.
45 The contemporary index describes this entry as "Monastery wch ye Philadelphians would have had".
46 Jane Lead to Loth Fischer at Utrecht, dated 9 July 1697.

We had 2 sheets of ye Journal to send you, but ye Printer being at a distance disappoints us. Timothy & Lydia wth Onesimus greet you.[47]

47 Out Letters July 13.
A Mon^{sr} Mon^{sr} Loth Fischer a Utrecht. July 13. Sub. Jane Lead.[48]
The Baron of Borquertrode.[49]

53 Out letters July 16.
A Monsieur, Mon^{sr} Loth Fischer à Utrecht. Sub. Jane Lead.[50]

For ye better security of our Letters, if perchance any Plot should be I desire y^t you may address ye rest to Mr Vandeput,[51] who may be trusted. We expected y^t Eutychus might have been in England before this.[52]

54 In Letters July 17. 97.
For ye Lady Jane Lead in Hogsden Square in ye middle of ye East side. sub. Luce. Ol. d. B.[53]

My son will shortly see y^t all what he hath from his Father is lost. For ye Elector now King in Polen hath pawn'd ye Diocese Meisen to ye Papists for 7½ ooooo Rychx dalders,[54] so y^t we ye Farm, wch was before a monastery, shortly must give over.

A Letter of ye Baroness de Burkertrode:[55] Amsterdam enclosed

I pray heartily not to trust upon y^e fine words of a man, for Friend Meshman saith me yt Ludolphi is against you, & not for you,[56] & this does also communicate all out of England to D. Schmiedberger,[57] & they do Allude in y^e known

---

47 Timothy = Francis Lee; Lydia = Barbarie (1653–fl.1720), wife of Francis Lee and daughter of Jane Lead [cf. Acts 16:14]; Onesimus = Richard Roach (1662–1730) [cf. Col. 4:9, Philem. 1:10].
48 Jane Lead to Loth Fischer at Utrecht, dated 13 July 1697.
49 Baron of Borquertrode = possibly Augustin von Burkersroda.
50 Jane Lead to Loth Fischer at Utrecht, dated 16 July 1697.
51 Possibly a son of the London merchant Peter Vandeput (c.1611–1669).
52 Eutychus = possibly either Franz Ferdinand von Knyphausen (1673–1725), or Friedrich Ernst von Knyphausen (1678–1731), sons of Baron Dodo von Innhausen und Knyphausen (1641–1698) [cf. Acts 20:9].
53 Luce. Ol. d. B. = Lucie Ölgard von Burkersroda writing to Jane Lead at Hoxton Square, dated 7/17 July 1697.
54 Augustus II the Strong (1670–1733), Elector of Saxony, who had converted from Lutheranism to Catholicism in June 1697 to gain support for his claim to the Polish throne.
55 Baroness de Burkentrode = Lucie Ölgard von Burkersroda.
56 Christian Meschmann (c.1628–fl.1704) merchant of Amsterdam; Ludolphi = Heinrich Wilhelm Ludolf.
57 Dr Isaac Schmidberger (fl.1697), Behmenist physician and correspondent of the Amsterdam based Behmenist Johann Georg Gichtel (1638–1710).

Blamings. That your meeting grows on is well good, but I believe yt it shall give many hindrances for you & our dearest mother, & possibly be a stop in printing of ye Diary,⁵⁸ wch I should see not fain.

[In letters 4th August 1697, continued]
For ye Lady Jane Lead in Hogsden Square in ye middle of ye East side. France unto ye Briel. Utrecht 22 July O.S. sub. G. i.e. Gideon.⁵⁹

Now as to our known Patron,⁶⁰ he also is sollicitous for his son y^t he might come into acquaintance wi^th Karthold,⁶¹ so y^t he expressly write if he did it not on your behalf, he would expressly give orders to his son, who as now will be at Brussel & go over Ostend for England, to come again home, y^t he might not speak this ungodly & impious nay & most perillous man for young manns, to wit Karthold; for because he did know his impious | principles to seduce ye youth, therefore he was very solicitous & did pray you to enquire close after this thing, & as soon as his son should once speak wth him / Korthold / to advice it immediately to him / ye Patron / then he would know w^t to do. For y^t Korthold ye first espouse had forsaken & marryed another,⁶² was a principle wch he had reached already some years ago ye youth to wit y^t in ye first covenant was ye Polygamy well ordered, & in ye 2^d annihilated but in ye 3^d yt is now to come should be recovered, wth 1000 other things.

The medecin is not yet sent to ye Patron, but he does query of you if ye said med[icine] was sent, & he / ye Patron / hath proved it by some other person whether he himself also should prove it? whereupon he is desirous to hear your answer, but Dear Friend I cannot consent it, because Kartholt had indeed carried ye false Magia in former times, therefore I pray to be cautious in your councell as to this matter. Our Patron is also desirous to have a right descrip-

---

58   The second volume of Jane Lead's *A Fountain of Gardens* (London: 1697), which contains prefatory epistles by both the editor Francis Lee (5 August 1697), and the author (29 July 1697).
59   Loth Fischer at Utrecht writing to Jane Lead at Hoxton Square, dated 22 July / 1 August 1697.
60   Baron Dodo von Knyphausen.
61   Dr Karthold or Kortholt, subsequently described as an "instrument of Belial". He may have been a relative of Christian Kortholt (1633–1694), Lutheran professor of theology at Kiel and a prolific author who had two sons. They were Matthias Kortholt (1674–1725) a poet and philosopher, and Sebastian Kortholt (1675–1760), who lectured on rhetoric and moral philosophy at Kiel University and also corresponded with Leibniz.
62   Kortholt had married Catherina Barenz or Beerens, a spiritual woman of Zwolle. He afterwards abandoned her and attempted to annul the marriage, claiming it was merely a betrothal.

tion of ye conclusion of ye Feast of Tabernacles y^t consists in a little bisked singet into wine & eaten also.

To our Antagonista yet in Amsterdam I have not yet answered,[63] because I do know y^t he will & must have ye last word, & if I y^r sweetest words write to him, he will dominate over y^r soul, & if any one y^t will grant not, then he shuns not to give such bitter words y^t I au^t it yet more secure to hold my peace, especially because he commonly is wont to say, I have this man written a Letter, whereupon he after a few days did dye. And then from another, this man has had already about his neck ye rope to strangle himself because he is gone from us away & would not follow us. Therefore I aut as yet better to keep my pen back y^n to write. tho as you think it well, I shall write as you did prescribe me at last.

The Treatise of ye Everlasting Gospel Message is sub Prælo,[64] & I hope it shall be absolved in 10 days.

I have received Litt. G. g. of ye Diary 2^d Part.

My Dearest Bro. & Sisters Tim & Lydia, Onesimus & Hephzibah.[65]

94^a The Solar Oil may be used internally for a Podagnius 9 drops in warm wine & to sweat thereupon.[66] Outwardly to anoint ye nodes there withall, & covered with a plaister. The Tincture hath mirable effects in Pestilential heat feavers & all sicknesses given in 28 to 30 dropt. We can bring & exalt this medicine thus high that it doth give as well luystre in ye darkness as a Carbunckel & is no Corrotion therein. The Plaister is good against all viciousness hath a special magnetick virtue to resolve & heal: for it ceaseth not till it hath drawn out all stragnesst hetrogenum:/ it may stick hard in ye body so deep it will. We cannot as yet have the medicines thus high because ye time is too short, but after some months I will send it, & y^t in Forma Pulveris which is wholy fi in ye Fire, as then this Oyle is also fi in ye Fire. Some drops thereof let fall upon Chrystall y^t is melting tinctureth it. But the Powder, if we make it is over six & is yet to be solved in every liquor. I have also found out the way the make red glass, upon y^e old manner in Fenestrarum orbiculis & is but to be done with a liquor wherewith but is to be anointed so it does make an ingress into y^e glass & how

---

63 Antagonist in Amsterdam = unidentified.
64 Jane Lead, *A Revelation of the Everlasting Gospel-Message* (London: 1697), which contains an undated prefatory epistle by the editor Francis Lee.
65 Tim[othy] = Francis Lee; Lydia = Barbarie Lee; Onesimus = Richard Roach; Hephzibah = possibly Mary Sterrell (*fl*.1712), French Quaker author of *A New Years-Gift, or a Token of Love* (1693) [cf. Isa. 62:4].
66 Kortholt; indexed as "Chymical Whimsies". The hand is quite different here and may indicate that these two pages were subsequently inserted prior to binding.

many things should I not number up that all do flow from out this Ground. I have seen with admiration how a spotted Diamont did lose its spots through our spiritum nay how another hath put off its cloudy & obscure coat. If you can have some stoner of that kind, wch they do call Phoeincres, wch are Diamonts y^t have a luystre which is wholy little they may be polisht as much as they will, as also scotie great Pearles, wherein is no glance at all or y^t are else black & not ripe, then I will let you see w^t this universal spirit is able to do & work thereupon. Our Menstrum does | extract all 3 principles of ye Gold &   94^b drives it over ye Alembic. We can have ye 3 Principia apart, as in ye Oyle, ye Sulphur, the Tinctur, ye Salt, & each one hath its particular operation upon y^e ☉, ♃ ♄ ☿ to strengthen ye Praedicates thereof & to separate the Heterogenea so as y^t by this medicine is to find perfect health & long life you writes from ye Quintessence of ye Gold, as if did remain a Caput Mortuum, but y^t is only an extraction ♄ per extractionem & not per viam Putrefactionis In capite mortuo does stick ye most noble Treasure but the true s [blank] is required thereby. Our Menstruum is Universalissimum for it doth resolve & reduce all things in their primam massam catholicam & separes ye 3 Principia, & gives each one in ye Hands of ye Artist in P [blank] y^t he may unite y^m joyntly in perfection what we see therein is not to be exprest by any penne. Yellow Deamonts we can make wholy white, in a short time. Be pleased to send some of that kind, & to weigh them for to see ye truth then you can make ye prove with more of them for great advantage in Quantitate, & made a contract with Leffman Bordens or another Jew.[67] If you may have ye History of the Water-Birds in Borussia, I pray to send it to me. There are some here who have begun to publish abroad wherein many thing of me or of my matters are inserted. I have opened my meaning over ye Historie fro[m] ye Birds curieuse enough, as also over ye Query concerning ye Spirit which did bring ye Key to ye Treasures according to ye ground of ye Truth very deep. Be but pleased to give more Information to me thereof then I can serve you therein. I have set down my sentiments of it but I do keep it back | till   94^c the others shall have opened there meaning. How [ ] Qu[ ] se se habent ^ apud [ ] in Germania? Methincks even as here in England [ ] where many are the motions, but that do macke only Pra[ ] ye Figures, & are perswaded by themselves y^t they have ye Being [ ] wch must exert it self also in Powers & deeds & not with words & [ ] or Figures only yet every one does stand in its order. I know many ways which I before did not know we are all men & do err in many ways. I was expecting also to find a more pure & unmixed Being in Catherin

---

67   Leffmann Behrens (c.1630–1714), Jewish financial agent resident at Hanover.

Berenz,⁶⁸ but it hath been also in Figures, wherein hath been well [ ] Praeludium unto another thing wᶜʰ we yet did not understand but have found out the true Bride wᶜʰ I did desire & long & loock after [ ] so many things have been prefigured from yᵗ year of in wᶜʰ I am yᵉ world.

95   For yᵉ same again.⁶⁹

I do see out of Kartholds Letter yᵗ yᵉ History of yᵉ Abbot is also known to him & happily to others also, wᶜʰ is done not well for yᵗ must be & abide secret things, there may result out many inconveniences; therefore I must entreat yᵗ they must be more cautious in our mothers house. I would fain also know whether Karth[old's] Medicine had yᵉ prised effect & though it had yᵉ same I can nevertheless have no good Idea of him. For yᵗ wᵗʰ yᵉ second wife is an impious & wicked Trick. But it seems yᵗ he & she have been ranting, yt they let copulate them orderly. Here in these lands this would be capitale crimen, where on yᵉ one side maritus, & on yᵉ other conjux still were alive.

Timothy & Lydia her Son & Daughter.⁷⁰

That you would make a contract wᵗʰ Leffman yᵉ Jew at Hanover were well good,⁷¹ if he would trust & send pear[l]s diamonds & jewells for England.

Make also a contract wᵗʰ yᵉ Jew of Court.

103 Out Letter. Aug. 7th 97.

A Monˢʳ Loth Fischer a Utrecht. Aug 3. sub. Jane Lead.⁷²

The Baron of B[orquertrode] is still here.⁷³ We hear yt he has been lately endeavouring to get himself introduced to yᵉ Lady Overkirke as designing to be a su[i]t[or]:⁷⁴ but it is not probable yt she will entertain such a Person on this acct.

We hope more in a little time to send you yᵉ 2ᵈ Vol. of yᵉ Diary compleat, wᵗʰ somewᵗ else yᵗ has been lately opened relating to yᵉ Temple structure. We hear nothing yet of Eutychus.⁷⁵

Wᵐ Lee in new George street near Spittle Fields.⁷⁶

---

68   Catherina Barenz or Beerens of Zwolle.
69   [Loth Fischer?] to Jane Lead.
70   Possibly a note inserted by the Archbishop of Canterbury's agent.
71   Leffman = Leffmann Behrens.
72   Jane Lead to Loth Fischer at Utrecht, dated 3 August 1697.
73   Baron of B[orquertrode] = Augustin von Burkersroda.
74   Lady Overkirke = a member of the Nassau d'Auverquerque family.
75   Eutychus = possibly Franz Ferdinand von Knyphausen or Friedrich Ernst von Knyphausen.
76   William Lee (d.1721), brother of Francis Lee, silk dyer of New George Street near Spitalfields, London.

A Pious friend of ours Mr Ripendale is returning to Holland in 4 or 5 days,[77] & if he can find out y^e Baron, he is to endeavour to perswade him to go along wth him.

Mr Dykeman,[78] Mr Freher.[79]

For ye Lady Jane Lead in Hogsden square in ye middle of ye East side. Utrecht 12/2 Aug. 97. sub. Loth Fischer. G.[80]

Silas hath been sick,[81] my last demonstrations to him have found some place in him concerning ye Love Feast & anointing,[82] but nevertheless he hold yet a scruple wch I shall see to draw out.

Barach hath also sent me a Letter of K. & Deughman / wch seem to be united / wch I send a Transcript here of ye same.[83] I thrust not yet fully wth this medicine 1. because I have found K. in willfull deceit. 2. y^t he is much inclin'd to debauchery. 3. because his present wife hath yet a husband. Therefore I would fain yt you might enquire into all his doings & walks, yt we might judge wth better fundament, happily would be also reveal'd to you.

Dear Mother, out of ye Heavens w^t it is, & how we might do herein. The Transcript of K. & Doughmans Letter is this for Barach some time ago hath K. had acquaintance wth a person from out Holsatia/ if I Bar[ach] remember well/ wch shall be of particular qualities, & who hath experienced many wonderfull things, wch because she hath done many wonderfull cures through some secret medicine, at last hath had a testifying in herselves yt she should manifest ye same medicine to Korthold. Therefore he had accompanyed himself wth her, & began ye cures, upon wch they did set into effect many signal cures; but before 3 weeks or somew^t longer, was her in her mind opened yt she must have for a Husband Korthold. | wth whom she should performe a signal great work

---

77 Mr Ripendale spoke German. His travel diary indicates that he had met August Hermann Francke at Halle in March 1697, and Jane Lead, Barbarie Lee, Francis Lee and Mary Sterrell at London on 9 July 1697. See Halle, Archiv der Franckeschen Stiftungen (AFSt) [hereafter AFSt], H D 60, fols 120–124, 193–197.
78 Heinrich Johann Deichmann (1665–fl.1703), a future secretary of the Philadelphian Society.
79 Dionysius Andreas Freher (1649–1728), an immigrant from Nuremberg.
80 Loth Fischer at Utrecht writing to Jane Lead at Hoxton Square, dated 2/12 August 1697.
81 Silas = unidentified [cf. Acts 15:22–40].
82 The Love Feast was a heterodox ritual celebrated in different ways. Essentially it was a variation of communion using a mixture of bread and wine.
83 Barach (possibly also Barak) = unidentified [cf. Judg. 4:6–22]; K = Kortholt; Deughman = Heinrich Johann Deichmann.

/ over wch Dr Shott had pronounced from him K.[84] / whence she had opened this matter to him, but he by reason of y^e marriage wth Catherina Barenz,[85] was fallen into a vehement strife, so as yt he had almost given up y^e spirit therein if not a help was found for him. But this wife ye strife of K. feeling in herself did come three times on this behalf into a great anxiousness and vehement strife, y^t her whole countenance was altered, & had layn almost in Agone, whereupon K. as he tells me had wrestled vehemently in prayers, & thereupon all had been opened to him w^t Dr Shott had pronounced for him Anno 1694 & 1695 & because this was thus bright and clear in his mind had to resign his will into ye will of God, & understood & known yt w^t Cath[erina] had played before him in ye figure he was to perform wth this Lady of ye Berg in essentiality, whereupon he had caused to be coupled wth her upon a due manner. Then had Cather[ina] had also an opening thereof yt it should be so, & had wished him ye bless[ing] of ye L[or]^d. yt ye Covenant & ye Grace of ye L[or]^d should depart never of K. tho ye L[or]^d might castigate him wth castigating of men sometimes. As soon he K. had given him therein, had he had yt blessings in ye medicine, as a confluence of all was happened to him, & had great peace & rest in his soul, therefore he now is almost minded as others are. He is mighty desirous for you, as also I myself y^t you (to wit Barac.) might come over | into England for we cannot write all things. To mention yet some w^t shortly of her person, she is a first born of King Carl. ye 2^d first espouse wth wch him had coupled here a Bishop,[86] & several Princes have seeked to marriage her, as she then should also ye Duke from Albemarle,[87] & should be given her here in Eng[land] a Dukedome, but she must go out of En[land] by an inward moving, when an Angel did appear to her & told her yt she must go away out of England cloathed in white. Cather[ina] must for ye time as she was at Lubeck. A.M. bear upon her breast, not knowing w^t it did signify; but now is y^e effectual name of this Lady A.M. [/] Karth. shews a great love to you dear broth[er], & because to you & Deb[ora] all things

---

84   Dr Shott = Dr William Scott or Schott physician to George William, Duke of Zell.
85   Catherina Barenz or Beerens of Zwolle; in 1694 she had sent money to Johann Kelpius (1673–1708) and was afterwards mentioned in correspondence between Kelpius and Deichmann.
86   This woman, whose initials appear to have been A.M., claimed to be the eldest natural (i.e. illegitimate) daughter of Charles II of England. She was an alchemist who apparently promised Kortholt that she could produce the Philosopher's stone. Kortholt and Barenz both feature in Breckling's *Catalogus Haereticorum*. See Viktoria Franke's chapter in vol. 1 of this collection, p. 185n140 & 141.
87   Since the title had become extinct with the death of Christopher Monck, 2nd Duke of Albemarle in 1688, this probably refers to Henry FitzJames (1673–1702), an illegitimate son of James II who had been created Duke of Albemarle (Jacobite peerage) in January 1696.

are known best w^t wth him & Catharina hath passed, therefore to entreat your confirmation & sentim[en]t also to give in this work. Huenrq Douchman.[88]

I Barac believe this matter must be examined very deep & not judged primo intuit well or ill. We will answer him in generalibus & not disapprobate it or prove till ye Jaspins the self hath inquired into it very deep, therefore pray to write as soon as possible for Eng[land] how hee must behave us therein, for I do not believe yt all these particulars, & especially yt they have written to us here, is known to her.

K. letter to me runs thus. London. Junii 20.[89] Dear Broth[er] we had expected you here (N.B. hence appears yt in Engl[and] is nothing kept secret w^t we do wright in confidence to our dear mother.) & I myself especially or particularly. It is very accept to me yt you | Dear Broth[er] hath given ye testifying concerning Catharina Barenz, to ye master of ye mint at Zwolle, yt it hath only been a figurative marriage, who did aime at another more glorious essentially & it is seen in very well, & do see it in himself thus, as I then always have avoyded ye carnal acknowledging wth her, as I do now see experience how well all things have been. Therefore she is now wth me as a friend but not as an espouse, as I then do see well wt it hath been for a figure, & she herself also. I pray also to give part hereof to ye Debora,[90] & y^t she would write me her sentiment thereof. We will yet come together there in great harmony, for mighty things do open then in ye nature, not by words & voices but by deeds & wonders. I do cure here by ye blessing of God all morbos desperatissimos, Cancrum, Podagram, Pthisius, Fistula wounds,[91] & find therein ye blessing of God, whom I give ye honour who knows to draw out & exalt those y^t are his own.

This day 31 July St[ilum] Ve[rtere]. I received a Letter of our fellow Brother Zoller at Leipsig advising in confidence & secrecy y^t they well had received ye description of ye Love Feast,[92] but Matthias was quite not contended therein, & s[ai]d y^t he y^t elder in ye Love who had declared to you his practice in receiving of y^e Love feast did know very well & yt he were Dr Hattenbatch,[93] & he was in admiration over this thing & did see yt yourself was not confirmed as out of God but now did return again to y^e weak elem[en]ts, whereas you had testifyed

---

88 Huenrq Douchman = Heinrich Johann Deichmann.
89 Kortholt at London writing to (Barach?), dated 20 June 1697.
90 Debora Germ[ania?] = unidentified.
91 I do cure here by y^e blessing of God all diseases without hope, cancer, gout, consumption, fistula, wounds.
92 Johann Jacob Zoller (fl.1704) of Leipzig, correspondent of Johann Georg Gichtel.
93 Dr Johann Salomon Hattenbach (1650–1699), a physician who held conventicles at his home in Lübeck and who had introduced the ceremony of the Love Feast to certain Pietists.

122 already in ye revelation of revelations from ye kingly Priesthood | yt this was ye sign or mark of ye Priesters,[94] yt were gone out from all ceremonial & figurative service of God, & many such words more. And tho Zoller had wee had to perswade him another thing, yet it had not satisfied him, therefore he had give him yt counsel, yt he would set down his scruples & send them to you, wch he had begun to do, & would send them after a week by me to you, wch I shall expect & send. Dearest Freind you will see from hence how cautious is to be gone in publishing some things as divine Revelations, for because ye expense of Swark or Deb. Germ. being at Lipsig in ye past winter hath opened to our friend Matthias yt Barah had been this elder of Love & brought you to their sentim[en]^t in keeping ye L[or]ds Supper, he does perswade himself & conclude yt this love feast is not given you by immediate revelation but received by perswasion of men. And it doth find now little faith by him /our Matthias/ because Barah does say yt he had received it by divine Revel[ation] whereas he knows yt Deb. Germ. hath commenced it & brought it in use [se]v[er]all each one who did but speak somew[ha]t of Xt. and especially because he /Matthias/ also did know how much ye pretended Revel[ation] of Bar[ach] & Deb. Germ. were to be esteemed, as [se]v[er]all well more had given out somew[ha]t for Divine Revel[ation] & yt was fallen out quite contrary—Epaphras is resolved to depart from Lipsig & to come & dwell at Utrecht—I believe yt this will be ye ground of no receiving neither ye Love Feasts nor ye anointing by our Friend [Silas?] & Jaeli, because they know this elder of Love intimius even Deb. Germ.[95]

123 Tychicus at Frankfurt near ye Mayn hath an office of 50 florins salary,[96] whereby he scarcely could have bread but yt was his comfort, yt he God in his prayers earnestly intreating had heard a voice you shall receive this office; then he had also seen ye same words written before him in silver letters, so as yt he had thought he must accept it. Item he had seen a heart in vision wch had through him a bundle of twiggs for correcting & therein written these words, I do love & make sorrowfull. His superior or B[isho]p is a man sayd he in words not impious & had ye renown from some Friends at Frankfort, who are also half of ye world, & half Gods, yt he was a pious man, but he can not suffer those who do read & esteem ye Books of Lead.

Tychicus was cast out of his office, & was become mad some days after.

Tewesday y^e 29 July St[ilum] Ve[rtere]. I was invaded by such an hellish power, yt I must suffer some hours as if my end was at hand, but God be thanked

---

94   Jane Lead, *The Revelation of Revelations* (London: 1683).
95   Epaphras = unidentified [cf. Col. 1:7, 4:12]; Jael = unidentified [cf. Judg. 4:17–22].
96   Tychicus = Johann Jacob Weinich (1649–1713) [cf. Acts 20:4, Ephes. 6:21]; he was a correspondent of Baron Dodo von Knyphausen and Francis Lee.

yᵉ enemy must depart & it is now somew[ha]ᵗ better again. Our Patron writes yᵗ Eutychus yᵉ 24 July s.v. would be at Ostend in order to go Angl[ia].⁹⁷

Epenetus's estate is sorrowful enough.⁹⁸

The friend out of Friesland sent as you did mention of lately for collecting by yᵉ Earl of ye Lipp. to a good work. I pray to be cautious of, for he is an acquaintance also wᵗʰ all our enemies. As to your councel to discover | yᵉ matter of yᵉ Love feast to our Friend [Juering?] at Wesel,⁹⁹ it will not be expedient, for she is also acquainted wᵗʰ our antagonist of Amsterdam, & yet wᵗʰ an other who is an intimus of yᵗ Antagonist who dwells in this city, so yt it would in no wise secret more but known to each one of our enemies.

Our Antagonist who dwells in this city hath a close acquaintance wᵗʰ Mʳ Scheller who is now also here in this city,¹⁰⁰ but wᵗ he doth here I know not. I have conjecture yt he our antag[onist] shall seeke to enquire something in Eng[land] by this Mʳ Scheller, for this was ye day before yesterday at my house, & would have included a letter for Eng[land] but my espouse sayd I did not write. Therefore be cautious against ye s[cor]pions.

124

For yᵉ same. Utrecht Aug 5/15 sub L.F.¹⁰¹

124

The Beloved Bro. Fish[er]. hath communicated me in your name some extracts out of Lett. concerning yᵉ Love Feast wᶜʰ is in it self very good, but pray give me leave to open my thoughts in simplicity of heart about this matter. First I was minded to write about this point to you 3 quarters of yᵉ year ago, as I did hear thereof yᵉ first time by yᵉ Friend Swarzin from Lubeck,¹⁰² wᶜʰ was here wᵗʰ us, especially because your books do speak yᵉ contrary. viz: yt we must go out from all outward figures & works, wᶜʰ yet by this ceremony or outward begun work could lightly receive a great crack yt yᵉ readers of them might be brought in doubts | whether ye same might have flown out of yᵉ H[oly] G[host] purely, or dictated by him. For because he had opened or manifested such exact things therein, would he indeed not have forgotten to dictate also this means of yᵉ Love Feast, wᵗʰ out wᶜʰ yet he did lead you & other precious souls so many years into yᵉ greatest & highest mysteries &

125

---

97 Baron Dodo von Knyphausen, possibly writing about his son's intended voyage to England.
98 Epenetus = unidentified [cf. Rom. 16:5].
99 Unidentified woman.
100 Probably the Mr Scheller, a young student of divinity, who had accompanied Heinrich Johann Deichmann and Francis Lee on a journey from the Dutch Republic to England to meet Jane Lead. Scheller departed for Holland on 1 August 1695 and by July 1697 seems to have settled at Amsterdam.
101 Loth Fischer at Utrecht writing to Jane Lead, dated 5/15 August 1697.
102 Swarzin or Swarsin = unidentified.

revealed them to you. Secondly because this ceremony draws his beginning of one wch you does name an high Elder of y^e Love. /viz: Dr Hattenbach at Lubeck[103] / who hath introduced it by y^e so named Pietists, & also hath celebrated it by you wth bread, as they ordinarily are wont to celebrate it, but after he was departed from you did you again change ye manner of celebrating it, & use it by commixting bread & wine together, & yt 3^d manner is this now transcribed manner wch I received thro our Friend above mentioned. Here I do acknowledge ingennously yt I am a little doubtful yt you hath received it not only from Dr Hattenbach first & then fallen out very unstably into these 3 several or distinct manners. For why should ye H[oly] G[host] have not presently shown you immediately ye true manner & revealed it to you, & first make such intimations therew^thall. And 3^ly I do fear yt it will go therew^th even as wth ye common sup[per] of ye L[or]^d, wch is but a sectary custome & imitation of y^t w[ha]^t ye Apostles did once. 4. I desired well to know whether we could come not into ye perfect thing & mark w^thout this outward means for we can w^thout this fix ye earnest imagination into ye broken | rised & ascended body of our saviour Je[sus] Xt. by our prayings praisings & thankings. This I would propose to you intreating to be pleased to answer me not unkindly thereupon, & yt circumstantially & upon all these 4 points. From me & Broth Zoller it shall be kept very secretly,[104] wch you well might trust upon. I do see actually yt we can eat & drink also w^thout ye outward bread & wine, & also partake of yt rised body.

There is written from out London de dato 26 July this, on ye next past Munday betwixt 12 & 2 ye clock at night was here seen in ye air against south west of this city a Fiery Ball like ye moon in greatness, & did give a sound as if a gun was fired, whereupon it did spread itself abroad wth a g[rea]t fiery stream very suddenly wch did stretch out his tayl against ye north, & let fall down upon ye earth a great many sparks of fire likes flames. This token did give 2 minutes of time such a bright shine as if it was about ye clear midday, whereof many men wch did see it as well in ye city as upon ye land were very dreadfull. Pray be pleased to open me your thoughts thereof.

Just now I receive a great letter of Silas who is wholly alarm'd yt our Friends in Engl[and] have published ye History of Tremellius, & still thereby have set down a superintendent near Magdeburgh. If Sila hath taken this evil ye publishing of ye History of Tremell[ius] w[ha]^t will he say if he shall hear y^t ye History of spirits wch appeared to ^ye Abbot hath been printed also? W^th such great ones

---

103   Dr Johann Salomon Hattenbach.
104   Johann Jacob Zoller.

as ye Ab[bot] is, it is not good to publish their secrets, especially because in | 127
Duchland is quite another state yn in Engl[and].

Sequitur Transcriptum or extract above mentioned.

From out ye letter Dr Schott to our Patron.[105]

The sister of Mary Stuard's hath marryed a merch[an]^t at Hanover already before 20 years, & have generated together 8 children, yn she did run away from him & was wanting 8 years, but now she is return'd to him because it seems yt she hath found no better Taverne. She & her sister have long laboured in chymicis wth Hollgrave ye other sister wch I know not shall no ways be better, & conjecturally of yt same kind as this is.[106] Huenrq.[107] Dr. Schott.

Karthold is a meer instrument of Belial yt I say no worse thing, & if he should further visit you, I would fain believe yt Satan endeavoured to hurt ye good cause by him. And because his now wife is one yt can exercise yt false magia I desired yt our Patron might have no correspondence wth him, much lesser use his sent so called medicine. For I believe yt K[arthold] this his new wife hath already used carnally w[he]n he & she were by ye false magus Hollgrave, for he was at that time an incarnated Devil, & their life hath been very over sodomitical.

I pray communicate to me in confidence w^t he hath opened so as to have had a pact wth ye known wife; & concerning ye ring found by Epenetus whether ye inscription, Inseperable was written in ye English or High Dutch tounge.

Highly Honoured & Beloved in the Jacinct Property[108]   139

Wherefrom you have given out a true shine & Lustre, as from ye magnetick virtue of the Eternal Stone, wch doth cause no little joy in me, for Unity is ye deepest Essence of Divine Love: y^r answer to ye Lett^r of Silas shews from w^t precious deep those Mysteries have unveiled themselves in you, & doth evidence y^t the true Sophia hath incorporated herself with y^r Understanding whereby you have fathomed that wch the Line was too short in others to reach. For God hath given you the Key to unlock wisdomes Gates, what was wanting in me more fully to explain & clear up in y^e Diary, you have worthily made out for the

---

105 Dr William Schott to Baron Dodo von Knyphausen.
106 Hollgrave = Dr Hollgraffen, an associate of Quirinus Kuhlmann (1651–1689), John Bathurst (d.1694?) and Kortholt.
107 Huenrq = Heinrich Johann Deichmann.
108 Jane Lead to an aristocrat, possibly Baron Dodo von Knyphausen.

better information of yᵉ Doubtfull. As for wᵗ was written at that time it was only as private Memorandums for my-self not knowing yᵗ it should ever be brought forth to publick View. The which I have suffered to go abroad in yᵗ Simple way in wᶜʰ it was opened in me. The First eternal Form of the Son of God must of necessity have passed through the Womb of the Eternal Virgin of yᵗ which was before all Eves Births, & is the same spiritual body wherewith he is now glorified: & this takes not off or derogates at all from wᵗ is due to the Human Virgin yᵗ brought him forth. Now as to the Difference yᵗ is between the fall of yᵉ Humane Race & of the Angels, God in his wisdome did favour mankind by cloathing them with an Elementary body, whereby the fierce fiery Property in them was mitigated & humbled. Whereas if they had been naked, of such an humane Body without the Qualification of yᵉ Water, their condemnation might | have been much more grievious & durable. But this is not enough to make against yᵉ final restitution of both natures; wᶜʰ I need not now farther enlarge on; yᵗ being I hope already sufficiently cleared up in yᵉ Gospel Missage:[109] to wᶜʰ you may refer our Silas. And as for the Ordinance of Anointing, we did not take upon us to bind any of our united stones but as we found any of them to be free & satisfied in their own spirits to practise it, they would not disdain or slight it tho veiled under a Figure. For we can witness yᵗ we have found great growth & establishment thereby. However it is much satisfaction to me, yᵗ yʳ Honour doth so entertain the beleif of it, as to observe it; not doubting but that you will from it meet, with us, yᵉ same refreshing. For the wᶜʰ our spirits here shall write with yours most intimately for a blessing to descend through it. Now the Feast wᶜʰ ensues after yʳ anointing is after this manner: We take yᵉ Finest Biscuit Bread, in Form of little round Cakes wᶜʰ we do consecrate & immerse in ye same wine, wherewith we celebrate the Love-Feast wᶜʰ having remained in yᵉ Cup a sufficient time to tinge it throughly is taken out with a Little spoon & distributed to each one yᵗ is present a whole Cake & after this we drink also of the same wine, wᶜʰ is as yᵉ Bridal Cup, & Token of Nuptial Joy. Thus we begin to keep the marriage Feast of the Lamb every New Moon, & other solemn seasons as occasion requires. And as Christ spoke of yᵉ eating | his body & drinking his bloud so we may say of this, in the spirituality thereof, yᵗ we do essentially participate of his life herein: But whether others yᵗ are of the same Templ-body with us can joyn & comply with us in these Institutions or no, we leave it entirely to their freedom. Yet we cannot cease to desire & with the same good & benefit to them, wᶜʰ we ourselves do reap hereby. ---- I shall at present make some demur in yᵉ conveyance of yʳ Letter to K[arthold] till I hear further concerning yᵉ boasted

---

[109] Jane Lead, *A Revelation of the Everlasting Gospel-Message* (London: 1697).

effects of his Medicine. For I have not hitherto learnt y^t he has completed any Cure. And am very much satisfied to find y^r Lordship in y^t sedateness of mind as not to be made credulous by puffed up sounds. For indeed I can never look upon him as one baptized with ye Holy Ghost to make a true & right Magus; but rather as a guilded one & one fitted to act in ye dark Kingdoms Exploits. For he knows how to put on an Angelical Form: & he wants notability or parts to carry on some great design under a plausible covering. And as for his adulterous marriage it is such an abominable thing, as her own Daughter doth decry it down to the life, & spares not to divulge the wickedness of them in many criminal circumstances. So y^t for me & my family we will have no interfering with such persons: neither has he ever come near us since his marriage wth her. For I do look upon it as scandalous but to maintain any com[m]unication with such as do lye under such real stains. Wherefore I hope I need not advise y^r Lordshipp not to be tempted with his golden Nails | now as for any knowledge of the History of ye Abbot perhaps it may not be so considerable as y^r L[or]dship may at first suspect, in him, who might possibly seek thereby to draw you out on that subject. For it is ab[ou]^t a year since we received through Gideon a short High-Dutch Narrative ab^t a little Black Man y^t gave the Key of a certain mountain to a Gentleman y^t afterwards became Epileptical but without any name or distinguishing Character either as to Person or Place;[110] wch was translated by Deuchman, & so come to ye knowledge of some others as a matter of no great secrecy, being paralleled with several others much of the same nature. However y^t shall serve to make us all for ye future more cautious; for we are not ignorant of prying spirits, y^t would take their advantage even of ye least Hints: And as to all things relating to our correspondence, we are resolved to be most reserved & obscure in y^t critical time. Wherefore also we have been much solicitous on account of the Dear Eulychus,[111] whom we have long expected. But you are fearfull I see least he should be infected, by one whom you have formerly known to be a corrupter of youth. For wch I cannot blame you. But there is but little fear of his coming ⟨[ever?]⟩ to us hither if the Gentleman might be prevailed on never to go to him. & since it was in y^r L[or]dships thoughts to send him to England, all our aims would be to serve y^r ends in sending of him; as having

142

---

110 This account was communicated by Loth Fischer and translated by Heinrich Johann Deichmann. It was printed as "A Relation of the Apparition of a Spirit, keeping the Treasures of the Earth, and of his Delivery of the Key of a certain Mountain in Germany, to a Considerable Person, and what thereupon ensued", in *Theosophical Transactions* for March (1697), no. 1, 43–45.

111 i.e. Eutychus = possibly Franz Ferdinand von Knyphausen or Friedrich Ernst von Knyphausen.

this prospect y^t there might be such a good thing hid in y^e inward ground of his heart, y^t after y^e little heats of youth are overpast, would spring up in your similitude, & so become a son of Consolation to you in truth. However as to his coming or not coming at y^s time it is left intirely to y^r own free disposal & satisfaction after weighing all the circumstances. If you send him we shall be ready to receive him & to serve you in all y^t we can study to do for him. As for Deborah she has much honoured me in joyning me with y^r L[or]dship accord-

143 ing | to that alliance & denomination wherewith we stand in ye higher world to see ye new offspring of a spiritual generation upon ye Earth; wch I therefore do most gratefully accept & should be glad to have a Letter from her or Barak. I did expect to have heard y^t they would have been with you personally before this time. I would not y^t any of y^r first foundation stones should lose their heat & vigour towards one another but keep it warm y^t the building may go on prosperously from Rank to Rank wch I doubt not but y^r Lordship will promote & countenance all manner of ways In ye Confidence of which I rest.

Y^rs most obliged ever to love & honour

Jane Leads

144 Silas and Jaël are not willing to receive the Institution of the anointing, but Bar[ach] and Deber. have received it. Chrysoprasis is not yet arrived by Sila.— Of late I did read over again the Epistle of the Blessed Pordage of the microcosmical stone,[112] & set down thereby my own Remarks, how the microcosmical process of the stone does accord therewithal. It is too prolix therefore I dare not molest therewith our Beloved Gid[eon] for Translating it.[113] Me thincks that the Birth of the manchild, and of the microcosmical stone in us are one and the same though it doeth not take away the Birth of a special manchild, who out vies the others in Gradu exaltations—. I dream scantly ever of the Octavia

145 without trouble; therefore I do discharge me | of all imagination, as much as I can possibly, as I then also within a whole year have dreamed nothing, except 2 Dayes ago I have hath again with her & her mother a combat, over wch I were awacked the Clock 2 in the night, but did fall again a sleep. and with the same dream awacked again the Clock 3. If I can I will yet by this Post send the Dream to Gid[eon]. I write also the things concerning the abbot, who will communicate is to you. So I must conclude this with heartily salutation to you, and all

---

112 An unidentified work by Dr John Pordage (1607–1681), possibly "A thorough philosophical letter on the lawful stones of wisdom" (no date). Cf. J[ohn] P[ordage], "Twelve Foundation Stones of the New Jerusalem", printed in Jane Lead, *A Fountain of Gardens*, vol. 1 (London: 1697), 180–182.

113 Gideon = Loth Fischer.

that are present with you, and in hope of the happy arrivement at London of Eut[ychus] abiding unchangeably

B. 3 Augusti old stile 1697

Faithful known servant | & Blessed & worthy virago.

I tell you here for your Information that N° 1. here following is a Letter written by Dr Schmiedberger at Graven-haage to Fr. Joh. Gichtel at Amsterdam, and by this send also to our Friend Silas, & by this to our Patron, from which it is come to my hands. N° 2 is a Transcript of the Letter, which the abbot writes to Silas, and I should out of this Letter well nigh conclude that he had not sent your Letter to the abbot. N° 3 is an extract of Kartholds Letters to our Patron.

N° 1.[114]

I must communicate to you, that besides that Sect, which according to the Pretension or rather Pretence | of Dr Schotten,[115] does wait upon the Incarnation of the Father, yet another in England under the Direction of Jane Lead breaks out which have published their acta Philadelphensia in this 1697 year of the month martii & aprilis & so will continue all months, wherein the son-in-law of Jane Lead, Ly, & an English man, as also some Dutch men, do collabour, as a studiosus Deuchman, and one Frecher,[116] which besides & above that they, according to their pretence, Jane Lead do beleive to be the apocalyptical woman apoc. 12 as is to be seen in the last Tractax of her, called the Fountain of Gardens or Diarium,[117] yet doe | averre that among them /: from out the Daughter of Lead :/ shall be brought forth a new Christus, who is to be a Partaker both of the celestial & terrestrial nature even as Quirin Kuhlman,[118] because he did converse with these men and women, did appropriate upon him before this time, that he, as Christ was the son of the Father, so he Christi, of the Son, & of his Kingdom should be, & sit down between the Father, which they afterwards did appropriate to a blind Gentleman, Bathorse /:[119] whom I at Amsterdam some years agoe did speak with several times, where he did tell me many things,

---

114 Dr Isaac Schmidberger at The Hague writing to Johann Georg Gichtel at Amsterdam (c. August 1697).
115 Dr Schotten = most likely Dr William Schott.
116 Ly = Francis Lee; Deuchman = Heinrich Johann Deichmann; Frecher = Dionysius Andreas Freher.
117 The "apocalyptical woman" was the woman clothed with the sun (Rev. 12:1).
118 Quirinus Kuhlmann (1651–1689), Behmenist poet and martyr.
119 John Bathurst (*d*.1694?), a wealthy supporter of Kuhlman's; he had lived at various residences in Middlesex.

and among other also that Quirin Kuhlman did cost him over 30000 Florens :/ who | should generate that sone with his wives Daughter in Law, but it became a Daughter that did die at Amsterdam, & because D Hollgrave hath perswaded him to do it is the son of this Hollgrave through Korthold pierced throughourly that he died, but Korthold hath retired him into England, with a woman after he had spended to Hollgraven, or the Devils Doctor as they are wont here to call him out of the rich purse of Gold of a Lord, who did seek the Lapis, that he should procure for him the Tinctur from the spirits of the earth.[120] Now after God hath annihilated these things altogether, this new English society seeks to establish | her Testifying through the authority of T. Bromly and Dr Pordage de novo,[121] and to draw all things to them through the writings of Jane Leade, that they send over to them their money, for printing of her books, & propose all things by her as an Oraculum, as before the cupidi novitatis have abused the simplicity of the Assenbourg.[122] And thus God doeth intrap the new-desirous ones, that seek wisdom in their own wisdom with the Greeks, while they go astray and err from the Divine Truth & simplicity of the Faith. 1. Cor. 1, 2, 3, 4. Whereto yet comes, that though Philadelphenses in England in their new actis do set down expressly a new relation of such a new Christ at Goodenberge in the Lordship of Baijraith,[123] from | Johann Wittgal & Anna his wife anno 1696 brought forth, which they write to have received from a Lutherian superintendend near Magdebourgh, whereby they bring in great peril & suspition, because already is made mention in the Publick Tiding of such a new sect, which doeth break forth in England. But that the new Christ at Goodenberg might be made manifest, a sone of a superintend out of Rugen, who being an adjutant among the miliz at Koppehagen, through many Inspeckings & Inspira-

---

120 A German version of this account up to this point is printed in S.J. Baumgarten, *Nachrichten von mertwürdigen Büchern* (Halle: 1756), 324–325, quoting a letter from Friedrich Breckling to Philipp Jacob Spener dated 1697.
121 T. Bromly = Thomas Bromley (1630–1691), author and associate of John Pordage.
122 Assenbourg = Rosemunda Juliana von Asseburg (1672–1712), daughter of Christian Christoph von Asseburg and his wife Gertraud Margarete. This noblewoman was the subject of a work by Johann Wilhelm Petersen containing a "Narrative of some strange Transactions and Revelations" experienced by her over about a dozen years. It was subsequently published in English translation as *A Letter to some Divines* (1695) with a preface by Francis Lee. She had also written to Jane Lead on 11 March 1696.
123 i.e. Guttenberg, a town near Bayreuth in northern Bavaria. This part of the letter resembles the contents of various letters from Friedrich Breckling dated May 1697 which refer to what was published in the *Theosophical Transactions* for March 1697. It is quoted (without source) in T. Wotschke, "Der märkische Freundeskreis Friedrich Brecklings", *Jahrbuch für brandenburgische Kirchengeschichte*, 25 (1930), 208–209 note 131. On Breckling, see Viktoria Franke's chapter in vol. 1 of this collection.

tions hath been wonderfully awackened & driven to go from thence over Riga to
Lubeck, and thus from thence coming to Goodenberg near | Culmback, found
that Child, & adscribes him these words: Hic /: scilicet Puer:/ est verus Deus
et homo, Jesus Christus, imago Coelestis Patris, et character Gloriae ipsius, qui
ab horâ nativitatis suae et adventus sui Rex in terrâ est, ut in Coelo, quiq[ui]s
eo ipso dum natus est, Regnum incepit, quod se extendet super totum mundum, regnaturus á mare ad mare, et cui genua om[ni]a incurvanda, et de quo
a Progenie ad Progeniem annumerabitur, quem ego confiteor Jesum Christum
esse. Scripsi 1696. 7. Decembris.[124] Haec habemus ex Relatione eminentis viri
habitantis prope Madeburgum et talis nova Generatio Spiritualis | et corporalis etiam hic in Anglia inter nos expectatur,[125] that that in Dutchland not may
have all conflux, and they do draw after them all and inchant by their acts, and
the mony no more may be sent for Rome, but may bring for England, where the
Devil /: because they beleive his final Salvation, & do make publick it in all the
world :/ will do again a good turn to them that they can cry out as others: Here
is Christus therefore I must make it known to my beloved Brother.

[N° 2.][126]

This Trouble in Saxen I was acquainted with already before | a year, through
even this effatum :/ of the spirits :/ but durst say nothing, know also yet many
things, that shortly have their effects, but wch I must conceal till they do follow.
The next pass 21 of the month was I warned for a great imminent misfortune,
and escaped through Divine Holy Direction & opening happily this mischeif,
so that I cannot enough praise the Divine Providence therein, while such a mischief was contrived me by the Papists, which I could not have escaped without
the conservation of the Divine Grace. And hath this been their last effort to stop
this high weighty worck & annullate it. But Gods Goodness and | Providence
hath changed the whole play, & opened me their subtile & exitiale designs, so
that, as if we may please to the Divine Providence, we through his assistance

---

124 This part of the letter refers to and quotes directly from *Theosophical Transactions* for March 1697 (1697), no. 1, 46–51. The translation reads, "This child is the true God and man, Jesus Christ, the image of the Celestial Father, and the brand of His Glory, who since the time of his birth and his coming is King on earth, as well as in Heaven, who, being born from Him [i.e. from God the Father], received a Kingdom, which extends over the whole world, [and] will reign from sea to sea, and to whom all knees must bend, and who will be acknowledged over the generations, whom I confess is Jesus Christ".
125 "This we have from a narration of an eminent man living near Magdeburg, and such a spiritual and corporal regeneration is also expected among us here in England".
126 Transcript of a letter from Theophilus Abbot to Silas.

shortly do hope a desired end, for which Ende the spirits do long also after it to give God thank through this inclosed Song, which principally doeth aime at the present state of our Church, & that is very spiritual & most considerable.

This is the Song which the Spirits do sing.

We give thanck to thee o God ever & ever, that Thou hast conserved pure thy word, this Place also | with a bright shin, & beg Thee, cause that surely, the more & more, does spread out it self the pure doctrine, for thy Honour.

2. The Treasure is dear & pretious, therefore restrain & keep down by force the spite of the enemies, keep thou himself the Protection, that they quench not through craft & murdering this bright light, let not find place their counsel, that against us runs early & late.

3. Give such men, that without fear & schunning shew us the true way, which thou hast prepared for unto salvation, with they spirit, do help & succur them, that not with force may be brought in unto us the dark night of the old abominable ones.

4. Wherein is not the littlest sparck of light, in anguish & grief, of comfort and Joy, thy word only can be comfortable the same doth conserve, by yough & old, until the end, and throw down headlong shortly or suddenly, that which does rob us the word and Sacrament. This is the Song, which we must pray for Thancksgiving to God for that averting of the mischief that was before Hand which is given us by the spirits, I leave it to your worthiness to your worthiness reasonable Judgement,[127] whether it may be possible to the Satan to entice to such a thing a Christend and | God only trusting Christian even in these perillous times when the Papist do thus mightily labour against us.

Theophilus Abbot.

Here followes N⁰. 3. Or an extract of Kortholds Letter to our Patron.[128]

I do not doubt, but you would have received the transmitted medicine. The Father of my dear Espouse hath appeared her at bright Day according to the Laws of England pertain to her 10000 R[i]x[-dollars] for a Pre bequeating, & even so much from the King, when the King is returned into England, then I shall pretend them. Could you procure me a Recommendation unto my Lord Danckelmann it would be good.[129] My dear Espouse does | stand in a great magia, & I doubt not, but it can the King in England yet be conserved long

---

127 Presumably the repetition is a transcription error.
128 Extract of a letter from Kortholt to Baron Dodo von Knyphausen.
129 Lord Danckelmann = Eberhard von Danckelmann (1643–1722), then Prime Minister of Brandenburg-Prussia.

alive, through means of my medicine, if it was proved first in your City, and then might be recommended to him from thence, which would help very much. I would transmit enough for the whole Brandenborough court. The Elector would give my well a good salary. You may well have heard of the Philadelphian Transactions. In the same is an Query of a Treasure. Why do you not inquire by me thereof, I do know the Ground of the matter. The J.L. is simple, and hath had one a little of an arising, but that is by far not to be found by her, what they do see by her, that w^{ch} | is published is for the most part set down by others.[130]   160
I did make me at first great conceivings thereof, but after I did speak herself, I found all thing very small, they are but words. Several things of my own are intermixed in the Transactions. They are the one against the other, and do more take upon them, than they can perform, they do discover them day by day more & more, whereof you shall perceive shortly enough to hear of, and if you will find it to happen thus, then you may easily judge, from out of what spirit it hath been written.

Wy do see the Begin of them all, and their Ende also, but they | can see   161
us not, for we do stand over and above their Principle. I have many weighty things to correspond with you: For the Begin of the new Teime or age will bring great mutations. The true magi shall produce Deeds. It concerns me highly to know one Thingh from Paulus of the Mount :/ Berg :/ who hath been a Kingly Commissarius in Duinkirchen for to receive by a notarius out of the Church book Information from his marriage and other circumstances. It concerns me very much. From the state of J.L. and from many hondert spirits and their Distinction I am | hoping to give more account. I will send by Mr Stupendaal,[131]   162
who goes in Augusto from hence, & is an Ocular or Eye-witness of my cures, a menstruum, wherein is to be solved Gold without Labour, without any corrosiveness, that it can be loan in presently, which is yet by far not so good, than my great medicament.

Behold now, dearest Friend, with Translating such nauseous excrements I must spend my noble time and consume my vigour of life that is tired out wholly. I do acknowledge ingenuously, that if I had may known, that such loathsome things would be | intermingled, then I should have conveighed myself out of them.   163
Pluribus in super attentus minor est ad singula sensus.[132] Our known Patron writes, that Silas had taken pet & was greatly discontented with the Bringing

---

130   J.L. = Jane Lead.
131   Stupendaal = possibly Mr Ripendale, who had met Lead and her associates at London on 9 July 1697.
132   "He who pays attention to many things is inferior at understanding particular things".

him into such an open Report, by publish things, that must kept secret. And that without inquiring whether it might be consented or no? For because Dr Schmidberger hath many visits from all that come out of High Dutchland in
164 these Lands, he does spread out the things through whole Dutchland. | and his warnings do find the more Ingress, because of late expressly was set down in the openly tidings, that did arise a new sect at London in England, & that they did meet together in a certain Garden at London &c. & c.[133] which he does appliquer upon your meeting. Now here also comes inclosed a Letter for Korthold from Patron sub convert of Mr Deughmann which I could not translate, but Friend Freter will do it, and then I pray to seal & give them to Deughmann.[134] I pray God to lead our Patron, that he may cut off his Correspondence with him. Valete & salvete omnes. I abide
    your F.

138 [follows page 164]
"The Patron of Mrs Jane Lead D Knhijphsen[135]
A mons^r mons^r Deijchman a Londres."

169 A Monsr Loth Fischer a Utrecht. Aug. 17. Jane Lead.[136]
    Poor Catherina Barenz being no longer willing to abide wth K. as a Friend,[137] if she cannot be wth him as a Wife has at length taken fresh courage & is resolv'd to go for Holland, being this very day, as we hear, departed.

177 Out letters, 30 August 1697
A Monsr Monsr Loth Fischer a Utrecht. sub. Jane Lead. Aug. 25. 97.[138]
    Korthold is according to my sight most fitly qualified for a magus of ye Luciferian kingdome. Your visional Dream concerning Octavia I much expect. Eutychus after having been in Town 14 days has found us out ye Address given being mistaken.[139] He has taken his chamber in ye Pell Mell for a month, & after y^t he seems very desirous to come & abide wth us. In ye mean time ye weather

---

133 On Sundays in 1697 Philadelphian meetings were held in a room within a property occupied by Mrs Anne Bathurst (d.1704), who lived at Baldwin's Gardens in the parish of St Andrew's, Holborn (London).
134 The enclosed letter was from Baron Dodo von Knyphausen to Kortholt; conveyed by Heinrich Johann Deichmann; to be translated by Dionysius Andreas Freher.
135 D Knhijphsen = Baron Dodo von Knyphausen.
136 Jane Lead to Loth Fischer at Utrecht, dated 17 August 1697.
137 K = Kortholt.
138 Jane Lead to Loth Fischer at Utrecht, dated 25 August 1697.
139 Eutychus = possibly Franz Ferdinand von Knyphausen or Friedrich Ernst von Knyphausen.

being good he designs to take a view of Oxford, where Onesimus is at present.¹⁴⁰ He thinks to set out on Munday next & to return in a few days. Pray advise our Cyrus of w[ha]ᵗ I write.¹⁴¹

I know yᵗ you expect yᵉ concluding part of ʸᵉ 2ᵈ vol. of yᵉ Diary wᵗʰ yᵉ Preface: but our Printer having been under yᵉ messengers hand has caused a stop. But he being now set free you may by yᵉ next receive w[ha]ᵗ belongs to it.¹⁴² The name of yᵉ person yᵗ Scheller writes about is not so much as known to any here.

Very dear Matthias¹⁴³

Whom I do know in the Evangelical line & order you being translated hereunto, yᵗ in it you may fill up every measure & degree to minister dedicatedly in yᵉ Holy Sanctuary where the Humanity of Christ, as yᵉ Ark of the Presence may open his Testimony within, as a rising spring, yᵗ so you may know no drought, having yᵉ well of Life so near to you. This I hope is well understood by you, perceiving yᵗ yʳ spirit runs much into yᵗ all hidden vein of life. For it is a Foundation so deep as God will raise up a Tabernacle here from yᵉ most pleasant residence furnisht with yᵉ Oracle the Holy Table, the Alter of Incense, the burning Lamp the Pot of Manna, the sacred perfumes & ointment. All of wᶜʰ now in yᵉ day of yᵉ spirit, one essentially to be fulfilled according as yᵉ gift of wisdom doth come forth to open & reveal what virtual substance which may be extracted hence. Therefore I would not have the my dear Matthias to stagger at yᵉ taking up of yᵉ ordinance & Institution of the Feast of Tabernacles, with the Holy Anointing wᶜʰ doth give the livily representation of yᵉ Body of the Resurrection receiv'd & quickened by yᵉ Ghostly Presence. Now as to yᵉ 1st objection yᵗ is made, yᵗ in the Revelation of Revelations,¹⁴⁴ the drift & scope was to nullify | & abrogate the outward traditions & customs of the churches, so as to shew yᵗ the Kingly Priesthood is to consist of such as have gone out from yᵉ ceremonial & figurative services of God. I do answer yᵗ yᵉ spirit has indeed always drove me from yᵉ outward into yᵉ inward from yᵉ figure into the truth. But when it was again shown me, yᵗ as we were to draw off from yᵉ law of common use of such or such natural & elementary symbols, so it was also permitted us to take yᵐ up again, in a more lively & essential manifestation relating to yᵉ mistery of Redemption

---

140   Onesimus = Richard Roach.
141   Cyrus = unidentified.
142   The second volume of Jane Lead's *A Fountain of Gardens* (London: 1697), contains prefatory epistles by both the editor Francis Lee (5 August 1697), and the author (29 July 1697).
143   Jane Lead to Matthias = unidentified (no date).
144   Jane Lead, *The Revelation of Revelations* (London: 1683).

& transmutation of the very elementary body & the offering up & restitution of y^e Creatures. For I would that you should understand y^t y^e divine magia will act through some external figures & mediums; as Christ himself has given us an example of, by washing of his disciples feet, laying on his hands to cure ye sick, breathing the Holy Ghost by an outward visible breath, commissionating his Apostles to go forth & anoint ye sick with oil, &c wch appears to be a sufficient foundation to go upon; Besides w^t I have received of a later commission & ordination, wch was to commence higher degrees in passing through ye dying body to ye Resurrection & then through that to ye glorification thus feasting upon Christ anew in his Kingdome of victory power & glory. Of which three degrees of | eating & drinking you may remember y^t I have spoken ab^t fourteen years agoe in ye Preface to the Heavenly Cloud.[145] And much about ye same time I with some few others, did privately practice it as in a Festival Commemoration of ye Resurrection. But by various changes of Providence as by death & otherwise, a cessation hereof was caused; till it was again opened to me afresh upon Dr Hattenbacks coming over hither & making such a motion wherewith ye spirit concurred.[146] Therefore as to ye second objection I can safely maintain y^t it was not originally derived from him, as you may suppose, but from ye spirits own dictate & conduct. Neither is ye spirit of God bound to deliver all his mind at once but raiseth up his own ministration gradually. The first part w[he]ⁿ we celebrated with this Elder of the Love, doth properly appertain to ye Resurrection: but ye second part wch we have since celebrated, & is nominated ye Feast of Tabernacles, doth reach yet higher & to this is annexed ye Anointing.

And therefore in ye 3^d place it is not like to be made a sectarian custom, neither is it to be imposed upon any body, but only recommended to such as are of ye Lords private disciplehood, who shall be perswaded | in their own minds of the fortitude they may gain hereby. For y^s is the day wherein we are called for to put on ye L^{ds} Body for our munition hiding for ye many prying adversaries we have as well in ye right as ye left. And as to y^r quere in ye last place, whether we may not arrive to ye perfect thing without such outward mediums; I do not at all deny but y^t we may participate through ye strong throu the strong attractive drawings of faith ye Divine Body,[147] even without these. But as Christ was thus evidently set forth in his humbled & crucified state before ye eyes of the Primitive Christians. So is he now set forth in like manner before our eyes in his

---

145 Jane Lead, *The Heavenly Cloud Now Breaking* (London: 1681).
146 Dr Johann Salomon Hattenbach.
147 Presumably the repetition is a transcription error.

exalted & victorious state, by ye use of these mediums & representations wch do more vigorously raise up & quicken to a deiform unity according as some have made the proof of.

By the Jacinct I have receiv'd a copy of his most weighty lett^r to you:[148] & have found in my waiting there upon ye the spirits who do communicate wth him, have passed through such regions for refining that they are restless till they have given Intelligence in order to ye lifting up ye kingdome of light here below, y^t may answer to y^t above. I have for some years been acquainted with ye mystery of separated souls of several degrees & orders, who have communicated excellent knowledge, especially in ye supracelestial affairs, & ye matters of ye mount sion state. Therefore I have a Faith y^t y^s way of commerce wth spirits of y^s rank will in a short time be better understood & so be of great use for counsel & conduct for to such as may be chosen for an high & publick work. Now I would be farther informed after w^t manner these spirits do appear, in what figures & at w^t times, as also what mediums they speak through. It might possibly be convenient for this Abbot to read ye part of the <u>Enochian Life</u> wch treats from my own experience of the communion of ye Saints above & below:[149] & if you shall judge it fit, you may recommend the same to him. I have of late felt a mighty | strong attraction of many departed souls to draw my spirit among them, for ye declaring ye Immutable Love of God, for redemtion out of all centries & worlds. And they appeared to me while I was speaking on y^s wise to them, so still & so attentive, as if they would drink in every word with great alacrity & rejoycing. But y^s I commit as a secret to you & our own disciplehood.

    I perceive you have had notice of the Institution of an Holy Feast of Tabernacles, of ye anointing accompanying it: wch I wish y^t you with our dear Jael might be with us partakers of as of as real eating & drinking with Christ in ye kingdome of ye Resurrection wch is sealed by ye anointing. And tho it may appear perhaps in ye Thoughts of some as to much a price of formality, & inferior to the dispensation we are at present under yet we can say by experience y^t in ye solemn use thereof we have found spirit of life to enter through it. Neither is ye feast altogether a new Institution, as it may seem to be hinted in ye description; for I now remember y^t ab[ou]^t fourteen years agoe I had a special order & direction from y^e Heavenly Court & Council to observe it as a symbol of y^e Marriage supper | of the Lamb which I accordingly did with a few of us for seven days at a time, but by several circumstances intervening as death &

---

148   Jacinct = an aristocrat, possibly Baron Dodo von Knyphausen.
149   Jane Lead, *The Enochian Walks with God* (London: 1694).

other removings. I was left alone in this matter & had wholy laid it aside, till it was new again by another opportunity put into our hands. So my dear friends I only offer to you, as we in joynt Fellowship do stand together to come & feed with us upon ye Body of Love & to be baptized with us in ye burning oil of the Holy Ghost.

193 To ye Lady Jane Lead. v. sub. G[ideon].[150]

It would be indeed well if ye Sardius & Beryl wth their matched did come sometimes together for celebrating ye Institution of ye holy ointm[en]^t, but in ye last nominated, Silas he is yet not convinced in his mind, & doth suppose that for ye acceptation & confirmation of such an holy Institution were required wonders. But yet I am hoping y^t they shall be convinced yet. They understand not y^t ye outward signs or vehicula vel conjunctionis et receptionis media[151] must be proportionated wth ye outward Body in wch they live, & y^t Logos himself hath become medic[a]e natur[a]e, & for this end also is Bread & Wine as a leaven, whereby heavenly flesh & bloud, as an incorruptible seed is sown into ye outward till ye Heavenly hath penetrated totam massam.[152]

Tychicus is Weinich,[153] & is minister amongst 30 Families in a village or countrey town. He & Locher are at Zur[i]ch.[154]

195 To m[o]ns[ieu]r Loth Fischer.[155]

I thank your Lordship for ye extract of ye Relation out of Moscovia wch is truly very wonderfull, & deserves more exactly to be enquired into, & especially who they are y^t have been admitted into ye City & Temple to see ye customes & ceremonies of this Hidden People, & whether they may have any knowledge of Moses & X^t & w^t ye sentiments of their High Priest or Priests, w^t adoration they pay to or before their Images if they pay any, or whether they may

---

150 Loth Fischer at Utrecht writing to Jane Lead at Hoxton Square (no date).
151 "vehicles or means of connection and reception".
152 "the whole lump"; cf. Gal. 5:9.
153 Johann Jacob Weinich.
154 Heinrich Locher (*fl.*1704), a banker in Zürich who collected money for the printing of Jane Lead's works. See Hans Schneider, *German Radical Pietism*, trans. Gerald Macdonald (Plymouth: 2007), p. 47 n. 63.
155 The contemporary index suggests that this was a letter sent from Jane Lead to Loth Fischer. Although the contents indicate that what has been transcribed was from a different sender to a different recipient, this letter was doubtless connected with "An Extract of a Relation of an Ambassadour in Muscovy", which contains a brief description of the 6th Dalai Lama. See *Theosophical Transactions* for May and June (1697), no. 3, 182–184.

be one Philosophical or Historical monum[en]ts for ye preferring of a sacred coleula or magia amongst them[156] or ye memories of y^t & eminent Philosophers & magicians would be well worthy of Enquiry | but ye manners of their life & conversation ought to be in ye first place looked into.

---

156 Coleula is not Latin and its meaning is unknown. It is possible, however, that the word was mistranscribed and that colenda was meant; i.e. sacred worship.

2   **Answer by Richard Roach, Rector of St. Augustine, Hackney, to Five Queries Concerning His Philadelphian Beliefs. Endorsed by Archbishop Tenison (12 pp.) [2 November 1697]**[157]

1. Whether the Holy Bible is not a complete rule of Faith & Morals?
2. Whether there is to be expected any new Revelations of any necessary doctrine of faith or rule of life?
3. If a man pretends to a new Revelation, whether he can convince another of the truth of it without a sign shown him?
4. Whether the Revelations to which Mrs Jane Lead pretends in her first & second volume of the Fountain of Gardens be true? How they can be proved to be so? To what ends of Christ Jesus do they serve, which cannot as well or better be served without them?
5. How come you who profess yourself to be of the Church of England & in holy orders, to minister in a separate public assembly: at the same hour when God is worshipped in the parish churches: and in which you become a fellow minister with woman preachers?[158]

1   1. Query. Whether ye H: Bible is not a Compleat Rule of Faith & Moralls?

An: The manifestations of ye will of God to his People, & ye Rule of Faith & Life wch he has given them, have been graduall; according to ye state & ye Capacity of ye Church: & consequently its Perfection & compleatment is graduall also. That given to ye Jews in ye Law of Moses was a Compleat Rule to them; whereby they might believe & practise ye will of God, & attain Salvation. Yet not so compleat but that ye Addition of ye other parts of the Old Testament,

---

157   LPL, MS 942, no. 141.
158   On 23 August 1697, through the intercession of a "Great man", Roach appeared before the Archbishop of Canterbury. At this meeting he gave Tenison a written account of the "extraordinary experiences"—the "opening of ye spiritual senses, visions, voices, transports &c"—with which some people in England had been favoured. Roach entitled this document "An Address and declaration in testimony of ye Rising Powers of ye Spirit & Kingdom of Christ ... in way of Apology to the Church of England for his late proceeding with wth ye Philadelphian Society others in Proclamation of the Kingdom of Christ". Nonetheless Tenison sought further clarification as to Roach's Philadelphian beliefs, requiring him to respond to these five written queries. Evidently Roach's apology together with the lengthy answers presented here dissuaded Tenison from taking further action, since Roach remained rector of Hackney until his death. Roach's academic colleagues, however, were not so forgiving and he was later expelled from his fellowship at St John's, Oxford in March 1698—ostensibly for non-residence but more likely for frequenting conventicles. See Bodl., MS Rawlinson D 833, fols 6^r–7^v, 83$^{r–v}$.

yᵉ Historicall, Propheticall &c. made it more perfect; by opening, Illustrating, & spiritualizing yᵉ Law of Moses; & preparing by degrees, thro yᵉ Representations of Christ to them more clearly than yᵉ Law did, by Propheticall Figures, Scenes & Descriptions of his Person, offices, Kingdom &c. for yᵉ bringing in of yᵉ Gospel State.

The Church being thus prepared, in Gods Determinate time yᵉ Revelation of Christ was given, wᶜʰ is likewise compleat as yᵉ Law was in its time; & for such a state of yᵉ Church. & here tho yᵉ 4 Gospells of yᵉ Life, & Death, & doctrines of † [i.e. Christ] contain in em all that is to be believed & Practised; & are sufficient to salvation: yet yᵉ Acts of yᵉ Apostles, yᵉ Epistles, & yᵉ Revelation of Sᵗ John have been added as a further Degree of Compleatment. As yᵉ Ancient Prophets made way for yᵉ coming of Christ in a State of Humiliation & suffering, so there is given likewise a Gospel Prophecy; giving us Expectation of, preparing us, & leading us on to greater things, to a ministration and Kingdom of † [i.e. Christ] far more Glorious. As then yᵉ Law, with its Prophecy of yᵉ Gospell, was then a compleat Rule of Faith & Practise; yet not so as to exclude wᵗ God had farther to manifest in yᵉ Gospell: so is yᵉ Gospel of † [i.e. Christ] Crucified, & giving Rules for yᵉ following state of his Church, wᶜʰ was to be a suffering state in Conformity to himself, in yᵉ like manner compleat; yet not so as to exclude wᵗ God has further to manifest upon yᵉ opening of a greater Ministration; wherin yᵉ Power, & Glory of Christs Kingdom may be manifested: wherin yᵉ Church, Redeemed from its suffering state & partaking of this Glory, may have new things concerning yᵉ state of this Kingdom to be Believed; & higher Duties in consequence herof bound upon them; as there shall be greater | Assistance & grace poured out in yᵉ H: Spirit of God to enable men here on earth to Know, Believe, & Live more according to yᵉ Pattern of yᵉ Angelicall state & after yᵉ Laws of Paradise it self. As yᵉ Gospel is Founded upon yᵉ Law & is yᵉ fulfilling of it so is yᵉ succeeding Ministration of the H: Spirit & yᵉ Glorious & Triumphant Kingdom of Christ Founded upon yᵉ Gospel & suffring state; & is yᵉ Explication & Fullfilling of that. Which contains a sufficient Answer [margin: "2"] to yᵉ second Query viz: Whether there is to be expected any new Revelations of any necessary Doctrine of Faith or Rule of Life. In conclusion there are such at this Day, who by yᵉ Blessing of God may say wᵗʰ Sᵗ Peter 2 Ep: Cap: 1.v 18, 19. And this voice wᶜʰ came from Heavn we heard when we were wᵗʰ Him in yᵉ Holy Mount: We have also a more sure Word as Prophecy, to wᶜʰ ye do well to take heed; as a Light that shineth in a dark place, untill yᵉ Day Dawn & yᵉ Day Star arise in your Hearts.

3. Qu: If a man pretends to a new Revelation whether he can convince Another of yᵉ Truth of it without Any sign shewn Him?

An: St John Baptist came wth a Revelation of ye Kingdom of ye Messiah, & proclaimed it to ye Jews, & prepar'd his way warning all to Repent & be Baptiz'd, & make themselves ready for the manifestation of Him as Matth: 3.2. Repent ye for ye Kingdom of Heavn is at Hand. & all this without sign or miracle, Luke 10.41. John did no miracle: but all things that John spake of this man were true. Agreeably hereto may ye Approaches & beginnings of ye triumphant Kingdom of Christ here on earth, be Reveald, Publisht, & Proclaimd, & his way made ready in ye Hearts of many Persons, standing free from Prejudices, & having been long much conversant in ye more Spirituall part of Religion: and this likewise without a sign or miracle to vouch it. The Reasons of Both may possibly be, that such a time & Dispensation Approaching & entring, there may be many other signs of Discernment, of another Nature, as Rationall conclusions, calculations, concurrent circumstances, wth those Footsteps & Appearances of ye Expected Ministration & Kingdom that may be discernd by ye sagacious Inquirers into, & waiters for it; wch tho they are beneath Demonstration & miracle, may yet amount to a Morall evidence, & be a sufficient Motive of belief.

It is here also to be well observed that St Johns preaching & publication & Baptism were not with that strict necessity that evry one must believe, & be obliged to receive it on | pain of Condemnation: but was offerd as a mighty Advantage, help & Preparation for ye Gospel, to those that could receive it. While there was less Evidence than Miracle it was without rigorous Imposition; but after ye Kingdom of ye Messiah appeard, & was confirmd by many Signs & Wonders, ye obligation became more binding & necessary. So in like manner at this Day what is reveald & offerd for Preparation of ye Triumphant Kingdom is not rigorously Imposed on any; but prest earnestly, that they may receive & enjoy a Peculiar Favour of God, in ye great Benefit of being ye First fruits therof. And ye warning now given to ye Christian world is to Return to ye Purity & Spirituality of ye Gospel; which is at this Day so much excluded by received opinions, Traditions, & Systems of our own; and Buried under ye less Materiall part ye outward Form of it; even as ye Ministration of ye H: Baptist preacht up ye strictness & Purity of ye Law; lest our Lord coming & finding all things so Disorderd & perverted should smite ye earth with a curse.

4. Qu: Whether ye Revelations to wch Mrs Jane Lead pretends in her first & second Volume of ye Fountain of Gardens be true? How they can be proved to be so? To what ends of Christ Jesus do they serve, which cannot as well or better be servd without them?

An: These two Books are but part of that Persons writings: & can be little understood, being most deep & Mysticall, without ye Perusall & Understanding of yᵉ others; which are more Introductory. Nor can these others be well understood but by such as have knowledge of yᵉ Mysticall Divinity; wᶜʰ is by most neglected: yet will be found when throughly search'd into, to contain yᵉ most sublime truths, & yᵉ most Spirituall Part of yᵉ Christian Religion: being yᵉ manifestations, Experiences, & Entertainments of such as have lived a more retired & Abstracted life, Devote to God, & more conversant with him than those of yᵉ mixt & outward Life. Such Books are Preparatory of yᵉ Spirituall Kingdom of yᵉ Messias, asserting chiefly & Primarily yᵉ Kingdom of God within us; shewing yᵉ method of yᵉ souls Progress, Purification, & Ascent to God in yᵉ Interior way, thro a holy communion with, & Participation of him, in a manner not to be conceived but by such as have been made Partakers of it. Those of this Author are offerd further as Propheticall; describing yᵉ Glories of yᵉ Approaching Kingdom; as well as directing yᵉ Preparations for it: Particularly yᵉ Revelation of Revelations printed A[nn]o 1683.[159] And these are yᵉ Good Ends of Christ Jesus to wᶜʰ they serve, & that in a Peculiar manner.

They bring an Evidence with them to such as are well prepared & Initiated in yᵉ Mysteries of yᵉ Kingdom, nor have there been wanting Hundreds that have felt yᵉ Power of them; & given their Testimony: severall of which in reading them with some other late writings of this kind, have been made not only assured of yᵉ truth of them from that Demonstration of yᵉ Spirit of God they found in 'em; but have in an extraordinary way been made Partakers of yᵉ same Spirit; yᵉ Divine Powers & Joyes, in an unknown manner, pressing in upon & flowing into 'em; themselves giving a Conviction for beyond wᵗ all yᵉ Powers of Reason could amount to.

4

But these are such as stand in yᵉ meek & Childlike Spirit, & in great simplicity; not full, & Prepossest allready wᵗʰ Receiv'd Opinions, nor Prejudices agᵗ any thing yᵗ yᵉ good God may give out for Manifestation of his will; or further good to his church. By what Instrument soever. Not reading them as Censors wᵗʰ a curious & Inquisitive eye, bent chiefly to find out some thing amiss, in an opposing & objecting Frame of Spirit, by wᶜʰ a check is given, & a Stop is put to yᵉ mild spirit of God: but as Inquirers, & Learners, as yᵉ true Children of yᵉ Kingdom; & as yᵉ Disciples themselves of yᵉ B: Jesus were warned & Instructed to be, looking chiefly & wᵗʰ desire after wᵗ there is of God to be learnd, & wᵗ good hopes there may be of Blessing & Benefit to his People: & rather apt to overlook & allow for yᵉ frailties & weakness of yᵉ Instrument. In yᵉ Moderation, Impartiality, teachableness & calmness of this temper yᵉ H Spirit has a more ready Passage; & communicates more freely its divine Light & Influence.

---

159   Jane Lead, *The Revelation of Revelations* (London: 1683).

The more or less Persons are thus qualified, Prepared, & Initiated, the more or less are they capable of Discerning & Receiving ye Spirit of these writings, such as are thus qualified in Spirit, tho not Initiated, altho they may not understand them throughly, may yet do it in such Degree as to Partake of ye Benefit; & may quickly be brought to understand & digest them more fully.

There are also Externall Evidences of such writings that may be collected from ye ordinary Topicks from whence we usually Judg of ye sincerity & truth of any writer; taken from ye consideration of ye subject matter it self, its nature, tendency, & Ends &c. wch sort of Evidence may otherwise be more fully deduced.

At Present these writings are not offerd but to such as can receive them; nor Imposed upon any. They are offerd as yet without a sign, according to ye Answer to ye preceeding Query, chiefly to such as are highly spiritualiz'd & enlightend; & also to such as are looking after & Advancing towards ye Approaching dispensations, as most capable to Discern them. Such as cannot it is only desired they would suspend all censure & opposition for a while; lest they should even tho well meaning but | under prejudice & zeal for ye common traditions, or ye present minestration be found with St Paul fighting ag^t God: but wait whether in ye office these, & other late writings of ye same Nature, in concurrence with ye great things that are moving at y^t day, may not approve themselves to be of God; & to be, as it is hoped it may be in a short time, confirmd also by outward signs, for ye conviction of such as are to be brought in in a lower Rank after ye First fruits; whose Faith & Discernment could not rise so high, as to believe under absolute Demonstration & Miracle. It will be best either for ye Discovery of ye Truth, or towards ye Partaking of ye Benefit of it, as proving so to be, to pray earnestly to ye Father of Lights & Opener of all hearts, for ye Spirit of Wisdom & Sound Judgment; & be especially zealous in doing his will, that they may know of ye Doctrine whether it be of God: for it must be said both of such as shall read & understand, as well as those y^t Receive & give forth these Revelations of ye Spirit of God: A man can receive (or take to himself) nothing except it be given him from Heav'n. Which is ye answer y^t St John Baptist gave for Himself.

5. Qu: How come you who profess y^r self to be of ye Church of England & in H. Orders, to minister in a separate Publick Assembly: at ye same hour when God is worshipt in ye Parish churches: and in wch you become a fellow minister with women Preachers?

An: There cannot be a Separation from a Church where there is no Disallowance of its establishment; nor any Article of it[s] Faith denyed, or Article of its Constitution opposed.

This Appearing in a Different Assembly is but an Addition of Different Practice, upon an extraordinary emergent occasion; & wch ye Church of England it self would provide for & allow, if satisfyed of ye truth & certainty thereof.

The difference is of Place only, not separate from ye Body of ye Church; but in conjunction with it: being a meeting only for ye Improvem^t, & exercise of Religion, in ye more spirituall part therof.

All churches must own a great declention from ye purity & spirituality of Religion, & ye Apostolicall Practice of ye Church of Christ: & cannot blame ye Aspirations & Endeavours of their members for ye Recovery of it in themselves, & in ye Particular Church wherof they are members.

Such Endeavours & Practice are not Inconsistent wth ye Establishm^t of ye Church of England: which in its constitution could not intend to debar or exclude ye Extraordinary Gifts & Powers of ye H: Spirit, & ye Exercise of them, if they should by ye Blessing of God appear & receive again within it.

Such Endeavours & Practice are not Inconsistent wth ye Reformation; but most agreeable to yea ye very Design & Intention of it.

Such Practice of different Assembly's where every | one tho not in holy orders had liberty to Prophecy, & speak their Experiences for Edification, (as it was common in ye Jewish Temple it self, & in ye Ancient Christian Church) is no new thing under ye Reformation; & in ye Church of England it self: but known in ye earlier & purer times of it to be an allowd practice. According to that of St Paul 1 Cor: 14.26. How is it brethren? When ye come together evry one of you hath a Psalm, hath a Doctrine, hath a Tounge, hath a Revelation, hath an Interpretation. Let all things be done to Edifying. In wch words the Apostle only orders & directs ye Practice of it.

The laying aside of such Assemblies was but about ye latter end of ye Reign of Queen Elizabeth: being prohibited only for some Abuses of it. & this yet was done contrary to ye Opinion & Judgment of ye Metropolitan of that time.

It highly deserves to be considered, that while ye Holy Spirit was in ye Church, as there was at first full Liberty for ye exercise of its Gifts, so as ye Particular Constitutions of Churches arose, this Liberty was still preserv'd: nor as ye Forms came in, was ther[e] any Abridgm^t of y^t Liberty thereby, while it continued. Since ye Cessation of ye Spirit it has been thought convenient to use a Form; & therin to depend on ye ordinary Assistances of ye Spirit: yet not excluding its Undoubted Right if it should again Return.

The Form being at this Day Establisht, & in Generall use, & ye H: Spirit of God Reviving as yet but in Lower Degrees, it condems not ye Form in its present use: but only claims its Ancient Right & Liberty, for its free Exercise & Increase.

It highly Deserves to be Considered by all Churches in their Forms at this Day, whether since this Right & Liberty cannot well be allowed Promiscuously wth ye common use of ye Forms; & since some among them might be capable of meeting & Receiving ye Advances of ye H: Spirit, but ye Generality not, & so not to be deprived of or hinderd in their present use of their Form; it be not expedient, upon a Return of ye H[oly] Spirit, & w^t it might Justly claim of all, to allow of a more Private retirement, & place of Devotion, as of a Chancell, or an Inward Court; wherin a more Particular Attendance might be given to it, & for such as are Partakers therof; to keep warm & cherish what they have received, to Exercise their Gifts, & to serve God with them. Which being in Union wth ye outward Congregation could not but make ye solemn service of God more Acceptable to Him; & Procure a greater Blessing upon ye whole.

As yet, for want of such Convenience; & Necessitated for these Good Ends now mentiond; upon Great, & to us most evident & daily Experiences of ye Extraordinary Powers of the Holy Spirit of God, begun allready in ye Church; Wee meet, not separate from Our Proper Congregation but in Union therwith; only as in an Inward Court of ye same Temple, wch Union we think a Different Place can no more Hinder, than the Different Places wherin ye Holy Rites of ye Church of England are celebrated, can hinder ye Union of ye Whole.

7 Hence our Meeting at ye same hour with them can not wth due construction, be thought Unjust; & counted a separation; but even necessary to, in such circumstance (and even the very Act of) our Communion.

But yet, to give as little offence as Possible, we meet only in ye Afternoon: & not in ye Morning, wch is ye Time of Declaring & solemnizing our Union of Communion with the church, in ye Celebration of ye Holy Supper: which is ye Test, & Symbol of it. So that even without ye Reasons assigned it could Amount to no more than Absence upon some cause or other; & this being as has been Declared only a Locall Absence, for & with a more Reall & Perfect Union, it is well hoped it may, for those Great Reasons & Causes alledg'd, be thought Justifyable: & not only so but Directly for the Advantage & Benefit of the Church.

Hence it is hoped there may be collected sufficient Reason, why one in Holy Orders of ye Church of England may minister in such an Assembly. Especially having experienced a new & more powerfull unction by partaking of ye blessed effusions of ye H: Spirit of God; wch he finds himself obliged to attend: yet in such manner as he doubts not when throughly considered will give no just offence either to ye Church of England or any Church whatever, but will prove in ye event for ye advantage of ye whole. And it may prove ye joy & Glory of ye Church of England in Particular, that ye Holy Powers shall break forth in its members; & as ye divine unction may appear, in an extraordinary manner to have taken hold of & communicated it self to many of its priests & pastors. He cannot forbear wishing & Praying, altho he be at present counted beside himself, that all ye rest of his Brethren might be not only such, but in higher degrees participating of ye holy unction from God; the sufferings & Reproaches for it only excepted. Nor can he doubt but that this good thing wch broke forth in ye Bosome of our Church, & thus unwilling & refusing of it self, to seperate from her: & as loath to be rejected by her, shall hereafter spread it self, till ye Blessing be Universally distributed; & ye Inner court receive & comprehend ye outer: And as it is evident that ye same is likewise communicated to severall of our Brethren dissenting from ye Church of England; that it shall make ye like progress among them till we come to forget all our little Animosities & Contentions; & drown 'em all in ye overflowing Love of God, & of each other; & unite Hand in Hand, in free & full communion for ye Cause of God, & ye Promotion of the Kingdom of our Lord.

As to ye Case of womens speaking in ye Congregation; it appears plainly to have been in use in ye Apostles Dayes: | & the Restrictions of ye Apostle, as ye Learned Grotius on ye places informs us, belong not to such as had ye extraordinary Gifts. And however this Great man may be tax'd of Inclining in a place or two to favor of a notion of his own; yet this is a Case wherein he is wholly unconcernd; & left to ye free Determination of his Reason, & Knowledge of ye History & Practice of ye Apostolicall Church.

* And it is a great confirmation of this exposition, that other Commentators (& even Dr Hammond himself), being perhaps unwilling to give an Interpretation y^t should favour this thing; are here forced to use such evident shift, & elution of ye Text. viz. that ye womens Praying & Prophecying here in ye Congregation is meant, only their hearing others Pray & Prophecy; & so joining mentally with those that do it openly. The evasion is here under ye equivocation of ye word Praying; wch is applicable indeed to both speaker & Hearer, but when rightly distinguisht denotes ye Actions of two different Persons, & that two Different wayes. But this seems plainly detected & confuted by ye other word, Prophecying: wch whether it denote ye declaring future events, or expounding, or speaking to edification, ye Principall significations (of it) cannot / there being here no such Ambiguity, be applied to those that hear it. Or, wch amounts to ye same we may indeed, tho in a different sence, be said to Pray wth him that Prays; or ye Reader: but not to preach wth ye Preacher. It is further observable, how ye same words Praying & Prophecying in ye first verse applied to ye ma[ ]; & denoting & also Interpreted to be ye Act of ye Speaker, are immediately resumed again in ye next verse; evry man Praying or Prophecying with &c. But every woman Praying or Prophecying &c. where there can be no colour of suspicion but that ye Apostle means by 'em in ye second, ye same that he meant in ye first. And for any to Interpret ye former Roundly of ye speaker; &

presently without ye least shadow of Reason here appearing for it or pretended to appear, to Interpret the same words Resumed again, in a different sence; to denote ye Act of ye Hearer, is altogether Precarious & Elusive.

. . .

* Now that those were of an Inferior degree to ye divinely Inspired, & Learners rather, on whom ye Apostle layes this Injunction; & most probably more forward to speak then others, & troblesome in asking Questions in ye Congregation is sufficiently favord by that passage; If they will learn let them ask their Husbands at home: But as to those womens speaking who had ye Propheticall Gifts, we find St Paul speaking of their exercise of 'em, 1 Cor: 11.5. But evry woman praying or Prophecying wth her head uncoverd dishonoureth her head. Where he plainly owns ye Practice of it; & only Regulates ye mode or manner of doing it: & inlarges to ye 16 verse, in giving Reasons why it should be done in such a way; now ye correction, & diligent Regulation of ye mode of any Action, evidently presupposes, & allows ye Action itself And it is great confirmation &c.

9   But farther; upon supposall that ye Apostles Injunction afterwards was Intended to bind these also who had those Extraordinary Gifts; (tho it be hard to think he should change his opinion & Intention in ye next chapter but one, after he had orderd such a Regulation) yet hence tis plain it was ye allowd Practice of ye Church for a time; Restraind, it at all so, for some Irregularities, & Restraind as a thing that might almost have been permitted to continue in ye Church as it began. Which may be enough for ye Present occasion; as will appear, as ye thing shall be considerd more Fundamentally.

Now as ye Woman was First in ye Transgression so ye Curse lay heaviest upon that sex: and one Particular Branch of it was a deposing Her from that Joint Autority with her Husband, wherin she was to Rule with Him, as a King & Queen together in equall soveraignty; to an Inferiority & Subjection far below ye naturall subordination of her sex. Thus we find it Imposed by God Gen: 3.16. In sorrow shalt thou bring forth children: & thy desire shall be to thy Husband, & He shall Rule over thee. But tho ye Curse laid on ye Female was ye heavier, yet ye man had this too, & y^t heavy enough as Gen: 3.17. Cursed is ye Ground for thy sake; in sorrow shalt thou eat of it all ye dayes of thy Life: in ye sweat of thy face shalt thou eat bread; till thou return to ye Ground: for out of it wast thou taken: for dust thou art & to dust shalt thou Return. Nor was he at all to insult; or to value, much less misuse his new gaind superiority: being himself likewise so far degraded: but to wait jointly wth her in Humility & Patience, till ye Curse of both should be taken off by ye Promisd seed of ye woman. wch was to be done gradually in ye Ages & Periods of time determind by God for ye Accomplishment of it. Indeed yᵉ effects of yᵉ womans being deeper in yᵉ Transgression & curse appeard very evidently in yᵉ first Ages of yᵉ World, in yᵉ little Regard had to yᵗ Sex, or mention of them, or Record of their Age, in yᵉ writings of Moses & from yᵉ time of Purification; being so much more for a Female than a Male. &c tho yet here there was some Regard, as in yᵉ Mention of yᵉ Age of Sarah, yᵉ Type of her who should afterwards bring forth yᵉ Promis'd seed. & Greater yet about yᵉ Dispensation of yᵉ Law, where a woman was Joynd with Moses & Aaron to lead yᵉ People of Israel, as Miriam. & afterwards some of this sex were still raisd up, tho but rarely, to be Prophetesses, Judges & Deliverers of their Country. Such were Deborah, Jael, Huldah, Judith &c.

But afterwards in yᵉ Blessed Virgins conception & bringing forth yᵉ Son of God, there was a mighty Reparation of yᵉ Dishonours of that Sex; wᵗʰ a condescension & Favor to it far beyond wᵗ the other could ever Boast of. After wᶜʰ there Appears a more gracious Regard of God to yᵉ Sex in Generall. The Malignity of yᵉ Curse | of Both being so much abated; & yᵉ severe Denunciation on yᵉ Mans part of Returning to yᵉ Dust, Eluded & Escap'd in yᵉ Person & Humanity of Christ; Dying indeed, but not seeing corruption; & in his Resurrection triumphing over Mortality & Death: with a like escape & Triumph on yᵉ womans side, being Restored from yᵉ Curse of a preternaturall subjection, to an earthly Husband, to become a spouse to her Maker. & hereby yᵉ means set on foot to Derive a like Blessing & deliverance to both Sexes, in yᵉ Resurrection of yᵉ one from yᵉ Person of Christ Jesus. Also for yᵉ working off yet more fully & perfectly this subjection & Inferiority of yᵉ Female to yᵉ male; & Restoring it to its joint Autority & soveraignty herewith: ev'n till both uniting, & rising above yᵉ Power of yᵉ Grave be so joyned & made one in Christ their Head, as to make good that of yᵉ Apostle, in an eminent manner: that yᵉ man is not without the woman, nor yᵉ woman without yᵉ man in yᵉ Lord: & that there is neither male nor Female, but all one in Christ Jesus.

We cannot doubt but that there shall be such a totall freedom from yᵉ Curse here on earth, in those holy & blessed ones that shall be made partakers of yᵉ First Resurrection, mentioned Rev: 2.4, 5, 6. & that in yᵉ Glorious & Triumphant Reign of Christ, all this Inferiority & Subjection must be by this Time all wrought off & wholly removed; that both together may Reign & Triumph with Him. In order to wᶜʰ we may observe our B: Lord began to Regard yᵉ Female sex more graciously & converse with them freely, & sufferd them to minister to him of their substance. & also at his Resurrection afforded them yᵉ Peculiar Favor of Appearing first to them; standing then on Types (as yᵉ Event may demonstrate) of his second & spirituall Resurrection within us, upon yᵉ Approach of his Triumphant Kingdom, being to be declared & Publisht first, & cheifly by that sex. And lastly, at yᵉ effusion of the H: Spirit made them equally partakers of yᵉ Extraordinary Gifts.

What was so far effected in ye Restraint & Abatement of ye Curse by ye virgins bringing forth ye Promised seed, is to be compleated & perfected as that Glorious woman mentioned Rev: 12.1. Appearing as a great wonder in Heaven, cloath'd with ye sun, & ye moon under her feet, & a Crown of 12 stars upon her head of whom ye Church is but a Representative; shall bring forth that Manchild wherwith She is in Travail: who is to be caught up to God & to his Throne; & afterwards to come & Rule all nations wth a Rod of Iron v.5. when ye son of God who came before in a weak & fleshly birth, in Ignominy & Contempt, shall again be manifested in a more spirituall manner In ye Kingdom, Power, & Majesty of his Father as it follows v.10. & I heard a voice saying in Heaven, now is come Salvation, & Strength, & ye Kingdom of our God, & Power of his Christ. For ye Accuser of our Brethren is cast down.

This is a thing to deep to be, as yet, & withall too large to be here Discours'd of but those that are more acquainted wth ye state of ye Spirituall & Superior worlds, & ye great Appearances therein; those that have had Instructions from & concerning | the Wisdom of God, w^t Glorious Representation & Figure therof is brought forth & exhibited in ye Heavens; that know why in so peculiar a manner the Divine Wisdom is all along in ye H: Scriptures, & by other deep writers, Represented as a Glorious Virgin; & also how far she is concerned in this wonderfull Birth; & how particularly Justified to, & Presiding over this ensuing dispensation; will not be at a loss to understand ye mystery; or be offended at ye Forwardness of ye Female sex (ye Time of this their servile subjection thro ye Curse now wearing off, upon ye Approach of ye Kingdom) as now conscious of their native Right, & beginning to exert themselves; & becoming by ye Favor & Commission of God ye First & cheif Publishers of ye Internall & Spirituall Resurrection of Christ, & his H: Spirit within us. & Proclaiming to others ye Glad Tidings of his Return. Nor will they think it at all strange if ye Divine Wisdom or the Eternall Virgin shall at this Time Animate & Favour in an Especiall manner, that sex by wch she is Represented.

Here we must not blame them if, as probably they will, they outstrip, & run before us in ye Glorious work of this Day. & less can ye man be offended at y^s Recovery & Restoration of ye Primevall Parity. Which will be the Restitution of his lost Crown & Glory; according to that of ye Apostle, The Woman is ye Glory of ye Man: But will have cause to Rejoice in Prospect of ye full accomplishm^t hereof; whereby he shall receive again his virgin Bride pure & perfect, & rais'd again to be an Equall match, & to be a meat help for him, as at first design'd by God. Thus again, as at first, & now more gloriously in ye Triumphant Kingdom of their Lord Reigning as King & Queen with him in Joint Authority & in their equall native soveraignty; as one in themselves & also one in Him.

Hence it is concluded that tho such women also as had y^t Extraordinary Gift of Prayer & Prophecy in ye Ancient Church were really Intended in ye Apostles Prohibition of women to speak in ye Church; by reason of that subjection commanded by ye Law of their first Transgression: (wch yet is not Granted) It may yet be enough for our present purpose, that this part of ye subjection, by ye curse, was so near wrought off by ye Promised seed in its [place?] of Humiliation, being born of ye Virgin; & ye Freedom of that sex so far Asserted, as to Admit them for sometime to a degree of parity in ye Apostolicall church; in ye free & Publick Exercise of ye Gifts of ye H: Spirit conferd upon them; even tho it should be supposed ye Restraint of ye Apostle was laid on those who had received them, as well as others; & y^t ye time of their full & free Allowance was not yet come, by reason of some Remains of ye Imposed Law of subjection still in force against them. But these remains upon ye succeeding of a more glorious Ministration, wch is to be ye Fullfilling & Perfecting of ye Former, for | ye Reasons, & by ye methods all ready mentioned are to be wholly disannull'd & taken out of ye way. Nor can even an Apostolicall Injunction of a Particular Practice or Inhibition of a thing, not convenient in such a case & in such a state of ye church, be obligatory any longer than that state & ministration shall continue; & when ye Reason of it ceases; & ye Reason for a different practice shall appear. For as much as ye Holy Spirit cannot bind it self by a Rule of Church Practice given us, & proper only at such a time, so as that it shall not be Alterd in a new & Fuller dispensation; when ye Proper Time for such an Alteration shall come.

To conclude, the Prophecies of Joel concerning ye full pouring out of ye Holy Spirit upon ye Handmaids also, so y^t Both ye sons & daughters should Prophecy, will surely Require that at ye full completion therof they should not be Restraind from ye free exercise of their Propheticall Gifts. Those then that maintain that Prophecy had its full completion in ye Apostles Time cannot well Account for it but as it appears there was (at least for a Time) an Allowance of its free exercise. But those that expect a more full Accomplishment & Generall Effusion of ye H: Spirit as they can better Account for ye first & Imperfect completion, so they have sufficient Reason to conclude it must then at least be without this Restraint; in full Freedom & Liberty for both sexes to exercise their Gifts, & speak forth in ye Powers of ye Holy Ghost ye Wisdom, & Praises, & Glory of God. And that this Restoration & Advancement of ye Female sex to ye same Freedom & Dignity with ye male shall prove in ye event, ye Glory of this Age; and ye compleatment of our Triumph, & Perfection of our Redemption by Christ Jesus from ye Curse & Thraldom of theirs & our First Transgression.

Mr Roach Philadelphian his Answer to some queries 2d Nov. 97.

3 "The Life of the Author"

An Autobiographical Account of the English Visionary Jane Lead (1624–1704)

The following text is an English translation from the German by Leigh T.I. Penman of Lead's "Lebenslauff der AVTORIN" ["The Life of the AUTHOR"]. It was printed in Jane Lead, *Sechs Unschätzbare Durch Göttliche Offenbarung und Befehl ans Liecht gebrachte Mystische Tractätlein ... Neben der Autorin Lebenslauffe* (Amsterdam: 1696), pp. 413–423. The original German version—probably by Loth Fischer of Utrecht—was itself based on a now lost account, most likely dictated by Lead about the time she went blind in late 1695 to her amanuensis Francis Lee (1661–1719). The amanuensis, it appears, also added a brief preamble (paragraph [1]), before sending it to the translator.

The Life of the AUTHOR

[0.] Because our dear author sent, at the translator's friendly request, a short account of her life for the appreciation of the lovers of her writings, he has not failed to append and impart it here.

[1.] Following the frequent enjoinings and reminders of several friends, it was deemed necessary to provide an account of the circumstances in which the author of this and other tracts besides was first called and granted her God-given high-Talents, which she did not omit to do, and in the following fashion.

2. Concerning that time, in which the Spiritual Life was born within me and began to impel me, so did this occur in the sixteenth year of my life,[160] around which time some inner promptings began to grow within me and become prominent, through which I became convinced of the vanity of youth.

3. My parents, who raised me in matrimony, lead honourable and modest lives according to the custom and manner of the universal English church, and were esteemed in their honesty around the Norfolk countryside where they lived.[161] | My father, who was called the squire Ward, had me educated in all good outward manners and morals befitting the dignity and class of his house.

---

160 About 1640.
161 Jane had been baptized on 9 March 1624 in the parish of Letheringsett, Norfolk; a younger daughter of Hamond Ward (c.1577–1651) and his wife Mary, née Calthorpe (1582–1657).

4. But I shall pass over this and more besides, and move on in order to provide you with a report of the descent of my high gift, through which I have been born out of God. This occurred and did make itself manifest by means of a beam of Godly light, which burst into my mind and faculties, at a place and time where one might least expect or even suspect such a thing to happen. It occurred namely on Christmas day, the so-called Yuletide feast, when I was among a happy company indulging in music and dance.[162] Suddenly I was overcome by a feeling of sadness which welled up within me, by which I became convinced in both thought and feeling that I did not find myself here upon the path to Heaven. And a strange voice addressed me and said: "Withdraw from this, for I shall lead you in a different dance in place of this vanity." After hearing this message I at once retired and withdrew from the party, so that I might alone contemplate these rare words, an action to which God's indwelling spirit did further impel me.

5. And although my friends and relatives were amazed and did inquire of me precisely what had happened, yet I, at first not knowing what I had experienced, kept hidden from them the true matter and revealed it unto no one, with the exception of a preacher, who was chaplain to a certain knight that dined regularly with my father.[163] | He, chancing upon me in his study as I was reading in a book, did ask of me why I shunned and did not partake in the happenings in my father's house? And I revealed to him how and why I was impelled and moved to my present disposition, whereafter he gave me the advice that I should hold fast in the hope and belief that God, despite the struggles with which I was beset, had something good and great in store for me. His words, although they granted me some comfort, could offer but little help in my condition, because my many sins (through which I recognized the decay of humanity) were all too horribly known and apparent to me. Above all, I carried a constant burden in my mind because once, when I was relating a small matter I had inadvertently told a falsehood and a lie. This did afford my soul great fright, for the words of the Revelation to St. John chapters 21:27 and 22:15, that he who loves untruths and lies shall never enter the New Jerusalem, weighed upon my mind. And I could not stop pondering those minor matters, my words as well as thoughts, in which the evil of sin lurked; and my dwelling upon this caused me a spiritual perplexity which lingered three entire years. Although

415

---

162   Assuming Lead's recollection was accurate then this had occurred on Christmas Day 1640 at Letheringsett Hall, Norfolk.
163   The chaplain may have been William Gurnall (1616–1679) and the knight Sir Valentine Pell (1587–1658).

my parents undertook and spared no effort and industry to free me from these melancholy fantasies (as they called them), or, better said, to suppress the thing which God had awoken within me, all of their efforts did come to naught, and did not stop me from taking to heart that which afflicted my soul, | so that I was forced to spend (as I said) three whole years in this despondency, without comfort nor joy.

6. After sometime had passed, however, I perceived within me a great drive and impulse to depart for London. And because I had a brother there, who was a recently-married merchant,[164] I wrote to him in secret and implored him to request of my father that I might come to London. This he very politely did, and my father approved, so that in the nineteenth year of my life I went there in the hope of encountering a religious right which could heal that malady with which God had stricken me.[165] To which end I spent half a year following my arrival intensively attending public as well as private rights and services, yet the least thing did not touch or resonate with the condition of my soul; until God, seeing my misery and wretchedness, finally led me to stumble upon a congregation which, in an extraordinary fashion, introduced me to the richness and breadth of His love and grace. The foremost marshal on this path was one named Dr Crisp, whose first sermon I did hear touched me in a most wonderful way.[166] His chief subject and emphasis was the matter of the new covenant, through the discussion of which he answered and refuted all the various objections and counter-objections which had toiled within me, as if he had been sent by God himself precisely to the end that he might absolve me from doubt and take away my scruples. In all honesty I departed from this first service with joy (just as the chamberlain of Queen Candace did from Philipp),[167] | and the sorrow had disappeared and been lifted from my face.

7. This liberal spiritual right was entirely different to any other I had ever heard, and I immediately committed to follow on this route, and to hear nothing from any other but those on the same path. In so doing I was daily fortified in the belief and the assurance of the love of God. This belief and assurance stood painted before my mind's eye in the form of a paper with a seal pressed upon it, so that I too believed I was beyond all doubt sealed by the spirit of promise.

---

164 Probably Hamond Ward the younger (c.1605–fl.1661), then living in St Clement's Eastcheap.
165 She was actually 18.
166 Dr Tobias Crisp (1600–1643).
167 Acts 8:26–40.

This was further witnessed by a new spirit of prayer which was granted to me at the same time. And as such I went forward comforted, because I held the virtues of the good society to be the best and true instruments to pursue my spiritual healing.

8. After about a year, however, my family wished to have me once more with them at home, as they noticed I was refreshed in my mind and freed from my sadness. Although it was difficult for me to separate myself from my religious community, I acquiesced to this request out of an indebted obedience. For my parents suspected that I had been led astray, and poisoned by errors, and were worried that I might, without permission, accept a marriage proposal by another who had chosen my spiritual path. And their fears may well have been realized, had not my brother intervened against he who did unknowingly stand in the way of my return home. And although this situation was indeed no small temptation for me, | God did not fail to grace me with further assurance of his love, through the indwelling provision of many doctrines and teachings, which accompanied me on my path as soon as I arrived at any desolate place. For although in these deserts I had to go and forgo the springs of outward refreshment, the Spirit indeed followed and nourished me everywhere.

9. After some time had passed a man was proposed to me as a candidate for marriage, of whom my parents well approved. Yet because he accorded more value to outward things as opposed to matters indwelling, I refused to accept the proposal and accede to the marriage. Thereafter I dedicated myself to my Lord Christ as his Bride, and had little inclination or desire to marry a mortal person who was not as one with my Lord, and of his same Spirit. And on these grounds I did reject all candidates and comers, until finally, in my twenty-first year,[168] a very devout, god-fearing and devoted man did announce himself to me,[169] whom God had inwardly illuminated with a degree of His Light. Our acquaintance was made on account of the fact that he was the son of the brother of a certain knight who had married my mother's sister.[170] This knight was entrusted with the care of his dead brother's son, in addition to the goods

---

168 About 1644.
169 William Lead (1620–1670) of King's Lynn, Norfolk.
170 Sir Valentine Pell, who had married Barbara Calthorpe (1592–1667) at St Luke's, Norwich on 2 March 1617. His sister Mary (1588–1633) had married John Lead (1578–1639) at St Margaret's, King's Lynn on 9 December 1613, making him an uncle by marriage of William Lead.

and chattels bequeathed to him. For which reason the knight, after the father's death, did summon this nephew from London (where he at that time idled) to live in the Norfolk countryside.[171] | Because my mother and sister took care to visit each other often, this merchant, whose name was Mr. William Lead, was often present, and after about a year we were married.[172] We lived together in love and unity for twenty-seven years, and did together raise four daughters. Two died in childhood, while the other two married; one of these departed this world leaving the legacy of a granddaughter, also blessedly departed, while the other is still alive.[173]

10. In his forty-ninth year of age God withdrew him [William Lead] from these outer principles, and transferred him to the upper regions, which was for me a not inconsiderable test and temptation toward sin, given that I had lost such a magnificent husband.[174] Immediately afterwards a great suffering in the face of worldly sorrows and obstacles began in earnest. For my husband had invested and risked a large part of his possessions to an agent overseas, who received the entirety of them following his death, therefore robbing a widow and children of what was rightfully theirs. Of these goods he relinquished nothing. And although I was left therefore mired in a manifold, deep and most desperate poverty, so was I all the more inspired to collect an enduring treasure in Heaven. Thus I determined to remain a widow in God, and to remain fully and wholly faithful to my eternal and constant Husband, to seek advice and help from him alone. And I have lived now twenty-three years as a widow,[175] and dedicated myself wholly to God, and have thereby healed my body and soul.

---

171   In May 1639, just months after the death of his father, William Lead was living at "The Three Golden Lions" in Lombard Street, London. He remained in the capital during the early part of the Civil War before occasionally staying with Sir Valentine Pell at Dersingham, Norfolk.

172   Jane and William were married between 15 June and 14 July 1644, possibly at Letheringsett or Dersingham.

173   While two babies may have been christened at Letheringsett or Dersingham before 1647, two were certainly baptized at St Margaret's, King's Lynn: Mary on 18 January 1649 and Barbarie on 24 February 1653. One daughter who survived into adulthood was known by the initial R. (d. before 1696). The other was Barbarie (1653–*fl.*1720), widow of a man named Walton, who married Francis Lee on 12 November 1695.

174   William Lead died on 5 February 1670 and was buried the next day at St Botolph without Bishopsgate, London.

175   Accordingly, this account appears to be dated 1693. Yet it should be stressed that Lead's memory began to deteriorate with age so that her recollection of certain dates is not always reliable.

11. In the year of our Lord and Saviour 1668 | I was visited once again with a vision from God, of a hitherto unexperienced intensity, as my previously printed works, and in particular the secret writings and manuscripts which I still have in my possession, demonstrate.[176] In this vision I was given to understand that the loss of outward things, and all impediments and various sufferings served only to prepare the path by which the heavenly powers and gifts could descend into our souls unhindered, and make us forget and abandon all that perpetually distracts and opposes the outward person. And the more heed and notice I took of this new reprieve, or dispensation and benediction of prophecy and revelation, the more did new revelations daily inspire me and break forth, to the extent that I knew not where to turn, nor where I could find anybody who might accept and understand what had revealed itself within me. Until it finally came to pass, after diligent searching and enquiry, that I struck upon a society gripped and moved by this selfsame spiritual benediction. Within this society the foremost leaders on this path were, among others, those high-illuminated men in recognition of the deep secrets of God, Dr Pordage, Mr. T. Bromley and Mr. Sabberton.[177] And both parties did much rejoice that they had found each other and come together, and were thereby strengthened in awaiting the Lord; and the daily exercise and strengthening of their respective individual gifts.

12. Following this our society and apprenticeship | (if I may be permitted to use the English expression) grew mightily in size, ultimately coming to number more than one hundred persons. Of the much reputed elders, Dr Pordage was the foremost, and he became a special instrument to encourage, impel and assist me in strengthening this dispensation, or distribution of grace and divine benediction.[178] For he took me into his house, where I lived in his presence, so that we might become better and more precisely cognizant of the interior expectation of God's coming, and united in the spirit of the secret devotion. And he saw and greatly rejoiced at recording the new heavenly revelations which followed and which were permitted me.

---

176 In *A Fountain of Gardens*, however, Lead's *"First Vision"* was dated April 1670; some two months after she became a widow. Moreover, elsewhere Lead maintained that the "Spirit of prophecy" had been declared unto her "since 1670".

177 Dr John Pordage (1607–1681), Thomas Bromley (1630–1691), and Joseph Sabberton (*fl.*1643–*fl.*1680?).

178 Francis Lee reckoned that Lead's "familiar friendship" with Pordage began in either August 1673 or 1674.

13. In this fashion we lived together in great spiritual happiness for around six years, until he [Dr Pordage] came to the end of his life and died in his seventy-eighth year of age,[179] leaving behind him the blessed memorial of a true godly life and an upright spiritual monument to God's work. I can say in all modesty and truth that I never knew anyone who possessed such a high and splendid recognition of the deepest secrets of God. Following his departure from this world our society has been much scattered and distracted, and only a few of the leaders on our path, whom I mentioned previously, are yet alive. I myself am of such an advanced age that I cannot reasonably expect to remain much longer in this body. For this reason I strive ever harder, by all means available to me, to shine and reflect out that light with which God has visited me, | so that it may be spread to all the nations and all four corners of the earth. For this is certainly and infallibly the highest and most noble service that there has ever been, so that the world may be led to the light and acquainted with the same, even though at this time there are few who believe and are given to understand or to recognize it. Concerning my own part not the least doubt dwells within me. For even if I shall inhabit this body not much longer, yet might I still be permitted to see part of these prophecies fulfilled both to the world at large as well as privately. The day is near and shall truly come, upon which my writings shall become of great use and service to some, although they shall be only few, who might through reading the same outlive or recover from perils and death. Blessed, favoured in abundance and known by the Lord are they, who shall become instruments in spreading further and to all, the awareness of the deep and mysterious things which belong to the Kingdom of Christ. So long as I yet inhabit this body I do hope and wait for the blossoming of the age of the Lily, of which some features have really already begun to break forth.

14. For this purpose I have related a true report concerning particular parts as well as the entire course of my life, showing how God, since the time of my youth until this very day, has led me, so that all, into whose hands my books and writings pass, | may know in which way and manner the spirit of God has raised me, and brought me to this high recognition. God gazed upon the lowness and humbleness of his servant-girl, and yet deigned her worthy of being entrusted with such a great treasure.

---

179 Lead was welcomed into Pordage's house from roughly March 1676 until his death in December 1681. Most likely this was in the London suburb of St Andrew's, Holborn where Pordage occupied a property at Red Lion fields.

15. And although an account of the many challenges which I have had to endure, when God was yet with me at all times, might be discoursed upon more largely and in greater detail, I especially wished to concentrate above all on the revelations, which have appeared to me and accompanied me since 1670, so the God-seeking reader might in several ways observe and learn how I was always led further and did progress from one degree to the next in the embodiment of His wisdom. With this I shall conclude, and plead with all power, that the golden voice and source of this Spirit shall break forth abundantly and be taken up by all nations, so that they may be prepared for the great day of Christ's return, and the return of the Lord, in which we all want to hope, believe and await. Oh come soon Lord Jesus!

This is a truthful, factual account related by
JANE LEAD.

4   Francis Lee, "A Faithful Account of the Last Hours of M[rs]. Jane Lead, by One Who Was a Witness of Her Dying Words"[180]

[Copy found in Henry Peckitt MSS written and presented to the Swedenborg Society. A contemporary German translation was published as *Der Seelig und aber Seeligen Jane Leade Letztere Lebens-Stunden* (Amsterdam: 1705) and referred to by Christopher Walton as a German translation of "The last hours of Jane Lead by a Friend". This German version is significantly longer (by about 50 per cent) than the copy held in Swedenborg House and also varies in several particulars; the Swedenborg MS for example, ends abruptly and there is nothing here about Lead's burial and epitaph. The published narrative is also in the third person rather than as here in the first person, suggesting a more impersonal account for wider circulation. The German account was eventually retranslated into English by Samuel Jackson as "The Last Hours of Jane Lead by an Eye and Ear Witness" (*c*.1833) and is preserved among Walton's papers.[181]]

1[r]   After this blessed woman, in the year 1702, had finish'd her own Funeral Sermon * [marginal note: "* That I suppose was her living Funeral Testimony"][182] her whole soul was ingaged about that great change of this mortality to with that of immortality which is in Heaven. She was often told by many pious souls that she would yet live longer to see a great change in the church of God for the best, of which she had many great inspirations from the Spirit of God—many of them she hath set down in her own Journal. So she hopeth patiently for that
1[v]   promised Revelation of the children of God. | She repeated again of an assurance that the spirit of God had revealed to her, that there would be a great and glorious change in the Church of Christ near at Hand, so near that some now living would see the beginning, and that the real Desciples of the Lord would soon be wonderfully brought forth to the terror of the great ones of this world.

This will be the shoor mark whereby the first born of God will be known from the rest of the World; so that the destroying angels which have the seales of the wrath and indignation of God in their Hands to pour down upon the Earth shall
2[r]   have no power to hurt them: so she spoke of this as to herself with holy fear | and trembling before the Lord. He would not let Moses go into the promised Land, neither let David build him a Temple, but the Lord gave him the model of it. The Lord will send those onley who he sees fit in his eternal wisdom, that no flesh may have the praise.

---

180   London, The Swedenborg Society, MS A/25.
181   London, Dr Williams's Library [hereafter DWL], MS 186.18 (1), 33–75.
182   Jane Lead, *A Living Funeral Testimony* (London: 1702).

As soon as her funeral sermon was published followes the accident which certainly would have been her death, but the goodnes of the Lord restored her again, for the good of her self and others of Gods children.

The next spring, in March, as she wrestled in faith & prayer, did the enemy of souls tempt her faith | and patience greatly, as she was at Home alone she fell down a whole pair of stairs and laid for dead [line crossed out] she was very heavy and her left arm was broke and for many days they did not expect her life.

It pleased God to bless the means that she was most wonderfully restored in three months, so as to go about the House without much pain in her arm. [marginal note: "I have heard say she was in Lady Mico's Colage at Stepney"] Soon after she came to town to see some of her Christian friends to bless and praise the Lord in fellowship with them for restoring her again in this world; she also sent provision to them to refresh their poor Bodies also.

After this she went not much out as the days were sharpe but spent | the spring at Home in reading, praying and admiring the goodness of God in her Garden.

She was so well as she had not been a great while. Now all her pious friends believed her end was not so near (as she herself believed) in hopes the Lord would enable her to finish what she had begun in her writing about the great change in the Church of Christ, only to let her live to see the beginning of it.

Many of her heavenly words was omitted to be set down, as none of her Friends did believe her End was so near:

Her words of her last recovery was so great blessing to all her friends who had the pleasure to hear them, yea for truth she did raise her very soul up to God to praise him for his | wonderous ways in his providence to her so well before as after this great accident, so many of her deep expressions was not understood by some of her Friends, just as the Disciples of our Lord did not understand when he told them of his sufferings.

She herself was after [crossed out] led through the spirit of God to a different spiritual progress as she neaver had experienced yet. The Lord did reveal himself wonderfully to her in the Temple of her soul, she was tried or punished seven times as gold is purified in the fire.

So she stood the trial, and received a fresh zeal of the power of the Resurection of the Lord, for which she openly praiseth the Lord. After this it was strongly imprest | on her mind to explain herself more of that change in the true Virgins that follow the Lamb, or their mark by which they shall be known from them that worship the Beast, with some hard advice & caution to all them that wait for the Revelation of the Lord.

Her intention was that this was desired for the special use of all the true ministers of Christ, especially for them who are really called from above to that high prevalidge as the continuation of her before mentioned funeral sermon.

After this she was composed in her soul, and said she had now nothing more to do as she expected her self to pack up to travel Home: so according to the will of the Lord in what manner he pleases to call her, so she testifieth to us with caution that in her last dying hours | we must expect not much of her. She believeth she would dye sudden or if not the poor body would be to weak as not to have power to say much therefore it was best to be ready when we are in health. After this she prepareth her House within and without.

She stood ready clothed in the spirit for the blessed bridegroom of her soul to meet him. Her friends expect a change which soon followed. They did see in her most astonishing pangs of death which was of different natures—her whole body was for some time as that she would compare it to nothing else but a heap of nasty rubbish, so that in her Flesh was a continual fountain of corrupt matter; therefore she called her Body her great Burthen, a great load, a prison, a old stitched | coate, that she had no pleasure to be shut up therein & as alone to suffer therein to the will of God.

Her soul wished for such a Body in which she might say I come O Lord to do thy will.

At first she was taken with a Hectick Feaver [painfull?], in April 1704, which returned so often as she took nourishment wch brought her body so weake that she brought everything up again, that her poor body was quite altered—all her friends belieued her sicknes would be long and painful.

The Darts of Death took possession of her Body—the Beastial part which is under the curse that no remedy could remove. Under these tryals she felt the wrath of God often, which she bore with great patience & humility, tho' she did triumph through faith in the cross of Christ.

This painful sicknes lasted about 4 months from before Easter till in August, | [crossed out] in which she was for some days a little better [crossed out] when she was very careful to make good use of, she used to say how I am a little better come let us think on our Friends, let us write to them or let us come together to praise the Lord whilst he has given us time again.

She said I pray you hinder me not to make good use of the time whilst I have strength, let us be in earnest for our God, let us mis[s] no opportunity let nobody hinder us to think of the Lord whilst it is day.

Sometimes she would call to her pious Friends and beg them to assist her in the work of the Lord which might serve to his honour and praise.

Sometimes she called the Scripture to be read to her, which is the marrow & substance for every care through which she was very much comforted.

But other times she was very much comforted in reading of the lives of some great Disciples of Christian & could let her heal | to the truth of it; at the same time she said she was not come to such a great step, as those great men, tho' she blessed and praised the Lord for what he had done for her Soul and wait till she was in one Faith and Hope with them.

She wished that Christ might be more transformed in his members below, as he is in his members above. She said the Church triumphant was not compleat without the Church militant as the above or not idle, but in constant exercise to praise the Lord with the angels & just so sh[oul]ᵈ the Church below ascend above or bear one with the church triumphant to bring Heaven down on Earth.

She was very thankful when she heard the word of God read to her always examining herself outwardly & inwardly with deep humility, which her words and feeling oppressed as Job & David | who said prove and try my veins.

Some Friends did read to her Cardinal Petrucci's Spiritual Letters, which then came out in English,[183] they treat much of the Christian Perfection the Love of God, which Doctrine agrees perfectly with her own Heart: she was very much pleased with that great saints writings.

It pleased the Lord to try her with various crosses of different natures from within and without was that of her Family—here she found at present greater Trials than she had experienced in ten years before & she was in prayer often with God, most whole nights she wrestled with him, like Jacob in faith, that the Lord might fulfill the fourth petition of the Lords prayer to her Family. She told me when she | had so wrestled with God, that always something was sent for her family, for which she first praised the Lord and then distributed the same, only for the greatest necessitie these outward tryals was not to be compared with the Burthen of her soul which were various. The Church of God as in her captivity here, laid much at her Heart for whose redemption she earnestly prayed—the next that oprest her very much the German and English nation and outward worship for their reformation. She powerfully prayed to God, tho' she suffered greatly of both, that she might be more transformed with the Image of her Lord and Martyr.

She had great compassion and mercy with all who shewed but a willingness to follow the Lord.

She was very much grieved in her soul when she heard of some Profesors | that did not walk agreeable to the Scriptures, that when she heard of such at Home or abroad it was a dagger went through her soul. Then she had much at

---

183   Pietro Matteo Petrucci, *Christian Perfection, Consisting In the Love of God: Explain'd in Several Letters To a Lady, &c.* (London: 1704).

Heart the Society to which she belong'd, that all of them might walk in the Footsteps of the Lord and Marter; besides all this was a continual death in her body present, so that she lost all the feeling, sweet [crossed out] injoyments of God. She was intirely stript of her sweet comfort of her Beloved, that it seemed to her as if the Lord was now turned her Enemy. She was now quite stript of those great gifts and graces which she before enjoyed of her Beloved, which he himself had worked in her through living truth. She had long waited and wrestled with God for a Society of such souls with whom she could be united as in the Lord, so as to be realy of one Heart and mind in the love of the Lord, | such as the Holy Ghost has given us a model of in the Church of Jerusalem of which she often has mentioned in her writings expressly of the Tree of Faith & in the Ark of faith,[184] as well as in the three messages to the Church of Philadelphia.[185]

8r

Tho' she had over come many great trials yet wear they not to be compared with what she suffered in her sickness about 2 months before—all the power of darkness powered in upon her, which burthen was in her last hours great trials to her poor soul, which was as so many Deaths to her; yet under all these Trials which she suffered for Christ sake, did she earnestly seek to see such a congregation of souls who might truly be inwardly united to the Lord Jesus Christ to the glory of God—these was some of the forerunners of her last battles and trials with death and Hell: tho she was under all these great trials inwardly & powerfully strengthened |—tho the Lord did hide his Face from her, and had drawn a vail before her Face that she could not see her Beloved. She said the holy Comforter did now hide his Face from her, which made her inwardly cry out and mourn that he whome her soul loved seemed a stranger to her, tho she said he only seemed to be so, in truth he was not, but was even then more present in her & with her as in the center of her soul and did pray and wrestle with her, that he might give her Enemies the last blow or beat them quite out of the field. After this as she felt a little ease, she told me that she was led from God in a deep mystery which could not be expressed by words, which she never in her life had experienced.

8v

She died in the latter part of the year 1704.

---

184   Jane Lead, *The Tree of Faith: or, The Tree of Life* (London: 1696); Jane Lead, *The Ark of Faith: or A Supplement to the Tree of Faith, &c.* (London: 1696).
185   Jane Lead, *A Message to the Philadelphian Society* (London: 1696).

5   Notebook in the Hand of Christopher Walton[186]

pp. 1–14: "Three Epistles, addressed by Francis Lee to the learned and pious Pierre Poiret in Holland, in the years, 1701, 2, 3, respecting the Philadelphian Society and Mrs Jane Lead—translated from the original Latin copies of the author's own hand, so far as the indistinct writing thereof could be deciphered" (translation by Rev. Robert C. Jenkins, 1871).[187]

Epistle I (1701)[188]

Beloved brother in Christ—The eternal rock be thy strength and health in that of all thy beloved companions in Christ Jesus [^ "re Mrs Lead"]. Now at length is brought to light fully completed [^ "being published"], the Mystical Diary (Diarium Mysticum) the 3^d & 4th vols. thereof, embracing a further period of about seven years, being brought down to the year 1686.[189] Whence again she begins a new curriculum of several following years i.e. of the pure life of faith: which resulted with the Enochian Walks (pub. 1694)[190] some other pieces old as well as new—but few however written by my venerable and dearest mother still remain, which might be printed for the nourishment of the faithful, and the increase of the Church of the first born. The verses which are in the Heavenly Cloud are her own.[191] Those however which follow the Glory of Sharon are not hers, but by my beloved brother R. Roach.[192] Also those which are prefixed to the first volume of her Diary and are inscribed Solomon's Porch,[193] also

1

---

186   DWL, MS 186.18 (1).
187   Pierre Poiret (1649–1719), correspondent of Francis Lee and formerly a follower of Antoinette Bourignon (1616–1680), was a student of mysticism and prolific author who published mainly in French and Latin. For contemporary copies of the original letters in Latin, see DWL, MS 186.18 (2), a.
188   Partly printed in [R.C. Jenkins] "Miracles, Visions, and Revelations, Mediaeval and Modern", *The British Quarterly Review*, 58 (1873), 182 (with a different translation); and in Serge Hutin, *Les Disciples Anglais de Jacob Boehme aux XVIIe et XVIIIe siècles* (Paris: 1960), 195–196 note 24, 253 note 36.
189   Part one of the third volume of Jane Lead's *A Fountain of Gardens* was issued at London in 1700, and part two in 1701.
190   Jane Lead, *The Enochian Walks with God* (London: 1694).
191   Jane Lead, *The Heavenly Cloud Now Breaking* (London: 1681).
192   Jane Lead, *The Wars of David and the Peaceable Reign of Solomon ... Containing ... II. The Glory of Sharon* (London: 1700).
193   "Solomon's Porch: or the Beautiful Gate of Wisdom's Temple. A Poem; Introductory to the Philadelphian Age" in Jane Lead, *A Fountain of Gardens*, vol. 1 (London: 1697), sigs. *E^r–*H^v.

two poems on Matthew and Numbers in vol. IV,[194] which latter have a deep savour of eternal wisdom (Sophia) now that we have finished the Diary, we will with God's help address ourselves to the Heavenly Cloud and the Revelation of Revelations |, hoping for some little fruit thereupon.[195] When these two tracts were published at first, they were much sought after and praised: with all the rest of her works there was altogether another result, so that now all books published in her name be despised and trodden down, and derided by the wise of this world. Yet the learned Dodwell the author of the "Cyprianic Dissertations" and of many other works, a man celebrated throughout all Europe, thinks them not to be altogether despised, wherefore, as my most excellent friend, bearing in his breast a pious and sincere heart, he wrote an Admonitory Letter to me on these revelations, wherein he propounded many things which will be profitable to the victory of truth;[196] and I doubt not that his name as soon as it is made public, will lead all the learned of England, and those endowed with the discernment of pure reason, to the consideration and examination of these books. It is true that he attacks the heresies of the Gnostics, the Manichaeans and Origenists, and that not made secretly but openly; but while he attacks these he attacks the whole English clergy, in order that he may awaken them from sleep, and thus provide for the defence | of the doctrine of the Trinity.—I replied to him and gave him full liberty to bring forth what had been written on either side, since he seemed previously to have asked this of me. To the great God of all these things are committed and surrendered, in order that His cause may at length come forth victorious. It is necessary that gold should be tried with fire, and so it is with truth. A learned divine moreover is now writing an eclectic theology which contains many things but little agreeable to the common reformed theology, a work truly full of erudition, whence it has greatly pleased so many, although it lacks [de] the mystical and sacred wisdom of the kingdom of God from the logical ["deepest"] and most profound principles, and co[ ] by the authority of all ages. And though it may be complained with too much justice, that but too little public and manifest profit has accrued to our ["Philadelphian"] body from these books, nevertheless God may have secretly touched the hearts of many, and may direct the hearts of the pastors

---

194 "The Cloud of Witnesses" (two poems on Matt. 11:9 and Num. 21:17–18) in Jane Lead, *A Fountain of Gardens*, vol. 3 part ii ([London]: 1701), no pagination.
195 A new edition of *The Heavenly Cloud* together with a postscript was printed at London by John Bradford in 1701. This was followed by a new edition of *The Revelation of Revelations*, which was also printed at London by John Bradford in 1701.
196 Francis Lee's correspondence with Henry Dodwell was partly printed in Christopher Walton, *Notes and Materials for an Adequate Biography of the celebrated Divine and Theosopher, William Law* (London: 1854).

into his inward truth, preparing them to lead his beloved flock by the streams of living waters.—Your letter of explanation (in French) M^rs *** has translated as an Apologetic Preface to her "Theologia Germanica";[197] she sends you also her salutation. She has written to *** which | you have doubtless received. You have offered her a most acceptable gift, and have marvellously bound her to yourself in the bond of eternal love. You have satisfied all—the truth is on your side. The Theologia Germanica or genuine theology is defeating and triumphs over the defeat of that which hath been corrupted & interpolated by the blind reason of man. But I humbly ask you that you do not indulge too much that authority of your own understanding which is so clearly seen by you (and would it were so with myself), even where reason and light demand it, or at least seem to demand it; nor believe too readily every narration or information that you receive. For many things are familiarly related among friends which, though like to the truth, are not the truth. What I now say applies to some works of Jacob Böhme, recently translated into our language, though this is of less moment. Our adversaries will readily catch and cavil at trivial points. His work Forty Questions on the Soul came out here in England a little before the martyrdom of King Charles the First,[198] and was put into his hands and read by him with great admiration, for he quickly perceived that something remarkable was concealed under the enigmas [^ or "emblems"] of the writer. Two noblemen brothers, who first fought against the King, but afterwards stood on his side, showed great regard | for this Jacob Böhme and as they had access to this most pious monarch, the opportunity was not lost to them.[199] Our friends thus assisting up to the return of Charles II, the son of the King, the remaining works of this divinely taught Author were brought out under the auspices of the Earl of Pembroke, who had received our Pordage most friendly in his house.[200] But Charles the II returning, such writings as these pleased neither himself or his court. So much did he act to the contrary that there was a light courtesan among his favourites who ridiculed Böhme.[201] Such was the custom of this King and of his court. But the Duke of Buckingham who was on intimate terms with the King,[202] and was also an alchemist (as was the King himself)

---

197   *La Theologie réelle vulgairement ditte la theologie germanique. Avec quelques autres traités de même nature* (Amsterdam: 1700).

198   Jacob Boehme, *XL. Qvestions Concerning the Soule*, trans. J[ohn] S[parrow] (London: 1647); cf. Jacob Boehme, *Forty Questions of the Soul*, trans. John Sparrow (London: 1665).

199   Charles Hotham (1615–1672) and Durand Hotham (c.1617–1691).

200   Philip Herbert (1619–1669), fifth Earl of Pembroke; Dr John Pordage (1607–1681).

201   Alternative translation: "On the contrary, satires ridiculing Böhme and his doctrine were his delight".

202   George Villiers (1628–1687), second Duke of Buckingham.

found an opportunity to promote these books, in order a little to satisfy his [^ "avaricious"] thirst after gold.[203] Nor must I omit to mention that the son of Pordage for no insufficient reason (as it appears to me) has been placed on the household of the Duke.[204] The golden mountains promise themselves much from this, but they constantly bring forth mice, and nothing more. There is however a certain chemist here in London, very experienced, who confesses that he has gained more profit and real science from one of the author's books than from a hundred (more or less) books of other authors.[205] The same person has compounded from his receipts, a very simple medicine by which he has become restored to health | and to the use of his limbs, when no remedy of aid could be found from other ordinary physicians.—a gate seemed thus to be opened which might discover an access towards the unfolding mysteries of the divine kingdom. But our well-versed adversary hath found hitherto many, yea very many works and obstacles, whereby the way of the Lord, the way namely of peace and truth, may be hindered and closed. But the head of the Dragon hath been bruised, and we shall be freed. Clouds and tempests have gone before the face of the glory of Israel; the light therefore will soon arise to those who look for it and prevent it.—Your books "On Learning" and "On Education" are judged by several pious and learned men, to be eminently necessary for this nation: wherefore not only your book "On Learning" but many other treatises of the same kind written by truly enlightened spirits, we trust will soon at length be brought out in our own tongue. As soon as all preparations that have been duly made, so that the unified parts, if not all, yet at least the greater having been everywhere removed, a way or method may be prepared as God now at least points out to us.

The recent censure of the Scotch Presbyterians has given occasion for kindling a greater light, not only in Scotland but also here in England; and without doubt the noble utterance of Zerubbabel shall be confirmed to the age which has now begun. | and what is beyond the conception of many Religionists, that the women shall prove the more valiant. The treatise of the blessed Virgin A.B. "On the renovation of the Gospel Spirit" might be profitable to many.[206] That, as well as what that [invalid?] John Engelbrecht hath written "On the Three States" ought to be greatly encouraged as I think, among our people.[207] It does

---

203 Alternative translation: "… in order to satiate the hunger for gold".
204 Samuel Pordage (1633–1691?).
205 Possibly Albert Otto Faber (1612–1684).
206 Antoinette Bourignon, *The Renovation of the Gospel-Spirit*, 3 parts, was published in English in 1707.
207 Although there were contemporary English translations of works by Hans Engelbrecht

not become us to be idle in the Vineyard of our Lord, for already it is nearly the eleventh hour. What is that <u>Northern Prophet</u> doing who lives at Amsterdam?[208] What are the Jews doing? What of the good song which they call Hosanna? Many spirits have gone forth from the throne of the Majesty on high both on the right hand and on the left. May the right hand of the most High preserve us, and the angel of the Lord protect us lest our feet slip in any direction. May the light of God be over thee, my brother, for evermore. May the dewy cloud be over thy house and all that dwell therein, and may thy rest be in the tabernacle of the Lord. May the Lord hear thy prayers and be propitious to thee, and the power of the Holy Ghost cover thee. This is and ever will be the prayer of thy most devoted in the bones of Christ. F.L.

Epistle 11 (20 April 1702)   7

Most illustrious and beloved in Him who was and is and is to come, Love— from our Wetstein, alike yours and ours.[209] I have received "The Threefold Life" (or state) edited by your care | and have read it with fruit.[210] I translated also 8
to my venerable Mother the greater part of the Life of <u>Saint Elizabeth</u> (of Hungary) and of <u>Werner</u>, that holy youth,[211] and she will express to you by letter her opinion hereupon. In regard to what you write about the life of the <u>Marquis de Renty</u>, it has been already sometime translated into our language (and that, as it is believed) by Burnett Bishop of Salisbury although a most bitter enemy of the Church of Rome,[212] and the knowledge of it for many years has

---

(1599–1642) in manuscript, the earliest extensive publication of his writings in English was *The German Lazarus; Being A Plain and Faithful Account of the extraordinary Events that happened to John Engelbrecht of Brunswick* (London: 1707). It contains a commendation by Pierre Poiret.

208   Possibly Oliger Pauli (1644–1714).
209   Several booksellers with this surname were active in Amsterdam including Hendrick Wetstein (1649–1726), as well as Rudolph and Gerhard Wetstein.
210   Possibly a version of Jacob Boehme's *The High and Deep Searching out of The Threefold Life of Man through The Three Principles*. According to Christopher Walton, a copy of Boehme's "Two dialogues of the super-sensual life" was in Francis Lee's hand rather than William Law's [DWL, MS 186.13 (6)].
211   *La Vie de Sainte Elisabeth, fille du Roy de Hongrie, Duchesse de Turinge, et premiere religieuse Du troisiéme Ordre de Saint François* (Paris: 1702); Pierre Poiret, *Le Saint refugié, ou la vie & la mort edifiantes de Wernerus ... mort à **L'an 1699* (Amsterdam: 1701). An English version was eventually published as *The Edifying Life and Death of John Verner, A French Protestant* (Dublin: 1810).
212   *The Holy Life of Monr. De Renty, a Late Nobleman of France ... Written in French by John Baptist S. Jure. And Faithfully Translated into English, by E.S. Gent* (London: 1658). Lee was

been acquired by me as well as by my venerable mother. Nor do we doubt that these <u>Three Lives</u> will through the watering of the Holy Spirit, produce much fruit in this age; and that they are in truth the most solid apology for mystical theology.—Wherefore we render thanks to the God of Light that he has given such heroic examples to these latter days, and that he hath granted to you strength and disposition to accomplish what you have done in your work. Your ~~usage~~ of Mrs. A. B. ought to be very dear to us.[213] Would that all who think themselves servants and children of God, could discern this genuine and lively image and I suppose the real merits of the original. They would not then rashly undervalue that <u>Life</u> which he hath vouchsafed to honour.[214] But we are fallen upon very difficult times, in which every one wishes to be, and to appear to be, a judge even though he have not judged himself.—and this, before that infallible judge comes who will reveal all the hidden things in

9   the | hearts of his saints, discriminating all that is mixed, and separating the wheat from the chaff. Let us await this oracle as you yourself say, "in the pure ground of a purified heart, where only Christ shines and judges",—the oracle, I repeat, which under the law was called typically the <u>oracle of judgement</u>, and which none but the High Priest was authorized to put forth. Christ therefore, our great High Priest who enters into the secret recesses of the purified heart, alone has in himself this oracle of judgement, and hence it is above all things to be guarded against that any should judge before the time, that any instrument of God, even the very least, should become a subject of contention among pious men. One thing may be profitable to me, another thing to another. That which is profitable to the other might not be to me. This is equally in the hand of God, and more honourable (it may be) than that which I so highly prize. For I regard only my own advancement, but I do not discern that by which my advancement is brought about. As regards that Utrecht friend of whom you speak, as he is sincere and pious without hypocrisy, we well know that he will do nothing seriously and wittingly to hinder the progress of the Word of God, & to bring His instruments into contention. But if through ignorance of fact, or the relation of others, or too great zeal he should do this in a single instance,

10   GOD himself will shew his mercy, | will open his eye, will purify the ground of his heart, will free his mind from every prejudice, revealing to him the hidden

---

       probably referring to the second edition of this work published by Benjamin Tooke at London in 1684, although the translator has been identified as Edward Sheldon (1599–1687).

213   Antoinette Bourignon.

214   [Pierre Poiret], *La Vie de Dam^{lle} Antoinette Bourignon. Ecrite partie par elle-méme, partie par une personne de sa connoissance* (Amsterdam: 1683); [Pierre Poiret], *La Vie Continuée de Dam^{lle} Antoinette Bourignon* (no place, no date).

things of darkness, and manifesting the light of the tabernacle of Glory in the day of his advent. Entering into the inmost recesses of his spirit, that one and only master shall nourish and teach him continually that he fall not again, and prevent the very least of his fellow disciples from giving any offence. May the merciful GOD grant also that we ourselves may be preserved unto the coming of the Lord Christ, from every scandal of this kind, and from all rashness and arrogance of spirit, and that His peace may remain with us. The Lord stands before the door, let us walk carefully; let us watch, one and all: for snares and nets are spread everywhere; on all sides there are the stratagems of the Prince of Evil. Everywhere wars, private and public: everywhere the warfare with or against GOD [Greek: ...]. Let us fly then to our arms which are spiritual, and in the power of God, not carnal or worldly power: in order that the kingdom of our peaceful King may be established among us, and remain with us for eternity. Come quickly, O Prince of Peace. Gather the peacemakers unto thyself, and grant that we may all live in one according to thy mind. May that gift be ever sacred and solemn to us. "The Peace of Christ be with thee always" and with all thine. May it increase daily, may grace be multiplied, and may the fruits of the Divine spirit become more and more increased to us; Which is and ever | will be in the prayers of thy most obliged and devoted in Christ. F.L. April 20th, 1702.

Epistle III (20 April 1703)

May His work be perfect, I pray the God of Love himself; and be confirmed in all the friends and children of God. May it be perfect and confirmed in thee my beloved Brother, may it be so in each of us who are here fighting and labouring under the banner of crucified Love; that your love and our mutual brotherly love [Greek: Philadelphia] may never fall away and never perish; but that bearing all things, believing all things, hoping all things, enduring all things, the head of Satan may at length be bruised, and all his machinations and stratagems to disturb brotherly concord, may prevail nothing. I doubt it not to be most true that he who hath his name from <u>accusing</u> hath now by daily use become most fully proficient in his art of <u>accusation</u>; and that in order to produce discords between the brethren, sometimes (as you know secretly), he should move the very elements in a supernatural manner, whereby the appearance of things, which in reality were never done nor said, might be put forth. Not a few examples of this kind are well known to me, and <u>daily I experience the singular subtleties as well as the mere fabrications and pure inventions of that ancient enemy</u>, and this ever more and more | every day. I know well that the Baron de N. whom I love sincerely (intire amplector) could never have pronounced such words as are reported of him;²¹⁵ though he has never written about this controversy, nor indeed have you. The truth was clear both to me and to my venerated mother. Meantime we greatly lament that our most faithful Utrecht friend should have reported such things, as we were sure that he never desires to relate anything, or to speak of any one unless he firmly believes that what he relates was said or done; whence we do not hesitate to believe that they are mere fabrications and imaginations produced in the senses by the cunning adversary. Thus it is that brother often crucifies brother, and among the angels of Light and faithful fellow servants, there arises sometimes a severe temptation. That golden saying of Tauler we see daily fulfilled: "What remains for us my lord and master, than to receive lovingly these messengers sent from heaven by God himself in order to exercise our patience and faithfulness?" But among my papers I find opportunely a writing of mine to yourself, which as I am uncertain whether it reached you, and as it contains my old sentiments, I will not refrain from exhibiting here *********. Here you have our sentiment and our wish. May almighty Love grant that these things may be imprinted on the hearts of all the faithful; that we may dwell as one on Mount Sion, that the City of Peace may descend | from heaven, the bride of the Lamb the Peacemaker adorned for her spouse. I greatly joy that Les Torrens de Madame Guyon have fallen into your hands,²¹⁶ and it is most gratifying to me that you are giving your attention to the editing of the treatise. May the merciful God grant that the messenger who brought intelligence of her recent liberation from prison, published in the newspapers, may not only be found true, but that rich fruits may spring therefrom to the glory of our Divine master. The life of that poor unlettered holy servant maid Armelle Nicolas, of which you make mention as about to be published by you, I look for with eager desire, on account of the vast benefit which may accrue from it to rightly disposed souls.²¹⁷ Your letter, our beloved Wetstein who is now staying with me communicated to me. I wrote immediately to Mr Fischer in regard to Engelbrecht's works,²¹⁸ to enquire about them, and to ask why the German edition had been interrupted. I expect his answer. That, as soon as I receive it, I will communicate to Wetstein. My mother is now confined to her bed,—still very dear to her spouse, and affording us an eminent example and corroboration. Some others have now become much edified by

---

215 Baron de N. = unidentified.
216 *Les Torrens spirituels* by Jeanne-Marie Bouvier de la Motte-Guyon (1648–1717).
217 Pierre Poiret, *L'Ecole du pur amour de Dieu ouverte aux Savans & aux Ignorans dans la vie merveilleuse d'une pauvre fille idiote, païsanne de naissance & servante de condition, Armelle Nicolas* (Cologne: 1704).
218 Loth Fischer (d.1709).

the example of her patience, resignation and faith, who thought dishonourably of her before. Whatever is ordained for us may God be glorified, through His Christ, not only "in the highest" but "in the deep". We all embrace you. May grace and peace be in your | dwelling and remain with you eternally. F.L. April 20th, 1703.

6   Six "Epistles Addressed to Some German Associates of the Philadelphian Society, Resident in Holland, upon the Decease of Mrs. Jane Lead (Ostensible Founder of the Said Society), by Francis Lee, Her Son-in-Law and Executor. Their Date is Sept or Oct 1704, and They Are Here Transcribed from Lee's own MS".[219]

15   Francis Lee to an unknown aristocratic lady (c. September 1704)[220]

Madam. It having pleased the Infinite Good to call up his dear and faithful handmaid, M^{rs}. Jane Leade, by loosing the bonds of her mortal flesh, about a month since,[221] and thereby delivering her from all the evils and calamities of her long exile from the land of her eternal nativity; I did, according to her special appointment, as well as according to the obligation I stood in, both by spiritual and natural affinity, acquaint presently her greatly esteemed friend in Christ, Mr Poiret,[222] therewith: | and did beg him at the same time that your Highness might have notice hereof, together with the communication of her Blessing and continual remembrance of you, and of her Christian farewell and exhortation to as many as she has left behind, that we may all hold fast what we have received, nor sinking or wavering but taking heed through the patience of the Cross to secure our standing, that we lose not the price of our High calling in Jesus Christ. But feeling an inward drawing at this time in my spirit, and being jealous that I might not fully enough in all things perform the will of deceased, I have resolved to write to your Highness expressly by the hands of our Beloved Brother Mr Loth Fischer,[223] as perfectly understanding the will and meaning of my blessed Mother in what relates to your progress and advancement in the life of Christ, wherein only the true nobility consists. Now she was not insensible that you were encompassed about with many difficulties and temptations on every hand, so that it might be very hard for you to stand in this perilous day; and that more especially by reason of the birth; which made her pray that your faith might not fail, and that the strong blasts of the north wind might

---

219 DWL, MS 186.18 (1) [Notebook in the hand of Christopher Walton, pp. 15–31]. For copies of the original letters, see DWL, MS 186.18 (2), b.
220 This woman may have been a member of the Sayn-Wittgenstein-Berleburg, Sayn-Wittgenstein-Hachenburg or Sayn-Wittgenstein-Hohenstein families. Luise Philippine von Sayn-Wittgenstein-Hohenstein (1652–1722) was a correspondent of Johann Dittmar, while Countess Hedwig Sophie von Sayn-Wittgenstein-Berleburg (1669–1738) was a Pietist who promoted religious toleration.
221 Lead died at Hoxton on Tuesday, 8 August 1704.
222 Pierre Poiret (1649–1719).
223 Loth Fischer (d.1709).

not hurt the tender buddings of the spirit, nor the little foxes undermine that inward vineyard which is planted in you by Christ. But she had a confidence that you would be preserved, as a beloved lamb, by the care of your Good and Gracious shepherd: and that the trying | of your faith would beget patience and perseverance, so that you might be made perfect and intire. Keeping close to the heart of Jesus and thereby wanting nothing. She heard likewise with much joy that your illustrious father the Duke,[224] was himself not without some good relish for divine and spiritual things, though not fondly carried forth after the manner of some but well poised with Prudence and Wisdom, for the better and more effectual management of that which might otherwise be easily miscarry through immoderation or precipitancy. Therefore your Highness entering into stillness, and into the deep and silent introversion, thereby to attain the habitual prayer of the Divine presence, and abstraction from the world, is what I am sure my venerable mother would have pressed on you: that so you might come to be perfected in Love, and to be filled with the springs of the Heavenly wisdom. And she would further doubtless tell you, that after all the highest advancements that you can possibly make here, after all the sweetest spiritual enjoyments, and sensations, after all the most familiar intercourses of spirit with spirit, and divine colloquies; and after all the highest raptures, and most intimate union with God in Christ, and whatever can be named of this kind; you must be truly content to be stripped of all, and to stand naked; yea to have your very flesh separated as it were from the bones, piece by piece, through that spirit which is able to divide betwixt the joints and the marrow, and which | overseeing all things, goeth through all understanding, prize of subtle spirits. For my dear Mother after that she had finished and published her Funeral Testimony,[225] which she was willing to have come out in her own life-time, as she was endeavouring to put all things in a readiness for her longed for dissolution, was made to pass through this state of exinanition, in conformity to her Saviour, the beginning whereof I may date from that terrible fall of hers in March 1703, which was attended also with many onsets in the spirit. But God was powerful in her all along, giving her the victory over all, through Jesus Christ. So soon as she was a little recovered from that dismal shock, which was not without a peculiar Divine influence and blessing, as I can testify upon my certain knowledge; she was excited to continue her former testimony by a strong driving of that spirit which had hitherto so wonderfully conducted her. This she accordingly did, and so made another short treatise, declaring chiefly the state

17

18

---

224 Duke = unidentified.
225 Jane Lead, *A Living Funeral Testimony* (London: 1702).

of the first Resurrection in Christ; which by her order is now in the hands of Mr Fischer, who labours in the translation of it, that it may be in readiness to be brought forth in your language, as any shall be stirred up by God to promote its Publication.[226] This she would have called <u>The Royal Stamp</u>. And as this is the last of all her writings, so that soft Divine unction which flows through it gives the confirmation of the rest, but more particularly of her first of all, which is <u>The Heavenly Cloud</u>.[227] It is mostly | Prophetical; but she was confident with an holy reverence that the testimony of Jesus, which is the true spirit of prophecy, would accompany it in the fulfilling by an impression of his own stamp and character according to what is therein declared. This I am by many arguments fully satisfied of, as well as by that infernal taste which is above all argument: but the seasons are in the Father's hands, and that may appear near to us, and at the very door, while (we) may be yet at some considerable distance off. However it be, let us be in a preparation: for the day and hour may come when we think not of it; which was a main end, of her leaving this her last legacy to those that are called as elected to be of the first fruits of the kingdom. Among which that your Highness may be numbered together with the Prince your Father and sealed with the true stamp and seal of the living God; as I know it to have been the prayer and intercession of my honoured mother in Christ, so shall it not fail to be of me her son.

 Who am—Madam—your Highness's—for all Christian services—most obedient & oblig'd serv[an]t—F. Lee.

19 Francis Lee to the same unknown recipient

Madam—a little before the blessed decease of my most honored Mother, she gave some advice concerning your son, and his affairs, to Mr Fischer to be communicated to your Ladyship which I doubt not but you will have received; and she had also a mind to have written to | your Ladyship expressly, had not her weakness increased so fast upon her. She had always a very sympathising affection with you, and a most deep concern for your son, the Baron, as one that had been given up under her tutelage and care: and though all the things have seemed to run cross for so many years, yet will I not yet despair but that your

---

226 Jane Lead, "The Resurrection of Life, or The Royal Stamp and Sign which has been imprinted upon those who have been Resurrected with Christ" (1703). The English version is no longer extant, but a German translation was published as *Die Auferstehung des Lebens: oder das Königliche Merck- und Kennzeichen so denen aufgetruckt ist, Die mit Christo auferstanden sind* (Amsterdam: 1705).

227 Jane Lead, *The Heavenly Cloud Now Breaking* (London: 1681).

and her prayers will in the end bring down the desired blessing for him; and that so much the more possibly as she is now entered into the sanctuary above. The Lady which he pursued is said to be given away to another. But other designs are still in his head, which when I saw him last he appeared very confident of compassing: but what they were I cannot tell, or even guess. Your Bill of £31 was payed into his hands, and I pressed him hard to be a good husband [of it?] and to discharge in the first place what was most necessary. He made an overture by a third person of returning again to love with us, but my dear Mother on account of her sickness diverted it. Nor were we indeed willing to do anything herein without first acquainting your Ladyship to know your will and pleasure. After this he retired somewhere into the country; as I hear; what may be the effects of it time will shew. He said he would return at the end of two months, and more than one is already expired. That he may return to himself and as a Son of so many tears bring joy into your Bosom at last. I shall without fainting hope and pray, as being truly Madam, most obliged to serve you and yours.

Francis Lee to "Archippus"[228]

21

My worthy Friend and Brother in the Life of Christ. I am obliged to give you an account, as well as the Brethren dispersed in Germany and Holland, of the call of Christ to our venerable Mother to come up and abide with him in the superior sanctuary where all things were ready; and of her passage thenceforth through the Dark Valley of Death, with many strong and strange combats underwent by her, that her victory might be the greater, and her triumphs the more glorious. Whereof having given a pretty full narrative to our beloved Fischer, and to several others through his hands, I am persuaded that he will not be wanting to communicate of the same for your benefit and edification as well as that for any other hidden names in country, who have not defiled their garments or denied the faith.[229] According then to the last Will and Testament of my Mother I am to acquaint you with her remembrance of you in the eternal bond of love; to encourage you for the noble profession which you have hitherto made and your patience in the hour of tribulation and temptation; to exhort you to a steady perseverance and continuance to the end in what you have received of the Heavenly Gift and ministration, for as much as your labor shall not be in vain in the Lord;—to thank you for all your kind demonstrations of a particular office and love to her, for the sake of the Divine treasure

---

228 Archippus = unidentified [cf. Col. 4:17; Philem. 1:2].
229 Subsequently published as [Francis Lee], *Der Seelig und aber Seeligen Jane Leade Letztere Lebens-Stunden*, trans. Loth Fischer (Amsterdam: 1705).

entrusted with her; and to assure you lastly of the truth of God's covenant and promises, | not only to the faithful, but also to their seed after them. Therefore as concerning your Son, or Sons, her mind was that you should not be at all discouraged; but making an offering in the spirit of the fruit of your loins to the God of Heaven, there to rest in hope, laying the full and whole charge upon Him who is the Father of all immortal and eternal spirits, who cannot sure be less careful of their eternal welfare than you; and will doubtless accept those prayers which are offered up in faith on that account. Further in her name I entreat you to salute all the Brethren and Sisters known to you. Beloved of God, and sanctified in the blood of the Lamb; exhorting them to all patience under the cross, that they may be made meet to receive the Royal Stamp and character of the first and blessed resurrection. It was also her Will, that her friends and correspondents should be everywhere admonished to examine and try with the utmost diligence the many spirits that are gone forth at this day: and especially to take great heed of all that follow the deeds of the Nicolaitans and of all that lie in the bed of spiritual fornications. Likewise she was deeply concerned for several high and sublime spirits, which may have received some touches of the Divine Wisdom, and been attracted by some sensible Lights and Graces: and indeed for the great mixtures which are generally everywhere found even among the very children of the Kingdom themselves. Wherefore she most powerfully recommended humility unto all, according to the deepest and truest ground of it; and I am strongly | pressed to inculcate it, as from the Lord, and from her; that every one may prefer one another in all loveliness of mind; not sitting down in the judgment seat, but waiting for the Day wherein all things shall be revealed that are now hidden: doing every one his own business; and remembering above all the commandment and pattern given by the Lord to his Disciples when he washed their feet. Beside this, according to her, we ought to be grounded in that humility, with the whole circle of Christian graces and virtues, which is comprehended in charity, which never vaunts itself, or is puffed up, but is long suffering, kind and condescending, rejoicing in another's good; and bearing, believing, hoping and enduring all things; as in the tracts of a True Philadelphian may be more fully seen, which are subjoined to the Third Message to that Society.[230] Such would she have us all to be, as there are described. And may the good God so pour out the grace of his Spirit abundantly upon us at this time, that such we may actually come to be, and so be found in the time of the First Resurrection, wherein the name of our God, and

---

230   Jane Lead, *The Messenger of An Universal Peace: or A Third Message to the Philadelphian Society* (London: 1698).

the name of his City shall be imprinted on us, and on all that are unmoveable in the faith and love, in living characters. And which was the sum of her last Testimony and agonising prayer: and wherein I doubt not but yourself dear brother in Christ, will concur with her, and with me, who am—in the patient waiting of the Kingdom of our Lord—your fellow Traveller and friend.

Francis Lee to "Tychicus"[231]

In the Fountain of Life, Light and Love, Blest and Beloved, By order of my Mother of Blessed memory I am with a hearty love greeting to certify you and them with you called of God in Christ Jesus to wait in the true spiritual Temple, of her late passage to the glorious mount of God, though through a dismal vale of darknesses and deaths; that the measure of the sufferings of Christ might be filled up in her, and in all the great Saints and Elders of the Love; and that by these she might be consecrated and consummated as her Lord was, for an eternal Priesthood in the heavens, with, in, and under Him, the Great Mediator and Priest for universal nature. Not long before she departed from us, to be present with the Beloved of his soul, she received advice of what you had written in May last to the dear brother Fischer: and was well satisfied that you were called to see, that the cross of Christ did not consist in words and habits; but did lie far deeper. She was truly a woman of the Cross, notwithstanding she was so highly blessed and favoured of God: and I am instructed by her (and I hope also from the Lord) to declare to you and as many as are in fellowship with you in the truth, that ye take heed of ascending before ye have descended into the deep of deeps; that ye humble your souls to the dust, and with deep yearnings of heart cast yourselves down at the foot of the Cross of Jesus; and that ye make no images unto yourselves of anything in the heavens | above, abstaining from all idols though never so fine. As for the rest, it is no great matter how ye appear outwardly, if excesses and scandals be avoided. None have ever been more mortified to the world than some that lived in Prince's Palaces: and none have more despised the pomps and fashions thereof, than some who have been so humble of heart, as not to be willing to distinguish themselves from others, as if they were better than they. If the essential glowing flame of the Holy Ghost be in you, then you need not be taught this of any one: but you, as taught of God, will discern the spirit from which this is sent to you and your fellow brethren. This one thing yet remains, that ye all seek after the ancient ways and stand in the Paths of old; not neglecting or slighting, as the manner

---

231   Tychicus = Johann Jacob Weinich (1649–1713).

of some is, the established oracles and records of truth, delivered down to us for the perpetual building up of the Church of God.—for as much my dear and blessed Mother took always great delight in having the Holy Scriptures read to her, as often as we met to wait together upon God: we having in our daily course just finished the whole Bible a little before she was called from us into glory. This therefore I must further in her name advise and admonish, that there be a holding fast to that which was delivered to the saints of old, that so every one may build upon the true foundation of Christ and his apostles; not laying any foundation of their own. For I can say that as Christ | was the foundation in her, so all His words, had a more peculiar influence and power upon her, than any others; as proceeding from His blessed mouth immediately. During her sickness she called to me frequently to read, and I found her much refreshed with the Psalms of David, and some select portions in the Prophets, and in the New Testament: (when I asked her where it was her pleasure that I should read to her, she answered, know you not? Anywhere in the orthodox Scriptures.) And as I have received several instructions and consolations lately in visions of the night, which I take to be from her spirit; so once she appeared calling to me with my dear Wife to wait upon our good God in our daily ministration, strictly also cautioning as not to lose any opportunity of retirement and holy introversion that presented itself. I made then several reflections hereupon for myself and others: and wrought with a mighty drawing power upon me to obey this call. The testimony of Jesus is true in all the generations of his Saints; but the time of glorification is not yet. And though it may be near, yet the present mortification and putrefaction must precede it. This I know to have been her mind: and I think also it is the mind of God. Into whose powerful protection, and most wise and gracious conduct I commit you, my dear Brother, with all that love the Lord Jesus Christ in truth and sincerity, abiding under the Cross—your and their servant to the death.

27 Francis Lee to Meyer J.L. Hachenberg[232]

Immanuel Jesus liveth.—In his spirit and life truly indeared Brother,—you having been one of the first that was powerfully stirred up to converse by letter with Mrs Jane Lead, my dear and honoured Mother for the sake of the divine gift entrusted with her for the children of the cross and having yourself been under some peculiar visitations of the Divine Wisdom; I cannot omit to send you, when she so dearly esteemed and commiserated, her love-valediction, Greeting

---

232 Possibly Johann Caspar von Hachenberg, or a relative.

you from the eternal fountain and root of blessing, with grace, peace, wisdom and power. It was her earnest desire and prayer that Christ in you might tread down Satan under his feet, to the confusion of the wicked agents conspiring against you; and that he would speedily deliver you from all those powers of darkness that have received a permission to afflict you in the outward man, for your higher perfection and consummation; but which cannot in the least touch your inward spiritual man, which is kept as under the hollow of the hand of the almighty, and which being hidden for a little while, shall be gloriously manifested with the children of the resurrection, in the approaching blessed kingdom of our Lord. In which that we may meet and rejoice together, after having passed through many tribulations, and being washed and purified in the blood of the most holy Lamb, who was dead, but is now alive, living and reigning for ever, is the faith and | hope of your very affectionated and sympathising Brother under the cross of Jesus, unknown in the flesh but known in the spirit,—F.L.—The dear brother Fischer can communicate to you several edifying and comfortable particulars concerning this late change and passage.

Francis Lee to Madam Tisshenn of Rotterdam[233]

In the bowels of Jesus, very much indeared Friend and Sister,—In these you were tenderly embraced by my blessed Mother, who is lately entered into her seat, in the eighty first year of her earthly pilgrimage, and who left to you, and all her friends, the children and servants of the living God, her most Christian valediction and blessing; with prayers and sighs thereon not to be expressed, pouring out her soul, truly simplified, that the name of Jehovah our everlasting Righteousness may come to be hallowed on earth as it is in heavenly places, and his most Holy Will to be universally obeyed in simplicity and singleness of heart; and committing you to his wisdom and power, that ye may be preserved blameless in the faith, abounding in the love of God and of the Brotherhood, and so therein advancing day by day from grace to grace, till all come to the unity of the spirit, for the effectual gathering in and establishing of the Church. Which all her writings arrive at; and in the faith whereof she surrendered up her spirit to the founder and builder of this temple, which is to descend from above according to the patterns given to her. Now it having pleased | the wisdom of God, to call hence at this time our two chief elders as at once, there being but about two months distance from the departure hereof of Mad^{m}. Bothorse to

---

233 Possibly Madam Thijssen of Rotterdam.

that of my Mother;[234]—we being deprived of these two shining lights, might well be in a manner comfortless but that their God and our God still liveth, and the same spirit which rested upon them, shall not fail to be with us, and to work yet more abundantly as we abide steadfast with them in their ministration. But I must needs say of my dear Mother in God, that her steadfastness and constancy in the work and business of her Lord, was such as I had never known in any one person before: and that she appeared to me as Mount Sion that cannot be moved, in the midst of a multitude of furious storms and blasts continually made against her spiritual life in Christ, as well as not a few secret and most dangerous underminings. Oh how great is the power of God in His saints! ^ Hereupon she gave us to understand, that as wisdom's Day, whereof this she said was the dawning, should come to break forth, not a few others would be excited in like manner to follow so worthy an example; and she likewise added that it would be a good exchange to exchange the honours and dignities in this outward principle for those which are permanent and eternal with Christ in his principles and kingdom, which opens from within. For which end, it is well known how much she recommended to all the internal silence of the spirit, and abstractedness from all external objects, and whatever stands in nature's outbirth. Now I am to acquaint you as beloved Sister | and dear fellow pilgrim, with what perhaps may bear some peculiar relation to you, that in all that has lately come to pass, both with us and with you, there is a secret and hidden wheel in the midst of that wheel which outwardly appears; whence some things that are now dark will come to appear hereafter in their true light, all the wiles of Satan being laid naked. It has been the hour of temptation and judgment, and indeed begun at the house of God, that all flesh may be put to blush, and every lifted-up spirit may be silent. For if all this has happened to the green tree, what shall become of the dry? It was expedient nevertheless that my poor dear Mother should suffer all that she has been made to undergo, outwardly and inwardly: and that she should bear the reproach of all about her. But God forsook her not when she was most forsaken; though she would sometimes complain of the absence of her Beloved, and of the hiding of the Comforter. No: she fainted not, though she wrestled into blood: and the angel of the everlasting covenant whom she called upon, was indeed with her; and his arms were under her, as was powerfully testified to me. May He always be your Protector and Leader in like manner, that the gates of Hell may never be able to prevail against the seed of faith. Yea, may He guide all the house of Israel everywhere. Oh that

---

234 Mrs Anne Bathurst, widow, was buried on 1 June 1704 in the parish of St Andrew's, Holborn (London).

all false and treacherous spirits which are sent forth as busy agents be put to utter confusion.—Greet all that are with you who seek the | heart of the Lord Jesus, that are obedient to his new commandment; wishing them the constant increase of grace, peace, and wisdom from above: and that they make mention of us in their prayers, as we do of them; that we may be all led by the true Shepherd and Bishop of our souls, in all things, and at all times: being preserved in our passage through this most dangerous wilderness, till we arrive there where his virgin and Nazarite flocks do feed in the fullness of light, as at noon by the banks of the throne-river of Life. This is what pressed upon my spirit at this time for your, and for them that commonly love with you our Lord Jesus: and what will be, I verily believe, upon yours for us that are here, and particularly for him who desires to be known only—In the spirit and Life of Christ—your faithful and ever-bounden servant.

7   Miscellaneous Papers of Richard Roach (1662–1730)

J[ohn] B[athurst?] to Elizabeth Blagrave (Sunday, 12 June–Monday, 13 June 1687)[235]

3ʳ Dear Mʳˢ Blagrave
Sab[bath] June yᵉ 12 1687

I thought to have ritt to you about a dreme I had, by reson I understood it not, but thought yᵉ interpretation might be wᵗʰ yo: yet deferred, & supposed I might let it alone: yᵉ righting; but it is so often brought to me: & I seldom dreme:

I dremed I was at yoʳ hous in yᵉ paler, seting at yᵉ uper end of yᵉ tabell after diner: & all was taken away & yᵘ were seet at some worke, Mʳˢ Deboray walking by,[236] douing also some busines & I was set: wᵗʰ a larg silver tanckard before me, & it was half full of very fine wine: licke a white meskadin, I tuck a wine glas full & drank a litel & powred yᵘ out a silver taster of it, such as yᵉ wine cupes haue: wᶜʰ sure signified we had a wine seler & into ye tankard I squesed rosted aples, thay were licke backed & I sqesed them lik oringes, leving nothing but skin a core & I put nothing but yᵉ pure jusy pulp into ye wine & Mr Blagrave yᵗ son as dweleth wᵗʰ yᵘ set at ye louer end of yᵉ tabell i to see me make lames woll:[237] wondering at my curiosity to leve noe of ye pulp to ye skin: & core but leve them so drye & to let not ye lest bitt of skin or core goe in: but maid the pulp so pure, like juse of apill as are scraped: I seeing him so <u>exacktly mend me</u> I saed this is for yᵉ <u>children</u> of yᵉ <u>kingdom</u>: to <u>comfort</u> them: in ther jurneying: in yᵉ wilderness: <u>Plucking one him very concernedly & sad for I might tell yᵘ of the children did but now</u>; wᶜʰ <u>it is to comitt, wen sin knowingly; thay would neaer doe it this I can tell yᵘ by my</u> one experans: & I thought somebody com in & I remoued out of sight yᵉ tankard, & sad Mʳ Blagrave, I have not said all I have to say: for I have had all my sins set before me lick won ackt of sin & I thought there was noe possibillyty to set me to expeckt pardon: & yet I culd not rem[em]ber then any won sin: I had Ever comitted, it was sins of omisan & originall sin as others see but some yeres after I rem[em]berd when I was a Child about 6 or 5 yers of age, I had tould once a lye, but if that had then been brought to my rem[em]bers; I had surely desspard of Ever hauing marsy. And I semed as if I would have givin a leger acont of wot, I had pased threw, seing hell opened, & a gust going into it, & how I thought I culd justify god to all Eternity:

---

235 Bodl., MS Rawlinson D 832, fols 3ʳ–4ʳ. J[ohn] B[athurst?] (*d*.1694?) to Elizabeth Blagrave (*d*.1693), widow of the regicide Daniel Blagrave.
236 Mrs Deboray = unidentified.
237 Mr Blagrave = Charles Blagrave, physician of Clerkenwell.

as he was just: in so douing nay marsiful to keep me out so long: & much I had to say; but as before I forebore becase somebody cam in: I only sad to him S^r, I have not sad all: y^n Answd. noe, I had to houers more desease, as I shuld have said, y^t felt it I thought: it semes to me, as if som of ye children of ye Kingdom had sined some litil sin, & I was preparing: that thay might be comferted wth apells all refrched wth wine: but it did refer ye discors, to Mr Blagrave, becas I disliked my whole spech to him—but I knew noe reson for it; but my ernest pely, to children of sin, knowingly but won sin: & how grevos it is, by my one experans:

When sin is called to rembarans, & that none would sin won sin I had much of Mr Jefy Harde knowingly if thay knew wot thay did:[238] I knew not well his name—June ye 2d to words Evening: & after yr spirit came to me: it came after I had a jury in my self whether a member absent had as much streng by them selves or in wating a moung ye membars, for there fath, and loue opens in us, answers to there juse as Beman sa[i]th in one of his prefaces:[239] ye quschan y^u aske sath he shall be answered—not as I am more then any man—but yor queschon brings a keay to open the answer in me: so I haue often thought, we are beholdin more to them for there questions then thay to us for our answers, for if we have a treasur in us, yet if others has the Keys: we have ye benefit of the Keys: when thay com and unlocken us: to Learne also for our one yous; thes sperituall thoughts, were thus supled wth speritull uenyan & questions: such as may be y^u understud not so well before: nether did I know before, wt was givin to my sperit to answer ye som is as speritall convey, may be of profitabell: & our Knolig as much improued as temporall: if not more for our sperts are wiser, & more knowing then our bodis can exspress: & besid our bodis may be caled to serve to bels: a very good work: if we rem[em]ber who was chose for it: as Hevin and it is well, if we have noe other Excusis, when Christ cals us to folow him: besids, all trauell not won way exackly &c. therfor it is more then prouabell, of our sperits may haue ye parfektest comu[ni]an and ye knowleg more clere: I haue sent inclosed: wch I ritt one ye convey of yor Ang[e]ls spirit [several illegible words struck through]

Truly I shuld want a secrytary if I shuld right, all, as if discouered to me as is yousfull amoung y^u. Thes inclosed I desire to be retorned; for I right for my one benifit and som tims, so com[m]unicat: to quickin each other: as I find I am dircked & think not, it is I, as can right y^u any thing: nether would I have y^u

---

238 Jefy [Geoffrey] Harde = unidentified.
239 Beman = Jacob Boehme.

account me another way then wat I am. And Know my self to be: a pore weck ynorgnt nothing nether ~~Ask~~ I of angels or men: I thank y^u for that: wether seek for visions but only to serve god in sperit & in truth fathfully & constantly, not knowing when my lord will com: & anoyn me, wth that holy unstion from ye father wch shall teach us all things: & when ye onenting is apon me: & I am to dice ye preast of his, in cares: then all, as I desir of God to doue to tack care for some that I goe not out, when ye anynting oyle is apon me & to haue as much care of touching the dead as we can:

 I culd wish them papers first sent to Mrs Nelson were well parvesed & if not understud rather to haue them agane,[240] for thay went well coded, lick camills of spises from Canan I felt such wagons & loding of camalls, they caryed wth them: as I felt all the hose Emty: of when we have sett many goods in order, to send in wagons when we have | dilivered all out, as we [...] besyed to prepare we sell ye very hous emty y[...] wch, very refreshing and Esy to me; it being lick goods, we are glad when we haue sent them: as we are dircked: yet I know ther is something: in that to my cruckly as will be reveled in my time: by ye great ladin as I felt went wth them—y^u ritt y^u thought my sperit caryed somthing away wth me, it is lick I might: for my sole & body was much refrched wth y^u, & y^u haue oft refrched me in my bonds, & set me free taking them of for me: ye lord help us all to rise & praise god singing continually night and day, holy, holy, holy, lord god of sabath: & pray tell Mrs Debora my good frend: it has been offen apon me: she must desire notheng but resignashan & as I felt these words wth power from y^r self: in resignashan is Rest; wch rest ye culd bring us all unto: and folow ye lamb fuly; & where so ever he gose, for we must all, over com, threw ye blood of ye lamb ye Eternall son of god in us.

 I [recd?] at wot y^u right concerning Mr Bromly,[241] his labouring side will be satisfied & ye hungry will be feed, when ye rich is sent Emty away, it cals to mind wot his angill sad to me, som yers sencs: ye power is a coming forth, but I have much work to due furst: And we must heale: but we must begin to heale our selues furst & when I herd of his sight so clered and mendid then I though the heling might furst com amoung our selves: ye lord threw his mighty power: hele all our souls sikneses: that our bodis may be fitted for heling. [words struck through] my prayers was much for Mr Bromly wthout seasing: his spent dilivered his request: & I see him in [...] prayers [words struck through] pray rember me to Mrs Oxenbrig:[242] I thank she had forgot me but she coms and is in our sper-

---

240 Mrs Nelson = unidenfitied, although someone named Nelson was mentioned in Quirinus Kuhlmann's *Kuhlpsalter*.
241 Thomas Bromley (1630–1691).
242 Joanna Oxenbridge (d.1709), widow of Clement Oxenbridge.

itall asembely: Mrs Pocock is continaly wth me in a whitt figure:²⁴³ a wating wth me but I know not whether she is ded or living. She furst came in her outward signe to be fuly known. Pray tack care of ye inclosed for her: I wish y^u or she can read it, y^u may shew my righting to ye children of ye kingdom if yu think it may stay and comfort them in ther jurny to wards Canan: for tell them, we as are sent as spise to vew the good land: we know, that it flows wth milk and hony: but few of us is, yet fitted to Enter: tell Mrs Lawton she mus joy in her son:²⁴⁴ and rem[em]ber he is not hers but ye Lords, & if ye lord send for him it is Enof: if he not her father & ye father of her childeren; and if a Abram can after Isak he may have him: but we know not w^t is good and best for us, and our childeren: I send ye copy as I promised; but that is letill ritt and not I see parfittid: I shuld be glad to haue a leter from Mr Geff: H.²⁴⁵ tell danell he [comes?] & sings in me: I thank yu all for yr [desirs?] and co[u]nt myself yu^r servant for ye redemshun as to the glory and liberty:

JB Thur: 16:

[in margin of fol. 3^v]
Monday 13 [June]. My loue to y^u all: & pray for me: I had much off my aunt and M^rs [Po ...?] before y^r letter com wch I thank y^u for. Rem[em]ber me to Mr Bromly: in time I may right to him: but he is wth me

These for Mrs Eliz: Blagraue in pregen cort old baly London

Madam [Anne] Bath[urst] to a lady (1693)²⁴⁶

Madam

I am prest in spirit that your Ladysh[i]p should read & fully understand the 4 ch[apter] of John. O that we did but in part know what it is to drink of the River God and the new wine of the kingdom! Sure we should go no more to draw water, but find the fountain aflow, the well of Life within you. O is it not time for you to learn, the messiah is come. Came he not in the fullness of time to be born? Is he not risen & sent the Spirit? Surly wait we not for the Holy Ghost? Let us wait for the spirit, which not many days hence, but we shall be baptised with fire & the Holy Ghost. Have we only received Johns Baptism? To look for him that is to come, or look we for him that is already come to

---

243 Mary Pocock (*fl*.1649–*fl*.1691).
244 Mrs Lawton = possibly a relative of Mary Laughton (Richard Roach's niece).
245 Geff: H. = Geoffrey Harde (mentioned earlier in the letter).
246 Bodl. MS Rawlinson D 832 fols 5^r–6^v.

teach all nations; And what if this fire be already kindled, & a few live coals are scattered abroad? Was the sacrifices under the Law to be offered by fire, neither were to offer strange fire: If this were well understood, we should find a greater mystery than most understand; that our sacrifice of Prayer is to him which answereth by fire; And I hope we are better learned than to say we have not so much as heard of the Holy Ghost's fire, which indeed is a witness of the Life & Power of God within; not a dead letter, but a quickning spirit, a living breath of Life breathed in us by Creation, but manifested by Restoration & the new Creature, which we are if we be new born of the word & spirit, the word that giveth spirit. I am still opress'd in spirit that your Honour may be more honourable to get within the vail; that the mystery may be unseal'd of Christ Jesus in you, And if he be in you, what need of Jacobs well of water, since Christ the true messiah is come, to teach you all things? And we shall all be taught of God. Happy man & woman that is rightly taught to go to God the Fountain! For while | we go to broken sisterns that will hold no water, we seem to say, we will have none of him: And as Christ says, you search the Scriptures, and they are those that testify of me, and you think in them to have Eternal Life; But why come you not unto me, that you may have life, & have it more abundantly? Why wax you lean from day to day? God is not a barren wilderness, nor a thirsty desart, & He calls all to come & buy wine & milk without money or price; coming is believing his promises, which is that He will give his Holy Spirit to them that ask it, and that we may receive the witness of it, even the true witness-bearer, witnessing with our spirit, even the Baptismall fire, & here she that can baptise with fire, or rather is commissioned to baptise with the Holy Ghost & fire hath the true witness in him, and he or she that hath received the spirit of burning hath that in them, that Christ came on Earth to send, and that which his disciples felt when their hearts burnt within them, while Christ talked with them; which spirit of the risen crucified Jesus and his burning Love open the scriptures concerning himself. And if this Baptism is fallen upon you you need not men to teach you; but you will be a possessor of that promise, we shall not need for any to say to us, I know the Lord, for we shall all know him from the greatest to the least, & knowledge shall over the earth. Shall most of us believe this & pray for it, & yet cannot believe that some of these drops may fall before the great effusion of the spirit. I tell you sister, He is come and the fields is all ready white for the harvest, and some have tasted and offered up their first fruits already; and some do declare that the Lord is risen, and has appeared in his risen Love, and burning flames; yea even some women among us, but when they tell the disciples of it, it seems but as an idle tale; but we have received through free grace & rich & plenteous mercy, that which the Rabbis themselves could not believe, unless the Spirit, the Divine, manifest it unto them; therefor go not about to teach, but commend our lover, which the watchmen of the city would fain take | away. We know we are black because of fallen nature, but our beloved is come in to be Himself in us; and is He not better to us, than another Beloved? Yes, He is the choisest of Ten Thousand; for he satisfies the hungry. He is the bread of God, which if we eat we shall hunger no more. He is the water of life, which when we have well drunk, we shall thirst no more, nor go to the Preachers to draw; nay his flesh is meat indeed, and his blood is drink indeed, and except we eat his flesh & drink his blood we have no life in us; understand we this? The mystery of the Gospel is so great that had we ministers of the Letter it would be no great thing; for I count none ministers of the Spirit, but them that can give of the Spirit; for the Apostles they were but to preach & baptise, and as they spake the Holy Ghost with power fell upon as many as heard it. Waite we then at Jerusalem for the spirits teaching that we may be endued with power from on high, & receive that Holy unction which is able to teach us all things; And pray we for the spirits teaching; for He hath said every one that seeketh, findeth; unto him that knocketh it shall be opened. Were we more perfected Christians in the Letter, we should soon know, that if we ask the Holy Spirit it will be given unto us; And then we shall most truly say having received the spirit of truth, <u>never man spack like the witness of the spirit in us</u>.

These lines I commit to your Ladyship, finding your Sun near setting, & your moon in the wain, & you in the evening of your days, but near the dawn of eternity: I therfor tell you, the expected year of Jubilee is upon us, and God has opened the mystery, and there is according to the promise a worshipping eye to eye, the vail is rent, & our human flesh does not hinder, as it did not Moses & the Fathers of old, so now, seing Christ has rent the vail of all Human ordinances & is come in our nature, and has made us Temples of the Holy Ghost; what is there for us to doe but to worship in spirit, for God is a Spirit, & they who worship him must worship in Spirit & truth; And this is Christs doctrin: and if two or three are mett togeather in his name, in his spirit, which is the true | call, he will be in the midst of them; so that we are for Christ's worship, His form is the Holy Spirit of Truth; for if we have not his Spirit upon us, in us, & with us, we have not where withall to worship him. In the time of Ignorance God winked at man, yet now it is time to shake off dead works & serve the Living God; & that we may offer up living sacrifices; for that which died of itself, was not to be offered up in that day, & think we that God will be less honoured when he has sent his Spirit for us to worship with; We have two witnesses, the Spirit and fire, or the Spirits fire, by which we are to worship the Father in his own nature, which is Spirit. I can say I am not Eloquent neither before the Spirit spoke to me, nor since, but as I am minded so I write, and the Lord gives us understanding in all things, In the faithfull desire of her who is a child in these things, & this is the first attempt of such a nature, therefor may plead for itself while I am

your Ladyships humble servant A.B.

A[nne] B[athurst] to a friend (no date)[247]

D[ear] friend, I find myself better for as much as you are willing to come, & accept of the will for the deed; and so leaves you to your own freedom in person, but not in spirit, tho flesh profiteth little, <u>The Spirit quickens</u>, your person I leave till there is a more convenient season for [few?] to come. Tell Mr. R. from me,[248] the season is good for the spirits visits, and I expect a visite from him in spirit, & suppose he confine his person, yet his spirit must be with Jehovah the unconfined, and there I could bless him as Melchizedek did Abraham; for blessing there must be & not confined to one two or three. Mr Lee's child must be blesst,[249] it is not come to its rest, like father, & mother all three, <u>All must come to the Glorious Liberty, and none but angels can sing this round, the end hath the Beginning found</u>. Let him I mean M[r]. R. putt off his garments of mourning, shave & wash himself we should not mourn while the Bridegroom is with us; Let him go into the Garden of nuts & meet with his Beloved, and not let his Beloved wait till his locks are wett with the dew of the night; Is He not coming? Do we not hear the Bridegroom's voice? Why slumber we, is it not the voice of our Beloved? The Watchmen that go about the city say, so our Beloved more than anothers Beloved; But the Church the true spouse of Christ says of her Beloved, He is the Chief of Ten Thousand; and so I refer him to read the Canticles. Lett it not be said as Christ said of the Jews, I would have gathered you as a Hen gathereth her chickens under her wings but ye would not; the nett has been spread, if it had been on the right side of the ship, it would have brought more fish to the shore than the nett could contain: I say as formerly, O Love! O Love! It is the Right side of the ship which if the nett be cast in, brings more fish in than can be brought a shore, for they were fishers of men. I leave you with God, where I desire to find you.

A.B.

---

247 Bodl. MS Rawlinson D 832, fol. 27ʳ.
248 Mr. R. = probably Richard Roach.
249 Probably Deborah Jemima, daughter of Francis Lee and Barbarie, who was born on Whitsunday, 23 May 1697.

Letter of J[ames] K[night] to [Richard Roach?] concerning Jane Lead's death (22 August 1704)[250]

Dear S[i]r,

The loss of so great a person wou'd be very considerable, if there were no hopes of ther spirit's resting upon some of the living, but I have larger expectations, and look for ye revival of ye work with a greater vigour. She was a woman of ye cross, & acquainted with sorrows. Her days, like David's, were appointed to conflicts; and as ye troubles of ye Jews ended in David for ye sake of ye refreshments under his peaceful Successor, so perhaps with her life your sufferings may have ended; and by a true succession of blessings & seasons you may have a calm enjoyment of your past endeavours, and a happy & triumphant raign over all opposition. She entred into her rest in your year of rest, and was preceded by another of her sex, an eminent pillar of your society, ye same year; y^s mighty loss may be but ye surer pledge of ye near approach of a wonderful resurrection. Isaac was not bless'd, till ye death of Abraham Genes: 25:11 nor enjoy'd his Rebekah, till ye death of Sarah; so ye grand blessings of your family, and the perfect matrimonial union were not perhaps to come on till ye toils of ye first generation were completely ended with its death & dissolution. I pray God inspird you with such measures, as may be most for his honour & glory.

My humble service to M^r and Mrs Lee. I am S[i]r your real friend & Servant J:K.

Rebecca Critchlow to "the Reverend Mr [Richard] Roach at Mr John Roach in Westcote, Gloucestershire" (London, 20 August 1696)[251]

Dear Brother In our Lord Jesus

I reioyce in the grace of God that is in you and that the God of all grace is so eminently with you in your retirement that by the indwelling of his holy spirit the heavenly powers of the eternall one haue bin so evidently manifested not only to the refreshment and comfort of y^r own soul, and I doubt not to the benefit of such as y^u have converst with and preacht too if the Apostle reioyced that Christ was preachd tho out of envy I may well when I am sattisfied it is from loue to him and his members and tho in some circumstances y^u may in this

---

250 Bodl. MS Rawlinson D 832, fol. 33^r.
251 Bodl. MS Rawlinson D 832, fol. 37^r. Rebecca Critchlow (*fl*.1707), most likely the author of *Unpremeditated Thoughts of the Knowledge of God* (London: 1695), under the pseudonym Irena. This work was reprinted in 1697 and "Humbly offered to Consideration, by One of the *Philadelphia* Society".

differ from us yet I am well asured we are engaged in the same work and that the unity that is amongst us in the generall and more pertiquelar shall neuer be broken as it is founded in God and aims at his glory the gates of hell shall neuer prevail against it the enemy has made but one remarkable effort in the fame[..] since y^u went and some small asaults in the publick but I bless the lord in all his stratagems has bin defeated and conquerd by the power of God which has at times apeared strongly amongst us since you went and I hope there is some advance made thereby of the Christian graces of faith and love and the grace of patience I am sure has bin preacht to us by the practice of our exelent Christian frind Mr Wastin who has bin with us almost euer since y^u left us he has had A feauour and rhumatism but blessed be God pritty well again he designs to leau us two or three weeks hence my children and frinds giue their seruis to.[252] I hope it will not be long ere y^u return in the mean time forget not

Sir y^r faithful frind and seruant Reb Crichlow

Letter of Rosemunda Juliana von Asseburg (no date = 1696?)[253]

Beloved esteemed in the Lord!

I thank you indeed heartily with my sister for the kindness and Love, you have been pleased to shew unto us, since you were willing to take share in our sufferings, and would impart to us so good a Counsell in laying hold by faith on the Lord of life, He it is also only and alone, who hath plucked my sister out from death and restored Life to her again, His Almighty hand hath helped her alone, Praised be his Name in the eternities. He will also according to his great goodness and Love make me perfect, stablish, strengthen and settle me in Him, that I may be perfectly one with Him, as I do hope. May he also renew your strength, that ye may mount up with wings as eagles, that you may run and not be weary, and walk and not faint; The Lord will still more and more do good unto us, He will fill us with his Grace and mercy, He gives us beyond what we pray for or understand, our mouth shall be filled with laughter and our tongue with singing, for He that is mighty hath done to us great things, and Holy is his Name, nay He will yet do superabundantly more unto us, Blessed be He forever and ever. I commend you all into his faithfull Hands and am from the Bottom of my heart your sincere servant,

Rosemunda Juliana Asseburg

The Baroness of Reichenbach and my sister greet you many times.[254]

---

252 Mr Wastin = unidentified.
253 Bodl. MS Rawlinson D 832, fol. 46^r. Rosemunda Juliana von Asseburg (1672–1712).
254 Baroness of Reichenbach = probably Marie Sophie von Reichenbach.

Letter of L[oth] F[ischer] to Jane Lead at Hoxton (Utrecht, 16/27 June 1701)[255]

Blessed Virago, most endeared and venerable Soul, 47ʳ

Our Friend Matthias sends to me the following Scheme, which he received from another Friend, which is unknown to me: And because it seems not unworthy of communicating to you, I would translate it in your Tongue:

Here I do send to you, Sire, a conjectural [^computation] account about the years of the world collected by me. I do indeed know that it is diametrically contrary to your sentiments, but because it doeth flow not from out of my Brain, but from out of the writings of the highly illuminated Jac. Behme; I pray to receive it the more kindly and to commit the Event to the most High one. If that Friend and inventor of the mysterious Figures of the mentioned Writings in Holland* (* this is that Polon[n]us who refuted our blessed Pordage living in this Town:[256] my envious adversary) is yet living, I [..]ohld fain this to be commu[n]nicated to Him and hear its sentiments thereof.

3970 years are according to the Sentiment of Jac. Behem 3 Princ. c. 18 v 35 are passed from of the Begin of the world unto the healthfull Birth of Christ.

1765 Years will pass from the Birth of Christ unto the end of the world.

Sum 5735 Years will the world stand according to this after the will of God.

The first computation is, as was mentioned, of the blessed Jac. Behme.

The second is well indeed the Mine, yet builded or directed upon the Sentiments of that blessed man, and according to the Time of the Day in which the Lord deceased upon the cross accompted viz. shortly after expiration of the Third hour of that Evening. In these two Accounts or Computations as well as in the third summe springing thence does conciev a Mystery: because they doe goe all thrie, according to cabalistical computation in monadem or the number of one* [* whereby this, though but conjectural computation is confirmed the more] But the event or Consequence, be it more early or late, must be committed to the divine almightiness, and not made to be an <u>head</u> of the Belief.

From the first 6 days of Creation there could be insisted also a query of Decision, but it is now not necessary to do it.

But what the above mentioned inventory of the Figures of Jac. Behme hath answered I am ignorant, though that Answer was remitted through me to our friend Matthias:[257] for it was sealed, send to my house. But the Replick of the Friend of our Matthias as (* upon it) which was send also through me was this:

---

255   Bodl. MS Rawlinson D 832, fol. 47ʳ⁻ᵛ.
256   Polonnus = unidentified; Pordage = Dr John Pordage (1607–1681).
257   Matthias = possibly the unidentified correspondent of Jane Lead referred to in document 1 above.

A Short Replick/: siegen Anmerckung:/ upon the Answer of the Inventory of the Figures by Jac. Behme.

What the friend from out of Utrecht hath answered about the computations of Time I have seen, and first that he hath done great labour ~~of~~ in gathering of so in any old classicorum erroneous sentiments. Farther that he taketh for granted the first sentiment, as confirmed by Jacob Behmen, but the from thence derived other, as the absent and not canoniced, draws in to doubts, can be not otherwise, because the Mystery of Numbers is unknown to him, without which neither he, nor any other may receive the Opening to comprehend how that with this does concur, & agree: as also how every Number doeth reveal a Mystery, nay how the Begin treads back upon a wunderfull manner into the End; that I therefore in consideration of such certitude, and that it should be opened to me poor, worm alone, do offer to me creature eternall praise and thanks in a still admiration! The prefiguration & basis of my calculus or casting up viz. the Expiring or Dying of Christ upon the Cross, I have given to know already, but modum calculandi I leave to every one him self: because I shall burthen up this opinion to none by more Demonstrations, beeing content that it may stand to the Lord alone if it is thus pleasing to Him. Yet nevertheless I will yet this here add, that the Death of our Saviour after this computation hath followed, just about the 3 hour, 10 minutes and 48 seconds, say 3h 10′ 48″, in the afternoon. It may be ridiculous to whom it will. It did please me not a little that that Friend did allege from out of the 40 Questions de anima by the 6 Species of the Δ in the I Qvestion viz [paras] 78, 79, 80, 81, 82. Oh if he had obtained and understood the Numbers he would not have passed over or omitted the excellent 77 [para], wherein all is comprehended. That the dear Man Jac. Behme, hath known well the End of the Years of the World, I do not doubt, because to him hath been made known the Begin till to the Birth of Christ, as he then here doeth place | the End under the 6 species of the fire: which not is done without cause, but that he wrote not clearer of it, was not in his own, but in Gods will, without which no hair can fall from our head. Now while here is the speech of the fire, I will add what follows how viz. from out of the commun Astronomia is not unknown, that Christ the Lord hath beene born in Trigono igneo when [Mars] Maxima in [Aries] signo was passed before 6 years. Then is known also that we deliver now also in Trigoneo igneo ut Astrologica[m] loquor; whose Lordship or Dominium should reach till the Year 1782 &c. This I do give to consider further every one who but hath set not to his ground. I do conclude with this joyfull short-breath: Lord in thy Light we do see the Light! Hallelujah! Jah! Jah!

Now my dearest Friend I have heard with great admiration from the Dear Mr. Sprögel, that the Baron had been querulous toward him,[258] as if he has yearly more not than 50 lb for his subsistence, and though he did believe that the Lady his Mother did send more, but he received it not. Which is an impious Pretence, and therefore I do warn you altogether yet once not to give him any pence without a Quittance. For I do fear Satan will afflict you yet through him with such Speaches. And it was expedient to ask him with what Conscience he could speak such things? Mr Sprögel (may you say) had expressly told me, that he had done so. God may redeem him from that deceitfull spirit!

From this our Friend Sprögel/: who writes me yesterday that he doeth suppose to be home upon [Saturday] of the 25 of this Month st. novi:/ I heard also that Kuster now was with the Early, of which Mr Schitz doeth make often mention of, and that he had sent a Letter to Oliger Pauli at Amsterdam,[259] whith whom he was one Mind, and had published :/ as I hear from another Friend:/ a Treatise wherein he did command and make clear the writings of Oliger Pauli. All do raise before they do dy and are full grown men; before they are born and [soon?] wise than Solomon.

~~The~~ What doeth precede was written by me upon the last passed Fryday, as the 24th of this Junii st novi, but upon the following Saterday, I made a walck for a part of our city wall, but was so wearied out, though it was not far, that I could hardly reach unto my house, and had immediately a fit of a feaver, that continued the whole Night and yesterday again the whole Day and Night, and now [Monday] I am very miserable as being no member through the whole body wherein I did feel no pain so that I can write not more, than that here comes a Bill of Exchange from the Baronesse, and pray to greet the two Friends the students, & that their Letters [are?] best pr[..]aved, and as soon I received an answer from their Friends I should send it over. I do salute you hertely altogether and abide

Your most obliged servant and Friend L.F.

Utrecht [Monday] 27 Juni 1701 st novi.

From the Baron I have not yet received a Letter for the Lady he [ ] there!

"For the Lady Jane Leade, in Hoghsdon, over against the Land of Promise near London", "Franco unto the Briel"

---

258 Mr Sprögel = Johann Heinrich Sprögel (1644–1722), Lutheran theologian and Pietist leader active in Quedlinburg; also father-in-law of the Pietist historian Gottfried Arnold.

259 Oliger Pauli (1644–1714), wealthy Danish merchant and millenarian; he was the author of *Novus in Belgio Judaeorum Rex Oliger Pauli* (Helmstadt: 1701).

Letter of Jane Lead to Richard Roach at Oxford (c.1695)[260]

51r Dear Onesimus and son of Wisdom[261]

I would not haue you think that I haue neglected you because I did omite writing to you in answering your last letter to me the cause was my eyes are so bad that I cannot write at all my self which I hope you will take as a just exquse but be assured I carry you allwa[y]s in a dear rememberance as a soul upon my heart feeling an intrensical union in the spirit of the Virgin Wisdom as deputed by her to open veriety of her misterys in you which I perceiue you had some witness of hauing set apart forty days scritly to wate upon our deuine oricle we rereceiued many aduertisments both upon our own perticuler account and also yours all relateing to the manifestation of a further progress in Wisdoms principle wherein you were anointed to be a priest in her orb and a streeme of light did enter into you from her brightness, so I was commanded to lead you up with some others to the High court of the Princely Majesty who sealed to you a commission to go forth in the Power of a Holy Ghostly Ministration so you were conducted by Wisdoms Angel where a fountain did flow with Golden liqure into which you were to be plunged into which being done, you were fitly qualified for that function where unto you are called my dear Onesimus this and much more was opened to me conserning you by seueral remoues still Higher and Higher by which a deuine congruety is to be maintained in order to what is yet to be reuealed which though our person be at distance yet our spirits are to keep pace togethere in Wisdoms walkes till we shall haue opportunity

51v for a personal conuers where by those deep things that haue been reuealed | may the better be under by you I haue a little tretice which now is printed I do thing to send you by the carryer is titled the 8 worlds made manifested. I know not whether you haue had the paridicical laws which also printed which you desire them. I will send them. Thus my Dear Onesimus I shall conclud giuing all assurance of a concurrance mutually with your spirit in the prosess of loues Kingdom which I do now see is near upon and spreading in this our own nation and in forrine parts which in ninty six will giue a further proufe which Wisdoms Stare will cast her glance more brightly therefore let us watch and pray that we may see her day. So with my intire loue to you with my daughters seruice desireing still to hear from you which is all at present from your

most effectinet Mother to Loue and serue you Jane Lead

For Mr. Richard Roach Fellow in St. Johns Colledge at Oxfurt

---

260 Bodl. MS Rawlinson D 832, fol. 51r–v.
261 Onesimus = Richard Roach.

Letter of Jane Lead to Richard Roach (31 August 1697)[262]

Dear Son of Love 53ʳ
   I am well satisfy'd to hear that you are so well compos'd in spirit, and that you have the Divine Powers accompanying you even in the place where you now are that may defend you against all manner of Attacks. For which you have the concurrence of our spirits with you. And do as in a Glass see that all the tumults and hurly burlys of spirits will as mist vanish and dissolve. Therefore be strong in the spirit of wisdom and meekness, whereby all shall be overcome. We have obtain'd our Licence for Westmorland,[263] where there was a very great concourse of people on Sunday. And though there was some molestation from Boys and some rude fellows, yet there was a sober sort of company very attentive and inquisitive. We had no body but our own family and Hephzibah,[264] with the good honest man, who once before assisted. I would be glad if a door of providence might open for your return to us again. And according to some thoughts stirring in my mind I could wish that this Gentleman now coming to you, and having been recommended to you and my son Lee, might be an occasion to move for leave to come for London, if nothing more considerable than this offer itself. But I shall leave Divine Wisdom to guid you in all your Affairs. So offering you up to the influencing Powers of the Eternal World, and praying that you may keep fast on your Anointed shield | which no carnal weapon can 53ᵛ pierce. I remain
   Your most Affect: Friend and Mother
   Aug. 31. 97.
   Jane Lead.[265]

Dear Brother I could find no Certificate in your Table Box but these two which were in the litle one I here send you. I [hope?] Mr Lilly will send you what he has. Pray be exceeding cautious in your conversation, for I am to suspect that something may have come to the Archbishops ears from some friends not fully establish'd with you. The spies are many, and of serious kinds. Let all that is possible of civility be shewn to this gentleman, the Baron of Knyphausen, who comes by tomorrows coach: He is of a very disposition, but a stranger to all our

---

262 Bodl. MS Rawlinson D 832, fol. 53ʳ⁻ᵛ.
263 Westmoreland House, near Bartholomew Close (St Bartholomew the Great), a site formerly occupied by a Presbyterian congregation.
264 Hephzibah= possibly Mary Sterrell.
265 Jane Lead's signature has been added in a different hand and appears to be her autograph, with the letter itself probably in Francis Lee's hand.

Affairs. You may do well to bring him into the Company of Mr Conyers.[266] He designs not to stay above 2 or 3 days. When you can finish the verses pray let me have them. Epenetus greets you very kindly. We all [ ] you, and shall assist you to the utmost with our Prayers, as is our Duty. With my Affectionate service to all that are with you, and for you, I am

Yors faithfully

F[rancis] L[ee]

Letter from "Jael" to Richard Roach (no date)[267]

55r The Lord bless thee with power from on high my dear Brother Onesim[us].[268] I am refreshed by thy spiritual lines, the Lord reward thee all the good, thou doest attribute and wish me in the Lord my soul desires nothing more, then to be a meek instrument to the Lord according to soul spirit and body, and that withall I may thus entirely be retired an parted from all, like an earthen vessel is in the hand of its master, that suffers itself to be prepared to very use, not arrogating the least to itself, what he master doth and effecteth through it. I can tell you, my much beloved Brother, in lowliness of my mind, that standeth so composed here in as if I never had done or worked any thing, fit to be counted cast worth of all, it is also presently brought into an oblivion so that my right hand not knoweth what the left has done. But there is something much complain of, which is that the Gross elementary body makes me yet often so slow and lazy, and that also presently I am to feel the motions and stirrings of the old man. O that the resurrection state were once become so mighty and powerfull, that no motions at all might be perceived, of what hath but any likeness and uniformity to the old and natural man. The elementary cleaves to my natural temper, which I am yet dead by the mercy of the most high, but as soon as I am drawn out of the watchfulness, and then something as absurd, inconvenient or unseasonable happeneth, a hard word slippeth often out of my mouth, ere I am aware of which in examining myself I can not iustifie as having flown out of the meek spirit of Jesus, who[m] the natural man could find many excuses [ ]oaths & justifyings, Behold with these things I must now & then tire my self,

55v which I write | to this end, that thou, Blessed of the Lord, may [form?] higher esteem of me then is due or I am capable of. But I hope & wait upon the power from on high which will make me all new, wherein thou, my faithful Brother

---

266 Possibly George Conyers (c.1669–1726), who like Lee and Roach had attended Merchant Taylors' School and St John's College, Oxford.

267 Bodl. MS Rawlinson D 832, fol. 55r–v.

268 Jael = unidentified woman referred to in document 1 above; Onesimus = Richard Roach.

mayst assist me in wrastling and prayers for me before the Lord, I shall also not forgett thee, that thy growth may increase & multiply before the Lord, which gives thee all assurance to

Thy Faithful sister Jael.

Letter of Lydia [i.e. Barbarie] Lee to Mr Richard Roach, fellow in St John's College, Oxford (7 February [no year])[269]

Dear Brother

I received your kind and acceptable letter wherin I perceive our infinite louing Jesus and eternal Mother dos suffer you still to be afflicted and menaced by the infernall shades of Darkness: I may tearme them so by reason tis shewed to me that they shall vanish away tis but to make you a tried st[ ] therefore Dear Brother hold fast on the Chain of faith and then will your God be glorified in you: and your virgin Mother doth some times seeme to withdraw her self from you tis only that you may set a Higher value on the favours she does intend to bestow on you do not forget you have a pledg of her love already, therefore haue corage for you are to fight under the banner of your Great Lord and master and though he may suffer your cruel enemies for a season to threaten you you will come with a noble conquer in the end and they shall return to there own center again, for at this very moment as I am writing to you, many ill shapes was presented to my inward sight some compassing you about others with open mouths as though they would swallow you up, but then appeared your Jerusalem Angel with a flaming sword in his hand Brandishing about at which sight they did all soon fly away then did your Angel pour something of a golding liquore on your head whereby you were strengthened and so assended, it has pleased the Infinite God to open in me visional prophecy wherein I had a sight of you and many others, after much deficulty I saw you crowned and made King over a Citty upon mount horeb where the new Law is to be deliuered also another time I saw 2 pillars before another city wherin was many Glorious appearances on of the pillars your name was written by Gabrile the Angle with some other names under it; so not doubting but your Eternal Mother Wisdom will Crown you with trophy of Victory which shall be the prayers and ernest desires of your Louing sister Lydia Lee / Mr Lee giues his kind love to you begs your exquse for not writting to you.

---

269   Bodl. MS Rawlinson D 832, fol. 56^r.

Letter from unknown correspondent to ["Silas"?] (no date)[270]

Dear Brother in the blessed Spirit of our Jesus

In whom you have been made worthy to be called and to fill up in your Body the measure of his sufferings, I rejoice to find that you think not the weight heavy which is laid upon you, since it works for you a far more exceeding weight of Glory which will be manifested in that Day, when having passed through the Total Death of the Cross, and having been melted down, and purified many times in the Fire, you shall come forth in the Resurrection Power as most fine Gold, without the least dross, or the Alloy of any inferior metal, being tinctured throughout with your eternal Mothers Virgin stone, that so you may be fit to bear your Fathers superscription and Image, in the most visible Part of you. Be comforted therefore, and rejoice my dear Brother, that you having found favour to be called into the Apostolical number, having been thus exercised, that you might learn to follow the Pattern of the Great Apostle of the Gentiles, who was after so many ways, both Inwardly and outwardly, afflicted, tormented and buffeted by Satan; that he might learn to know nothing but Christ, and him crucified, thereby to be laid hold on and apprehended by him, so with him to Arise, and Ascend, and receive the all miraculous Gifts of the Spirit. My Brother remember that you have a supernatural Relation to this Apostle, and are joined with him in the same Faith, and the same commission; whence the Spirit of Wisdom in our Mother appropriated to you that mystical name, by which you subscribe yourself, that so at the same time you might be humbled to the lowest Degree, and yet at the same time know yourself to be a Brother and a colleague of him that was not inferiour to the greatest of the Apostles. For a further confirmation of this State in which you do stand, my Dearest has seen your Angel standing upon Mount Calvary, with six others, one known, and five unknown; encompassing the cross, above which [was?] the Lamb, with a triumphant Crown all of transparent Gold, having in the Forefront of it the living image of the Glorified Personality: and this Lamb had one wound, which was still flesh, by the sprinkling of which Blood, every one that came near to the Cross was Purified. But here you appeared under a new Figure, or name, that of Sylvanus, who is also Silas, being then given to you, presignifying how you are to triumph over the cross, and to make up an Apostolical Time with the Spirits of Paul and Timotheus, & whomseover they may be found, either here or abroad the six others that were joined with you in this society, or order were named Joanna, Mary Magdalen, and Mary the mother of James,

---

[270] Bodl. MS Rawlinson D 832, fol. 58r.

Cleopas, Alpheus, and Simon of Cyrene. After this appeared also the seven great Prophets and several of the highest orders, to whom you was joined, and many great things were after that [..feded?], which would be too long to particularize.

Richard Roach to dearly beloved brother and sister in our Lord (no date)[271]

Dear & Beloved Brother & Sister in our Lord. 94^r

Your Acceptable letters both I Received & was severall times about to Answer ye Former wch was sent before Christmas last but was still diverted. I hope for Gods opportunity. I Rejoice in ye opportunities of keeping warm & improving that love of Christ which he has shed abroad in our Hearts one towards another. & as it has been my Principle all along that no difference of sentiment should Interpose to any diminu[tion] of that Love so by Grace I have endeavourd both ye Promotion & Practice of it. We are in good hopes of some very good effects of our endeavours after a better accord & unity between those at Mrs Bathurst & us.[272] Mr Lee & I were there for some time since: & had a strong impulse to speak of this subject, & press them to such a unity as whereby we might all together unite our Talents & bring our vessels together in one for a more full opening & breaking forth of the Holy Unction & Powers of ye Blessed Spirit of God; wch it seems to wait for & earnestly excite us to [open?] our meeting together in one Accord in order to its more Free Descent upon us. A Little after I had some discourse wth Mr White who askt w^t we meant by Unity & said If we would have them unite wth us in those outward things they could not do;[273] if we meant by union an union of Love in Christ ye Foundation, there they were in union wth us. I Answerd It was neither of those that we meant here. But that ye prejudices disputes oppositions of spirit & Alienation of Love wch was in too great degree ye consequent of these might be removed; that we might converse | & wait on God sometimes together for those great ends before 95^r mentioned. Minding only those things wherein we do Agree. After some further Discourse he declared Himself ready to comply herewith & promisd to do His utmost to bring ye rest to an Agreement to have a general Meeting once a month; at M^{r[s]} Bathursts & Hogsdon by turns. In which I doubt not but you will concur & meet wth me in spirit, as it may be furtherd & effected by ye good spirit of God. For we have & shall always maintain a Love & Respect for you on

---

271 Bodl. MS Rawlinson D 832, fols 94^r–95^r.
272 Mrs Anne Bathurst (d.1704).
273 Jeremiah White (1629–1707), nonconformist minister, formerly a chaplain to Oliver Cromwell.

Account of that Good & Spirituall thing wch has been opend in you by ye good spirit of God jointly wth us. As a little outward demonstration & token whereof we send you ye enclosed. And should be glad to hear of your Habitation there being Attended wth ye Blessing of God energasing upon you both Inwardly & Outwardly. & that you had some suitable associates wth you. W^ch I hope may in time be effected. Mrs Lead, & Mr Lee & his wife wth Mr Sterrel are all Heartily Recommended to you. May ye God of Peace in this Blessed opportunity of solitude & Retiremt from ye world give you ye Blessed entertainm^t of converse & communion wth Himself.

I remain Dear Brother & Sister your faithful friend & Bro[ther] in Christ Jesus R[ichard] Roach

Account by Richard Roach (Monday, 14 August 1704)[274]

27^r Sunday, I went to ye meeting of our Friends at Baldwins Gardens, where Mrs Oxenbridge gave me an Account of a Visit & Communication in spirit from our late departed Friend Mrs Lead.[275] I stood a little in suspense at first, but thought if it were really so I should perceive something of it my self before I went away; as having stood nearly united wth them both, & as having my own spirit much open & pretty quick of sensation both of ye Influences of spirits on ye Body & out of ye Body. I perceived Mrs Oxenbridges spirit much opend & Inlarged & under very good Influences, but stood still & passive not pressing to unite wth her spirit in order to make any Discovery that way. When ye meeting was about half over, I was thinking again of this matter, & said in my mind, surely if Mrs Lead has thus visited our friend I shall not go away w^thout having some visit or sensation from her my self. Immediately upon y^t thought I felt as it were a sudden lightning flash as it were of Divine Power, & seemed to perceive Mrs Leads 27^v spirit wth me, (tho ye many spirits of ye Company then present | Influencing my spirit at ye same time hindered that clear Distinction at first wch might put it out of doubt, but afterwards it continuing with me, I felt ye Flame of Divine Love in her Heart kindling & uniting wth ye like Flame in my own, & Distinguish ye Touch of her spirit in like sensation to w^t I had formerly had of it while in ye Body, tho now more pure & Powerfull. So y^t I had scarce any possible room of doubting left. Afterwards ye same evening, I had some Repetitions of ye same Influences; tho not as ye First Flash wch opend them. I had also just befor I went

---

274   Bodl. MS Rawlinson D 833, fols 27^r–28^v.
275   Baldwin's Gardens in the parish of St Andrew's, Holborn (London); Lead had died at Hoxton on Tuesday, 8 August 1704.

to bed a sudden descent of Mrs Batthursts spirit upon me;[276] wch I distinguish'd very clear & plainly; in a strong & sweet union & entercourse of Divine Love.

The next morning I had some pleasant dreams & sensations just before I wak'd & it seemd as if I was wak'd by them; w^t they were I do not Remember; but as soon as awake my Spirit being now entirely free & clear, I perceived Mrs Leads spirit wth me wth full evidence & Assurance that it was for Influencing & Uniting wth my Spirit. Then presently I heard her call & Bid me come up upon wch I sprung upwards in my spirit & enterd into a more near Union with her; & felt ye Divine Power more strongly & sweetly concurring. This | drew me more out of my self into a sweet Intra[ncendent?], in a stillness beyond nature & Creature. Then I saw in Vision as it were a little globe descending out of ye High Eternity, wch opened & widened it self still more & more in its Descent. And I heard these words Articulately spoken viz The Eternity Display's its Self. And I had this Instruction & Admonitio[n] given me, not in words but in ye way of spirit communication, viz, that while God opend himself in these Holy Powers the creature must lye thus silent & passive wthout least motion from Inferior nature.

After this that morning my thought were expressed, concerning ye carrying on ye meeting at Mrs Oxenbridges likely to cease from being kept there unless some came in & took Mrs Batthurst Rooms for ye support of it; And ye private meeting at Hoxton now ceasing upon ye Death of Mrs Lead; & also w^t way providence might dispose of me upon this late change, for ye carrying on of ye work of the Kingdome. And then | thinking whether it might not be convenient for me to take M^{rs} B^s. lodgings for ye aforesaid ends, I found an entire Acquiescence of my spirit in it as ye way & will of God. And am not averse to think this motion to be pointed out & extended by y^{se} late motions and visits of ye Blessed Departed as an Instrument under ye Superior concurrent Powers of God: especially having observ'd severall times before upon ye departure of some eminent persons in our ministration, they have gon over as it were in spirit wth some peculiar visit & manifestation to some of another Family, or of a Divided Party pointing out Reconciliation or nearer Union: which has been observd to follow. As upon ye Death of Dr Murray, Mrs Batthurst; & Dr Gilman who have been made as ministering spirits among us of concord unity & Love; & that blessed be God wth very good effect.[277] As I doubt not but will be ye consequence also of this descent in spirit of our deceased Friend.

---

276   Anne Bathurst had been buried on 1 June 1704.
277   Dr Gilman may have been a relative of Caleb Gilman (1670–fl.1708); see Laborie, "Philadelphia Resurrected", in *Jane Lead*, 215.

Richard Roach, "What are Philadelphians, and what is the ground of their Society" (18th century)[278]

54ʳ "Wᵗ are Philadelphians & wᵗ is ye Ground of their Society?"

The church of Philadelphia mentioned in yᵉ Revelations is yᵉ Church to wᶜʰ yᵉ Great Promises of yᵉ Perfect State, yᵗ comeing of Christ in his kingdom, are made see chapter [blank]. The seven Churches being Figurative of successive church states in wᶜʰ wᵗ was there typically & in little Represented should be unfolded & fulfilled at large.

That we are now in yᵗ 6 Church period or yᵉ Philadelphian succession is yᵉ opinion of many of yᵉ Learned wᵗʰout, & is confirmed by Revelation among yᵉ Children of yᵉ Kingdom: & the Great Motions Mutations, Wars, Inwardly & Outward, yᵉ Testimonies to yᵉ Returning Spirit, & Witnesses to yᵉ Triumphant Kingdom, also yᵉ Judgmᵗ Work or Burning Day of Elias begun, in short yᵉ Universal Movement yᵉ general fermᵗ & Grand Crisis of yᵉ Day all concur to give us Demonstration of.

The Philadelphian Church then is yᵗ Church of Christ in yᵉ Wilderness, & fed there wᵗʰ yᵉ Manna of true & real Powers of yᵉ Holy Spirit of God in way of extraordinary Communication wᶜʰ yᵉ Churches in a visible pompous church state being or Apostasize from; & wᶜʰ stands in yᵉ Faith & Preparation for yᵉ

54ᵛ Glorious Kingdom & Reign of Christ wᵗʰ his Saints; and | this yᵉ Church Mystick & Catholick wherever dispersed throughout yᵉ Christian World, whose band of union & communion in its wilderness state is yᵉ Life & power of yᵉ Holy Ghost felt & witnessd among em & yᵗ [cement?] of Brotherly Love wᶜʰ their name imports.

These therefore are beyond all others to be found eminent in yᵉ grace of charity & Love as being yᵉ Church, or belonging to yᵗ Church State wᶜʰ is to Recover & Hold fast that Love to God & the Brethren wᶜʰ Ephesus first Lost. The k[ ] very of wᶜʰ will be yᵉ Holding fast yᵉ Crown, & bring in yᵉ Dominion & Kingdom of Christ & the overcomers here wᵗʰ Him.

The Philadelphians of this Nation then generally Speaking are that Part of yᵉ whole wᶜʰ are found here in yᵉ same faith & spirit. And who besides yᵉ general Qualification of Mystical knowledge & Experiences have been Actuated by a fresh Rising Gale of extraordinary Power, about yᵉ middle of yᵉ last century. Wᶜʰ opend first upon Mʳˢ [blank] Pordage & then upon Dʳ Pordage her Husband, Mʳ Bromley & several others, thro whom it was Propagated.[279] An

---

278 Bodl. MS Rawlinson D 833, fols 54ʳ–62ᵛ.
279 John Pordage had married Mary, widow of William Freeman, by licence on 17 January 1633. She was buried at Bradfield, Berkshire on 25 August 1668.

this was in order to Constitute the Kingdom witness in yᵉ Nature of yᵉ Love or properly of yᵉ Olive tree: as there was also about that Time a strong motion & descent of Power in yᵗ severe & fiery Spirit & Ministration of Mᵗ Sinai in Condemnation of yᵗ Pride Vanity Formality & [blank] of the Age upon yᵉ Quakers as yᵉ Candlestick [ ]ness to hold yᵉ Light of Primitive Truth & worship | of God by His Spirit Extraordinary Influence & Operation to those denied such worship, & servd only by yᵉʳ own talents natural & Acquired under yᵗ general Influence of yᵉ Spirit wᶜʰ is alike possessd by Christians & Pious Heathens. They held yᵉ Candle indeed but in Part, & Testified onely to ye Kingdom of Christ wᵗʰin; therfore to fulfill their testimony come forth yᵉ new prophets of yˢ Day in yᵉ severe & Sinai Spirit as they did & wᵗʰ greater commotion & bear testimony not onely to yᵗ Kingdom of Christ wᵗʰin but to yᵉ Glorious Kingdom & Reign of Christ wᵗʰ his Saints in yᵉ Restoration of yᵉ Universal Church & yᵉ Great Sabbath of yᵉ World.

55ʳ

The Philadelphian Testimony then being in yᵗ Love & for yᵉ Love in yᵉ pure Gospel Spirit or ministration of Mᵗ Sion, was a testimony in full is both to yᵉ Inward & yᵉ Outward Kingdom, & the Pravalence of Love & Mercy agᵗ Justice & Judgmᵗ, in yᵉ Peaceful Reign of Solomon succeeding yᵉ Davidical Wars wᶜʰ prepare its way. But some of these & indeed yᵉ major part of late have been led & kept their meetings more privately; while another party have been conducted & Animated to bear a Publick Testimony to yᵉ World both by preaching & writing. These in deed calld themselves a Philadelphian Society, & in modesty as being Apprised of yᵉ Mystery of yᵗ season, & under experience of yᵉ Rising Powers of yᵉ Spirit sent forth to warn others & be in Preparation themselves in order to become true members of the Glorious Church of Philadelphia wᶜʰ is to be broᵗ forth in this Church period, yᵉ Pillars of wᶜʰ are fixt for ever. Tho indeed severall of yᵉ others yᵗ were and in degree in yᵉ Spirit & under | the driving of this Church State or Period but was understanding yᵉ Mystery, Disownd then & do still disown yᵉ name. While others thought it yᵉ properest term of distinction for yᵉ waiters for yᵉ kingdom at this day; & some among us have had it confirmd & Applied in Inspiration.

55ᵛ

The Mystery of yᵉ Lily, or yᵉ Virgin Wisdome of God travailing in yᵉ Church & bringing forth yᵉ manchild or second Birth of Christ viz in Spirit & in yᵉ Power of his Father, is yᵉ central point to wᶜʰ all Scripture Types, Prophecies, movemᵗˢ & operations tend. And proves yᵉ Key of yᵉ Times and Seasons wᶜʰ are reservd in yᵉ Fathers Power to be opend in yᵉ latter day & dispensation of His Wisdom coming forth to Cover yᵉ Earth as wᵗʰ an Inundation of Light & knowledg. The Day of yᵉ Mother must precede that of the Birth. And if we can discern yᵉ one we be assured yᵉ other is not far off. Look we then for yᵉ Day of Wisdom opening Her sacred principle & giving forth Her spiritual Creatures. It is evidently true y^t we are in ye Time yt many run to & fro & knowledg is increasd; & some of ye Female Sex have been chosen & Distinguished wth Admirable Talents for ye Information of ye Age. But one Person especially been favour wth a most Wonderfull series of Manifestation & Revelation, expressly declared to be from ye Principle & Treasury of God Virgin Wisdome; giving forth her peculiar discoveries directions Advices & Cautions Adapted to the Present Season & Exigence viz for Preparation of her children to meet the Lord as now coming in | his Kingdom; wch is ye most direct Immediate & necessary work of ye day; & of unspeakable Advantage to those y^t can receive it. This has been published to ye World in ye Works of Mrs Jane Lead wch are over look'd by ye wise of ye world & almost unknown in her own country; but high valued in others, & testified to by numbers of all ranks & quality as to their Blessed & Powerfull operation upon their souls in such manner as no product of these latter Ages has been.

It was then under ye Inferior conduct of this extraordinary person, & ye superior Conduct of ye Eternal Wisdom, affording here her peculiar manuduction y^t ye Philadelphian society Engaged in ye Publick Testimony for ye Kingdom, went forth in ye year of our L^d 1697.

It was not in way of Disunion or separation from ye Body of their Brethren that these went forth into Publick Testimony but as [   ] by Private Impulse & Providential Conduct; & accordingly stood towards their Brethren, whom they left meeting in Private, in an open generous & Amicable Spirit; tho some offenses taken against them by such as finding no call to ye Publick Work themselves & not discerning theirs stood in opposition to 'em. This opposition & misunderstanding they endeavourd to rectify & to that end offerd a generally monthly meeting wth them wch was not Accepted.

Of those y^t went forth wth a Publick Testimony | some settled at Hungerford Market; but did not hold it. Violences wthout arising, & contention with in. The other who were under ye Conduct of J. L. held it out to ye Appointed time viz, their Six Years Testimony; Begin at Westmorland House & continuing it at Twisters Alley, at Lorimers Hall & at Hoxton. In ye Sixth year they had a prophetical manifestation y^t after their six days labour their seventh day or year should be their Rest or Sabath; wch was made good in their cessation from their Publick Testimony, by an express an express [sic] order from ye Lord. Upon wch they printed their Protestation agt ye ~~Great~~ Degeneracy & Apostacy of ye Christian Churches from their first Love, agt y^t Spirit of Faction & Party, agt ye Formality supineness & deadness of this Sardian Age & Spirit in wch ye outward Churches stand. And shaking off ye Dust of their feet for a witness against them shut up their meeting after having read it openly & disperse several of ye Papers among the People, on Sunday ye twelfth of June 1703. W^{ch} they declard to be ye finishing of their First Testimony.

About this Time was witnessed a fresh opening of ye Heavens & Descent of a gale of Power from ye Divine Unity for Healing & Reconciling & Inviting ~~our~~ their Brethren of Baldwins who were likewise making some Advances also, to full Unity & Agreement. W^ch was soon effected by reason of Mrs Leads being unable to go to London a meeting was held one Sunday at Hoxton another at | Baldwins Gardens: & after her Death at ye Latter onely.

This Descent of ye Powers of ye Divine Unity I my self was witness of wth a Visional sight of a Higher Sphere or Region opening, & ye word [ ]ringing Victory. Where it was also manifested to me that this Society had done its work & held out its Time, & Obtained ye Conquest. Also y^t ye Love had been Crucified in 'em by such a scene of suffering as had renderd them in ye Appointm^t of God not onely y^e [ ]ilors but also Devotes & Sacrifices for ye Nation, Averting y^t Dreadfull Judgmnt & trial of Gods anger otherwise to be pour'd out

This New Power & Animation Enabled me to Keep up in ye Faith & Prosecution of ye work & Ministration of Wisdom in wch I had been traind up from my first Acquaintance wth any of this Society having been Visited by ye Lord in an Extraordinary manner & from ye same Principle ~~viz of ye~~ from whence Mrs Lead had her Manifestations, viz from ye peculiar treasury of ye Eternal Wisdom; & this before I knew her or had seen any of her writings. And I am here obliged to speak of my self in ye conduct of this Historical Acc^t as being almost [words crossed out] left alone in pursuance of the ministration of ye virgin & the Door by her begun to be opend in these nations & also wth Relation to w^t is further to be manifested thro it, And Particularly having ye mantle of that great Saint upon her departure faln upon me, or poyti[n]g of her S^pt to go on wth ye work.

Now the sum & substance of y^e <u>Philaldelphian</u> testimony to ye world was 1. for pure & Primitive Christianity & to particularly con[ ] in most of ye principal Actions & matters relating thereunto. | in General ag^t ye In[ ]ations Adulteration & traditions of ye Latter Ages. 2. For Christian Love & Unity against ye divisions & contentions of ye Age. 3. For ye worship of God in Spirit & Truth, ag^t ye Literality & Formality of worship so prevalent at this Day. 4. Promotion of ye Glorious Kingdom; & Sabbath y^e of world coming on & its preparation Actually begun by the Precious Gales of ye Spirit in Grace & Love. 5. Declaration of the Burning of Elias in ye Spirit of Justice & Judge also to concur in this Preparation of ye Kingdom, & the Holy Warfare agt ye Enemies or opposers of it.

After ye Death of that Glorious Instrument who for ye Singularity of her call, Revelations, & Work was denominated by ye Spirit the Representative wisdom, I had a Visit in Spirit from her as descending from ye Heavens & saw a small Globe beginning to descend from ye Highest Region, wch grew larger & larger as it came nearer to ye Earth; not onely large from its being nearer to ye Eye, but as dilating itself in its descent. And I heard this Word, the Still Eternity displays it Self. The Holy Power ye Sacred Union opend in my understanding to see wch way it was proper for me to move, & where to Reside & as I discernd it gave a token of Attestation to it. That Conclusion was, that upon ye Death of Mrs Bathurst it being needfull some Body should [step?] into her Place for ye Support of ye Meeting at B[aldwin] G[ardens] & no other Appearing willing to undertake, it must be my Province & Lot. So I remov'd to Mrs Oxenbridge.

During ye Time of ye Hoxton work or Testimony there happen a division of some belonging to Baldwins Gardens & a separate meeting was set up, by some | a more narrow & severe spirit tho Reforming in some Points & particularly Declaring for a more close & strict waiting; In wch they have made Improvem^t & gaind a Blessing in Degree. i.e. to ye good part & Intent and also met wth signal rebuke on Acc^t of y^t wch was wrong in its origin viz. The Spirit of a Party, & Assuming ye Seat of Judicature over their Brethren in things beyond their knowledg & Talent.

This Party then Breaking off from Baldwins Gardens stood in great Opposition & Aversion to those of Hoxton then under their Publick Testimony. And particularly ag^t ye manifestations from ye Divine Sophia wch opend chiefly among those in y^t course & work. As also some of ye other Party also did. And w^n they Invited those of B. Gardens to a General Meeting wth them in order to a Better Understanding they Excepted against those of Hoxton in their Invitation to them. Ag^t wch Exception some of those of B Gardens testified in ye Meeting, wch ended wth out any thing effected in order to union. However I was orderd by Inspiration to be there & read ~~the follow Paper~~ a manifestation & Exhortation to Peace & Unity; to Charity & modesty in Judgmt & censure upon ye Call or Talents, or conduct of others in ye Spiritual way. There was also sent that Day from another member of ye Hoxton Society a Prophetical Denunciation in a Parabolical way Representing some spiritual Builders undertaking to Build, & to Appoint who of their Brethren should concur & who should not when suddenly a fire broke out, & after that an Earthquake wch devoured & | destroy'd among em, to their great loss & damage. This was made good in a Fire of Contention between the two Head Leaders which rose to y^t degree [ ] y^t chief of them Broke off & left them wholly. And ye other was sometime after Remov'd by Earthquake; i.e. as shatterd in ye temporal part.

~~After~~ Upon this I had a second comission to go to those y^t Remaind meeting as before, & give them a Love Invitation, in ye name of Jehovah Elijah to Return & unite wth the Original meeting from whence they were broken, where they should find rest & a Shelter from ye Storm y^t was otherwise coming upon them. Upon wch they Appointed me a Day to confer about ye matter; But nothing was then done. Afterwards two or three more of them were seiz'd in like manner by ye Earthquake. I.

In this Love-Invitation I was orderd to speak onely to ye good part & take no notice of w^t was Wrong among 'em. And it was given after my removal from Hoxton ~~from~~ to B. Gardens soon after this; He that was their cheif & broken off from them came round again & joynd at B Gardens as at first. And Another their principal members declard he had an admonition from God to joyn there, & did so accordingly.

We had some other spiritual Friends struck in about that time; & a fresh gale of the Divine Power arose at Baldwins Gardens meeting | wch had been Represented to me in vision some time before as under a Death work, wch I also experienced in spirit. And wth this fresh rising gale a Great Gathering was made, & many persons reachd by ye Divine Power, & Testimonies of strangers coming to ye meeting openly given. 59^r

~~One~~ The Reason of ye Fresh Rising Gale was the Spirit of Concord & Unity then Prevailing & ye concurrence of ye spirits of all ye three parties Reunited in ye same meeting. And it was a Beginning of ye Fulfilling of a Prophetical manifestation & exhortation at large to Peace & Unity upon ye death of Dr Murray declaring Him to have faln as a Lamb of sacrifice for ye division & contentions of those among whom he stood in a Peaceful Reconciling spirit;[280] & ye future union & unions y^t should after spring from it. This was while ye Hoxton work was going on, & ye other Party wholly separate.

Having Represented this meeting standing now in a good degree of union begun of its various parts talents & powers, & under ye peculiar Blessing of God in ye mutual exercise of 'em. I shall hence take ye occasion to shew ye nature of ye distinct powers & talents cheifly witnessd among this People; who in each Party are real witnesses of some extraordinary operations of ye Holy Spirit. Promising onely that in order to ye Preparation of ye Triumphant Kingdo[m] ye Universal Power Deity has begun to move; & y^t particularly eminent in this nation within ye last century.

The powers of ye Triumphant Love opening chiefly among this People renderd them ye Centre & magnet for Attraction of all other Powers & Parties in ye Spiritual | Ministration & so was joynd by some of ye more Refind vessels of ye dispensation of Mt Sinai, bringing in their Talent in concurrance. So y^t there are four great distinctions to be made of this People in General, wth Relation to ye Work of ye Kingdom carried on among them. As 59^v

---

280 Dr Murray's death is also referred to above in the account by Richard Roach dated 14 August 1704.

1st those that have their Powers & Talent Triumphant Power of ye Love opening as from a [new?] & peculiar centre in order to prepare for ye triumphant of Christ; is from God ye Father & peculiarly ye Principle of His Wisdome come in a superadditional work to that of Christ suffering & in order to Advance Him to His Crown.

2 Those that Have their Powers & Talent in a degree of Revival of ye Primitive Spirit & Operation of ye Holy Ghost in ye nature of ye Gospel suffering dispensation.

3 Those y^t have their Power & Talents from harsher Root of ye Reviving Sinai work & ministration: viz who have drawn ye origine of their spiritual Life or Power from ye Quakers, softened & meliorated by ye communion wth their Brethren in ye other Talents & Ministrations. Several of these who really Retaind a Degree of their true & Primitive power have joyned in a good Accord wth us.

4 Those y^t go forth wth ye Talent of ye Key for Open manifestation, & Proclamation, under y^t peculiar ministration of ye Virgin Wisdom opening from & in ye Father; as ye Virgin Mother of Triumphant Birth; Predominant & Regent in her Day & conducting Her peculiar Instruments thro various de[ ] to their Hights Attainm^ts & Elderships in any of ye pr[ ] works or Powers into a further Birth & childhood, is as | children of ye New Jerusalem dispensation. In a degree & in ye spirit of y^t Jerusalem wch is Above wch is Free & wch is calld ye Bride of God & y^t Mother of us all. Under wch Conduct & as Candidates in probation for this state those of ye Hoxton work & ministration were led. Into this last ye Powers of ye First [ ] are ^ former to subside & centre, for ye Holding part i.e. thro y^t Hour of Probation & Judgm^t that comes upon ye Preparation works & Instruments; & for opening y^t Door & giving Birth to a ministration beyond that of its preceding witnesses & preparers.

Those of ye third distinction or distribution of Talents are shown cheifly in ye other or Bow Lane Party, in wch ye severer root tho meliorated dispite it self in all its Peculiarities & Properties.

Those of ye Second Distinction, i.e. in ye Powers of ye Gospel suffering dispensation have continued Included in ye original Body & meeting, rather in a passive state than either judging their Brethren or concern in any divided or external movem[en]t as to their general carriage & character. Tho yet in times of Probation & strife of ye Dark Powers & wrestle also of ye Divine Powers of the suffering & triumph^t ministration there have been contests on one side for Christ suffering & on ye other for Christ Triumph[an]t.

Those of ye First distinction were cheifly the Ancient standers of ye Baldwins Gardens Meeting who Received ye Derivation of ye Love Powers fro[m] ye First Instrum[en]ts. These Powers were also experienc'd by in ye Hoxton society: of these last very few are left at this day. And ye testimonies of this kind viz ye triumphant kingdom could scarce be | born of late years yea have been much opposed in ye First mentioned meeting.

For after ye Fore mentioned gale of our Primitive Power opening had continued some few Months; A jealousy & distast opend from the Harsh & severe Root among us, upon ye rejection of some Proposal thought by some principal persons unadvisable; wch occasioned a wrath & an opposition wch bro^t a damp upon ye Holy Powers. Hence came Publick clashings & contentions wth wch ye Spirit of Justice & Judgm[en]t struck in to clear off w^t was defective on both sides. Those of ye severer side opposd those in ye Liberty of ye Love; & these would maintain their Liberty & Testimony. And there were some Excesses on both sides. But especially in ye Opposition to ye Ancient Spirit & Testimonies of the Love, & of ye Glorious Kingdom of Christ yet to be Reveald; in wch Testimonie, I was chiefly concernd, having manifestations from God ye Father & from ye Centre of ye Divine with wch they generally opposed as not coming forth in ye common way & manner of their own talents. I was directed to bear as much as possible wth ye opposite party, & take in w^t ever ye Spirit of truth should give forth thro their talents, what so I might partake of 'em in conjunction wth my own wch I endeavour as much as possible to do; & stand in ye part of | Healer & Reconciler; & it was shown me that the testimonies of y^t spirit on one side or ye other should not be mixt with natural resentm[en]t ag[ains]t others if they could not receive 'em. By these directions in y^e power of God assisting I kept my ground & continued my testimony thro all opposition till God saw it fit I should w^thhold it for a time, giving me an express order to [remove?] from & making one of my Greatest Antagonist wth whom yet I kept in pretty Amicable corrs= y^t mean of direction thro y^e Spirit where I was to settle: I was orderd to draw off gently because of many friends that thought hard of it. Accordingly was providentially calld to Stanes for about three weeks, where I had a Great Manifestation from God of y^e Elias Day Coming on, & ye determination of many of ye cases & Difficult points that were in debate; wch I was orderd to send to that other Party; part of wch I lent amongst them but as I found it was not freely received I stopt ye Rest & so retird to my new Station & soon in to ye country for ab^t a quarter of a year. Afterwards by direction I set up a little meeting in St Jones where I had Liberty to Breath in ye Divine Life wth a few select persons according to my talent; & had | a fresh & peculiar gale Accompanying it as long as I held it. Sometime before my removal from B. Gardens one there had a strong power & Impulse came upon Him ~~there~~ & declared open A Famine Coming upon them not of Bread but of ye Word of ye Lord. W^ch was made good afterwards in ye cessation of the Testimonies of ye triumphant kingdom, & ye original Powers of ye Love & ye prevalence of ye severe & Sinai

Powers among them wch Occasiond upon my Return ye Following Testimony. wch upon an order from ye Spirit I went & Read among them. As not wholly ab[sent]ing from that meeting, but going as I was directed; & as for ye meeting ~~held~~ in my own chamber holding it onely on a work day [lest?] it might be Interpreted a Separation.

61 [pasted in slip]
These have a talent of ye Spirit wch they have closely Attended upon; & that rather of ye Gospel Suffering Spirit than that opend in ye original Philadelphians, viz. of ye Triumph[an]t Kingdom: in ye new Accession of ye Fathers Power, & y^t Principle of ye Divine Sophia opening: which these have opposed in those y^t Enjoyd them; & these latter endeavourd to Apprize them of & Invited them to a concurrence in unity; to wch also ye Former have made some Advances; but it is not yet fully wrought out.

Richard Roach, "An Account of the rise & progress of the Philadelphian Society" (18th century)[281]

63^r "An Acct. of ye Rise & Progress of the Philadelphian Society"
Tho ye name of a Philadelphian Society be peculiarly Appropriate to some Spiritual People in England who have Appeard under that Denomination, yet is yet a more general term belonging to all that are in ye Faith of ye Coming of Christ to his Glorious Kingdom, & under a Preparation for it: & bears relation to ye church of Philadelphia, Rev. 1.11. wch is Representative of a successive Age of ye Church bearing y^t title & under y^t character & Spirit. Hence ye name of a Philadelphian Society has been us'd in other countries as Holland, Germany &c.; & is not a name of a peculiar sect or partie, but of such as in all Parties are found in ye Spirit of Brotherly Love & ye Faith of ye Kingdom. And hence it is that ye Philadelphians in England calld not themselves a Church but onely a Society.

63^v As there was among ye Jews a sort of | people calld ye Essenes, who livd a more Speculative & Abstracted Life; & were more conversant wth ye Mysteries of Religion & thereby better Prepard to receive Christ as it is said these generally did; so in ye Christian Church there has been a People also, thus inclin'd; & looking beyond ye rest y^t keep in vulgar mock of Opinions & Traditions of ye Age wherein they Live; & Endeavour to cultivate ye true & Primitive Christianity; & Inward work of Regeneration; & to knowe & partake of ye Primitive Power

---

281   Bodl. MS Rawlinson D 833, fols 63^r–66^r.

& Spirit of Religion; & Attain a real communion & Conversation wth God. Such have been ye Mysticks in all Parts & of all denominations; who have overlookd & shot beyond ye Particularities of their own Church or Party as in an Outward Visible Form, & kept to y^s Interior ~~way~~ or Spiritual way; in wch there may be observd as Great a Harmony & Unity even amo[n]g those of Externally different denominations, as there is among those ~~of~~ in the Outward way & Forms a Disunity & Disharmony.

It was then from some of this Inward Mystical way in England that ye Philadelphian Society had its Rise: & that wth a fresh Concurence & Holy Gale of a Divine Life & Power opening first & Principally in Mrs [blank] | Pordage wife of ~~Dr~~ John Pordage Doctor in Physick: who married her for ye Exellent Gift of God he found in her; wch gift he also became in a high Degree Partaker of. ~~Sometime after two Fellows of All Souls College in Oxford~~ Mr Pordage was Intimately Acquainted wth Oliver Hill a Great Mystick of S^t. Johns College in Oxford,[282] who was very familiar wth Dr Everard;[283]

W^th the Doctor & his wife were joyned some others & they began to wait together & Exercise ye Gifts of Prayer Exhortation Singing & under a Living P[owe]r & operation of ye Holy Spirit. And not long after were joyned to 'em two Fellows of All Souls College in Oxford. Mr Thomas Bromley & Mr Edmund Brice:[284] who having Heard a sermon Preachd in Great Power by D^r. Pordage at S^t. Maries, the University Church; went together to Discourse wth Him, & receivd such a satisfactory Acc[oun]t from him that they Immediate Joyned themselves to this Little Society, & Continued among 'em to their Dying Day. Also ye Earl of Pembroke at that time being convinced of ye Extraordinary Power & operation of ye Spirit among ['em] joynd Himself & waited w^th 'em.[285] This was at R[eading?] where for sometime they | kept up a Continual oratory both day & night Relieving one another by turns: wch close watch they were obligd to keep by reason y^t upon ye Fresh opening of

---

282 Oliver Hill (c.1630–fl.1702), admitted pensioner at St John's College, Oxford on 23 August 1648. He was made a Fellow of the Royal Society in 1676 but then accused of plagiarism. His "strange" whimsies were disregarded and he was considered a fool and enthusiastic Quaker.

283 John Everard (c.1584–1640/41) was a Cambridge-educated, multi-lingual Doctor of Divinity and politically radical preacher who also had a deep interest in alchemical, mystical, Hermetic, philosophic and Rosicrucian texts—several of which he copied and translated from Latin into English. His name had been posthumously coupled with Pordage's in a pamphlet issued in 1645.

284 Edmund Brice (fl.1648–fl.1696), translator and schoolmaster.

285 Philip Herbert (1619–1669), fifth Earl of Pembroke.

Heavens & Powers of ye Spirit desending there was an opening also of ye Bottomless Pit, & Inroads of ye Sp^ts of Darkness to disturb & war ag^t them; & so much ye more as ye P[owe]rs of Dark world Broke in upon y^m so much ye more did ye Powers & Influences of ye Light world open; & ye Heavenly Visions voices Raptures & Enjoym[ent]ts were given to enable them to Conquer & bear down ye infernal oppositions. After some time, w[he]n Mrs Pordage was deceased M^rs J[ane] Lead was Joynd in ye work wth Him: whose Extraordinary gift of Revelatio[n] ye D^r gave great Regard to & Attendance upon. After the D^r died.

65^r   Afterward they met in Baldwin Gardens in ye House of Mrs Joanna Oxenbrigd wth whom Mrs A. Batthurst combind who were two Principal persons in carrying on ye Spiritual work: & both Enlightened persons and both having great & wonderful experiences & manifestations fro[m] ye Heavenly world.

Abt this [*hour glass symbol*] M^rs L^d was relivd at Stepney at ye Lady Micos College. Still by a Providence she was drawn forth into a newe Publick Station & went again. And was by means of Mr Francis Lee latte Fellow of St John Baptists College: who in his Travels having Heard an Ac[oun]t of her when he Returnd

65^v for | England, sought her out & became Intimately Acquainted wth her: & after married her Daughter: And they took a House together in London, & had some Private Meetings there; after ye manner of those before mentioned wch was without any thing of study or premeditation but waiting for y^e [Appearance?] of ye good Spirit to gifte them utterance in Prayer in Speaking to Exhortation in singing &c.

Ab^t this time Mr Richard Roach Fellow also of St John Baptists College in Oxford was Visited from above wth Extraordinary Communications; & being by his Friend & Collegue bro^t. Acquainted wth Mrs Lead Mrs Bathurst & others, under ye Divine Visitation; Contracted a Friendship wth them & began to frequent their meetings & sometime after joynd himself in ye House wth Mrs Lead & her son & daughter.

In ye year 1697 Mr Lee & Mr Roach combined together in a Design to put out the Acta Philadelphia or Theosophical Transactions; wch being a New Alarm to ye World. It made the Meeting ~~of~~ at Baldwins Gardens to become Publick, & so many flockd & crouded in that they were Constrained to take a larger Place, ye Room where they met being but a Private Chamber & Mr Bathurst ~~very~~ [^then]

66^r Aged & Sickly not being Able to bear so great a love | & ye Disorders attending it.

Wherefore it was Agreed to Remove thence & meet at Hungerford Market, in a large Convenient Place; where Mrs Lead & her Family were Present: but finding it inconveniant by reason of ye great Distance from her Habitation, being now [ke ...?] to Hoxton & In Consult wth ye Rest Concluded since there were

Persons enough to carry on ye Meeting at Hungerford Market w^thout them to take another Place; wch they did from after at Westmorland House & carried on a~~ another Meeting by themselves.

The Hungerford Meeting met wth great Opposition, & Violences from ye rude Multitude; & Continued for about Half a year till Divisions growing also among themselves, they were not Able to hold it any longer, & so that Party laid down their Publick Design.

Those at Westmorland House met wth Somw^t better Success.

"Reasons for the Foundation and Promotion of a Philadelphian Society offered to the consideration of all Christians" (no date)[286]

"N°. 1. Reasons for the Foundation & Promotion of A Philadelphian Society offerd to the consideration of all Christians" 80^r

Whereas ye state of Christendom is at this day miserably torn & rent through ye manifold divisions and sects of it, all equally pretending to be ye True Church & Spouse of Christ: Whereas also all that ye Learning, Wisdom and Power of man is able to do, has hitherto instead of Healing, serv'd rather to widen ye Breaches of all Partys: and whereas likewise there is not a Church any where visible, that is so one, as to be without all discord; so Holy as to be without spot or wrinkle; or so Catholick, as to be void of every degree of partiality and particularity; it hath pleased ye God and Father of Compassion to stir up powerfully in this Day some Persons as well in other Countries as in this kingdom, deeply sensible of ye Imperfections & corruptions of all Churches, & Congregations whatever, but especially of their want of charity for one another and of their want of y^t faith which o[u]^r Blessed Lord has describ'd as a Grain of mustardseed: & soberly considering the Insufficiency of Human Learning, with regard to so Glorious an Attempt, as is ye Re-union of all the torn limbs of Christianity; and the Folly of y^t Wisdom as well as ye weakness of y^t Power, which is of this world in all y^t is without or above its sphere; to wait separately & jointly, in obedience to our Dear Lord & master, wth all Humility, Resignation, and Perseverance, for Power from on High; whereby the Day of his kingdom, may come to be wittness'd, and Proclaim'd in all Parts of ye World; for wisdom from above which sits on the Throne of God, & is y^t Spirit of Revelation, which alone can enable any to see into, and to Govern in all Spiritual Affairs; and lastly for that Divine Learning, concerning which it is prophecyed that all shall be Taught of ye Lord, and which is y^t secret path wch ye vulters eye, neither has espied

---

286   Bodl. MS Rawlinson D 833, fols 80^r–81^r.

or ever can espy: That so the Church and Bride of Christ may be hereby prepared and adorned to meet her Beloved, being made throughout conformable unto him; through ye vital operation and Resuscitation of his One holy, and Catholick Spirit in her.

80^v 2dly Wherefore we do not at all pretend to Appropriate, or confine this Spirit to our selves: or by consequence hereof | to set up for a new sect, or Church. But we do only propose that our Assembling and convening together, may be in order to keep warm that spirit of Love, which is shed abroad in our Hearts towards you all, and to strengthen one another in his Holy and Apostolical Faith: which (Primarily) concerns the Revelation of the kingdom & Glory of God within the soul: that so by waiting diligently upon and holding fast what we have all ready received of it, we may be at length, with others whom God shall call to be of the first fruits of a Virgin-Church that may exactly correspond with the Titles, whereby her soveraign Head stiles himself writing to her; being made <u>Holy</u> as he is Holy, <u>True</u> as he is True; and bearing together with him the <u>key of David</u>, or the seals of the kingdom as Anointed with him, and consecrated by the Holy Ghost into the Preistly, Prophetical, and Royal order.

3. This is that Perfect <u>model</u> which we have before our Eyes and do press after: but which we acknowledge our selves very short of arriving to. Therefore we look not back, though some of us may say that we have been made partakers of the Holy Ghost, and have tasted in some degree of the Living Word of God, and the Powers of the World to come, or of the future Blessed Age: But as if we had hitherto attained nothing, so do we strive to reach out to the mark of the <u>Philadelphian Prize</u>.

4. At present we are but as the rough he[w]n stones that are design'd to enter into the Foundation of a goodly structure; in much weakness and Imperfection, in much superfluity and mixture, wch great unevenness and some rubbish, (and thus it was in great measure even with the Apostolical Church of <u>Corinth</u> tho so highly Gifted:) All which must be first done away, and the stones prepared apart for their place in the same, till being fittly cut and polished, they be at last (by degrees) all brought together and the Tabernacle of <u>David</u> then finished;

81^r Before the personal Glory of the | Lord from Heaven, the true <u>Son of David</u>, in the power of his <u>Father</u>, will descend to fill it.

5. Our practice we would have to be <u>Apostolical; abating</u> from temporary, and particular constitutions; conformable to the truth and power of the good spirit of God, without whose inspiration we can never perfectly love him, nor worthyly magnify him; as he will be magnifyed and loved, when his Holy will shall be done on earth as it is in Heaven, and his kingdom be also established Here as it is There.

6. We receive the Holy Scriptures of the Old & New Testament with the deepest veneration: and the Hope which we have for the full completion of every promise & prophecy therin contain'd can never be moved.

7. Our work is to persue Peace and Love towards all men; and to submit to every ordinance of God, the supream governor of the world; to kings and all that are set in authority over us; according as he in his wisdom thinks fitt, for the good of the same in the administration of secular affairs.

Whoever would be further satisfied as to our Faith and Practice may find them described in the spiritual writers Antient and Modern, and more perticularly by some of our own Society.

There was printed also a Paper containing propositions extracted out of these Reasons, wth Scripture proofs Adjoyned (A n°. 2).[287]

Richard Roach, "An Account of the Philadelphian Society in England" (18th century)[288]

"An Account of ye Philadelphian Society in England"   82^r

The Philadelphian society wch first appeard publicly in London in ye year 1697, were part of a Society of Spiritual People who for above 50 Years had met together after ye Primitive way of Attendance or waiting for ye Holy Spirit, to Assist and Activate them in Praying or speaking to Edification of each other. And these are supposed at first to have had their rise at least in part, from some English Mysticks, wth whose writings they were Conversant: & afterward from a fresh Gale & Excitement of ye holy Sp[iri]^t for Revival of ye work of God, & Preparation of his kingdom. This first experienced by M^{rs}. Pordage ye wife of D^r. John Pordage Author of ye Theologia Mystica: who married her for her excellent gift; & became himself partaker of it. After this M^r. Tho. Bromely, Author of ye way to ye Sabbath of Rest, perceiving there was a power & presence of God more than ordinary wth them, joynd himself to y^m, wth others. Also M^{rs}. Jane Lead Author of ye Heavenly Cloud & ye Revelation of Revelations came in; & ye numbers Increasd & they kept Private Meetings, being blest wth a singular Revelation of God; & also at times molested & opposed by ye powers of darkness warring ag[ains]^t ye rising power [*manuscript torn*].

In ye year 1697 Mrs Lead, who livd before privately at ye Lady Mico's College in Stepney near London, Mr Francis Lee (after her son in law) being found   82^v

---

287   A version of this document was printed as *Reasons for the Foundation and Promotion of a Philadelphian Society* ([London: 1697]) [LPL, MS 942 (130)].

288   Bodl. MS Rawlinson D 833, fols 82^r–88^v.

wth her took a house in London & had a meeting on a week day; & ye Sunday meeting ~~was~~ for ye General resort of those who were of this way was held at Mrs Ann Batthursts in Baldwins Gardens, London. Soon after was added to Mrs Lead Family Mr Rich^d. Roach, formerly collegue with Mr Lee, both sometime Fellows of S^t. John Baptists College in Oxford. These for a while attended both meetings. About ye Spring of ye year the former being under a strong driving & Excitem[en]^t for it they concerted together to put out ye monthly memoirs calld Theosophical Transactions by ye Philadelphian Society consisting of Conferences, letters, dissertations Inquiries &c for ye Advancem[en]^t of Piety & Divine Philosophy. The Publication of the Acts gave an Alarm to ye world, so y^t their meeting at Baldwins Gardens began to be crowded wth such numbers y^t they were constraind to become more Publick & to Divide ye meeting. Accordingly there were two other meetings opend, ye one at Hungerford Market; wch by reason of ye Rudeness & Violent oppositions they met wth from ye multitude, & some [ ] among y^mselues were forced to desist not holding out a full year.

Mrs Lead & her Household opend Another meeting [ ] Westmorland House & had a great Conflux of People [ ] more favourable & civilizd; yet by degrees [ ] tumults Increasing they took another more [ ] place [ ] Twisters Alley in Bunhill Fields. And some [ ] | considerable time after (they met more publickly again in ye City at Lorimers Hall. After y^t they removd ye meetings to Hoxton ab^t a mile from London; where Mrs Lead wth her Family then liv'd.

The Meeting at Baldwins Gardens was still kept up & held by such as chose to be more private; & some differences began to arise amongst y^m & offence to be taken ag[ains]t such as were engaged in the Publick work; wch these strove to compose & to preserve a good understanding & unity wth them, as not separating from y^m on acc[oun]t of any disagreem[en]t, but following w^t they thought their call & Abetm[en]t to Proclame ye Kingdom openly: leaving them to their Liberty to continue Private according to their sentim[en]t or desire.

On ye First Day of their Meeting at Westmorland House they read Publickly their Reasons for ye Foundation & Promotion of a Philadelphian Society wch are as follow

n° 1. From these Reasons extracted & printed several Propositions confirmd by Scripture places annexed; wch are here subjoind

n° 2. At their meeting again in ye City at Lorimers Hall where they had a vast Concourse of People they read openly ye Declaration of ye Philadelphian Society upon Easter Sunday A°. 1699 wch was afterwards Printed wth an Additional Declaration as follows

n° 3.

(Nota bene * here comes in a half sheet by itself thus marked *)

* Nota bene
[This comes in Page 3. after the Relation of the Philadelphian Society.]
There had been a Great Alarm in this Nation & an expectation raisd in many, of some Appearance more than ordinary of ye Power of Christs Kingdom, to be manifested in ye year of our Lord 1697 by ye writings of Mr Tho. Beverly, who had pointed out that year,[289] & even a particular day in that year viz. ye 23 of August to be signalizd by some manifestation of ye Power of ye Kingdom. But nothing appearing openly & great enough to Answer the expectations, even Mr Beverly himself thought & ownd himself mistaken; & look'd on to ye year 1700. For ye small ~~beginning~~ & contemptible beginnings of ye Kingdom work in its Preparation & Proclamation by ye Philadelphian Society were overlook'd or ridiculd almost by all; yet beside its breaking forth in that notable era of ye year 1697; there was something yet more peculiarly & providentially signal in point of Time; for one of ye members of this Society being in Holy Orders of ye Church of England was Excited to Bear a testimony of ye Kingdom to that Church & to ye Clergy in particular. Accordingly in a Providential Juncture he unexpectedly was calld out, & an offer made him of Introduction to ye Arch Bishop | of Canterbury, by a Great man, who of his own accord came to [^ and clergyman] Mr R[ichar]^d Roach & declar'd that it lay upon his Spirit to engage him to discourse wth some of ye eminent clergy upon those extraordinary things ~~which~~ concerning wch he had spoken wth him in private & offerd further to give ye said clergy man Introduction to ye Arch-Bishop or any other whom he should choose. This offer was accepted, & ye person that made it appointed ye day, wch prov'd to be ye 23 of August, & y^t w^thout any design of either ye persons concern therein, as has been solemnly declar'd.

Mr R. at his Appearance before ye Archb[isho]p deliverd his Testimony of ye Kingdom in writing, Address'd to ye Archb[isho]ps & Bishops & other of ye clergy of the Church of England. It contain an acc[oun]t of ye extraordinary experiences, consisting in ye opening of ye spiritual senses, visions, voices, transports &c wch some persons in this nation were at this time favourd w^thall, & particularly of wch himself had had ye Actual sensation. He received several queries in writing from ye Archb[isho]p to wch afterwards he Returnd Answers at large: & had leave to come several times after for Conference upon those matters: After wch ye Archb[isho]p dismissed him saying to this purpose I perceive you are rooted in y[ou]r Opinions; however I will not be a persecutor nor give you or your ~~Society~~ Friends a disturbence.

This Society in its &c.

---

289 Thomas Beverley (d.1702), an Independent minister and prolific millenarian author.

84ʳ   This Society in its various stages went thru many & great Tryals both Inwardly & outwardly but those engaged [ ] parted by yᵉ Great Power of God
84ᵛ   & yᵉ [ ] of yᵉ Holy Spirit, wᵗʰ Concurre[ ] | in a wonderful manner: so yᵗ they were enabled to fulfill yᵉ Time of Their Testimony wᶜʰ was six years towards yᵉ end of wᶜʰ thro yᵉ scandalous & malicious reports raisd ag[ains]t them they were required by yᵉ Recorder of London, (upon Address to him, as after specified), to print their Publick Vindication & Justification, in challenge to yᵉ world to prove any of those crimes wherwith they were charg'd: wᶜʰ they readily assented to, & printed it forth with; & it is as follows

nº 4. Just before Conclusion of their Publick work having by virtue of yᵉ Recorders warrant taken up a person for making riot & disturbance in their meeting, he bro[ugh]t afterwards an Action ag[ains]t their Constable; whom they stood by, & had a Tryal at Hix's Hall, in wᶜʰ they overcame & cast their Adversary.

After this it pleased God to give yᵉ manifestation of his will for Laying down yᵉ Meeting, thro Mʳˢ Jane Lead, at yᵉ end of six years. Also another of yᵉ Society had it signified to him by yᵉ Spirit, sometime before, that they were to undergo their six daies labour in six years Publick Testimony, & in yᵉ seventh they should have Rest.

And now by consent laying down their meeting & Finishing their Publick Testimony to yᵉ Kingdom, they [ ]ed & got ready to disperse among yᵉ Com-
85ʳ   pany upon yᵉ day of their Appearance in Publick, the Protestation | of yᵉ Philadelphian Society; wᵗʰ a Declaration of yᵉ Reasons & Grounds for their Finishing at this time their first Testimony, wᶜʰ is here adjoynd.

nº 5. Now as to yᵉ Expression in this Protestation of Finishing their First testimony, it is to be understood wᵗʰ relation & Allusion to yᵉ Revelation witness in their course; first in a Saccloth Testimony; 2 a Resurrection Testimony. 3 an Ascension Testimony. The first Testimony then of yᵉ Philadelphian Society, is supposd to be in Saccloth & Ashes, in suffering & contempt. The 2ᵈ. in greater Liberty & Immunity. And so in about three years & a half from yᵉ time of their mystick death or cessation of their first Testimony, viz. in yᵉ year 1707 there was Actually a Revival & Resurrection of yᵉ Philadelphian Testimony in Publick,[290] in wᶜʰ several persons, who had been concernd in yᵉ First, appeard & bore their Testimony again, yet in such manner under yᵉ conduct & protection of yᵉ spirit, as not to be expos'd to Injuries & Insults as before. And there is yet another testimony to be born by some of this society & spirit, wᶜʰ may answer to an Ascension Testimony, as in yᵉ open Heaven of yᵉ Church, for wᶜʰ there

---

290   See Laborie, "Philadelphia Resurrected", in *Jane Lead*, 213–239.

is now a Preparation & Expectation: even by some concernd in ye first or Saccloth testimony. And this last is expected to be on one hand wth greater power & demonstration of ye spirit, & on ye other wth greater condescension to ye visible Body of ye Church: wch will prove ye means of its Admission & Acceptation or y^e [open?] door of Philadelphia into ye Temporal state & [blessing?] as she had before into ye spiritual. In order | to w^{ch} (it is observable that this Society of whom some as that of its Principals, were of ye Church of England, & one of them in Holy Orders, declard that by these Proceedings they meant not any separation from ye Church or party to wch they before belongd; but held ye unity wth them. And he who was in orders of ye Church of England did notwithstanding these engagements on all occasions offerd, preach or perform any office in ye Church according to ye Form & Prescription therof. This indeed in way of submission & condescension as S^t. Paul becoming all things to all men in order to gain some; but yet taking some steps as Liberty from ye Form in way of Assertion of ye Right of Primitive Christianity; & hearing a testimony for that.

And this was thought by those concerned in the Society a peculiar honour & token of ye love unitive Spirit of Peace & Love therin, in that persons of all Perswasions were found therein combining & overlooking ye particularities of their own sect & Harmonizing in ye unity of ye Primitive Spirit & Faith of ye kingdom.

The substance of ye Philadelphian testimony was

First for ye Primitive Christianity in general.

2. For the Spirituality of Religion opposition to ye Letter & Form, so prevailing in this day.

3. For Charity & Unity, in opposition to ye spirit of contention & division [so?] generally prevailing | among the various sects & Parties of Christendom.

^ The Proclamation & Propagation of the Kingdom of Christ

This Society in their sufferings looked upon themselves as devotes & sacrifices for the good of others, & ye breaking ye way of ye kingdom Blessing among them in sad due time. And as their Appearance & testimony was a death work so it involved many others at their expiration in a state of suffering wth them, who were either in ye spirit united, or who had conceivd greater hopes & expectations from them, as appearing witnesses for ye kingdom, & giving declaration of ye actual experiences they had among 'em of ye Reviving Powers of ye spirit. Now to such as had such great expectation from y^m this sudden finishing their testimony as in death gave a great offence, & occasiond troble & suffering with many reproaches, especially to many abroad who were their intimate correspondents. But in their Death ye Power of Life was experienc'd, to carry some on still in their work, more privately, & in order to ye Remaining testimonies, as before mentioned.

As to their opinions more particularly, they Believe there is some thing good, or of God in all Parties, & That to be a ground of mutual charity among 'em.

They own all yᵉ <u>mystick</u> writers, in yᵉ Inward way & conduct of yᵉ soul by yᵉ Holy spirit, that among all parties.

86ᵛ They believe that yᵉ extraordinary Powers yᵉ spirit have been more or less in all Ages | of yᵉ Church, tho sometimes & generally in the latter Ages retiring from yᵉ <u>visible</u> church [state?] into yᵉ <u>Wilderness</u> of Privacy.

That there will be a <u>Elias day</u> burning as an oven for Purgation of yᵉ churches, & also for reconciling the differences therein, & restoring yᵉ <u>Primitive Christianity</u>.

That in order hereto there will be a further <u>pouring out of yᵉ spirit</u>, & a revival of yᵉ <u>mighty works</u> as in yᵉ times of old.

That there is first to be a <u>Reign of Christ in spirit</u> before his kingdom comes to be manifested more externally.

That there will be at last a <u>Restoration of all things</u> not onely of mankind, but even of yᵉ lappsd <u>Angelical</u> hierarchies to their primitive station & glory.

Those yᵗ would see further of their opinions may find an account of 'em in yᵉ <u>Theosophical Transactions numb. 2</u>. In yᵉ <u>Propositions</u> extracted out of yᵉ message to yᵉ <u>Philadelphian Society</u> by <u>Jane Lead</u>; as also in yᵉ Preface to her Book entituled <u>The Wars of David, & yᵉ Peaceable Reign of Solomon</u>: And more at large in their writings, of wᶜʰ for Conclusion of this Account I shall subjoyn a Catalogue.

Catalogue of Books written by yᵉ Philadelphian Society.

<u>Theologia Mystica</u> or yᵉ <u>Mystick Divintiy</u> of yᵉ Eternal Invisibles. By <u>Dʳ. J. Pordage</u>.
<u>The Way to the Sabbath of Rest</u>
<u>The Journeys of yᵉ Children of Israel</u>
<u>An Account of Dispensations calld Extraordinary</u>
These three by M̶r̶. <u>Tho. Bromley</u>
<u>Theosophical Transactions</u> by yᵉ <u>Philadelphian Society</u> consisting of Memoirs, Conferences, Letters, Dissertations, Inquiries & for yᵉ advancement of Piety & divine Philosophy.
<u>The State of yᵉ Philadelphian Society</u> by F[*MS. trimmed*]

87ʳ Books written by M̶r̶s̶ <u>Jane Lead</u>.

<u>The Heavenly Cloud</u>
<u>The Revelation of Revelations</u>

The Enochian Walks wth God
The Wonders of Gods Creation, in ye Eight Worlds
The Tree of Faith
Three Messages to ye Philadelphian Society printed diffirent
The Fountain of Gardens. 3 vol:
The Everlasting Gospel
The Wars of David & Peaceable Reign of Solomon
The Ascent to ye Mount of Vision
The Signs of ye Times
The Funeral Testimony. These by J. Lead.
Unpremeditated thoughts of God By R.C.
The Key of ye Scripture
Elias or ye Trumpet Sounding to Judgm[ent]^t On ye Great Storm.
Solomons Porch. A Poem introductory to ye Philadelphian Age.
Lyra Davidica a collection of Hymns & Spiritual Songs. These 4 by R[ichard] R[oach]
A Perswasive to Moderation, among ye divided parties. Item
The Restoration of all things. By J[eremiah] W[hite]

There remain not yet printed at least in Engl[and] Several Extraordinary tracts written by Dr J. Pordage as

A Treatise of ye Angelical World
Of the Dark World
Of Seeds & Tinctures
Sophia or Spiritual Discoveries: wth others
A Treatise of ye Resurrection. By J.L.

The works of Mrs Ann Bathurst; wth ye Remains and Experiences of many Enlightened persons of this society.
 [margin] * Essay of ye Possibility Expediency & Necessity of Revelation both Private & Publick in this Latter Age of ye Church
 Stella Magorum, or the Star in ye East leading to | the Second Appearance 87^v
of Christ in his Triumphant Kingdom: consisting of several Concise Tracts: viz. the Stumbling Blocks in ye way of ye Kingdom. The Central Pass, or ye Birth-Gale of ye triumphant Ministration. The Key of ye Kingdom. The Individual Reign & ye threefold Process of ye Kingdom. Of ye Time & Seasons, & ye Number of ye Beast. Of ye Two Witnesses of ye First Resurrection; & ye Manner of Christs Appearance. The Process of ye Church Periods from Christ suffering to Christ Triumphant, & thence on to ye Consummation of

all things. The Creation in Consort, or a Hymn on ye Glorious Advent Thus by R[ichard] R[oach].

There are many other Compendious Tracts by ye same hand written as Compendiously & yet fully as might be on most of ye Curious Subjects relating to ye Kingdom, & also ye Controversies of ye Age. As, ye Stratagems of ye Great Enemy ag[ains]t ye Children of ye Kingdom. Of ye Virgin [birth?] of God; & ye Birth of ye Manchild. Of ye Tree of Life & of ye Knowledge of Good & Evil. Of ye Holy Trinity in Unity, wth its Illustrations & Figures in Nature. Of ye Restoration of ye whole lapsed Creation. Of the State & Regions of ye departed Souls. Of Liberty Free-will & Free grace, Predestination, Election, Reprobation &c. With discoveries of ye Secret Methods of Providence in mercie & [ ] in ye strange Appearances of this latter Age, both wth relation to ye Mystery of Iniquity & of Godliness. These under ye peculiar conduct & Assistance of ye divine wisdom & Holy Spirit have been prepared in private, & in a half hour of silence; & are as it is supposed to make a part of ye third & last testimony in y^e [ ]& powers of Philadelphia, wch has a little real & [ ] strength i.e. of ye victorious Love: by wch it holds out y^e [ ] course & carries ye evening light obtaind thro ye [ ] of Judgm[en]^t succeeding; & thro ye death obtains the Return | of ye Resurrection, or Morning Dawn of ye Kingdome; wch goes on to the Perfect noon. And thus according to ye central & centre holding power of ye spirit of Philadelphia or Fraternal Love (wch Ephesus lost), & in obedience to ye peculiar caution of our Lord to y^t Church she here, as elsewhere, Holds fast that wch she has receiv'd, & no one takes her Crown.

I shall onely add this Remark; ye Philadelphian Society of England broke forth wth its Testimony of Grace & Peace in ye year 1697, in wch year the outward Peace also of ye nations was proclaimd. Upon ye Rejection of the Testimony ^ The evening light to y^s nation vergd to Dusk, & ye night of Judgment. ^ the War brake out again in ye beginning of ye new century: & ye Divisions or Spiritual wars in this nation broke out in greatest violence dividing even ye national church ag[ains]t it self & its Inferior Clergy ag[ains]t its Bishops in ye House of Convocation. And in ye Conclusion of the work the Philadelphian Society, as shaking off ye Dust of their feet ag[ains]^t those y^t had rejected their Testimony in ye Love, were oblig'd to sharpen their declarations & denounce ye Judgm[en]^t Work to succeed. The same year in wch they seald their testimony & printed their Remonstrance or Protestation ag[ains]^t ye rejection refusal of ye offerd Advent of Grace in ye rising powers of ye kingdom. Upon ye eve & morning of Advent, according to Church Rubrick wth us of this nation; came forth ye Signal Judgm[en]t of ye Great & terrible storm: on acc[oun]^t of wch ye Church of England there being appointed a Day of Fast & Humiliation | it was observd the storm broke out again on ye very day of Humiliation upon y^s Account of it,

& y^t wth some of ye same ruinous effects as before as it were signally speaking ye Resolvd will of Heav'n, that ye Judgm[en]^t work should go on in this nation. W^{ch} as it has had it course ever since, & is yet proceeding in some measure amongst us, yet it is wth mercy intermixed & in a measure bounded by ye sp[iri]^t of grace the Philadelphian period of ye church in wch we now stand: wch spirit as it may have prevailed here & there more privately, so will at last more openly & generally prevail & out wrestle ye judgm[en]t work & season & Binding ye power of wrath & division, & bringing forth <u>Peace</u> & <u>Concord</u> & ye manifestation of ye Grace & Power of ye Kingdom into a more general <u>Acceptation</u> in ye visible church, as led by ye Grace of divine Providence, thro its work & night of Judgm[en]^t also, to y^e <u>Dawn</u> of ye kingdom as now more clearly evidencing it self in <u>demonstration and power</u>.

To ye truth & faithfulness of this narrative according to ye best of my information & Judgm[en]^t & as one concernd in all ye affairs & designs of ye society from ye Beginning to ye End (of its public work) I have (as occasion may require) set my Hand wishing & praying for an Excitem[en]^t & Resurrection of y^e Faith of y^e kingdom, & y^e Blessing of it y^e worthy person y^t has requir'd this Account; & all to whom it may prove usefull or Acceptable.

* Richard Roach. FINIS.

Hannah [= Johanna Halberts?],[291] "A visional Dream of a Woman at Utrecht concerning M. Lead's departure out of the Body."[292]

I Hannah ----- when I was visiting here some time ago a Friend, I found two Books, one being a mystick of a Roman Catholick Doctor, which when she gave me into my hand, said: This Book I would have you take along with you to read, but since I had read it already, I took the other viz: The Heavenly Cloud and Revelation of Revelations of M^{dm} Lead, which I had never seen before, and therefore begged, that she would lend it me, but therein, it shall be given you they are Dreams from an old English woman; But her mother replyed: Do you give away such a Book, which might yet serve for our reading: I answered: Pray lend it me only, which she did. But at my reading of it, I wonderd, that such a Person was now in the world, and the more I read it, the more my Desire encreased to see this Person, and at last it was answerd me by an Internall word: you shall see Her. But a considerable Time passed away, where I saw no oppor-

89^r

---

291 The sender is identified as Johanna Halberts in Johann Wolfgang Jaeger, *Historia Ecclesiastica, cum parallelismo profanæ, in qua Conclavia Pontificum Romanorum fideliter aperiuntur et sectæ omnes recensentur*, vol. 2 (Hamburg: 1717), part ii, 103–104.

292 Bodl. MS Rawlinson D 833 fol. 89^{r-v}.

tunity to see Her. At length betwixt the 14th and the 15th of August at night I saw in a Dream a wonderfull vision. I beheld a Matron sitting, to my appearance very pious and modest of a grave deportment and civil look. She was pretty well in Age, not very tall (as she seemed to me in her sitting Posture,) but lusty and fatt. She was of a pale dead colour, and cloathed (or rather covered only) with a black vestment, like a Rain-Cloath from the Top of her Head to the Feet; The cloath ~~was~~ being a vail of black silk, as if she was in mourning. But within the Vail of Silk, she was stark naked, Her Breast being open. At which I was greatly surprised, when I beheld this pious and grave Matron (as me thought) that her Heart was thus open and being much ashamed thereat, thought it to be contrary to Honesty, and so intended to go away. But it was said to me, that I ought to draw nearer to Her, and look | more closely to see, what there was upon her Heart. Then, when I did cast my Eyes on Her Breast, behold, I saw the crucified Saviour hanging there upon the Cross, His Blessed Mother being on one side, and John on the other, at which I wonderd yet more greatly, But it was further said to me, that I should approach yet nearer, and behold the Cross, that was there more closely and narrowly, wch I did with great fear and Trembling, then I saw, that upon Her Breast were blew swoln veines, and that Jesus with his Blessed mother, and his Disciple John were there hanging on the Cross living, I say, living, and not painted or printed. I marvelled at this vision so much that I folded my Hands, and lifted my Heart up to God, worshipping Him in an amazing manner. But when I began to pray earnestly [~~revrently~~], the Matron opened her Eyes, and turned Herself towards me, for to speak, but when she saw that I prayd, she spake not. I continued a considerable while in praying and then awaked, and this vision rested long on my Mind. But on the 30th of August I was called to M^m from L., who told me, that one Meschman at Amsterdam had visited and told her that iust then he had heard from Loth Fisher that M^m Lead was deceased,[293] and when I heard this, it was spoke to me at that very moment. This is the interpretation of thy Dream, and so I related the Dream to that M^m, and ~~withal~~ when I asked ~~of her~~ for the day of her Departure, ~~which when I did~~, behold, Mr Fishers Daughter being at the house of this M^m enquired for me saying, that she had looked for me at my own House, and found me not there, and therefore came now to ask something of me. At which we were amazed and Heard, y^t M^{dm} Lead had departed on the 5th day of August according to the tenor of my Dream.[294]

---

293 Christian Meschmann (c.1628–fl.1704), merchant of Amsterdam.
294 A variant copy is preserved among Francis Lee's papers; see LPL, MS 1559 fol. 1^{r-v}. Both this variant and the text transcribed here should be compared with the version printed by Jaeger.

8   Letter from Richard Roach to August Hermann Francke (London, 2 February 1726)[295] [Translated from the Latin by Diego Lucci]

O Reverend Father, and beloved brother in Christ,

I think that some news about me and my fate reached your ears long ago, at the time when I was involved in the Philadelphians' affairs with Mother Lead and Brother Francis Lee, and I was known among the Spiritual Friends under the name of Onesimus. After that proclamation of the Kingdom of Christ there was a long silence and a prophetic time of around half an hour, during which hardly any utterance about Christ's Kingdom or of mystical theology was heard in public. For came to an end the lecture, or rather the assembly of spiritual theology, in a corner of the Anglican church, an assembly then also openly recognized from its approach, and constituted by the followers of Dr. Horneck,[296] and maintained thanks to the work and activity of Dr. Coganus,[297] or Coughen (both are acceptable)—certainly of that Coganus who had been a companion and friend of Dr. J. Pordage and T. Bromley, during those then wonderful progresses of the powers of the celestial kingdom, which was then supernal and breaking out. Thus was fulfilled the prediction privately made by the spirit among the Philadelphians—namely a prediction of a future hunger; a hunger, however, not of bread or of natural food, but of God's word (namely, spiritual food, of which there was great abundance in that time).

---

295   Berlin, Staatsbibliothek Preussischer Kulturbesitz Handschriftenabteilung, Nachlaß A.H. Francke (Kapsel 30—England betreffend), fols 300–302 [signatur 30/42:1].

296   Anthony Horneck (1641–1697), Palatinate-born Church of England clergyman who had drawn up strict rules for the conduct of religious societies for young men.

297   John Coughen (c.1638–1717?) was the Dutch-born son of an English merchant resident at Amsterdam. He was educated at Cambridge University, ordained at Ely but then converted to Quakerism in 1663. Thereafter he studied medicine at Rotterdam and Leiden. See Hessayon (ed.), *Jane Lead*, 51, 59, 77, 229, 230, 232.

CHAPTER 11

The French Prophets and the Scottish Mystics: Prophecies and Letters

Michael B. Riordan

Introduction

In March 1709, four prophets arrived in Edinburgh proclaiming the end of the world in a series of ecstatic "warnings" they claimed to channel from the Holy Spirit.[1] The three girls and one boy were emissaries of the "French Prophets", a largely English millenarian movement—despite its name—that first appeared in London in 1706. In Scotland, the prophets attracted the interest of a group who championed the teachings of the Flemish Quietist, Antoinette Bourignon (1616–1680). This group—the first to call themselves "mystics"—believed that men and women had a duty to follow the Holy Spirit in everything they did, and that Christ would soon appear to convert the world to their beliefs. Some therefore accepted the prophets and started to prophesy themselves. But other mystics remained unconvinced and argued that spiritual reformation would not appear by outward signs and wonders.

This debate was sparked by the actions of Katherine Pringle, Lady Abden (1682–1747), one of the Scottish mystics. Late in 1709, Abden delivered a series of prophecies that outlined Bourignon's ideas. Some of the prophets believed Abden's warnings were inspired by Bourignon's writings rather than the Holy Spirit and accused her of being tempted by Satan.

This edition attempts to uncover the debate by publishing, for the first time, a selection of Lady Abden's prophecies along with a series of letters between the prophets.

---

1 Edinburgh, National Library of Scotland (NLS) 9847, fol. 9^r, Archibald Lundie to James Lundie, 7 April 1709.

The French Prophets[2]

France

The French Prophets emerged among Huguenots from rural Languedoc, who resisted the attempts of Louis XIV and his local intendants to crush religious dissent. Calvinists in the Cévennes mountains traced their heritage to the Cathar heretics of the fourteenth century, who saw themselves as a pure elect.[3] Their obsession with religious purity predisposed the Cévenols to resist Louis's attempts to secure religious—Catholic—order. Aided by the mountainous landscape of the region, known as *le Désert*, the Cévenols continued practising their faith in secret, while their Protestant coreligionists converted or went into exile.[4] They believed that they would find support in Protestant nations, which had been at war with France since the Glorious Revolution of 1688. The accession to the English throne of William III, champion of international Protestantism, seemed providential. William's ancestral home, the Principality of Orange, bordered Languedoc. From 1688, children in south-eastern France began to prophesy their deliverance at William's hands in ecstatic trances.[5]

In 1701, Louis sought to impose his grandson, Philip of Anjou, as heir to Charles II, the late king of Spain. Anxious to win Louis's favour, his representative in Languedoc, Nicolas Lamoignon de Bâville, ramped up the execution of Protestants.[6] Against this backdrop of persecution, 8,000 prophets appeared across the region. In 1702, one of them, Abraham Mazel, pronounced an order "to take up arms, for the cause of God" to liberate their imprisoned brethren.[7] On 24 July, inspired prophets murdered the inspector of the Cévennes, the Archpriest Francois de Langlade du Chaila, sparking a civil war between these "Camisards" and the government. The Camisards' army has been characterised as "military theocracy", because their strategy was dictated by prophets, many of them children. The war was fought between 1702 and 1704. Jean Cavalier surrendered in May that year, quickly followed by other Camisard leaders.

---

2 Hillel Schwartz, *The French Prophets: The History of a Millenarian Group in Eighteenth-Century England* (Berkeley, CA: 1980); Lionel Laborie, *Enlightening Enthusiasm: Prophecy and Religious Experience in Early Eighteenth-Century England* (Manchester: 2015).
3 Jean Cavalier, *Memoirs of the Wars of the Cevennes* (Dublin: 1726), xi–xii, 218; Maximilien Mission, *A Cry from the Desert*, 2nd ed. (London: 1707), 6.
4 Laborie, *Enlightening Enthusiasm*, 16–21.
5 Ibid., 21–24. See also Lionel Laborie's chapter in vol. 1 of this collection.
6 Laborie, *Enlightening Enthusiasm*, 24.
7 Georgia Cosmos, *Huguenot Prophecy and Clandestine Worship in the Eighteenth Century: "The Sacred Theatre of the Cévennes"* (Aldershot: 2005), 89.

England and Scotland

It was men acting under Cavalier's orders who brought the prophetic tradition of the *Désert* to the streets of London. Durand Fage, Jean Cavalier of Sauve and Elie Marion arrived in England in 1706, where they began to deliver prophecies in French.[8] These early prophecies foretold the Fall of Babylon in order to raise an army of Huguenot refugees to fight the final battle against their Catholic enemies in Languedoc. Soon they had over four hundred English and French followers from all levels of society. English prophets prophesied the conversion of the Jews to Christianity as the prelude to Christ's Second Coming. Their "warnings" were delivered in dramatic, agitated trances, which supporters claimed showed that the Spirit moved inside them. From 1707, their words were published in a series of *Warnings of the Eternal Spirit*, a printed record of God's work on earth.[9]

Until 1708, the prophets confined themselves to London. In February, they travelled to Enfield and Colchester, and in October delivered warnings in Birmingham. The prophets first came to Edinburgh in March 1709, but their mission was judged disastrous, and they gained few, if any, Scottish followers.[10] The most telling episode was the publication, by a London newspaper, of letters that revealed the group's divisions.[11]

The prophets received a better reception when they returned to Edinburgh in late May 1709, under the leadership of Thomas Dutton (1679–*c*.1741). Dutton had gained his reputation as a London magistrate, and acted as secretary to the radical Whig lawyer, John Scrope. He joined the prophets in September 1707 and started speaking under the prophetic agitations.[12] Dutton's decision to take the mission north may have been influenced by the fortunes of his previous employer. Scope became Baron of the Scottish Exchequer in 1708. Dutton's mission to Edinburgh achieved greater success than its predecessor because he won over establishment names. The Queen's Advocate, David Dalrymple, refused to intervene to prevent the prophets taking to the streets of the city.[13] They attracted supporters among Scottish Episcopalians, including

---

8   See Lionel Laborie's chapter in vol. 1 of this collection.
9   Laborie, *Enlightening Enthusiasm*, 82–83.
10 *Warnings of the Eternal Spirit, Pronounced at Edinburgh, Out of the Mouths of 1. Anna Maria King. 2. John Moult. 3. Mary Turner. 4. Ann Topham* (Edinburgh: 1709); Glasgow City Archives and Special Collections, Mitchell Library (GCA) MS 563620 (Dutton-Cunningham Letters), thereafter Falconer MS, 16–44.
11 *The Post Boy*, 22–24 September 1709.
12 Laborie, *Enlightening Enthusiasm*, 257.
13 NLS 9847, fol. 11ᵛ, James Lundie to Archibald Lundie, 12 August 1709.

the daughter of the Principal of King's College, Aberdeen.[14] Between July 1709 and January 1714, home-grown Scottish prophets delivered hundreds of public warnings to men and women in towns and cities from Edinburgh in the South to Aberdeen in the North, Glasgow in the West to Dundee in the East.[15]

Despite high-ranking sympathisers, many Scots looked on aghast. At the start of 1710, the prophets had to flee a violent mob in Edinburgh. That September they were detained in Edinburgh's Tolbooth, while the same fate greeted them at Glasgow, which they reached the following month. In January 1710, one follower, John Gyles, was imprisoned for twenty-three months—an extraordinary length of internment for the period.[16]

The prophets' supporters were largely drawn from Scottish Episcopalians, which increased the suspicion of the Presbyterian establishment: a petition from 1709 alleged they were part of James Greenshields's campaign to introduce the Anglican service into Scotland.[17] Greenshields himself dismissed the suggestion as rubbish and the prophets as enthusiasts,[18] but the petitioners had picked up on the interest shown by one group of Episcopalians: those who defined themselves by their "mystical theology". It was the apparent compatibility of the prophets' message with their own beliefs that caused some of the "mystics" to embrace them.

The Scottish Mystics

The Anglophone language of mysticism was devised in the 1630s by exiled English Catholics to describe the practices of monastic contemplation.[19] After the Restoration of the monarchy in 1660, English Protestants—both Anglicans and dissenters—adopted the language of mysticism, which they believed could promote true Christian piety in a corrupt society.[20]

---

14 NLS 9847, fol. 11ᵛ, James Lundie to Archibald Lundie, 12 August 1709.
15 A sample can be found in NLS 2686, 1–2, 23–42, 157–172, 176–178, 238–248 (Edinburgh); 51–53, 62–79, 83–92 (Aberdeen); 9–17, 174–175 (Glasgow), 48 (Dundee).
16 Falconer MS, 259–260 (Edinburgh mob; Gyles); NLS 5166, pp. 22–31 (Glasgow Tolbooth); Acc. 8592, unpaginated, warning of 15 September 1709.
17 Edinburgh, National Records of Scotland (NRS) CH1/2/28/3, fols 221ʳ–223ᵛ, petitions to the General Assembly from citizens of Edinburgh and Haddington, August 1709.
18 Gloucester, Gloucestershire Archives, D3549/6/2/2, memorial of James Greenshields.
19 Victoria van Hyning and Elizabeth Dutton, "Augustine Baker and the mystical canon", in *Dom Augustine Baker 1575–1641*, ed. Geoffrey Scott (Leominster: 2012), 85–110.
20 Sarah Apetrei, "'Between the rational and the mystical': the inner life and the early English Enlightenment", in *Mysticism and Reform, 1400–1750*, ed. Sara. S. Poor and Nigel Smith

In Scotland, Restoration mysticism was represented by moderate Episcopalians, who sought to reunite the Scottish church, which was divided between Presbyterian and Episcopalians. Church government, they argued, was irrelevant to salvation. What was relevant was each believer's personal relationship to God. The Scots thought that Protestantism lacked the devotional literature to restore this relationship, and therefore turned to the Catholic contemplative tradition, which afforded the tools to reunite the creator and his creatures.[21]

The Scots believed that the best way to encourage piety was to distribute mystical literature to those unacquainted with the "interior way".[22] They produced lists of mystical authors, which formed the basis for the catalogue contained in *Bibliothecca Mysticorum Selecta*, compiled by the Lutheran pastor, Pierre Poiret (1646–1719).[23] Mystical literature flowed between mystics in Scotland, London and continental Europe. During his studies at the University of Leiden, James Lundie (1686–1777) arranged for books to be sent to Scotland through his brother, Archibald (1674–1759), minister in the East Lothian parish of Saltoun.[24] The Aberdeen physician, Dr James Keith (d.1726) moved to London in 1705 or 1706 and acted as librarian to the Philadelphian Society.[25] Shortly after his arrival, Keith proposed "Raising a Stock to Print Books of Mystical Divinity".[26] The project was boosted by the will of Rebekah Hussey (1668–1714), the unmarried daughter of Lincolnshire MP, Sir Thomas Hussey. Keith's fellow physician, George Cheyne (1671–1743), persuaded Hussey to donate £300 to cover printing costs.[27] An indication of the popularity of the project can be

---

(Notre Dame, IN: 2015), 198–219; Liam P. Temple, *Mysticism in Early Modern England* (Martlesham, Suffolk: 2019). See also Ariel Hessayon's chapter in this volume.

21 Michael B. Riordan, "The Episcopalians and the Promotion of Mysticism in North-East Scotland", *Records of the Scottish Church History Society* 47 (2018): 31–56.

22 John Nichols (ed.), *Illustrations of the Literary History of the Eighteenth Century*, vol. 4 (London: 1822), 408.

23 NLS Adv. 25.5.53, fols 3ʳ–5ᵛ, "Catalogue de plusiers auteurs qui on ecrit de matieres Mystiques et qui les ont eclairies".

24 NLS 9847, fols 3–22, Lundie correspondence; Huw Scott, *Fasti Ecclesiae Scoticanae: The Succession of Ministers in the Church of Scotland from the Reformation*, vol. 1 (Edinburgh: 1905), 393; Robert A.L. Smith, *History of the Clan Lundy, Lundie, Lundin* (Glasgow: 2005), 374–375.

25 G.D. Henderson (ed.), *Mystics of the North East* (Aberdeen: 1934), 56; "Keith, James", in Royal College of Physicians, *Lives of the Fellows* [*Munk's Roll*] (http://munksroll.rcplondon.ac.uk/Biography/Details/2519); London, National Archives, Prob/11/612/108, will of James Keith; manuscripts from the library can be found in Oxford, Bodleian Library, Rawl. A404–405, A354, C602, C858, D42–44, D1262–3, D1338, H74.

26 London, Dr Williams' Library, Walton bundle XL.20.

27 London, National Archives, PROB 11/546/79, will of Rebekah Hussey; London, Henry Hoare and Co., HB/8/T/15, George Cheyne to Robert Apreece, 19 August 1714.

gleaned from one of Keith's letters, which indicates that forty-two per cent of subscribers to Jeanne Guyon's twelve-volume *Commentaires sur le Vieux Testament* came from Scotland.[28]

The mystics became notorious in the 1690s for publishing the works of Antoinette Bourignon. Bourignon claimed that the Church's division represented the Age of Antichrist and believed that men and women needed to be reformed to prepare themselves for Christ's Second Coming. The solution, she claimed, was to be found in mystical prayer. Men and women should pray continually, "whether he eat, drink, walk, or take his rest". This was an argument that appealed to Scottish Episcopalians. In 1699, the Ludnies' cousin, George Garden (1649–1733) wrote a Latin *Apology* for Bourignon, which he and James Keith translated into English.[29] As a result, Garden was deprived of his ministry at St. Nicholas' church in Aberdeen, which allowed him to put Bourignon's vision into practice. In 1701, Garden "abstracted himself wholly from the world" and formed a retreat in London, where he lived "most christianly".[30] This retreat formed the basis for the mystical community he started at Rosehearty, the ancestral home of his patron, Alexander, 4th Lord Forbes of Pitsligo (1678–1762).

Existing scholarship focuses on Garden's circle at Rosehearty,[31] but mystical literature was distributed throughout Scotland to groups who attempted to put mystical theology into practice.[32] Particularly important for our purposes is the retreat formed at Craighall in central Fife by Sir Thomas Hope, 6th Bart. (1685–1729). In October 1709, Craighall was the setting for the first Scottish prophets to speak under inspiration, and as late as 1713 the prophets were delivering warnings from Craighall.[33] It is within Hope's circle that we find two people whose roles proved decisive: Katherine Pringle and James Cunningham.

---

28   Henderson (ed.), *Mystics*, 130.
29   John Byrom, *The Private Journal and Literary Remains of John Byrom*, vol. 2, pt. 1, ed. Richard Parkinson (Manchester: 1856), 129–130.
30   Edinburgh University Library (EUL) 2097.8, fol. 28ᵛ, Mungo Murray to Colin Campbell, October 1701.
31   Henderson, *Mystics*; Geoffrey Rowell, "Scotland and the 'mystical matrix' of the late seventeenth and early eighteenth centuries: an exploration of religious cross-currents", *International Journal for the Study of the Christian Church* 14 (2014), 129–144.
32   Michael B. Riordan, "Mysticism and Prophecy in Scotland in the Long Eighteenth Century", PhD thesis (University of Cambridge: 2015), 84–85.
33   EUL La.III.709, 308–314; St. Andrews, University Library, 1012, 572–574, records of prophets' meeting, 2 October 1713; Henderson, *Mystics*, 203, George Garden to James Cunningham, 11 November 1709. The latter has been misdated by Henderson from later copies. The correct date is provided by the original, within Sir Duncan Rice Library, University of Aberdeen (AUL), MS 3320/6, i.e. 11 November instead of 17 November 1709.

Lady Abden's Prophecies

Katherine Pringle, Lady Abden (1682–1747), was a single mother. Her husband, John Wardlaw had died in August 1705, three months before Katherine gave birth to their daughter, Christian.[34] To cope with this situation, Katherine turned to mystical literature. She read Jeanne Guyon's *Moien Court* (1685) for "half a year before she joyn'd" Dutton's mission in July 1709.[35]

Over the winter of 1709, both Katherine and her infant daughter delivered warnings in Edinburgh, Stirling and Linlithgow.[36] Katherine dictated her warnings to James Garden (c.1685–1772), the nephew of Bourignon's translator. The surviving manuscript—which is published below for the first time—is a copy of Garden's transcriptions, entitled "The Last Revelation that shall be putt in print to the sons and children of men".[37] The warnings do not appear in chronological order, and so we can surmise this is a copy taken from Garden's originals. The manuscript opens with an instruction to James to "get a quair of paper" and to "make it into the form of a book". "There I shall have my secrets more plainly delivered to the world than it has been heretofore", the Spirit speaking through Abden informs us.[38] The prophecies are given between 3 October and 26 October 1709 at Linlithgow and Stirling. The warnings take up 376 pages, divided across 66 chapters, each discussing a disputed theological question or scripture passage.

The "Last Revelation" combined Bourignon's ideas with a defence of the prophets' form of ecstatic prophecy. The manuscript systematised Bourignon's ideas, which had been propounded in letters to her disciples. Abden's "Last Revelation" is both simple and systematic, despite being delivered verbatim. The book argues that through practising mystical prayer humanity can be restored to its primitive state. Adam was created in the image of God, with "a glorious Luminous, angel body" and two sexes.[39] Adam's fall from angelic hermaphroditism occurred when "it"—Abden uses the neuter pronoun—turned its desires away from God and placed them on worldly matters. Men and women have ignored the many prophets God has sent to renew His message,

---

34 NRS CC20/4/16, testament of John Wardlaw, registered 7 June 1707; NRS CC20/4/18, testament of Christian Wardlaw, registered 18 July 1719.
35 Henderson, *Mystics*, 248, George Garden to James Cunningham, March 1710.
36 Katherine Pringle, Lady Abden, "The Last Revelation that shall be putt in print to the sons and children of men" (thereafter Abden, LR); Henderson, *Mystics*, 217, James Cunningham to George Garden, 2 December 1709.
37 Abden, LR, fol. 3.
38 Ibid., fol. 1.
39 Ibid., fol. 4.

and so have become increasingly distant from their creator. God has tried many times to reconcile Himself with creation, by sending prophets to renew His message. But men and women have not listened and become increasingly distant from their creator. Abden's prophecies offer a way to recover God's favour by owning up to the faults of humanity and accepting the punishments He chooses to inflict upon the world. Abden believed that this can only be done through continual prayer, which will serve to reunite men and women with their creator.

The "Last Revelation" wove into this mix many doctrines that Bourignon had judged "accessory principles", unnecessary for salvation.[40] These included Abden's lengthy defence of the freedom of the will and her critique of the Calvinist doctrine of predestination. If God limited our wills as predestinarians implied, we would have the capacity "to make acts of love to him".[41] Rather more worrying was her view that because humans were so corrupted by the effects of the Fall, they required a state of purification—"purgatory"—after death in order to fully reach divine union, which is necessary for salvation.[42]

The "Last Revelation" combines Bourignon's mysticism with a defence of outward prophecy. Bourignon warned against trusting in signs and miracles. Outward prophecies could not "make us discover the Spirit of God", because they "may be done by the Operation of the Devil".[43] In contrast, Abden argued that false spirits cannot deceive those who follow the true Christian path. Drawing on Garden's *Apology*, she argued that women have been more likely to "experimentally [feel] the wayes of God moving in their soul" because they are not burdened with speculative knowledge.[44] Abden was one of several Scottish women who took Garden's defence as a justification of their peculiar role in the divine plan. These included Margaret Irvine, wife of the Jacobite Hugh Rose of Clava, and Katherine Gordon, wife of Thomas Orem, a local antiquarian.[45] Abden placed herself among several "illiterate creatures", like Irvine and Gordon, who were sent to remind people of their duties to their neighbours and to God.[46] Prophets were needed, in her view, to renew the faith whenever men and women failed to live up to their Christian duties.

40　Falconer MS, 247.
41　Abden, LR, 121.
42　Ibid., 45–53.
43　Antoinette Bourignon, *The Academy of Learned Divines*, vol. 2, trans. George Garden and James Keith (London: 1708), 5.
44　Abden, LR, 201.
45　NLS 9847, fol. 11ᵛ, James Lundie to Archibald Lundie, 12 August 1709.
46　Abden, LR, 280.

The Debate over Abden

Some of Abden's fellow mystics in Scotland believed her warnings to be divinely inspired. Archibald Lundie found their "Humility and Resignation" matched the writings of the "profoundest Mysticks".[47] Lord Forbes of Pitsligo was so impressed that he sent a manuscript copy of the "Last Revelation" to Andrew Michael Ramsay (1686–1743), tutor to Thomas Hope's son. In 1708, Ramsay had moved to London, where he attended the prophets' meetings, and became concerned about the credulity of his Scottish friends.[48] Pitsligo, by contrast, followed the prophets with great interest and may have delivered warnings himself. In 1712, reports circulated that his sister Jean had done so.[49] Pitsligo's neighbour, John Forbes of Monymusk (1680–1715) became inspired after hearing Abden's warnings in Edinburgh and would later go on to sing songs in Aberdeen under the Spirit's direction.[50] Abden's "Last Revelation" also circulated among Hope's circle in Fife,[51] and by the start of 1710, it was being read in London, so that the prophets there "may know the Holy Spirit's will therein", as the prophet James Cunningham put it.[52]

Others, however, dissented from this positive view of the "Last Revelation". They believed Abden's prophecies were an undue blend of inward piety and outward ecstasy. Letters published by G.D. Henderson in 1934 reveal that the leader of the Rosehearty mystics, George Garden, was particularly sceptical. Writing to James Cunningham, Garden argued that the prophets' ecstatic "warnings" were incompatible with mysticism, which required people to be still and silent so God could perfect them from within. The true Christian had no need to engage in outward shows of ecstasy, which were a sign that prophecies were not divinely inspired. God's truth ought to be "manifested in a small and still voice", and not "agitations of the body". The agitated prophets would "rather pull the soul out of its silent state, than preserve it" there.[53]

The letters published below reveal that the London prophets also doubted whether Abden's "Last Revelation" was divinely inspired. According to the process laid down by Thomas Dutton, doubtful cases had to be "considered by three mouthes of unsuspected authority" before it could be confirmed that

---

47 NLS 9847, fol. 12ʳ, Archibald Lundie to James Lundie, 12 August 1709.
48 NLS Acc. 4796/104/B, Forbes of Pitsligo to Andrew Michael Ramsay, 20 November 1709.
49 NRS GD124/15/1081, letters to the Earl of Mar from Jean Forbes.
50 AUL, 53, 59–63; NLS 2686, 59–63; EUL La.III.708, 57–59.
51 See note 33 above.
52 Falconer MS, 249, James Cunningham, letter of 10 January 1710.
53 Henderson, *Mystics*, 216, James Cunningham to George Garden, 2 December 1709.

prophecies proceeded from the Holy Spirit.[54] Some of Abden's warnings had already received the censure of the prophets in London, including the Swiss mathematician Nicolas Fatio de Duillier (1664–1753). The Spirit declared to Dutton that the "Last Revelation" was not of divine authority.[55]

Dutton believed that Abden's warnings had been inspired by Antoinette Bourignon, not God. The Scottish mystics' failure was their temptation "to contenance doctrines not obviously contained in the Word of God".[56] Abden's claim that her revelations contained substance absent from Scripture made her prophecies highly suspect. Dutton advised the prophets in Scotland to stop reading mystical books and instead embrace the Spirit's teachings.[57] He argued that, while mysticism could help to get at the "spiritual" sense of Scripture, it could not uncover the Bible's literal meaning. Bourignon and Abden, he argued, erred by taking the mystics' spiritual teachings, rather than the Bible's plain meaning, as their guides to leading a holy life.[58]

The case of James Cunningham of Barns (c.1680–1716) suggests that Dutton was unsuccessful at calling the Scottish prophets away from mysticism. Before encountering the prophets in 1709, Cunningham's rising debts and poor health had made him retreat from worldly activity. His sense of dejection led him to the *Santa Sophia* (1656) by the English convert to Catholicism, Serenus Cressy (1605–1674).[59] Contemporaries regarded Cressy's work as an important synthesis of mystical theology. It provided a scale of prayer for those at various stages of spiritual perfection. It was while following Cressy's rule that Cunningham heard Lady Abden deliver warnings in Edinburgh. She spoke of the duty "ev'ry man and woman" had to "retire [...] into their closets, humble themselves in my sight, hold their peace, be careful that their imagination do not interpose, that they may be altogether still".[60] When he heard this, Cunningham was convinced it answered a pre-existing "resolution and desire".[61] There was no "distinction betwixt the Spirit which" had been communicating "itself to me and that of this [prophetic] dispensation".[62]

In July 1710, Cunningham embarked on a prophetic tour across Britain. Hundreds of his warnings survive, which combine mysticism with prophecy. In one

---

54 Falconer MS, 87, Thomas Dutton, undated letter.
55 Ibid., 82–83.
56 Ibid., 112–113, Thomas Dutton, letter of 22 November 1709.
57 Ibid., 119, Thomas Dutton, letter of 6 December 1709.
58 Ibid., 120.
59 Ibid., 293; Henderson, *Mystics*, 200, Garden to Cunningham, 11 November 1709.
60 Henderson, *Mystics*, 201–202, Garden to Cunningham, 11 November 1709.
61 Ibid., 203.
62 NLS Acc. 4796/104/B, James Cunningham to Andrew Michael Ramsay, 6 December 1709.

example, the Spirit speaking through Cunningham called on men "to have no wills of [their] own". They must "disengage the Heart, from this world". The test of a true spirit was "internal soul-satisfying peace", which provided "serenity, and joy, in the midst of all outward suffering". Outward things, by contrast, were an "abomination" to God.[63]

As will be seen in the letters printed here, Cunningham encouraged other mystics to embrace the prophetic mission. Both Jean Forbes, the sister of Alexander, 4th Forbes of Pitsligo, and John Forbes of Monymusk (1684–1715), Pitsligo's brother-in-law by another sister Mary, delivered warnings. Monymusk delivered public prophecies in Aberdeen.[64] He "afterwardes dipped in my Lord Marr's insurrection in the year 1715, and was obliged therfore to flye the country". Monymusk died in a shipwreck on route to Holland.[65] Cunningham continued to deliver prophecies until November 1715, when he was captured at the Battle of Preston.[66] George Garden and other mystics remained sceptical. Garden's letters to Cunningham continued to circulate well into the eighteenth century, cautioning others against embracing the prophets' cause.[67] But these arguments did not stop mystics from joining the prophets. As late as 1740, Isabel Cameron, Alexander Falconer, Margaret Irvine, Lady Clava, Helen Middleton, David Spence, Katherine and Kenneth Gordon, all "continu'd firm in the Faith of the glorious manifestation of our Lord by his Spirit".[68]

The Manuscripts

1. Dundee University Archives BrMS 2/5/4

Lady Abden's warnings were transcribed by James Garden from Abden's spoken warnings. There is evidence that multiple manuscript copies of the "Last

---

63 *Warnings of the Eternal Spirit ... Out of the Mouths of Margaret Mackenzie and James Cunningham* (London: 1710), 9.
64 NRS GD124/15/1081, letters to Lord Grange from Jean Forbes, annotated by Grange, "Mrs Jean Forbes Ld Pitsliggo's sister who follows the modern (mock) prophets & agitates with them"; Monymusk's prophecies can be found in NLS Acc. 2686, fols 51–79, 83–92.
65 Falconer MS, 210–211. A memorial, by his widow, Susanna Morrison, is printed in John Forbes, *The Jacobite Cess Roll for the County of Aberdeen*, ed. Alistair and Henrietta Tayler (Aberdeen: 1932), xvi–xvii.
66 Falconer MS, 344–368; NRS GD1/53/721, list of prisoners at Preston.
67 NRS CH12/20/11, fols 268–320.
68 Falconer MS, 397, 391 (misnumbered), letters of Thomas Dutton, 5 July 1737 and 17 June 1740.

Revelation" were produced, which circulated in Scotland and England. Pitsligo and Cunningham both sent copies to their fellow Scottish mystics. On 3 December, five weeks after Abden's final warnings in the "Last Revelation", the English prophet, Thomas Dutton, ordered that "every copy" in circulation should be marked as condemned as being not of divine authority.[69]

The only copy we can trace—held in Dundee University Archives—does not bear such a mark. It came to Dundee from the personal library of Francis Garden, Lord Gardenstone, at Laurencekirk in Aberdeenshire.[70] Gardenstone's father, Alexander, was a member of the circle of mystics in northern Scotland. It is one of two manuscripts in his collection that relate to the prophetic mission: the other, now BrMS 2/5/3, is a series of warnings by the Scottish prophets James Cunningham and Margaret Irvine, and three English prophets: Thomas Dutton, John Potter and Guy Nutt.

Most of the warnings contained in the "Last Revelation" are lengthy discussions of theology, ill-suited to a format such as this, and most of these were delivered in private, at Stirling and Linlithgow. However, between 14 October and 31 October 1709, Abden delivered public warnings at Stirling, which are shorter and sharper. They synthesise the general argument for Abden's lay audiences. They have been published here in the order in which they occur in the manuscript.

2. Mitchell Library 562590

This manuscript is our principal source for the Scottish mission. It contains copies made from original letters written by Thomas Dutton and James Cunningham to their fellow prophets in England and Scotland. The letters were transcribed by one of the named recipients, Alexander Falconer of Delgaty (1682–1745).[71] Additionally, Falconer has included two letters from John Forbes of Monymusk to James Cunningham.[72] In most cases, the recipients of the letters are unknown.

Falconer was the son of Sir David Falconer, President of the College of Justice, and uncle of the philosopher David Hume. An accomplished scholar, Facloner produced English translations of the works of the fifteenth-century

---

69 Ibid., 113, letter of Thomas Dutton, 22 November 1709.
70 Dundee University Archives BrMS 4/6/2/1, Brechin Diocesan Library, record of donations, 1856–1888, 7, 10; J.R. Barker, "Lord Gardenstone's library at Laurencekirk", *The Bibliothek* 6 (1971), 41–52.
71 See Falconer's note, Falconer MS, 30. The manuscript contains one letter addressed to him: James Cunningham to Alexander Falconer, 10 July 1711 (385–386).
72 Falconer MS, 211–217, John Forbes of Monymusk to James Cunningham, 22 March 1713 and 7 March 1714.

Florentine millenarian, Girolamo Savonarola, and the only known translation of Gianfrancesco Pico della Mirandola's life of Savonarola.[73] In 1710, he joined the prophets, and his faith in the Spirit's manifestations continued until at least 1740, when our manuscript stops, shortly before the death of its scribe in 1745.[74] The manuscript formed part of the library that Falconer collected for his wife, Mary Hay, Countess of Erroll, at her estate of Slains in Aberdeenshire. The Erroll Collection was purchased in 1918 by Glasgow Corporation, and is now held in the city's main public library, the Mitchell.[75]

Roughly half of the manuscript is devoted to a discussion of Lady Abden's warnings. I have selected letters from Thomas Dutton and James Cunningham, which illustrate both sides of the argument.

Editorial Practice

I have regularised sentence structure and capitalisation. Contractions have been expanded. Original spelling has, however, been maintained throughout. All dates follow the 'old style' calandar employed in England and Scotland until 1752. The year is taken to begin on the 1st of January, which has been convention in Scotland (unlike the rest of the British isles) since 1600.

A note on parentheses: I have used round brackets, "( )", to indicate those original to Dutton and Cunningham's correspondence. Angular brackets, "⟨ ⟩", represent editorial interventions by Alexander Falconer and the scribe of DUA BrMS 2/5/4. I have placed my own interventions within square brackets, "[ ]".

---

73   NLS 3859, Girolamo Savonarola, "The Simplicity of the Xtian Life"; GCA 562588, Gianfranco Pico della Mirandola, "Life of the Reverend Hieronmus Savonarola of Ferrara written by the most Illustrious Prince John Francis Picus Lord of Mirandula and Count of Concordia"; Falconer MS, 390.

74   NLS 9847, fol. 22ʳ, Archibald Lundie to James Lundie, 11 June 1710; Falconer MS, 391–392, Thomas Dutton to [Alexander Falconer], 20 July 1740.

75   NLS 3859, 1; F.M. MacPherson, "Philosophy and religion", in *Mitchell Library, Glasgow: 1877–1977*, ed. D. Crawford Soutter (Glasgow: 1977), 43–45; Mitchell Library corporate records.

1   'The Last Revelation that Shall Be Putt in Print to the Sons and
      Children of Men' [DUA BrMS 2/5/4]

Follows the publick warnings pronounced by the Lady Abden att Stirline   268

(*1*)   *Munday October 3 1709*
My freinds, this voice is sending no new doctrine to the world. The design of it is to enjoin people to putt in practice what has been revealed to them already. If this had been done as they ought, there had been no occasion for this voice. Is not God to be praised who sends a voice to such a degenerate age to instruct them what they ought to do? Can this be cald a false voice which teacheth to deny the world, to love your brother, to leave all attachments to sects & partys and to be all united in love to one another and to love God in all things & above all things? What is to be said then against this voice? If the world would allow themselves to consider the great corruption, the great wickedness, the great folly this age is guilty of, they would be glad to hear a voice teaching them the means & ways to over come the same. For whatever the world thinks of | their own circumstances, if they do not repent   269
and amend their wayes, they will all repent it one day, but who so repenteth & listens to the voice, obeys what it commands, shall one day be thankfull for the mercy.

(*2*)   *Tuesday October 4, Stirline*
My freinds, consider your own circumstances. Consider what originall sin has brought upon you. Consider how that by originall sin ye have forfeited the use of all the creatures. Consider nothing is due to any creature. Since God Almighty is so very kind to the degenerate race of Adam as permitt him the use of the creatures, he ought to use them with all moderation & sobriety; for by excess of any thing they throw themselves into some inconvenient circumstance or other. By too much eating or drinking they incapacitate themselves from doing service either to God or man. Ought not then every person to be carefull what they eat or drink? These who are continually upon their watch will be carefull not to exceed in any thing however delicious the fare may be. But these who are content to live in | sensuality will take every thing they are inclined to. But my   270
freinds, the straight road to Heaven is by mortification of all your affections, by subduing your corrupt inclinations, by looking on your selves as no thing [*sic*] deserving, nothing owning that ye can do nothing, acknowledging that ye justly deserve nothing. These that proceed on this foot can be discomposed by nothing, for by the acknowledgement of their deserving nothing they lay aside the presumptuous thoughts of craving or asking any thing. The acknowledge-

ment of their deserving nothing makes them affrighted that mercys should be bestowed on such worthless creatures as they are.

Now my freinds, these are all wayes and means to bring a creature effectually in favour with the Son who dyed upon the cross for them. My freinds, these are means to bring a creature in favour with the Holy Ghost who sanctifies, comforts & supports them. These who are wise will take the advice, but the foolish will have no regard unto it.

(3) *Same day, Stirline*

271 My freinds, consider how much it derogates from | the power of God Almighty to say that every person has not free will. If the race of Adam had not free will who is to blame for the damnation of any? When creatures that has not [*sic*] free will run themselves into every evil whatsomever [*sic*], they have not themselves to blame for it. Where doth it land then? Must it not land on God Almighty who permitts them to do so and so? If the world beleive their wills are limited, that they can do no more good than they are permitted & that they can do no more evil than they are permitted, the creature cannot return thanks to God for their preservation & salvation, for so & so they were permitted & beyond that they could not go. Such & such rewards were appointed for them and that they expected, whether they merited it or not. And so the wicked, so much evil was permitted them to do, that they behoved to do tho' upon the doing of it they should be thrown into Hell. Now who is to blame for their damnation? Do they not level it against God Almighty who maintain that argument of *predestination*? Horrid blasphemy so to speak. Can the world beleive the great God 272 that made it can do an ill thing to anything he hath made in it? No, it is | not in the least to be credited. These who beleive & maintain such blasphemous opinions sett themselves in a road to that place to which they sett the greatest part of the world.[76]

---

76   Calvinist theology centred on the doctrine of predestination, which divided mankind into a minority, the elect, who were bound for Heaven, and a majority, reprobate souls who would go to Hell. Abden turns the Calvinist doctrine on its head, by arguing that predestination is so blasphemous that those who maintain it will go to Hell. While it might be tempting here to draw parallels with English universalist movements like the Philadelphians, Abden's argument reflects the views of Scotland's "moderate" Episcopalians, who challenged the Calvinist consensus of the Church of Scotland from the 1660s. Drawing on Arminian theology, moderates argued that predestination impeded human capacity to act morally, and began to stress the role of the Christian's own will in his or her salvation. In 1692, for example, the minister of Dunfermline, James Grahame, argued that by exaggerating the "impotence of human Nature", and teaching that the "far greater part" of worshippers was bound for damnation, Calvinists propagated a message of "pure Fatal-

If the world would consider what God is and what he has done for the world, they would be far from entertaining such harsh thoughts of Him. He made the world. He made man in the world a beautifull perfect creature stamped with His own image, breathed in him the breath of life, gave him a soul & gave him a will to exercise the faculties of soul & body as he thought fitt.[77] It is not to be thought that ever anything was taken from man that was given to him. No, that cannot be beleived. Wele you have account of the Fall of Man what was the occasion of it, which was by turning the heart & soul from the Creator and placing them on the creature. And by this, he brought all the creatures in bondage under which it groans heavily to this very day. Now is it to be thought that Adam could have been deceived if he had not consented to the same by the free will given him. Ye never have it sett down that | free will was taken from him. Is it to be doubted then but it still continues with him? 273

Wele, the next thing to be considered is, ye all beleive by Adams transgression originall sin in him and by him has been convoyed to all that came of him. Now consider if it be consistent with the goodness, the greatness & mercifulness of God Almighty to deprive mankind from the use of free will?[78] Is it not to be thought that Adams good qualities as wele as the bad were convoyed to us who live in this very day? Whoever doubts of the same will find themselves mistaken, but whoso beleiveth & exerciseth their will given aright will find it of great use. They find by the use & exercise of their free will, they have power to resist evill & to choose that which is good. Great enlargements might be made on this ⟨subject⟩ but 'tis enlargement enough to the world to know they have a free will that they may shun the evil & do that which is good. But these who do not beleive it keep themselves in such bondage that no advice, no doctrine, nothing that can be said or done can prevail to make them do what they should, they beleive that every thing | concerning them are predestinated makes them spleet on either one rock or other,[79] they either spleet upon despair or pre- 274

---

ity", which made God appear partial. NRS CH12/12/210, "Mr Graham of Dunfermline His Account of Presbyterian Principles & Doctrine", 1–2.

[77] The theory of the luminous Adam has its roots in rabbinic Judaism. See David H. Aaron, "Shedding light on God's body in Rabbinic midrashim: reflections on the theory of the luminous Adam", *Harvard Theological Review* 90 (1997), 299–314. Abden's source for this theory is Antoinette Bourignon, *Le Nouveau Ciel et la Nouvelle Terre* [The New Heaven and the New Earth] (Amsterdam: 1679), 51. The work was not translated, but the relevant passage is translated in George Garden, *An Apology for M. Antonia Bourignon in Four Parts*, trans. James Keith (London: 1699), 45.

[78] Abden's discussion here follows Bourignon's own account of providence, synthesised by her disciple, Pierre Poiret, in *The Divine Oeconomy*, vol. 6 (London: 1713).

[79] To split (Scots, *spleet*) on a rock is to err fatally.

sumption. And truly if anything be thrown away, 'tis no matter what the fall be if they be cast upon a rock all is one ruine.

(4) Same day, Stirline

The world may beleive without force of argument, there is no new doctrine here, nothing here but what has been taught formerly. But my freinds, the occasion of this, this very extraordinary appearance, is by reason & upon account of the great degeneracy, the great ignorance, the willful opinions, the different & many divisions of sects & partys.[80] Let the world but consider their circumstances. Let them consider what wicked, corrupt creatures they are. How many evils they are inclined to. How many sects they go upon to take them to Heaven, not considering the true & reall road. Are they not then greatly indebted to the God that made them? Are they not then greatly indebted to the Son that's willing to redeem them? Are they not then greatly indebted to the Spirit | proceeding from the Father & the Son who is willing to comfort, support & instruct them? Are they not greatly indebted to the blessed Trinity, who are pleased because it is their will to do it, to speak to the world by a voice through the organs of illiterate creatures,[81] proclaiming to them to forsake the world, & every affection to part withall, to mortifie themselves in everything, to love their brother as themselves, to love God in all things & above all things, to lay aside all attachments to sects & partys?

Now let the world consider if they are not safe to take this advice whoever dictates it to them, but when God himself declares it is himself by all he can do. When he declares it is himself, calling himself by the name of Jehovah, which name a heretick durst never assume, a name so sacred that the preist [sic] under the law pronounced it but once a year. Who needs doubt then but this is Jehovah who speaks by the name of Jehovah.[82] My freinds,

---

80 The moderate Episcopalians argued that factionalism—"divisions of sects & partys"—arose because people concerned themselves with religious externals, rather than piety. They argued that these divisions arose over *adiaphora*—things indifferent to salvation. Divisions would disappear if we focused on developing our inward relationship with God. This theme is pervasive in their writings, but see, for example, [George Garden], "To the English reader, of whatsoever party or perswasion", in Bourignon, *The Light of the World* (London: 1696), iii.

81 "Illiterate" here refers to theological illiteracy, not an inability to read. Mystics privileged unlettered ministry. The Scottish group believed that women, like Bourignon, were better able to receive the word of God because they were unburdened by worldly learning. See, for example, Garden, *Apology for Bourignon*, 2. Abden makes a sustained case for unlearned ministry at LR, fols 201–202.

82 Abden's point is that the prophets were not merely relaying God's voice, but He was liter-

I know what the world calls for, they call for miracles to prove the mission, but this is not to be granted. Indeed, where there is a new doctrine introduced into the world, there's great occasion for miracles to | perswade them of the truth of it, but when there is nothing but a voice instantly proclaiming to putt in practice what has been formerly reveald to them, there is no occasion for miracles there. God Almighty is kinder to these that strive to serve him than to grant them miracles, for they may beleive that miracles are very dear bought, & to work a miracle to the wicked world is more than will be done, he knowing it only hardens them more and more, he knowing that they know the Devil can work miracles & so they are as far from beleiving as ever.[83]

276

Now my freinds, consider whats to follow upon the back of this extraordinary appearance. You will very speedily see the glorious appearance of the Son of God upon the face of the Earth.[84] This voice, however the Instruments may be persecuted, this voice, as I the great God that liveth & reigneth forever and ever, ⟨hath said it⟩ will sound in some part or other to the end of the world, and it is for want of preparation that hinders this voice from being sounded out of the mouth of every man and woman. There has of a long time, methods been laid down, | to prepare the world for this voice, but little considered, many instructions to self denyall and mortificaton, many instructions to silent prayer, many instructions for laying aside their own activity, that God might act all. Now if every person will but take this method to dispose themselves for an extraordinary effusion of the Spirit, they'l find it very effectuall, they'l find it working not only by them, but in them, in such a way & manner as can not be spoke to the world. The world may beleive what is said, for as truth itself has said it, it is truth.

277

---

ally speaking through their bodies. This became an active point of contention among the Scottish mystics. See note 133 below.

83   Most Protestant theologians argued that the age of miracles had ceased. Although many of the prophets initially believed in miracles, they came around to this "cessationist" argument in 1708, after predictions that the prophet Dr Thomas Emes would rise from the dead proved to be incorrect.

84   Bourignon claimed the true prophets called people to inward moral reformation. False prophets claimed to know when Christ's kingdom would begin. This was the Age of Antichrist, which preceded Christ's thousand-year physical reign on Earth. Following the lead of the French Prophets, Abden here calls for people to both inwardly reform *and* claims to know that Christ will appear "very speedily". The debate between Abden's supporters and critics, like George Garden, arose over whether she could hold both these positions concurrently.

(5) *Same day, Stirline*

Ye men of this generation, ye will not beleive the judgments that are immediately hanging over your heads. The judgments are very great, and as they are very great so are they very near, even, so to speak, att the door.[85] These that beleive will prepare themselves, but these that will not beleive must do [so by] their own wills. This, this, this very language was plainly spoke sixten hundred years ago and every age since.[86] Some person or other has been alwayes stirred up | to tell the same that every person might be prepared for the judgment they were to be brought to. Now consider the length of time. Must not the world some tyme come to an end? I hope the world beleives so. Wele have they not reason to be thankfull that before the great overthrow, which is to be very speedily, have they not reason to be thankfull that God Almighty is pleased to proclaim to the world by the mouths of so many, that the world is near an end, that now is gone out the midnight cry?[87] Now consider whats meant by the midnight cry ere we go any further. Consider a wicked corrupt generation, all in darkness by reason of originall sin and actuall transgression. Much may be said to discover the thick darkness that's overspreading the world immediatly, many parts of it who never heard of God. Is there any thing there but darkness? Great darkness. Yet Gods ways to them are best known to themselves. Consider again the Christian world, how much darkness is there? Some pretending one thing, some another, yea, to come nearer hand, so to speak, what darkness in every sect? Some thinking, I'm better than my brother, I do better things than he. If there were not great darkness would any person be guilty of doing so & so? | Wele then my freinds, is not this midnight cry very seasonable? Is it a cry to be sent to the farthest corner of the Earth to bring all to the knowledge of the God that made them, to bring all to the knowledge of the Son who redeemed

---

85   The French Prophets and the Scottish followers of Bourignon were all pre-millenarians. They maintained that the reign of Antichrist would soon end, inaugurating Christ's thousand-year reign on Earth, prior to the last judgement. The differences between them concerned whether anyone, apart from God, could place a date on Christ's appearance. Drawing on the Gospels' condemnation of prophets of the last age (Matt. 24:11, Mark 24:11; Mark 13:22), Bourignon argued that the surest sign that a prophet was influenced by the Devil lay in his or her claim to know the time of the apocalypse, and this was used by George Garden to condemn the prophets. For the French Prophets' apocalypticism, see Laborie, *Enlightening Enthusiasm*, 81–86; for Bourignon's view, see, for example, her *Confusion of the Builders of Babel* (London: 1708), 25; and for Garden's censure, see Henderson (ed.), *Mystics*, 213, George Garden to James Cunningham, 2 December 1709.

86   That is, in the Book of Revelation. Tradition (and modern scholarship) dates the Book of Revelation to the reign of the Roman Emperor Domitian, who reigned from 81 to 96 A.D.

87   Matt. 25:6.

them, to bring all to the knowledge of the Spirit who is willing to sanctifie, comfort & support them? This midnight cry which is now in the world in diverse places theroff crys to every party to be united into one.[88] It crys to every person to humble his own eyes in the sight of his brother. Now consider the world. Consider the cry & see who can say ⟨any thing⟩ against it? Further have we not sett down many threatnings against the Earth, the inhabitants theroff, before the great day of accounts? Look what the Revelation of St John the Divine, which was revealed to him in the Isle of Patmos, ⟨says⟩. Consider the judgement of the four horses.[89] Consider the plagues of the seven vials.[90] Now my freinds, these must come to pass before the end. Consider then if every person has not need to be very much prepared, for who shall be able to withstand one of them.

Consider the many Scriptures to persuade you of the truth of the nearness of the approaching plagues. Consider the | many wars for a long tract of years in diverse places.[91] Consider the famine in diverse places.[92] Consider the plagues begun of great deaths both naturall and supernaturall, so to speak, both by batle and by diseases.[93] Consider again the vessall preparing to send to the outmost corners of the Earth that Jew and Gentile may be brought in.[94] My freinds, the end is very near and these who do beleive will be prepared. These who are content to hold with the world will perish with the world. The world may beleive what is said for they will in a very short time see it come to pass.

280

---

88 The Scottish mystics were well informed of the international nature of the French Prophets' mission. The prophets' German warnings circulated in manuscript in Scotland, and James Cunningham was kept informed of missions as far afield as the Ottoman Empire (Falconer MS, fols 38, 157–168, 312).

89 Rev. 6:1–8.

90 Rev. 16.

91 In 1701, Catholic and Protestant states (including England) formed the Grand Alliance against France, which supported the claims of Philip, Duke of Anjou on the Spanish crown. The War of the Spanish Succession lasted until 1714. Many mystical movements, including the Philadelphian Society, called for peace in the conflict.

92 The ongoing famine in East Prussia killed forty-one per cent of the population. Cormac O'Garda, *Famine: A Short History* (Princeton, N.J.: 2009), 92.

93 A plague epidemic swept through East-Central Europe during the Great Northern War (1700–1721).

94 In 1709, the Society in Scotland for Propagating Christian Knowledge was founded. It aimed to spread Protestant Christianity to "popish and infidel parts of the world" (NRS GD95/1/1, Society Charter).

(6) *Wednesday October 5, Stirline*

How can I be but greived to see the great folly of them of this generation who have dayly signs and wonders openly held forth to them and they not thinking any thing att all of any thing that's done or said. Is not the wonder very great to see by the mouth of illiterate creatures, to hear words going from their mouths, sufficient to bring the world to themselves. Again, the thing itself may be miracle enough, but when the doctrine is such 'tis miracle beyond their comprehension. It is so. But it is what they may comprehend, the substance of the thing as | suited to the capacity of every person who hears, that they may all comprehend it. But the case is with the world, they think themselves doing right things, going in right roads to Heaven, not considering what they are doing. So great is their folly. If the world consider that they are of the world, they have demonstration enough to make them beleive it. They love the world and the world loves them, is not that very plain? Is not that the case & circumstance of many of this age. Indeed it is so. Consider again these who are so kind to themselves as to consider what they are doing & see their doings are not right resolves to do so, no more resolve to leave the world, to leave everything in it, without regard of any evill the world can say or do unto them. These who are so disposed will be amazed, wonder & admire this, this very appearance, and these who come this length will assuredly by degrees, as they are able to bear, get discoverys of themselves, which discoveries will make them be glad & thankfull to do & obey whatever is dictate to them without curiosity of having reveald to them what is to come. But these who are of the world, hold themselves with the world, sett themselves out of the reach of new discoverys, either with respect to themselves or others. Now what can the world expect? No miracle is to be | given unto it in outward appearance, for these who hold with the world, find every discovery of themselves miracle enough, and these who hold with the world run, as it were, into a dungeon, where they can neither hear nor see.

(7) *Same day, Stirline*

My freinds, the agitations of the body is what none of you needs to be surprized with. Go read the history of the Old Testament in its originall, there you'l find the prophets of old had bodily agitations visible to all that beheld them, and the reason why it is so is this.[95] Consider mortals. Consider poor finite creatures

---

95 A similar argument was made by Richard Bulkeley in *An Impartial Account of the Prophets: in a Letter to a Friend* (London: 1707), 13–15. These arguments received short-shrift from churchmen, like Benjamin Hoadly, who lambasted Bulkeley in *A Brief Vindication of the Antient Prophets* (London: 1709), 21–34.

whose circumstances are so very narrow, whose vessals so very small, that they are not able to contain such a large degree, they cannot hold such outpourings of the Spirit. If they were able to operate on after a still manner, they would be killed, but for their preservation it goeth out in shakings of the body & crunching in the throat.

Now my freinds, the next question was what occasion have we for this? What need have we that such should be pitched upon & sent to us, since we have all already thats necessary for us? You say, wele you have all that's necessary for you. Indeed. But where's | the man that puts in practice? None of you. You are all equally guilty. Are you not then all greatly endebted to God Almighty that is pleased to speak to you in such an extraordinary way & manner?

The next question is: We're all spoken to in an extraordinary way & manner by the voice of our preachers, what need we any more? If we were taught aright by the voice of our preachers, ye would need no more indeed.[96] But so it is that which proceeds from the brain can go no further than the brain, the product of fancy can go no further than fancy. Wele then, you may object, if fancy & notionall conjectures be all we have, what should we do, since none of these things can profit the soul. My freinds, I'l tell you. Read the Scriptures of the Old & New Testament. Take them in the literall sense, simply as they are sett down. Putt in practice what they command you, and you'l find them sufficient to carry you to the place ye think ye are all going to. There you'l find you're bid leave the world, forsake the world & all things in it, turn from evil & learn to do good, have mean thoughts of your selves, love and esteem your brother, shun all strife & envy & foolish talking & every other thing that's necessary for your support upon your journey.

But say they, tho' we do all these, yet something is missing. A preacher, a teacher, or, so to speak, a minister is necessary to administrate the sacrament of baptism & the Lords Supper. Indeed, you say wele, for these things are necessary, since they are commanded. But let me see the man that can or dare confidently own before God & man that he is possessed the Holy Ghost & where that is wanting, where is his right? Can they make Christians by pronouncing the words or performing the outward ceremonies? No, my freinds, they cannot. Tis themselves that must make the Christian, for tho' it were so that you all have gott Christian baptism, yet till such time as you enter the Christian war-

---

96 This judgement reflects Bourignon's anticlericalism. See, for example, *Light of the World*, 16: "I may say with a sensible regret, that I know no true Priests who are simple Ministers of Jesus Christ, only to declare and interpret his word; because every one of them abounding in their own sense, teach that which is most sutable [*sic*] to their inclinations."

fare, you are no Christians.[97] Till you enter the batle against the Devil, the world & the flesh, till that is done, what can you be cald? Can a stranger passing thro' a countrey call himself by the title of a such a man when he knows nothing of them? Is it not reasonable to think he can do so? Wele then, my freinds, you might all be engaged in these battles before you can be called Christians, tho' ye received the outward ceremonies. My freinds, make good use of what you have heard and if you have ears to hear and | hearts to receive, you shall hear the next point discusst, that of the Lords Supper.

(8) *Same day, Stirline*
My freinds, you need not be affraid that any of you are not be imposed upon against your wills. Who is willing to part with sin, to forsake their former ways by loving the world, loving any thing in it inordinately? Who is willing to part with these things? Who is willing to part with every evil word or inordinate thought or every thing that discomposes them in the least? Who is willing to part with these things may come to be instructed by the voice to do whats good & refrain from evil? But these who are content to hold with the world the things of the world, to hold fast their corruptions & passions, these people are prooff against the voice, they need not care to come where it is. They will not be infected with anything that proceeds from it. More you are not able to bear it, else it should be reveald unto you. But for advice. Go home. Humble yourselves heart & soul, in body & mind, before the God in worship, the God that made you. Enquire of Him aright for His sake that dyed upon the Cross for all that are willing to embrace His example. Go | enquire with all seriousness what this voice meaneth & if you be sincere in your petitions you need not fear but you will be answered.

(9) *Saturday October 8 Stirline*
My freinds, ye must consider that every circumstance & every thing that falleth out to the sons and children of men, there is an overruling hand of providence in it. Now consider the goodness of Almighty God, that's pleasd to afflict the sons of Adam to see if by these means they can be brought to themselves. Some no sooner sett their face homeward than they meet with one disappointment upon the back of another. Their mortall enemy is very carefull & vigilant to

---

97 Antoinette Bourignon argued that this was the last age of the world, where there are "no more true Christians upon the Earth", because men and women follow "churches [and] societys", which are governed by a spirit opposite to the spiritual example set by Christ: Bourignon, "Antichrist Discovered", manuscript translation of *L'Antechrist Decouvert* (Amsterdam: 1681), AUL, 512, 4, 15.

throw before them everything that may fright them from going forward. But these who are stedfast & resolute do not want assistance to overcome whatever they meet with. Now that is one way the children of God are afflicted. The next thing is, no sooner Almighty God perceives the child to have good dispositions whatever, His inclinations may be He has not so much regard to them, but if He sees their dispositions such as he can have any | delight in them, He's sure to cross them in all their purposes & designs, that therby they may be brought to themselves, they are sett in a fair road to seek to him whom all their mercies do proceed. Now my freinds, if these two thoughts could gett place in the world, there would be no ground for discontent in any circumstance whatsoever. For if people once beleived that temptations & cross dispensations proceeded from their mortall enemy, they would with resolution step over them all. Upon the other hand, if they could beleive that afflictions and cross dispensations proceeded from the father of all mercies, who knows best what is their need, they would willingly and chearfully embrace the same. But the case is with the world, they think if they use the ordinary means & way, they are not to expect temptations, and so with all the rest, they think if they perform the outward forms that's sufficient to keep them from being more afflicted than their brother. But let the world consider that when God loves, He chastens and corrects severely every son He receives unto himself.

(10) *Same day, Stirline*
My freinds, the common objection is there is no occasion for this voice or any thing that can be taught by it, seeing as we have the Scriptures & preachers to explain the same. Indeed, if whats in the Scriptures were putt in practice, there would be no occasion for this, this extraordinary appearance. No, if the preachers were all of one mind, all teaching the same doctrine, making the same explanations of the Scriptures, there were no occasion for this way & manner of teaching. But consider the divisions that are now among us. Some calling themselves by one party. Some by another & which is worst, the greater part holding predestination, which is an opinion so very dangerous, next to damnation itself.[98]

But my freinds, to return, consider the same objections were in the days of old when the prophets were sent to speak to a rebellious, wicked people. Their answer was We have no need of these. Have not we the Law of Moses. What need have we of this mad fellow, this trembling fellow.[99] Look the original &

---

98 For Abden's view of predestination, see p. 172, note 76 above.
99 See Luke 22:71.

ye'l see they expressed themselves so. Look the Bible in the Hebrew tongue.[100] Now consider what it was, these they cald mad fellows were sent to warn them | off. Was it not to putt the law in practice? Was it not the putting themselves in readiness & being duely prepared for the comeing of the Son of God in the flesh, that when he came the world might not be in confusion & disorder? Now can any acknowledge the uselessness of the prophets? For first consider there were many generations in the days of the prophets which past ere the Son of Man came, that's to be granted. Yet the prophets called to all to be prepared for His coming, as if he had been to come in every age. He came effectually indeed to every age to them that beleived and were prepared for him. In these days, we have but a generall account of one prophet after another. But to leave that. Consider now the mission of the immediate prophets.[101] Do they not call the world to search the Scriptures, put in practice the directions given therein? Doth it not call to every man to humble himself in his own sight & in the sight of his brother? Doth it not call to every man to be reconciled to his brother & to love him as himself? Doth it not call to every man to deny himself & take up his cross, which is the safest way that ever was taken to go to Heaven? All these things considered, do not they then who practice the same putt themselves in a right road? | Do not they then who use these means prepare themselves for the Second Coming of the Son of Man, which will be very speedily upon the face of the Earth? No man almost beleives because it has been told them long ago, but that is a greater argument for it.

Now consider the goodness of Almighty God who knew the stuborness of the wills & heart of man, who would not beleive one prophet or two prophets, so to speak, but he has prepared many to proclaim this news to the world. Such an extraordinary appearance requires extraordinary preparation. Extraordinary preparation requires extraordinary means to stir them up unto it. Now my freinds, let the world consider what has been said. Let them search it & try if in it there be any heresy. If they find any, they are not obliged to beleive it. If they find none, let me see how they can be answerable for not listening unto it. These that do beleive will find it of great advantage to them, and those who do not beleive it will find it great folly when there is no time left for repentance.

---

100   Abden here turns to considering the prophets of the Old Testament, "in the Hebrew tongue". She may not herself have studied Hebrew, but Abden almost certainly knew people who knew the language. James Cunningham mentions checking a point of detail with "those who understand Hebrew". Henderson (ed.), *Mystics*, 204.
101   The French Prophets' missions in Britain.

(11) *Saturday October 8, Stirline Castle*[102]
My friends, if you would consider your own circumstances, you would see great occasion for an | extraordinary voice calling unto you upon many accounts. The first thing to be considered is, ye are not to expect two paradices, one in this life and another in the life to come. My friends, it is not the having abundance in the world that makes a paradice. No, but it is a taking too much delight in the things of the world, which delight invites their stay, and where once they'r invited to stay, they lay aside due preparation for the life to come. I do not say they lay it aside altogether, but they lay aside what is absolutely necessary. So my freinds, it is not one person or two or three thats guilty of this folly. No every person is guilty of it that places his affections on any thing but the Son of God who dyed the cursed death upon the cross. Every person is guilty of it that places his affections on anything but the Holy Spirit that supports & comforts every person that's willing to dispose themselves to receive it. Now my freinds, for further instruction, I'l tell you how ye shall shun a paradice in this life. The first thing that's to be done is you must of absolute necessity have low & mean thoughts of your selves. Ye must know that ye are nothing & that ye can do nothing. So when once ye come that length that ye are | nothing & ye can do nothing, yet then acknowledge ye deserve nothing, then when ye're perswaded ye deserve nothing, ye'l with all humility & thankfulness receive every mercy, returning the praise and thanks that's due to the giver of all. Now a person so imployed will be constantly giving praise & thanks to Almighty God. For is there an hour or moment that passes wherin they do not receive some mercy or other? Is there not then perpetuall occasion to return praise & thanksgiving to God the giver of every thing that's good? But the world will object & say, there is so much originall sin, so much corrupt nature about me, that I cannot be imployed. So att all times, something else I must be taken up with. Know my freinds, every thing that takes you up, takes so much of your heart from God and if ye knew or could be perswaded how great necessity there is for giving God all the heart, ye would be far from keeping back any part from him. Ye know 'tis the heart he requires & that of necessity it must be given. Now Almighty God is pleased to send a voice intreating the world not to serve him by halves any longer. This voice calls on them to take their affections from the world and the things of the world. Now where is | there occasion for being frighted att this voice when these are the baits the Devil holds the world fast by. And consider in every other circumstance & that of giving the heart fully to God. If

---

102 The Governor of Stirling Castle was John Erskine, 22nd Earl of Mar (1675–1732), keeper of the signet, and a close ally of Robert Harley, 1st Earl of Oxford. Many of his duties were taken on by his deputy, Lt. Col. John Erskine (1662–1743), his second cousin once removed.

the world take the advice they cannot be the worse of it, but if they reject it, they may therby incur great danger.

(12) *Monday October 20, Stirline*

My freinds, there are many things spoken by our Saviour and His Apostles that must not be taken in the literall sense. Consider the petition of asking dayly bread. If bread were to be asked & no more, no more were to be expected, but it is permitted for the race of Adam to ask under & in name of bread every thing they want. But my freinds, the true meaning of the petition is ye know, bread is cald the staff of life,[103] bread is good for satisfying the appetite of the hungry creature. By eating the bread people seldom go to any excess. It will be long ere bread make people drunk. It will be long ere bread suffocate the stomach or dull the senses. Now consider, as the petitioners putt in terms of bread, so the creatures ought to be used with all moderation.

(13) *Sunday October 9, Stirline*[104]

Let not my children go from this place whatever | they should suffer. If they be sent away by force they have not that to answer for. Now my freinds, consider what state & circumstance you are all in. Consider what the Son of God was upon Earth. He sent His disciples abroad in the world to teach & preach. Wele let the world consider that text of Scripture, when the disciples returned saying, We saw one casting out Devils in thy name & we forbid him because he followeth not with us. Now consider, my freinds, the answer, these that are not against us are with us.[105]

Now let the world consider what this voice calleth unto them. Doth it not call to every person to forsake the world, the things of the world, to humble him self in his own sight & the sight of his brother? Doth it not call to mortifie the corrupt inclinations & subdue the passions? Doth it not call to everyone to bear of his brother? Now my freinds, let the world consider the voice & the Spirit that sends forth the voice. When 'tis duely considered, may not they of this place be affraid of the Spirt that acts in them contrary to this Spirit. These who will consider do wisely, but who so slighteth the instruction, can reap no profite or benefite ⟨therby⟩.

Here end the publick warnings.

---

103 In English translations of the Bible, to "break the staff of bread" (Lev. 26:26; Psalm 105:16) is to diminish or cut off the supply of food. The phrase "staff of bread" was common by the seventeenth century.
104 This warning is placed out of chronological sequence. See introduction.
105 Mark 9:38–40; Luke 9:49–50.

2   Dutton's Letters (October 1709-January 1710) [GCA 562590]

1. [London, October 1709][106]
Madam,
The Lady Abden's case has been a great exercise to us, as well as our friendes in Scotland and the more, because of her piety, humility, | zeal for God, and resignation to His will in all which to us she appeared verry [sic] exemplary, but 'tis not altogether so, as has been represented to you. For none of the Inspired, ever thought or said, she had not received the visit of the good Spirit, and also spoke by it, tho' they are also satisfied, both from the nature of the thinges, and more fully from what the Spirit has done and said concerneing the same, that she has been under a great temptation, and that many thinges spoke and delivered by her have not been the pure dictates of the Holy Spirit, but proceeded from the influence of a foreign spirit[107] tempteing and seduceing her to uttere her own thoughtes, or his suggestions, as from the Spirit of God; But she has not been condemned by the Inspired here in the manner that has been related to you, nor have I knowen any case of the like nature, in which the Spirit has proceeded with more tenderness, than her's, so that wee are | perswaded her lapse has not been wilfull but through inadvertency, want of experience and temptation, and which if it please God to restore her again, may be to the making her, the brighter Instrument in His hand. For none of these thinges happen by chance, but by the permission of Almighty God, who by His infinite wisedom, can and will over-rule all thinges, for His own glory, and the good of those who love and fear him, and putteing their trust in Him continue faithfull.

What the Spirit here has done in her case, has been only this one of her Orders sent to Mr. Fatio, was by the Spirit in Mr. Marion, taken and torn, but nothing spoke theron. The like was done by the Spirit in Mr. Lacy on another to him, but all that was publick, was only at a meeteing of the Inspired upon occasion of ane Order in the same letter to Mr. Lacy. The Spirit by T.A. declared that the Order was not from this Holy Spirit.[108] Indeed, in private I had something

---

106   The letter is undated in the manuscript, but we can date it by its reference to Lady Abden's "Last Revelation", which was delivered between 22 September and 20 October 1709.

107   "Foreign spirit": The Devil. False prophets were believed to be inspired by the Devil, rather than God.

108   Nicolas Fatio de Duillier (1664–1753), the Swiss mathematician and disciple of Isaac Newton, acted as a scribe to the Prophets and compiled a list of the inspired; Elie Marion (1678–1713) was one of the original prophetic émigrés from France; John Lacy (1664–1730) wrote the first defence of the English mission and was himself inspired in July 1707. "T.A".

83 to the same purpose, on some | other Orders of hers, and the Spirit likewise both by signes, and otherwise, has to me declared, that the book called the Last Revelation &c. spoke by her, of which I saw the beginneing, was not by divine authority.[109]

This is all, from whence wee draw no such conclusion, as to beleive she has been altogether under the power, and posessed by ane evil spirit, nor have wee any warrant so to doe. For tho' wee have not mette with any case exactly like her's, yet there is scarce any of the Inspired but what have been tempted in the like kind, in one degree or other, and wee are as cautious of ascribeing that to Satan, which proceedes from God, as in receiveing that, as from God, which proceedes from ane evil influence.

Tis shockeing indeed to thinke, that a person who once has received the visit of the good Spirit, shou'd come thus under the temptation, and influence of ane 84 evil one | and deliver things in the name of God, false and delusory, but experience showes us it may be so, and tho' wee cannot fathom infinite wisedom in it, yet wee are made to see, it is not attended, with such frightfull consequences, as at first view seem to appeare. Nay no more than wee might expecte, in a work of this nature, if wee thorroughly searche the Scriptures, and make that our rule; For if our blissed Lord at the beginneing of His ministry, was led into the wilderness to be tempted of the Devil, and the tempter had power either to move his body or give him visions, or both, who shall plead ane exemption? Whenas [sic] that temptation of his may be as well to instructe us in the expectation of such assaultes, as to shew us the way of over-comeing.

It is perhappes a great error and the fundation of a multitude of false and erroneous doctrines and opinions, that many good and sincere soules have 85 fallen into, to thinke themselves altogether above the prevalency of | temptation, and that they are arrived to that pitch of spirituall discerneing, that Satan could never impose upon them, which to humble them for, and to lett them know, that it must be the goodness of God, not their attainements, must so preserve them, perhappes they have been suffered to be imposed upon by spirituall illusions from Satan, which they have taken for great revelations from God, and this I beleive many of the mystickes have fallen into.[110] Now it may

---

could be Thomas Alderidge, who is entered on Fatio's list. Geneva, Bibliothèque de Genève, Ms. fr. 605, fol. 7ᵃ⁻ᵇ.

109 This is evidence that Lady Abden's "Last Revelation" circulated among the London mission in manuscript.

110 The doctrine of "spiriutall discerneing", defined by Paul in 1Cor. 10, was concerned with distinguishing true from false prophecy, that is, prophecy which was given by God from prophecies used by the Devil to deceive people. For the prophets' use of this doctrine

be in the wisedom of God in His thus comeing to restore all thinges to destroye the power of Antichrist, to lett us see by what wayes he has gained ane empire, in the Christian worled, and that good and pious soules are not yet totally freed from his subtile attacks, and so long as wee are fully satisfied by unquestionable evidences that the work is of God, and that the Spirit super-intendes the same, we have no reason to desponde, or distruste God on such occasions. For that the Spirit does and | will discover, what is from Him, and what is not, in tyme and manner as wee are best able to beare it, so that wee need never feare being deluded to our heart, if we take the measures for satisfaction, the Spirit admittes and directes, tho' wee admitte this for a truth, that 'tis the Spirit only is the infallible guide to His Church and not that any person, tho' sometymes influenced therby, must therfore be at all tymes infallible.

86

This lesson wee have by experience learned and therfore receive or embrace not any thing, hastiely, because that ane inspired person has spoke it, but because wee are satisfied, it proceeded from the Spirit of God, and this I beleive might occasione Mr. Lacy to wishe that our friendes at Edinburgh wou'd not obey every Order by the Lady Abden's mouth without a clear conviction it was the will of God, because of the temptation he saw her under, which till she were delivered from, might be attended with unhappy | effectes, and to desire that others of more experience might be sent to Scotland, by whom the Spirit might rectyfie, what was out of order there;[111] and we esteeme it a great condescention of the Spirit to our weakness, to permitte us on all Orders of difficulty, to waite till the same be confirmed by three mouthes of unsuspected authority, if wee are, where they may be had—and it rarely happenes, but wee have a satisfaction in our own soules, before they are so confirmed, which makes us obey, tho' never so hard, to flesh and blood, with great chearfulness and resignation to the will of God, tho' in all cases doubtfull where such a confirmation cannot be had, we look on it more safe to obey than otherwise, tho' the same shou'd afterwardes appeare, not to have been right. For what wee did as to God with a pure heart, we can hardly think will ever be imputed, as a crime, tho' it was

87

---

and its sources, see Michael B. Riordan, "Discerning Spirits in the Early Enlightenment: The case of the French Prophets", in *Knowing Spirits, Knowing Demons in the Early Modern Period*, ed. Michelle D. Brock, Richard Raiswell and David R. Winter (New York: 2018), 265–290.

111 The English prophets, John Gyles, John Moult, Guy Nutt, Samuel Noble, Anne Topham and Anna Maria King, made another mission to Edinburgh in January 1710. They stayed until March, when all except Gyles (who was imprisoned at Edinburgh) left for Ireland. Dutton himself made subsequent trips to Edinburgh in May and again in September. Another mission from England was reported in 1711. See NLS 9847, fols 15–17; NLS Acc. 8592, unpaginated; Falconer MS, fol. 296.

not He that commanded it, wherenas disobedience ought to have verry good groundes for it | to prevente it being culpable before him where there is not evident tokens of the person's being under a temptation.

Wee are daily taught humility and a childlyke temper and wee daily see more and more, the necessity of our being so. For there are many stepes taken by infinite wisedom in this work, which at the tyme present wee cannot see through, and therfore the setteing up our own widedom, would be the sure way for us to stumble and fall. Wee thinke it certain wee may come to sure knowledge of what is a work of God, but 'tis tyme alone must discovere, what he for wise endes may permitte in it, which tho' it may cloude can never altere, what is certainly from him, and the Spirit, declareing so frequently, that now our Lord comes to sitte as a refiner, wee expecte every thing that may be a tryall of every grace proper to a Christian.

Wee have often seen thinges, that have been our present exercise and tryall afterwardes become subjectes of our rejoiecing, and praise to God, both because of the effect it has had on our own souls and also because wee have been made to see that the widedom of the Spirit therin, far exceeded what wee could have directed, and that it was our blindness and ignorance only, that made it a tryall. I doubte not but that this cloud at Edinburgh will be succeeded with a greater brightness, so that wee shall discovere infinite wisedome in the permitteing of it. Wee had our slumberings of Dr Emmes, they at Birmingham one of the like nature, one at Pulham, one as hard to beare,[112] and now you have your's at Edinburgh, which fulfilles what the Spirit has declared, that all who received this dispensation should do it, on the same foot with us, and that none shou'd be gainers by standeing aloof, whilst wee were fighteing in the battle; So that now | wee looke for cloudes and darkness to be round about him, only the chosen and humble, will have this advantage to beholde and walke by the pillar of fire whilest the oposers, proud and wise in their own conceites, will be ensnared and confounded by the cloud of darkness.

Madam, Mrs. S-r[113] must make apology for this liberty taken by, your humble servant,

Thomas Dutton

---

112   In December 1707, one of the English prophets, Thomas Emes, died. John Potter announced that Emes would be resurrected on the 25 May 1708. The failure of this prophecy led to divisions among the Prophets. Stephen Halford caused similar controversy at Birmingham, when he claimed he would be resurrected. Potter and Nathaniel Sheppard led a mission to Pulham, Norfolk, in February 1709. They were arrested, tried and released. See Schwartz, *French Prophets*, 113–115, 136.

113   Not identified.

2. | London October 27th 1709
My dearest and good friend,

    Last night at Mr. Toveys, I accidentally mett with our good friend Mr. D-s, who amongst other discourse, was speakeing of his haveing been with Dr Keith, Mr J. F., Mr. Ramsay or some of them,[114] but which I don't well remember, and there heareing it related, that wee had condemned the Lady Abden of not being acted by the same Spirit with us, a thing altogether false and what has not entered into our thoughtes, nor the Holy Spirit given the least grounde to suspecte. I haveing good reason to know how readey the Devil is to blowe about any thing prejudiciall to this work, was uneasey till I had gone this day, to waite on Mr. F.[115] at his lodgeing, least such a report might be spread amongst our friendes at Edinburgh. But not meeteing with him there, I trouble my good friend with this, to assure you that if any such report, should come to you, 'tis groundless and false, and wee are all, both by the effectes it has had on her own soul and the excellent Warneings wee have seen and also by the testymony of the Spirit abboundantly satisfied of the Lady Abden being really inspired with the same Holy Spirit, which wee have all drunke of. And the Spirit her not approveing of some Orderes sent, only shewes, that she has been under a temptation and has also erred for want of experience | but does in no wayes destroye or weakene the authority of the great communications of the Holy Spirit to her, nor ought to lessene our friendes esteem of her, only caution them and her, always to be upon a holy watch against the ennemy who will be overcome by the power of the Holy Spirit with her. There are severall who are bright instruments now, that in their first comeing out had severall thinges, tho' not of the like kind, yet of as stumbleing a nature, as those of the Lady Abden but humility, patience and prayer, makes them all turne to the good of the soul exercised therewith.

    If any of these things tende to the weakning of your faith in this glorious work of God, you so far answer the Devil's end, in promoteing them. For that is his main design, therfore lett these things only stirre you up, to walke more clossly with God and submitte to His will, putteing your trust in him, who will bring you | through all trialls and difficulties, and give you perfect peace in him.

---

114 The Quaker, Joseph Tovey, joined the Prophets in August 1707. Mr. D-s is unidentified. The other three are Scottish mystics based in London: Dr James Keith (*d.*1726) arrived in 1706 to practice as a doctor. Andrew Michael Ramsay (1686–1743) came south in 1709 to serve the Earl of Wemyss, who lived on Soho Square. J.F. is possibly James Forbes, later 16th Lord Forbes (1689–1761). An undated letter (within NLS Acc. 4796/104/B) places him in London around 1708–1709, but we cannot be certain of his movements.

115 Presumably the same Mr. J.F. mentioned at the start of the letter, i.e. James Forbes, later 16th Lord Forbes. See note 114.

Lett the externall part of this work goe how it will which you must never make the fundation of your faith, because you nor any one could ever keep pace with the footstepes of the Almighty, and therefore such a faith would be continually fluctuateing, now in heaven, then in the deep, as the face of this work seemes to our poor understanding that cannot always fathome it.

My love and service to your good land-lady, with my thankes for all the kindness she shewed us. I hope God has given her satisfaction in this work. If not, lett her but bringe her mind, to a pure resignation to His divine will, and truste to His guidance in her own soul, and upon such a disposition seekeing. I questione not but God in His mercy will vouchafe her a clear discovery of His divine hand herein.

There is ane error which I find some of her friendes are yet to fall into, in makeing the measures of God's dealeing with a private soul in order | to sanctification, the rules of His procedour in a publick work,[116] which is altogether wrong, and no way warrented by the word of God, which I beg you wou'd all make the rule and guide, and then you will find abundant reason, to beleive that God has indeed sent furth His voice, and that His Spirit has given warneing in your eares, which that you may all take, and answere His end to the glory of His name, and your own soules eternall welfare is the prayer of your servant in the Lord,

Thomas Dutton

3. | London, December 6th 1709

My dear friend and brother in Christ,

The Lord does try us all to the uttermost, yet none beyond what He gives them strength to beare, therfore | if wee putt our trust in Him, wee shall never be confounded.

If our tryalles were to come one way all men could not be equally tryed. But your future experience will informe you, that none will be established in a firm faith in this work on easier termes, than you and I. As the Spirit required a childlyke disposition, that you might receive from it, the first impressions of faith, so assure your self, that same frame of mind is to be continued, that you may be established therin.

---

116 Mystics argued that salvation was achieved by theosis—participation in the divine nature. Dutton's point is not that this might not be a legitimate personal goal, but that this was not how word of Christ's appearance was spread. When he heard about the prophets' mission to Scotland, Pierre Poiret argued that the mystics should not accept them on the opposite grounds, that "the kingdom of God comes not from external appearance and demonstration", but from within (NRS, CH12/12/669).

The mystery of iniquity which beganne to worke in the apostolick age, and has continued to worke ever since, has so woven and twisted it's errors, with the divine truthes and so authorized them by great bodies of beleivers therein, that nothing less than the Spirit of truth operateing | with great power, and brightness is able to divide, discovere and selecte from error, the scattered truthes, and recommende them in their native beauty, once again to us mortales, and nothing less than a mind entirely freed from prejudice, and loose to all things but the divine truthes, will be able to receive them. The way to make Babel fall, is by removeing the foundations on which 'tis built. Don't be in love with error, either for it's antiquity, or for the great names 'tis recommended with. Nor judge after the manner of the worled, for they for the most part runne by extreames, when truth for the most part is in the middle. I shall be sorry if what I mentioned to you should prove too hard a tryall for any, but yet I could not safely acquitte myself, without letteing you know what the Spirit had intimated to me theron.

It matters not how great truthes may be contained in that work when spiritually and mystically understoode. I for my part am satisfied, that it has not come so purely, from the fountain as that it ought to goe furth, stamp'ed with the divine authority of this Spirit. There is none of the other Inspired I know who, I thinke have read it, nor do I care that they should, unless more occasion be given for a solemn waiteing upon God by all the Inspired theron. I wishe I could but converse with your friend Katherine Orne, Isabel Cameron, James Garden &c.[117] I beleive I could satisfie them, that you all have reason to blisse God, because hereof, notwithstanding the great tryall 'tis at present to you, but the injurious practise of opening letteres, forbiddes me to speake these truthes which few when presented naked are able to beare and which the worled wou'd make ane ill use of. But the divine | guidance you are under, will in tyme manfieste to you what I meane and then you will see that this tryall, was for your good, as well as God's glory.

If I might be heared, and to as many as will heare, I wou'd again advise, that the Inspired wou'd goe to the fountain, with that light God has given them,

---

117 Katherine Orem *nee* Gordon (*d*.1732) was the wife of Thomas Orem, historian of Aberdeen. She was the daughter of William Gordon, and widow of Robert Keith, incumbent of Ballantrae in Ayrshire. The others are Isabel Cameron and James Garden junior. Orem and Cameron were inspired by the Holy Spirit. Cunningham reported one of George Garden's nephews was with Abden, and "went on [the prophets'] Mission". This must be the "J. G-n" who acted as Lady Abden's scribe: James Garden (*c*.1685–1772), son of James Garden. Sources: NLS 9847, fols 11–15, Archibald Lundie to James Lundie, 23 August 1709; Henderson, *Mystics*, 201, 206–207, George Garden to James Cunningham, 11 November 1709; Abden, LR, fol. 1.

which will more illuminate them, in the reall truthes of the Gospell than any mystick author whatsoever. This is the dawneing of the day, which will cause those other starres to dissapeare whose lightes were appointed for the night only. Those authoures will indeed be of use to describe the warfare of a spirituall Christian, and excite you like them to persevere in a constant pursuit of holyness, and doeing of the will of God. But the Spirit by them delivered thinges darkly; It wrapte up in mysterious termes many noble truthes. | But then 'tis only one illumen'd by the same Spirit that discoveres them for the literalle meaneing is altogether wide of the spirituall intention, and the wildest doctrines imaginable might be drawn from some of the mysticke authoures, if wee take that literally which they meaned in a mysterious spirituall sense; and this I take to be one of the errors palpable in the Lady Abden's book.[118]

120

I say thinges (my friend) that you will hardly be able to beare, but I don't doubt of the tyme comeing, when you will find these sharp remedies produce a wholesom effect, to the great peace and consolation of your own soul and I should not be your friend did I not deale simply and freely with you. God has wonderfully supported you under the first shock, and will continue still to supporte you and by many experiences you will come to know your faith is of God.

121   This letter I writte to you, and it may not be proper for any otheres perhappes to see it, but I wou'd beg of your friend not to be fond of, or builde upon the mystick principles. Your experience will informe you, they will lead you into no truth, but what the Spirit will, in its own tyme, more clearly teache you, and for want of a right understanding of their spirituall meaneings, you may be led into many errors, which tho' the Spirit will rectyfie yet it may be with some hard tyralls.

I don't remembere the wordes exactly but the Spirit upon my aplication to God thereon, threw it out of my handes and said some wordes, importeing it's not being of divine authority, but did not any way intimate to me in what part the errors lay, which rendered the whole unfitt for publick view, whether in that which I had, or in that which remaines, or in both.

122   I hope you will have mutuall consolation in the company of our friendes and that God's presence will in ane extraordinary manner be amongst you. My

---

118   Abden, LR, 293 warning of 7 October 1709. Dutton develops his earlier point about the legitimacy of mysticism. It could be useful for private devotion, but was useless for Christian evangelism, as Poiret and the Scottish mystics contended. His argument that mystical language often obscures divine truth may have influenced Pitsligo, who argued in one of his unpublished essays (NLS Acc. 4796/104/2) that the "lesser mystics" were too obscure. Poiret concluded, in contrast, that mystics needed to try harder to communicate.

prayers are continually for you, and I truste I have a share in your's. I am not come yet to a full satisfaction in the mystick's silent prayers, but thinke it is best to follow the practise and advyce of our blissed Lord, and His apostles, to aske from God such thinges as wee stand in need of, yet always with a resignation to His will. I'm certain God reguardes more the sincerity of the heart than either the manner or form of address, and 'tis safest treading in the ancient pathes, especially after such examples. My Christian love to your friend, and all our sisters in Christ,[119] from whom I should be glade to heare, and to all otheres our friendes.

You will find that divine truth more and more veryfied daily: "I will confounde them more and more".[120]

4. | London January 14th 1709[121]
Dear Sisters in Christ
Isabel Cameron, Katherine Orne,[122]

I had answered to the request in your letter to Mr. Garden in one I had just before sent to Mr. Gordon.[123] That what was spoke in me about the Lady Abden book (the exact | wordes wherof I do not remember) only intimated that it was not of divine authority, and so not fitt for a publick view, but in what part, whether in what wee have, or in what wee have not seen, or both, the errors were, I had no intimation at all, and I am apt to beleive with you, that 'tis in some of Antoinette Bourignon's accessory sentiments, and in some of Jacob Behmen's mistick theology, literally applyed and understoode.[124] The reason whey after this was signified to me by the Spirit, I was so forward to send it down was least the agreement of it, with any ones former opinions, should have prevailed to have printed it, accordeing to the Order, before the Holy Spirit had been consulted by the body of the Inspired; not that if any were

---

119 Reflecting a view common among mystical movements in early modern Britain, Scottish mystics argued that men's learning made them proud and therefore less able to receive divine inspiration. Women were better able to "receive God's Divine Light" than men. This explains both why women were the first to claim divine inspiration, and why many were convinced by their prophecies. Katherine Pringle, Lady Abden; Margaret Irvine, Lady Clava, Katherine Gordon, wife of Thomas Orem, Helen Middleton, and Elizabeth Young, widow of Gilbert Keith, all delivered warnings under divine inspiration.
120 Quote not identified.
121 A slip for 1710.
122 Isabel Cameron and Katherine Gordon, wife of Thomas Orem (see note 117 above).
123 Kenneth Gordon of Cluny (d. before 1741), an Edinburgh advocate.
124 Abden's warnings contained many of Antoinette Bourignon's accessory sentiments, unnecessary to salvation. There is no reason to think Abden had read Jacob Boehme.

dissatisfyed therewith that single authority, should be esteemed sufficient to barre all further examination.

I look upon the great trialles the Lady Abden has gone through, to be lessons (amongst | other wise endes) given for your instruction, and I doubte not that good soul will yet again truste God, rather than man, and be brought back into His house. Her case shewes you what temptations the Inspired are exposed to, and how that faith and trust in God, are in ane especiall manner required in this day.

I rejoice to heare of the work of the Spirit goeing on, in order to gratifie you, for instruments for God's glory. Some of the Warneings of the Lady Clava I have seen, which have all the signatures of the divine Spirit.[125]

I have seen some specimens of the strange language spoke by our sister Orme,[126] which to the best of my memory, is either the same, or like, to what was verry frequent with me at first, and still remaines at tymes, to this day, tho' the meaneing therof I have never had, but 'tis it is generally attended, with a holy elevation of the soul as if I were singeing hymnes in the courtes of God, and I beleive is a token of a great effusion of the Spirit wherever it is given.

Remember now you are ministers of God for others, and therfore His operations in you will be different, than when he workes in you, only for your own sake. Be content to be any thing in the handes of the Spirit, so that God may be gloryfied therby; you have one advantage above many that are called, in that you had been before taught to deny yourselves, and in the happy advances you had made, towards a victory, over all the corrupt desires of nature. This work will shew you the truth of that doctrine and the reall necessity of all, and more than you had before been taught.

I doubte not, that you frequently experience, the peace of the soul, enjoyeing God, and consolations proper to the Holy Ghost the comforter, beyond what wordes can expressse; Treasure these up, for you will sometymes be suffered to be hungry, and know a day of want, which is not token of God's displeasure but ane evidence of His love. For our happynesss being in the | enjoyment of God, and that enjoyment arriseing on our right desires, God in His wise instruction, so chequeres the smiles of His countenance, with the seemeing hideing of His face, as the soul he loves, may continually be keept in ardent breathings after Him, and also know the value of His favours.

---

125 Margaret Irvine, Lady Clava, was the daughter of James Irvine of Crimmond. In 1701, she married Hugh Rose, the 4th laird of Clava, a Jacobite (*d*.1744). Some of her prophecies can be found in DUA BrMS 2/5/3, unpaginated.

126 Katherine Orem (see note 117 above).

Expect you to meet with temptations more strong and violent, and in which Satan will appeare more visible than ever to you he did before; for God is qualyfieing you to be instruments in His handes by whom He will comforte, directe and deliver those, whom Satan afflictes, and that you may know both his devices, temptations, power, and the condition of the soul assaulted by him, and be able to administere, advice and comfort, with a true sympathy, and knowledge of the case, 'twill be necessary for you to have gone through or experienced somewhat of the like kind your selves; not that this will be the only end, whey they are permitted. For they will | turne to the advantage of your own soules, many wayes, as well as be profitable for the sake of others. 128

Therfore always have confidence in God, who will never leave you, if you forsake not Him. Keep a soul truely humble, and teachable as a child, and then these trialls will be of shorter duration. Every great truth the Spirit has made me sensible of, has gennerally come through the fire of a temptation, by which I have been made to see, I really knew nothing, that none but God could helpe me, and so with desires to be taught, throw my self at the footstools of His grace, which proceedeing teaches, that the soul, that hopes to be taught of God, must come clean as a white tablet, or at least bringeing no precious opinions but such as it desires God wou'd raze out if they are not agreable to His will.

Be not startled at any thing that occurres in this work. For tyme and God's instruction will make it evident to you, every thing is | done and permitted, with infinite wisedom. What therfore you at any tyme understand not, wait only with patience, and when it is most fitt, both for your good, and God's glory, you will be made to see the wisedom therof. 129

Think not that you are only to speake warneings to mankind. No! That is only one branch of your ministry, but you are instruments in God's handes, to many other purposes, as your more knowledge in this work, will make evident. Therfore be always resigned to God's will, lett Him use you as he pleases.

I wou'd recommende to you the study of the Scriptures, rather than the mystick authours, not that I thinke some you esteeme, were not divinely illumin'd.[127] But whilest you may drink at the fountain, I wou'd not have you seek to the rivers, nor seek light from the starres, when you may have it from the Sun.

---

127   Dutton does not have any specific mystics in mind, but the attempts to catalogue a group of mystical authors who had received divine inspiration. This process began with Augustine Baker, and was taken up by Scottish mystics, like James Garden, who produced a "Catalogue de plusiers auteurs qui on écrit de matieres Mystiques et qui les ont éclairies" (NLS Adv. 25.5.3, fols 3ʳ–5ᵛ), later published by Pierre Poiret in *Bibliothecca Mysticorum Selecta* (Amsterdam: 1708), 321–351.

The Spirit now openes thinges more | clearly, because now the Sun is riseing, and this is the beginneing of the day, whose light will eclipse the starres, tho' of never so great brightness. The worled could not beare in plaine termes, then, what now the Spirit appeares in power he will have them informed of. Therfore his instructions were veiled with a cloud of mystick expressions, which made them uninteligible, to all but those, that obtained illumination from the same light. By which meanes, they passed undiscovered by the careless observers, and stole into the heartes of the seekers of God; and you may observe the nearer they came to this day, the more clear were they in the truthes, the Spirit now causes to be proclaimed, which as it demonstrates, on the one hand, the unity of the Spirit, so it proves on the other, the advantage you have with respect to light, above them in their day; but what I speake of here with respect to doctrines. For as to any | meanes they propose to bring you nearer to God in holyness of life, use it, till God enlightenes you in a more perfect way, which ever stand ready to receive. And be assured in the mean tyme (that you may not condemne any that walke not exactly in the path with you) that God reguardes more the sincerity of the heart, and the earnest breathings of the soul, than any way or mode whatsover; So that what bringes us to have, the most pure, and earnest desires, seemes to be the most perfect way.

A gentleman in the west of England, in a letter to Mr Tovy, takes notice of it, as a piece of providence, for which he blisses God, that when last in town in a booksellers shop he mette with, and bought, the apology for the writteings of Antoinette Bourignon.[128] He saies, tho' he had no doubt before of this being the work of God, yet that ingenious authour has aboundantly strengthened and furnished him with arguments, | he thought not of before. Besides that he finds these thinges and this appearance fortolde by Antoinette Bourignon her self, which judgment verry much differes, from some at Edinburgh, who have sent up word, that tho' her writteings dispose people to inquire, yet not to receive this message.

I hope God's Spirit enables you to remember me in your prayers, I assure you, you are oft a subject in myne. Lett me heare from you, and lett us builde up each other, in our most holy faith. Wee have many ennemies both within and without, both spirituall and carnall, but in the strength of God shall wee destroye them, and God's strength is with us to conquere, so long as wee obey his voice, and keep our selves from the accursed thing, from hideing in our heartes any thing impure in his sight. For as He is holy, the inhabitants of his kingdom, must be holy also, which that wee may all be, is the prayer of your brother in Christ,

Thomas Dutton

---

128 The Quaker prophet, Joseph Tovey (1667–1737); [Garden], *Apology for Bourignon*.

Pst. Pray my love and service to ⟨---⟩ I have writte this post a long letter to ⟨---⟩ none of my good friendes in Edinburgh must take it amiss, that I have not in particular by letter, acknowledged their kindness before, the tyme I have to spare is pretty much employed in writteing and yet I am sadly in arrear to many.

Cunningham's Letters [GCA 562590]

1. | Barnes 27th December 1709

As I'm well satisfied that what my dearest friend desires as to my letters being more full proceedes from verry good, humble and pious motives, so I know not, if any consideration of my own interest, be sufficient to justyfie my not complyeing with them. But then, my dearest will be so kind, as to writte me any particular subject, on which he wou'd desire to know my thoughts and then if any thing occure to me, either from my readeing or small experience that I thinke can be of use to you, I shall imparte it | verry freely and without reserve, leaveing the issue to God, who I know will never leave to themselves such as endeavoure to acte from a sincere intention of doeing His will in every thing.

What that person[129] affirmes of his own feeelings is verry easey to be accounted for, and I know nothing I need adde to what I said in my last on that subject, but this gennerale rule, that in all our spirituall exercises, we ought to propose nothing of sensible taste or pleasure, no particular method, in fine nothing, but the pure and simple will of God, receiveing all equally from His divine handes, consolation, or desolation, light or darkness, sweetnesses or ariditys, a sense of his divine beatyfieing presence, or ane insensibility of that and every good. All ought to be indifferent to us, since they are the effectes of that same infinitly wise, and tender care of our heavenly Father. Yea were we to make a choice, it shou'd be that God might please, to lead us in the dark and narrow pathes, where nature can find no support, nor nurishment, where we can reste on nothing but God, since this is the most safe and speedy way to perfection, and we shou'd be glade to do nothing but suffer here, that all our pleasures and enjoyments may be reserved for that tyme of rest, which our God has prepared for His own, and which is shortly to be revealed. Lett us, my friend, laboure to do nothing that may hindere us from entering into it.

You do well to read Molinos[130] or any other book, that can be a help to draw you, to your inward recollection, but I know not if 'tis absolutely safe to propose that or any other book as a generalle direction in our way to Heaven. The true

---

129 Andrew Michael Ramsay. In his previous letter, Cunningham worried about Ramsay, who was in "a very serious Strain" (Falconer MS, 236).

130 Miguel de Molinos (1628–1696), Spanish mystic and author of *The Spiritual Guide* (1675). Molinos gained European fame when his works were condemned by the Papal Inquisition. The case prompted outcry from European Protestants, thanks to the exiled Scottish minister, Gilbert Burnet (1643–1715), later Bishop of Salisbury, who wrote about the Quietist controversy in the first of his *Three Letters Concerning the Present State of Italy* (London: 1688), 1–51. Burnet's work was translated Dutch, German, Italian, and French. In France, the first letter first appeared separately as an account of the Molinist controversy.

mystickes have only wrote such thinges, as they found in their own experience. Now, tho' this must wonderfully influence the heart of a sincere reader, with some sparkes of that holy flame, that consumed their corrupt natures, and also pointe out unto Him, the generale way, which they all after their master, trode unto perfection, yet as divine grace alwayes accomodates it self, to the infinite varieties of our naturall tempers, and constitutions, 'tis scarce to be supposed that any two saintes now in Heaven did walke exactly the same footstepes, tho' indeed all in the same narrow path, and therfore, we can scarce affirme that any one of their examples, or experiences, is a sure and generale direction to us, by which to regulate all our stepes. The eternall Spirit of God, the light that shines in every one of our soules, is the only secure, infallible rule, and director unto us; all creatures, all dispensations of providence, in fine every thing shou'd serve only as so many powerfull calles to lead us inward to hear the gentle still voice of that one true sheepherd | which all his sheep do know, and will follow. All this would seem to make against Molino's system ament outward directors, but I had not that in view, not thinkeing as I said last, that 'tis of any use with relation to our present circumstances, and therfore I industriously avoide to entre into that enquiry. I received the letters you sent me, and as I much approve of Dr James Garden's, so I'm somewhat suprized at his brother's.[131] I can as little know my self in some characters he gives me as him in his way of argueing. Nothing in it stumbles me in the least degree, except what he sayes in one paragraph of a letter of Mr Dutton's to ** which I shall transcribe part of "what the first have done in her case, has been only this. One of the Orders sent to Mr. Fatio was by the spirit in Mr. Marion taken and torne; the like has been done by the Spirit in Mr. Lacy, in another to him, and all that was publick, was only at a meeteing of the Inspired upon occasion of ane Order in the same letter to Mr Lacy, the Spirit by T.A. declared the letter was not from the Holy Spirit, indeed in private, I had something to the same purpose on some other Orders of her's, and the Spirit likewise both by signes, and otherwise, has declared to me that the book called The Last Revelation, spoke by her, of which I saw the beginneing, was not of divine authority".[132] I confesse this, particularly the last sentence, lookes somewhat odd, and therfore I | wou'd gladely know from you, what truth is in it, and also if it were not uneasey, to have a full distinct account, of all that was done in that matter at London, and in particular if any of the

---

131 Cunningham's correspondence with George Garden is printed in G.D. Henderson, *Mystics of the North-East* (Aberdeen: 1934), 199–262. Cunningham refers to Garden's letter of 2 December 1709 (208–221). James Garden's letter has not been traced.
132 Garden's letter is printed in Henderson, *Mystics*, 215. Garden here quotes from Dutton's letter of October 1709, Falconer MS, fols 82–83 (see pp. 185–186 above).

Orders, that were condemned, are pronounced in the name of Jehovah.[133] Nor wou'd I think it amiss, that a particular exact narrative were written of Withrow's case, since you see it proves a great stumbleing-block to friends as well as enemies, to which I am perswaded, the true matter of fact, wou'd be the most effectuall answer, and our friendes at London might be wrote to about it, if you at Edinburgh are not sufficiently inform'd of all the circumstances.[134] I must beg your advice how to answere the Drs letter, for as in the one hand one that knewes his dispositions might think he only wanted fuller information, and to have all the reasonnes that conclude in favours of this dispensation, as fairly laid before him, as he seemes to have the prejudices against it, so on the other hand, I may by frequent experiences, have now sufficiently learned, what little effectes my letters or discourses, can have on this occasion. My last letter seemes but to have rooted his prejudices the more,[135] and what better success can I expecte from another? Probably God designes to use no humane meanes in this affair, to have no testymony from man that all the glory may be given to Him, to whom all is due. Lett me know also, what you thinke as to writteing to | Mr. Poiret. I have no copy of what I writte to Dr Garden, and so knowes not if it is proper to send it to one who knowes nothing of me, much less do I incline to writte to him.[136] You'l writte to me dearest every thing that occures. And send if you can, the book of Warneings, and don't fail to recommende me to the prayers of all our friendes. It has pleased God these ten dayes, to permitte that my life should be more exposed to unavoidable outward distractions than before, may His holy will be done, may I have strength from Him, to beare this cross, since I was indeed unworthy any longer to enjoye that profound retirement I had been blissed with some tyme before. I know my God, cannot quenche a flax that smokes never so little, and I truste he will make all to worke together for my good; To whom be glory, dominion and praise, worled without end, Amen.

Adieu

---

133 Henderson, *Mystics*, 216: "It seems still a prejudice to me and not a small one against this appearance, that all the warnings are given out as spoken immediately by God himself; not in the stile of the ancient prophets as messengers and embassadors from from God to declare his will, with a Thus saith the Lord; but as if it were God himself the great Jehovah speaking immediately by the organ of their tongues."

134 Abraham Withrow split with the mission over the failed resurrection of Thomas Emes in 1708. Withrow started to believe that only he had been faithful to the Spirit's command and argued that true prophets should embrace worldly poverty. Under inspiration, John Lacy alleged he had been possessed by a "lying spirit".

135 Henderson, *Mystics*, 199–208, James Cunningham to George Garden, 11 November 1709.

136 Pierre Poiret (1646–1719) was the leader of a European-wide drive to publish mystical theology and had connections with several mystical groups in Britain.

2. | [n.d., to the same]

The outward distractions, I complained of in my last, still continue, and all the comfort I have is to retire as oft as I can, and throwe my self without limitation or reserve into the handes of Almighty Love, to be done and disposed accordeing to His good pleasure, endeavouring to be indifferent, whether in consequence to that act I feel any returnes, of that inward silence and solitude I sometyme before enjoyed, or be left (for my | punishment or tryall) to suffer under the tormenteing images, of these things, which my heart had in its extraversion, gone out, after in any degree. I know my self unworthy to taste of the goodness of God, of these refresheing consolations, a moment wherof is far beyond ane age of wordly [sic] pleasures, and therfore 'tis my duty to lay my hand upon my mouth, and chearfully, from a principle of justice, submitte to what I now feel. Besides, I wante from my experience to know the truth of what I wrote to Andrew Ramsay. "That perfection consistes not in any particular virtue or state of prayer, but in ane absolute conformity to the divine will".[137] By these and such other considerations, I endeavour to supporte my sometymes droopeing spirits, and I often reflect on the infinite wisedom, love and power of our God, who can, when numerous armies of Egyptians (cruel infesteing thoughtes) surrounde us, when we appear shutt up betwixt the mountaines, and the Red-Sea, I say, he can than worke a mighty deliverance for us, and will infallibly do it, provided we follow that divine advice (Exodus 14.13), Fear ye not, stand still, and see the salvation of the Lord. Then indeed the Lord Himself, shall fight for us, while we shall hold our peace, silenceing all our murmures, distrusteing our own activities. This is again | revealed in the 20th Chapter of the 2 Chronicle which I'd recommende to your perusall.[138] I know not, my dearest friend, but you may use some such method in your own case, but lett us never truste to this, or any other act of our own. The consolations of the Holy Spirit can alone supporte a soul, under sufferings sent by Himself, who will never suffer us to be tempted, above what He enables us to beare, if we continually flye unto the Lord Jehoavah, who is our everlasting strength. As to anxiety, my friend, it ought to be entirely mortyfied and subdued. We ought not to be surprized to find any new imperfection in us, rememebereing that we have in our selves nothing else. This should but sinke us more into the view of

---

137 Paraphrasing NLS Acc. 4796/104/B, James Cunningham to Andrew Michael Ramsay, 3 January 1710.

138 After Moab invaded, the prophet Jahaziel told the Jews to trust the Lord in battle against the enemy. The key text is verse 17, where the prophet recommends stillness, or quietude, in spiritual battle: "Ye shall not need to fight in this battle: set yourselves, stand ye still, and see the salvation of the LORD with you, O Judah and Jerusalem."

our own nothingness, and make us so absolutely despaire of our own strength, and endeavours, that we may continually throwe our selves without reserve, on Him, who alone can worke any good in us, yea helpe us to thinke the least good thought. Any anxiety for want of any degree of virtue, can only flowe from the Devil or nature, and is a sign, that our desire of that virtue or degree, did flowe from some interested or selfish principle. The use we ought to draw from it, is, that it may prove a new motive to abbandone and silence all particular desires, since even when most | specious, they flowe from a corrupted source, in that generale one of the accomplishment of the will of God. May He operate upon us in what manner he pleases, advance us either speediely or slowly, deliver us from this or the other imperfection, or suffer us still to groane under it, as He sees can most conduce for His own glory, while we continue silent and passive under all these divine operations, which however different to our narrow viewes, are at the bottom the same, as all tendeing to the same ende, and wrought by the same unchangeable beeing, who is yesterday, to day, and forever the same.

I thank you for all the papers you sent me. I returne you Mr. Dutton's two letters; the last of them and somethings in the first, I think not proper to be showen, but to a verry few, I owne to you, my friend, 'tis the most shockeing thing I have mett with since I beganne to look into this dispensation. Tho' the substance of all he saies, may perhappes be true, yet there are some expressions in both, I think not so verry cautiously and prudently said. He is but little acquainted with the mystickes, or he wou'd find all to flowe from the same spirit, and all leadeing to the same end of draweing us inward to hear in the fund | of our soules, the voice of the one true sheepherd. I have in my former letters to you, told you sufficiently my thoughtes of the mystick writers and of the use they can be of, and of the conduct of the Inspired, and others in relation to them, so I need adde no more, on that hand. As to the Lady Abden's book,[139] all I ever saw of it, pleas'd me verry well; I'm pretty sure some partes of it beare the characters of the word of God, nor could I discovere any error in what I hear'd, or read of it (unless that which you observed, and perhappes that is none either) yet probably that verry thing has offended Mr. Dutton joined with the many accessory opinions in it all new to him. What the Spirit did or said by him of it, seemes to ammounte to less than so absolute a formal condemnation, tho' indeed I shou'd be far from adviseing it's being published stamped with the authority of the Spirit. I know not if any projected that till it shou'd be confirmed by more of the Inspired, but I wou'd not thinke it improper for

---

139 Abden's "Last Revelation".

more of them to beg the divine direction as to this point. You may, my dearest friend, thinke | me too rash in opposeing the sentiments of one who has been long under the immediate influence of the Holy Spirit, but I venture on it, only to your self and am so distrustefull of my own thoughtes therin, that I can't hindere my self to beg of God to blocke this matter entirely out of my memory; Far from inclineing to writte to Mr. Dutton himself, as you wishe about it. I shou'd only wishe to know if Katherine Orne[140] or others of our friendes are as weak in this point as I. I shall endeavour to writte something to Dr Garden again[141] next week and send it to you to furthere or not accordeing to your discetion. But I know less than ever what to say ament that particular of the | book.[142] How easey were it for him from Mr. Duttons to forme a scheme of the designes of ane evil spirit in this dispensation to overthowe mysticism. But O my friend, how does all these difficulties evanishes when God vouchafes one glimspe of His countenance. Pray writte me what becomes of good Mr. Gyles and of every thing else that occures.[143] I had yesterday a verry refreshing letter from—. She lately mett with the Lady Abden. But O! What poor accountes she gives of her self, and her state. She owies her self unable to argue, but yet is fully convinced of the delusion, but does not pretend by any higher | authority than that of Mr Patrick Middleton or Mr. Lacy.[144] I thinke I need say no more but recommende my self to the prayers of you and all our friendes. While I live, I will blisse the Lord, who has brought me into the knowledge of them and His truth, and will be unalterably yours
James Cunningham

3. | Barnes 7th March 1710 [to unknown correspondent at Rosehearty]
I can assure you, your letters are no less agreable to me, than you say mine are, but yet I know not, how far I can complye, with your desire in writteing more fully. I wishe always to writte to you, under a sense of the divine presence, and the more that is vouchafed unto me, the less occasion do I see for writteing much. I shall however touche at the particulars in your's, and if any thing else

---

140   Katherine Orem (see note 117 above).
141   Reading "again" for "against".
142   Abden's "Last Revelation".
143   John Gyles travelled to Edinburgh in January with John Moult. He was apprehended and placed in custody for 23 months (NLS 9847, fol. 15ʳ; Falconer MS, 259–260).
144   Patrick Middleton, deprived Episcopalian minister of Leslie in Fife (1662–1736); the prophet John Lacy. For Lacy's censure, see Falconer MS, 82–83 (pp. 185–186 above). According to Patrick Campbell of Monzie (1675–1751), after hearing Abden's warnings in Stirling, Middleton told her "she ought to reckon herself deluded considering the failures of many of her predictions". NLS Acc. 4796/104/B, Monzie to Andrew Michael Ramsay, n.d.

occurre to my mind, sett it down, without further reflection. I reckoned when I wrote my last that ⟨-⟩ had been in town, which made me propose a thing I see now the folley of. O! When shall all our activities be mortyfied, when shall I cease therby to retarde the work of God? Perform this in me, O Lord, for thou knowest, I can do nothing. I am much comforted with what you writte, that our friendes are not at all stumbled with this seemeing failure, I pray God they may all make that use of it, to disengage themselves, still more and more from the outward thinges, from all reflections upon, or anxiety about, them, leaveing the whole affair to God, who will in his own | tyme, show that every step made in it, was the effects of ineffable wisedom, of boundless mercy. Lett us make it all our study, to minde the one thing necessary. Lett us look upon all outward eventes, as so many occasions, or calles from God to turne inwardes, there alone we can find true peace, and quiet. Thou Lord will keep him in perfect peace, whose mind is stayed on thee, because he trusteth in thee. Lett us therfore truste in the Lord for ever, in the Lord Jehovah our everlasting strength. What you writte of ⟨-⟩ state and feelings is verry comfortable to me. 'Tis indeed our duty to draw that advantage from all our failieings, therby to become the more sensible of our nothingness, our innability to do any good, or resiste any evil, that so we may see the necessity of a more closs dependance on our God, of a continuall waiteing upon Him, and of elevateing our heartes unto Him, without ceaseing. I felt my self also on Wednesday under a more than ordinary influence of the Holy Spirit, but without any impression of Katherine Orne speakeing, rather indeed to the contrary. Thursday I went to ⟨-⟩ where I was keept by bad weather till Sunday, and all that tyme as my formall recollections, could not be so long, and uninterupted as while here, so I thought I felt a more continued sense of the divine presence, my mind never wholly turned outward, and the moment I was left alone, my state was more | recolected and silent, than ordinary. These 2 dayes again, I have been under great aridity and distraction,[145] my mind drawen outward, by thinges that uses not to have that effect upon it, and in prayer a thousand idle foolish thoughtes, forceing themselves as it were in. O! May I by all this variety learn in every state to be content, to have no will, no desire, no choice of my own, but blindly throw my self into his mercyfull handes, who I know will order all this for my good, if I continue to waite faith-

---

145   Jeanne Guyon argued that in a time of "aridity" or "dryness", one must "suffer the and suspensions of the consolations of God" and "wait patiently" that one's life "may grow and be renewed". Eccl. 2:3, quoted from Jeanne Guyon, *A Short and Easie Method of Prayer* (London: 1703), 20. The Scottish mystics were primarily responsible for Guyon's European influence. The translation seems to have circulated in manuscript in Scotland before it was printed. Henderson, *Mystics*, 44, 196.

fully upon Him. O! May He ever be praised, who not only powerfully calles, but in a manner irresistibly drawes his poor, unworthy creatures into wayes He has chosen for them and leades them in pathes they have not knowen. What tho' we should be led by this all gracious hand even to the valley of the shadow of death, since e'en there He has promised to be with us to supporte us by his staff (i.e. faith) to cause us understande his will, and ennable us to performe it?[146] O! May we never cease to praise Him, may we even in the way of his judgements still waite upon Him. Lett the whole desires of our soul waite upon Him. Lett the whole desires of our soul be still to Him, and then when he has wrought all His workes in us, he will in his own tyme and way ordaine peace for us. Lett us not expecte that perfect peace, till the war be at ane end, till all his ennemies in us be overcome, till He has by the brightness of his comeing, | subdued all our rebellious lustes, desires, thoughtes and inclinations, till all self-will, and self-love, all love to the worled, and things therof be destroyed in us, till every thing of the creature be done away, then shall all our soules, be filled with that peace of God which passeth all understanding, then shall the Prince of Peace, come and dwell with us, and make us one with Him, as He and the Father are one. When we consider that glorious end, lett us not faint and be discouraged, however dark and rough the way may seem, that leades unto it. But I have said too much. I shall not answere the letters you sent me till next week, and then I know not how to answere. When I have so many repeated proofes, how little good my activity does in this matter, may not that sufficiently teach me to give it over, I beg to have your advice herein. 'Tis indeed strange these at [Rosehearty] shou'd in this matter acte so inconsistently to their own principles. Cou'd the thinges they firmly believe divine, have stood against all the cautions, and try-alls, they wou'd now use. If a worldling shou'd repeat their wordes and applye them to Antoinette Bourignon, how could they shun the force of them but as we now do? Has not Antoinette Bourignon in innumerable places affirmed the present teachers to be the false Christes and false prophets?[147] Yet such ane insinuation now is thought unjustyfiable. Could our Lord forwarne us of false prophets and not tell us the markes, to know them by? And yet now by their fruites they are not to be knowen. You | suggeste a verry just answer, to what they say of signes and wonders, but besydes do not the Romish clergy pretende every day to outward miracles, and I beleive other sectes do the like, tho' these are not knowen, but amongst their confidents. If you know any thing of this particular, you'l please writte it, because I wou'd asserte nothing in fact, but what

---

146 Psalm 23.
147 Matt. 24:24; Mark 13:22. Bourignon discusses these passages in *The Academy of Learned Divines*, vol. 1 (London: 1708), 58–69.

cou'd be sufficiently avouched. The 17th Luke from v. 20 is paralell to the 20th Matthew and there we are expressly told "That the Kingdom of God is within us" in opposition to the "Lo' here", "Lo' there" of the false prophets.[148] This is a key to understanding all these textes, which 'tis needless now to enlarge on. But above all, 'tis strange, that to these, who read and admire the mystickes, internall silent prayer shou'd become a suspicious exercise, or that they wou'd have hindere soules from yeildeing to the divine attraction, therto to engadge them to a more low more humane method or understande our Saviour's directions according to the naked letter. Well! May God opene their eyes![149] Which I nothing doubte of, being persuaded that what they do, is through ignorance, and proceedes from a zeal to his glory. The Almighty may showere down His mercies on you all, and perfecte the work he has begunne, in the earnest prayer of &c.

---

148   Luke 17:20–21: "And when [Jesus] was demanded of the Pharisees, when the kingdom of God should come, he answered them and said, The kingdom of God cometh not with observation. Neither shall they say, Lo here! or, lo there! for, behold, the kingdom of God is within you."
149   Acts 26:18.

CHAPTER 12

Thanksgiving and the Apocalypse: Two Eighteenth-Century Sermons

Warren Johnston

Introduction[1]

The two documents included here are Joseph Jacob's *Desolations Decypher'd and the Kingdom of Christ Discover'd. In a Sermon Preacht the 23d of the 6th Month, 1705. Being the Day of Thanksgiving For the Late Success of the Army, Under the Conduct of John Duke of Marlborough* (London: 1705), and Richard Dobbs's *A Remarkable Accomplishment of a Noted Scripture Prophecy, as Applied to the History of England During the Last and Present Centuries, in a Thanksgiving Sermon* (London: 1762). Each of these documents contains an extended explanation of apocalyptic prophecy published in the form of a sermon for a thanksgiving day. Jacob's sermon was for the 23 August 1705 (Old Style [O.S.]) thanksgiving day celebrating victories during the War of the Spanish Succession, and Dobbs's for the 29 November 1759 (New Style [N.S.]) thanksgiving for military successes in the Seven Years' War (1756–1763). Due to their length and intricate exegetical structures in places, it is unlikely that the published forms of the sermons were delivered in-full from the pulpit on the occasion; however, there are elements of the sermons, such as mention of the specific events being commemorated and rhetorical structures addressed to the audience, that give the suggestion that some parts of the discourse were presented orally by the preachers on the thanksgiving days themselves.

It has been claimed that millenarian ideas were "too dangerous a doctrine for pulpit orations."[2] This assertion that Anglican preachers were not willing to share apocalyptic ideas with their congregations fit nicely into the perception that prophetic and millenarian convictions, Anglican and dissenting alike, were in sharp and rapid decline after 1660, and had been largely the product of the political and religious unrest of the mid seventeenth century. Yet the two

---

1 I thank Lionel Laborie for suggesting changes and additions that have made this chapter stronger. I also thank Lisa Parlee for helping me prepare the initial typescript of the sermons.
2 James R. Jacob and Margaret C. Jacob, "The Anglican Origins of Modern Science: the Metaphysical Foundations of the Whig Constitution", *Isis* 71 (1980), 259.

documents included here belie the disappearance of apocalyptic belief in England after the Restoration, proving its availability to those beyond the academic and scholarly pale by locating it in the early and mid eighteenth-century pulpit and press.

The difficulty in locating apocalyptic ideas in sermons is due, in part, to the nature of early modern conventions. Most printed sermon titles contain great detail regarding the place, date, occasion, and audience of a particular sermon's delivery, but often little description of the main subject or even the biblical text the preacher expounded upon. John Tillotson's 1692 *Sermon Preached before the King and Queen at White-Hall, the 27th of October, Being the Day Appointed for a Publick Thanksgiving to Almighty God, for the Signal Victory at Sea: for the Preservation of His Majesty's Sacred Person, and for his Safe Return to His People* is illustrative and gives some indication of the ambiguous and generic nature of such descriptions: not only is the main theme not indicated (though one might guess that the recent military campaigns and the return of the king to England would play some part), but tertiary or tangential expositions on biblical passages and theological ideas are impossible to determine. It is only by reading through sermons systematically and completely that such refrains become apparent. In this case, it was Tillotson's assertion that a recent naval victory over France at La Hogue was a signal that the destruction of the beast and mystical Babylon—notably accompanied by the mention of ships and sailors in Revelation 18:17—had begun.[3] Though the titles of the two sermons chosen for inclusion here are somewhat more descriptive of their subject matter, it is still not evident that their content focuses directly and entirely on apocalyptic convictions.

The presence of apocalyptic ideas in the interpretation of events of great national consequence built on the foundation English scholarly prophetic exegesis that was established in the seventeenth century. Both Jacob and Dobbs demonstrate some recognition of this tradition, if only in passing. In his explanation of the description of the Church of Thyatira, Jacob applies and acknowledges Henry More's exposition of the prophecies of the second and third chapters of the Book of Revelation (p. 226 below). More was a Cambridge scholar and one of the most prolific expositors of apocalyptic prophecy during the Restoration. In turn, Dobbs mentions Henry More also, as well as Joseph Mede, crediting "the learned Mr. Mede" with identifying the prophetic import-

---

3   John Tillotson, *A Sermon Preached before the King and Queen at White-Hall, the 27th of October, Being the Day Appointed for a Publick Thanksgiving to Almighty God, for the Signal Victory at Sea: for the Preservation of His Majesty's Sacred Person, and for his Safe Return to His People* (London: 1692), 31.

ance of the growth of popery during Charles I's reign (pp. 242 and 248 below). Joseph Mede was another Cambridge scholar and, until his death in 1638, was a contemporary of More's early years at Cambridge. Mede's *Clavis apocalyptica* (1627; second edition 1632) advanced the concept of the synchronization of Revelation's various prophecies, interpreting them as occurring historically and into the future over the same chronological period, but with each emphasizing different aspects of prophetic fulfillment. Mede's ideas, and More's later advancement of them, became the standard approach in English apocalyptic exegesis for the next century and a half.

Despite this fleeting homage to their famous predecessors, both Jacob's and Dobbs's prophetic interpretations deviate from that exegetical model. Each has their own particular views of the accomplishment of apocalyptic prophecy and each work contains variations on the understanding of prophetic meaning. In this they display the continued influence of apocalyptic belief in the eighteenth century, while also demonstrating that these interpretations were still vibrant and adaptable to a variety of situations and interpretations.

Joseph Jacob (c.1667–1722) was a dissenter who began his training as a Congregational minister after the Revolution of 1688–1689 and the implementation of the Toleration Act.[4] By the end of the 1690s he had a substantial London congregation and ministered to a new meeting house in Parish Street, Southwark. However, his strict rules, which included forbidding members from attending services at other churches and from marrying outside the congregation, caused his followers to dissipate by 1702. He moved on to congregations at Turners' Hall in Philpot Lane, and later Curriers' Hall, Cripplegate.[5] Jacob's severity and abrasive nature, as well as the suggestion of his ability to alienate his audience, is apparent in his 1705 thanksgiving sermon. The Preface to the work includes the statement of his expectation that his ideas would be labelled "Cant, or Nonsence" and that they would be censured (p. 217 below). His concerns about congregational purity are also evident in his condemnation of occasional conformity at the end of his Preface (p. 217 below).[6]

4　Alexander Gordon, 'Jacob, Joseph (c.1667–1722)', revised by M.J. Mercer, *Oxford Dictionary of National Biography*, online (http://www.oxforddnb.com/view/article/14572, accessed 30 December 2015).
5　Gordon, 'Jacob, Joseph'.
6　Occasional conformity was the practice of non-Anglican Protestants attending Church of England services to take communion in order to be able to serve in public office. The issue was being debated in Parliament during the time of Jacob writing, and it was eventually banned through legislation in 1711.

The circumstances that instigated the sermon are mentioned at its outset. Jacob opens with an acknowledgement of the successful government of Queen Anne (r.1702–1714) and the military prowess of the Duke of Marlborough (1650–1722) (p. 210 below), that "Heroick General" as Jacob calls him in the last paragraph of the sermon (p. 240 below).[7] It becomes apparent, however, that Jacob views the recent victory at the Battle of Elixheim, in the War of the Spanish Succession, as far more significant than just the advancement of English political and martial interests.[8] Choosing Ezekiel 21:27 as his central biblical text, Jacob applies the phrase "overturn, overturn, overturn" to characterize the year's achievements and, more importantly, interprets these events as significant indications of prophetic accomplishment. The bulk of the sermon is then devoted to an explanation of the meaning of apocalyptic prophecy.

To prove the applicability of his chosen text to the end times that lead up to Christ's return to earth to establish his eternal kingdom, Jacob explains "overturning" in reference to the meaning of a number of prophecies from Revelation, including the letters to the seven churches (chapters 2–3), the seven trumpets (chapters 8–9, and 11:14–19), the two witnesses (chapter 11:1–13), and the woman in the wilderness (chapter 12), as well as the time periods mentioned in association with several of these prophecies. The influence of the predominant characteristics of English historicist apocalyptic exegesis is evident in Jacob's "synchronization" of these prophecies as episodes occurring concurrently along the same timeline. However, Jacob departs from that tradition in several important aspects. Though he locates his own time, in the early eighteenth century, as contemporaneous with period of the fifth trumpet (p. 227 below), Jacob steadfastly refuses to assign specific dates to the beginning, and thus to the completion, of each of Revelation's prophecies. His comment that previous precise chronological designations had "foild all Mortals" and have proven other interpreters "Lyars" (p. 229 below) demonstrates his purposeful departure from a prominent element of historicist inter-

---

[7] John Churchill was made the Duke of Marlborough by Queen Anne in 1702, after his military successes against France. Marlborough achieved a number of important victories in the first decade of the eighteenth century, during the War of the Spanish Succession, many of which were celebrated by general thanksgiving days in Britain. The most famous of Marlborough's victories was at the Battle of Blenheim on 13 August 1704 (N.S.), where he led a combined British, Dutch, and Austrian army to victory over French and Bavarian forces: J.R. Jones, *Marlborough* (Cambridge: 1993), 90–97.

[8] This battle (also known as the Passage of the Lines of Brabant) occurred on 18 July 1705 (N.S.) in the Spanish Netherlands: James Falkner, *The War of the Spanish Succession 1701–1714* (Barnlsey: 2015), 110; "Chronology", in *The Oxford History of the British Army*, ed. David Chandler and Ian Beckett (Oxford: 1994), 434.

pretations of Revelation, including those of Mede and More, who had both attached dates to their prophetic timelines.[9]

Another variance is Jacob's refutation of the idea that the Antichrist is a single entity or institution. Typically, English exegesis viewed Antichrist, along with Revelation's images of the dragon, the beast, and the false prophet, as collectively symbolizing erroneous ecclesiastical doctrine and policy, and most often assigned it to designate the Roman Catholic Church and the papacy. Though he agrees that these images symbolize false policy and practice, Jacob denies the usual anti-Catholic interpretation, instead maintaining that these three figures constitute three distinct aspects of Antichrist's character. According to Jacob, the dragon represents Satan, who inhibits the people's ability to properly follow Christ. The beast depicts secular powers that oppose Christ's interests in the world, and the false prophet signifies corrupt ecclesiastical authorities and false churches. Though he avoids making explicit application of this imagery to particular contemporary persons or institutions, Jacob shows some animosity towards religious officials and churches in his explanations. He associates the attributes of the false prophet with those "who make Gods of their Priests" (p. 233 below) and he criticizes those who have high offices in the church but are "guilty of Wickedness" (p. 236 below). Jacob's dissenting stance is also evident in his characterization of the Reformation as having only occurred partially through "pretences to Spirituality" (p. 226 below), and more aggressively so in his earlier mention of the "the Sins of Apostatiz'd Professors" and the "Priests in our Age [...] their Faces so hid with the Hair of Whores" (p. 219 below).

As mentioned above, it is likely that Jacob enlarged his original sermon for later publication. Evidence of this can be found, for example, in his explanation of the meaning of the Greek letters designating the number of the beast, and the Greek phrases used to designate the man of sin and the son of

---

9   Joseph Mede saw the first six seals (Rev. 6–7) as the history of the early Christian church up to the time of Constantine; the seventh seal, which encompassed the seven trumpets, covered the period up to the fall of Rome (imperial Rome continued in papal Rome); the pouring of the seven vials (Rev. 16) coincided with the last two trumpets and signified the progress of the Reformation leading to the final destruction of the papacy. Mede placed his own time in the period of the fourth vial, which was being fulfilled in the events of the Thirty Years' War. Henry More largely followed Mede's interpretive framework, though his explanation of Revelation's prophecies emphasized the importance of the Church of England in fulfillment of the apocalyptic plan, with the second and third vials signifying the reforms carried out by Edward VI, Elizabeth I, and James I. More believed that he was living during the period of the third vial. See Warren Johnston, *Revelation Restored: The Apocalypse in Later Seventeenth-Century England* (Woodbridge: 2011), 11–13, 135, 140, 143 n. 81.

perdition that would likely have gone over the heads of most of his congregation. He also includes several tables (pp. 231 and 238 below) to summarize his ideas. These aspects, along with the overall length of the printed sermon (thirty-two quarto pages), suggests that the original work was augmented for publication.[10] However, Jacob's declaration of his purpose to "refresh" his audience members' "Memorys" (p. 225 below) regarding his previous discussions of the prophetic accomplishment of the end times, and later his intent to "discourse these Things unto our Information and Edification" (p. 239 below) in the future, intimate that apocalyptic exegesis was a topic that fitted comfortably into his public preaching.

Richard Dobbs (1694–1775) was a Church of Ireland clergyman. He was educated at Trinity College Dublin, where he earned his B.A. in 1723, M.A. in 1724, and his Doctorate in Divinity in 1750.[11] He was appointed rector of Tullyhogue, County Tyrone in 1731, and then rector of Lisburn, County Antrim in 1743, where he remained until his death in 1775.[12] His thanksgiving sermon was originally delivered in Lisburn in November 1759 but it was not published until three years later in London. Like Jacob, Dobb's apocalyptic views were inspired and influenced by his particular ecclesiastical outlook and affinities, and like him as well Dobbs believes the victories being celebrated are prophetically significant. However, unlike Jacob, Dobbs's position was fully in support of Anglican

---

10   This kind of augmentation of sermons from the form delivered orally was common in the early and mid seventeenth century, when *ex tempore* preaching or delivery from very brief notes was preferred. However, by the late seventeenth century it was becoming more usual to use detailed notes, and as the eighteenth century progressed, more and more preachers were writing out their sermons for delivery, a practice which facilitated the publication of a copy very close to the sermon given from the pulpit. See, for example: Arnold Hunt, *The Art of Hearing: English Preachers and Their Audiences, 1590–1640* (Cambridge: 2010), 12–13, 131–135, 180, 182–186, 393–395; Ian Green, "Orality, Script and Print: the Case of the English Sermon c.1530–1700", in *Cultural Exchange in Early Modern Europe, Volume I: Religion and Cultural Exchange in Europe, 1400–1700*, ed. Heinz Schilling and István György Tóth (Cambridge: 2006), 237–238, 240, 248; Josef Carlson, "The Boring of the Ear: Shaping the Pastoral Vision of Preaching in England, 1540–1640", in *Preachers and People in the Reformations and Early Modern Period*, ed. Larissa Taylor (Leiden: 2001), 282; Jennifer Farooq, *Preaching in Eighteenth-Century London* (Woodbridge: 2013), 9–11; Françoise Deconinck-Brossard, "Eighteenth-Century Sermons and the Age", in *Crown and Mitre: Religion and Society in Northern Europe Since the Reformation*, ed. W.M. Jacob and Nigel Yates (Woodbridge, 1993), 111–112.
11   W.P. Carmody, *Lisburn Cathedral and Its Past Rectors, with an Appendix* (Belfast: 1926), online (www.lisburn.com/books/lisburn_cathedral/cathedral-2.htm, accessed 30 December 2015).
12   Carmody, *Lisburn Cathedral*.

church structure and doctrine, and his interpretation of prophecy was much more specific in its application and viewpoint, as well as in its chronological precision.

At the outset of his sermon, Dobbs declares that the fulfilment of Revelation's prophecy of the seven churches is "particularly applicable to the national Church of England" (p. 243 below). He further argues that this prophecy is similar to the description of God's creation of the world in six days, which he uses as an analogy for the creation of the "present happy British Constitution" (p. 243 below). He then proceeds to explain this political "creation story" in a series of six successive twenty-year increments that summarized the political affairs of each of the periods. These began in 1620 with the emerging distinction between "the Promoters of absolute Power, and the Godlike Rule of a free Monarchy over free Subjects" (p. 243 below). His depictions of important constitutional achievements (parliamentary legislation such as the Petition of Right in 1628, the Bill of Rights in 1689, and the Protestant Succession in 1701) and the political setbacks (the promotion of absolute power, the dissolution of the constitution during the Civil Wars, and the brief period of Tory ascendancy at the end of Anne's reign) during these times make Dobbs's Whig sympathies readily apparent. With this explanation complete, the bulk of the sermon is devoted to Dobbs's paraphrase of the prophecy of the seven churches found in chapters 2 and 3 of Revelation, with particular reference to developments relating to the Church of England.

In expounding the meaning of this prophecy, Dobbs again covers the period from 1620 to 1760 in twenty-year intervals, with each of these periods corresponding to one of the churches.[13] As he had done for the political landmarks along this timeframe, Dobbs now identified the developments in the church over these years based upon his own particular ecclesiastical stance. The Church of England and its clergy had suffered at the hands of "Sectarian", "Puritan", and "Popish" interests (pp. 247–248 below), and were punished for its inadequacies by the removal of the church establishment in the 1640s and 1650s. However, "the faithful Sons of the Church of England" were rewarded with the reinstatement of the Church of England at the Restoration (p. 249 below). The final securing of the Established Church in the Revolution of 1688–1689 paralleled the constitutional settlement of the same period that Dobbs had described previously.

---

13 For Dobbs, the church of Ephesus (Rev. 2:1–7) represented the years 1620–1640, Smyrna (2:8–11) 1640–1660, Pergamos (2:12–17) 1660–1680, Thyatira (2:18–29) 1680–1700, Sardis (3:1–6) 1700–1720, Philadelphia (3:7–13) 1720–1740, and Laodicea (3:14–22) 1740–1760.

Dobbs's exegetical framework is highly original and idiosyncratic, departing considerably from traditional historicist interpretations that described the fulfilment of the prophecies of Revelation being carried out over more than 1500 years. Not only did Dobbs compress this timeframe into several centuries, but he also applied this prophetic accomplishment very specifically and narrowly to the political and religious circumstances of Britain. Such an explanation had the added benefit of fitting very nicely into the thanksgiving occasion with which the sermon was associated, celebrating as it did the accomplishments of the British constitution and the Church of England.

In addition to this national political and ecclesiastical progress, Dobbs also assigns apocalyptic meaning to several other events and developments in the seventeenth and eighteenth centuries. One of these is the advancement of scientific knowledge. Dobbs specifically identifies Francis Bacon's thought, "the Light of experimental and civil Philosophy" (p. 257 below), with the morning star in Revelation 2:28, and he includes the foundation of the Royal Society among the successes of the period after 1660 (p. 244 below). Like Isaac Newton, Dobbs also connects this improvement of knowledge with a growth in understanding of scriptural prophecy.[14] Elsewhere, however, he associates the flaws identified in the Sardian and Laodicean church prophecies with the Arian, Socinian, and Deist controversies in the first half of the eighteenth century (p. 258 and 261 below), as well as with the an overly literal understanding of scripture on the one hand, and the over dependence on "mere human Reason" on the other (pp. 259 and 264 below). Again showing his Whig colours, Dobbs marks the end of the Philadelphian church period with Robert Walpole's fall from political power in the early 1740s (p. 260 below).

In the final section of the work, Dobbs carries his chronological applications to their Millennial conclusion. Early in the sermon he identifies his main biblical text, Revelation 6:2, which describes the appearance of the white horse and its rider going out to conquer at the opening of the first seal. He connects this image with the armorial insignia of the Duke of Brunswick, who defeated the French in the Battle of Minden on 1 August 1759 (N.S.),[15] and with Britain's monarch (pp. 246 and 266–267 below), giving his apocalyptic predictions an immediate currency. Then, using this as an anchoring point, Dobbs lays out another series of twenty-year periods that coincide with the opening of the

---

14 See, for example, Stephen Snobelin, "'A Time and Times and the Dividing of Time': Isaac Newton, the Apocalyse, and 2060 A.D.", *Canadian Journal of History* 38/3 (2003), 546 and note 17.

15 This battle was part of the Seven Years' War. It was one of the victories being celebrated in the 1759 thanksgiving that this sermon was associated with.

seven seals and then the sounding of the seven trumpets: with the overlap of the seventh seal with the first trumpet in 1880, Dobbs predicts that the seventh trumpet will inaugurate the Millennium in the year 2000 (p. 266 below).

Like Jacob's, it is doubtful that Dobbs's sermon was originally delivered orally in exactly the same form as it was later published in 1762. Its length (over fifty-eight octavo pages) would have been prohibitive. However, it is not unlikely that Dobbs would have felt comfortable in delivering some shorter form of his apocalyptic message, along with its celebration of his particular political and ecclesiastical proclivities, to his congregation on the occasion of military and national triumph. And he, like Joseph Jacob, promised his audience an exposition of prophetic meaning (in this case the 2300 days in Daniel 8:14) in the future (p. 245 below), demonstrating he was clearly at ease with delivering such messages from the pulpit.

The presence of apocalyptic ideas in thanksgiving-day sermons demonstrates that not only were these convictions being presented publicly, but also that they are apparent in officially sanctioned occasions of great importance. Application of apocalyptic interpretations associated with these national public celebrations clearly disproves not only the idea that such belief quickly dissipated after the 1640s and 1650s, but also that the continued adherence to these convictions was something simply reserved for closeted study. Ministers were not necessarily reticent in sharing with their audiences their application of prophetic meaning to the circumstances of the day, nor did their voicing of these ideas equate with radical action. They appear as one way of understanding the significance of events of the day. This is evident in the two documents chosen here. It is also clear that both ministers had discussed such ideas about apocalyptic meaning and fulfilment with their audiences before, and that they would feel comfortable doing so again in the future.

A Note on the Texts

The spelling and punctuation of the sermons have been left in the form found in the original publication, except that obvious typographical errors have been corrected using square brackets. Some sections superfluous or redundant to the main argument of the sermons have been removed, and are marked by the use of ellipses (…). The original marginal notations in Jacob's sermon have been included as footnotes, with the original content identified by italic text. The original errata noted in Dobbs's sermon have been used to correct his text.

Desolations Decypher'd

AND

The Kingdom of CHRIST Discover'd.

IN A

SERMON

Preacht the 23d of the 6th Month, 1705.[16]

Being the Day of Thanksgiving for the Late Success of the Army, under the Conduct of JOHN Duke of Marlborough.

Publisht at the Request of the Hearers.

By Joseph Jacob a Servant of CHRIST Crucify'd.

Psalm XLVI.8. Come, behold the works of the LORD, what Desolations he hath made in the Earth,
Psalm CXLV.10, 11. All thy works shall praise thee, O LORD, and thy Saints shall bless thee: They shall speak of the Glory of thy Kingdom, and talk of thy Power.

LONDON.
Printed by J.D. and Sold by the Booksellers, MDCCV.

---

16 Jacob was applying the practice of some seventeenth- and early eighteenth-century nonconformists of not using pagan-derived names for the days and months, as well as taking the new year to begin in March. Designating the new year to begin on 1 January, the regular (O.S.) date of this thanksgiving was 23 August 1705, as confirmed in the notice for this thanksgiving day. See *A Form of Prayer, and Thanksgiving to Almighty God: To be Used on Thursday the Twenty Third of August next ... For the Late Glorious Success for Forcing the Enemy Lines in the Spanish Netherlands, by the Arms of her Majesty and Her Allies ...* (London: 1705), title page.

The PREFACE

[...]

As to the Ensuing Discourse, I Expect it to be Censur'd, as every thing from me is, by some sort of People, who yet would be thought Charitable, But this Subject is like to be the more Spoken against, because it will be so Little understood; as how should it, by those who spend so many more hours in reading of impertinent Newspapers than in searching into Gods Holy Word, with which whoever is unacquainted, he can by no means understand the Doctrine here delivered; a Doctrine founded only on Revelation, and therefore not to be known but by the teaching of the Spirit, out of the Sacred Volume of Gods Holy Word, in a way of running to and fro therein, or Diligently Comparing scripture with Scripture.

I am so much, both assur'd of the Truth, and perfectly acquainted with the Tenor of the things here delivered, that whoever shall please to call them Cant, or Nonsense, may be satisfy'd for me they may use their Liberty, only Let them remember that they must not only answer for every Idle word, but for every hard word also that is spoken against Christ, his Servants, or his Truths, all which I am Positive, are designedly Exacted in this Tract in which all Fantastical or Enthusiastical Extreams are avoided, and only such matters are asserted, as are deduceable from, and reconcilable to the whole Tenor of Scripture.

[...]

Of all that take upon them to censure this Discourse, or its Author, I shall expect the most bitter Cavils and malignancy from such, as most Cry up, and yet least of all practise Moderation, Peace, Unity and Charity; Matters of Great Worth, and chief Consequence, but so little understood, and so much less exercis'd, by many vain and unruly Talkers (in the front of which Let Occasional Conformists ever be plac'd[17]) that it should seem they have forsworn every thing about these virtues, but the Name of them.

[...]

Southwark, The 30th of the 6th Month, 1705.[18]   JOSEPH JACOB

---

17 Jacob is criticizing dissenters who take occasional communion in the Church of England in order to qualify for public services. See also p. 209 and note 6.
18 30 August 1705 (O.S.).

WHEN first I heard the Tydings of that Victory, for which we are now Assembl'd to praise GOD,[19] those Words came to my Mind, I will overturn, overturn, overturn it, and it shall be no more, until He come whose Right it is, and I will give it Him; which Words I could not but think so sutable to the Success, that I then determin'd with my self, if a Set time for Thanksgiving on that Occasion were appointed, as now it is, I would, God willing, speak from them, not only, because of that three-fold overturning of the Enemy,[20] for which we have met together to give Thanks, under the Government of an ENGLISH Queen,[21] and the Conduct of an ENGLISH General,[22] who loves Engaging better than Encamping, and Action more than Ostentation; unto a Grateful Commemoration of which, the three-fold overturning mention'd in those Words, may at this time excite us; But more especially, for that the Words lead us to the Consideration of those Many Overturnings God is bringing on the World, in order to the Erecting of a Throne for His Son, above all the Thrones of the Sons of Men: Of which, as the words I have mention'd do expressly speak, so God hath given us a Solemn Assurance, saying, I will make him who is my first-born, higher than the Kings of the Earth.

On this Account, I say, I was chiefly led to pitch upon these Words for the Theme of my Discourse this Day; we having in them so plain an Intimation that all the Overturnings which are begun in the Earth, will still be rouling on, and there will yet be a turning over of Nations, and all persons or things that therein are opposite unto the Interest of our Lord Jesus Christ, until He comes to rule and reign whose Right it is, unto whom the Universal Dominion (which so many have in vain aspired after) shall be given: Of which wonderful Revolutions, and the most glorious Conclusion of all, I shall now address my self to speak to you as I am able, from the Words I have mention'd, which you will find written in

EZEKIEL xxi. Ver. 27.

I will overturn, overturn, overturn it, and it shall be no more, until He come whose right it is, and I will give it Him.

---

19   The victory Jacob refers to is the Battle of Elixheim (or the Passage of the Lines of Brabant) on 18 July 1705 (N.S.). See p. 210, note 8.
20   This is Jacob's general theme throughout the sermon, which he takes from his central text, Ezekiel 21:27. He links this to apocalyptic prophecy (see the table on p. 231 below), but also uses it here to connect that theme to the military victory that instigated the thanksgiving occasion.
21   Queen Anne.
22   The Duke of Marlborough.

EZEKIEL signifies the Strength of God, or strengthn'd by God; which Name no doubt was design'd by Providence for this Prophet, to let him understand, what Strength he both would want, and should receive from God, for the Faithful delivering of his Mind to the Jews, unto whom he was to preach; a more obstinate Race than which there was not to be found in the World: Harder of Belief, and less capable of Impressions of Divine Truth, no Generation of Men were ever known to be than the Jews, which as God well knew, so he fortify'd this Prophet for his Service in ministring unto such, three special ways;

1. He gave him a Glorious Vision of his most Excellent Majesty,[23] that he being under a deep sence of what a Great God he serv'd, might neither fear what his Enemys could do to him, nor yet that he should want sutable Supplys from him;

2. God did most plainly and faithfully discover to this Prophet, the perverseness and malignity, the incorrigibleness and obstinacy of those unto whom he was to preach,[24] that knowing the worst of them, he should not be startl'd at what he should see or find by them.

3. God Almighty spirited the Prophet for his Work, by making his Face strong against their Faces, and his forehead strong against their foreheads, even like an Adamant did God make his Forehead harder than a flint,[25] so that he left him no room to fear them, nor to be dismay'd at their Looks, altho' they were a rebellious House, and impudent and hard-hearted Children!

And thus accoutr'd for his Service, God sent out this Prophet in bitterness and the heat of his Spirit,[26] to speak his Mind unto the Jews, who were at that time in Captivity;

[...]

That Man who will successfully expose the Sins of Apostatiz'd Professors (such as the Jews then, and many now are) he that will vigorously oppose himself to them, had need be made strong as Jeremiah was by God, like a defenced City, an Iron Pillar, and a Brazen Wall,[27] otherways he will be prevail'd against by his Antagonists; For as it was then, even so it is now, the Professors have Whore's Foreheads,[28] they refuse to be asham'd; The Foreheads not only of the People, but even of the Priests in our Age, are so Thatcht, and their Faces so hid with the Hair of Whores, that they do neither blush at, nor stick to commit such

---

23 *For this, see* [Ezek.] *ch. 1.*
24 *This we find in ch. 2d and 3d.*
25 *ch. 3, v. 8, 9.*
26 *ch. 3. v. 14.*
27 *Jer. 1. 18.*
28 *Jer. 3. 3.*

Abominations, as many among the Heathens would have been asham'd to be guilty of:[29] What need then have those of an invincible Spirit, and an undaunted Brow, who are sent of God to cry aloud, and to lift up their voice as a Trumpet,[30] against the Sins of such as would be counted his People?

[...]

I shall not have time to examine the whole Chapter, in which severe Judgments are threaten'd to the Jews, and their malignant Enemys the Ammonites; that is, to Professors and Profane; both whose Calamities are denounc'd in such moving Terms as might well invite us to overlook them, were it not that thereby we shall be prevented of seeing what in the Text doth more nearly concern us, as being altogether apt for the Day in which our Lot is cast:

The former part of this Chapter is taken up in Destructions threatn'd to the City of Jerusalem, and the Land of Israel;[31] After which Denunciations he comes here (as it were in a distinct Prophecy) to denounce Judgments against King Zedekiah, then reigning at Jerusalem;[32]

[...]

And indeed the Words obviously slide from those Times, into the End of Time; Here is a quick transition made, which is common in Scripture, from a present to a future matter; however Zedekiah and his overthrow may be here spoken of historically, there is a prophetical Intention held forth in the words, which is far enough from being as yet compleated; He begins with threatning Zedekiah's overthrow, but before he ends, he passes on to discover the overturning of all Antichrist, and establishing of the Kingdom of Jesus Christ our Lord.

In which sense I doubt not the Words are chiefly to be taken, for as no scripture is so of private Interpretation,[33] as to be confin'd to one meaning only, least of all are these Prophecys to be crampt, which should be extended to their full length, and this here reaches unto the Destruction of all the Enemies of Christ, and to the setting up of him over all; and so indeed judicious Expositors do understand the Words of my Text, nor can many Expressions herein be reconcil'd to truth, if they be not thus taken.

[...] As all sound Expositors grant the verse of my Text refers to the End of the World, so I doubt not the two verses to which it belongs, have a like reference; and as the former part of the Chapter, under the Name of Jerusalem, foretells

---

29 Here Jacob is attacking Anglican ministers.
30 *Isa. 58. 1.*
31 *See this,* [Ezek. 21:] *v. 1 to 24.*
32 *See v. 25, 26, 27.*
33 2 *Pet. 1. 20.*

the judgments that shall some on the Church of God, of which that City was a Type, so do these verses point out the ruin that shall befal Antichrist, of which that wicked prophane Prince of Israel here threatn'd, was a type, thro' whose sides, God fetches a far but full blow, at all Antichristian powers and principalities, whom he will overturn, in order to the Setting up of the Kingdom of his well-beloved Son.

And thus I understand the words, to be Level'd at the Great Antichrist in the Latter days, who is to be overturn'd, that Christ may be all and in all.

I know that prodigious and prophane misapplications have been made of these words, to such particular Princes, as Preachers from them have been prejudic'd unto:[34] But God forbid that we should understand these words to be meant only of one particular Limb or Member of Antichrist, altho never so Great, Suppose the Pope himself, or the Great Turk; This prophane wicked prince of Israel, here prophetically pointed at, is a Scriptural denomination of all those powers, who under pretence of Religion do oppose the Interest of Christ;[35] nor is this Strange, since however different they may be in Opinion, they are united in Opposition to Christ, They have all ONE mind to give their strength and power to the Beast, and therefore are called by ONE Name,[36] Thou prophane wicked Prince of Israel; by which certainly the whole Posse and Force, the Congluvies[37] and Confederacy of the Enemys of Christ are to be understood; all these are represented as ONE by blessed Paul, He calls all those powers who act against God and his Word, and that under a pretence of Religion too, he calls them all by a single name, That Man of Sin! That Son of Perdition! That wicked One![38] It's most absurd to imagine that he Intends here

---

34   *So one Wesley of Chesthunt preaching before Sir R. Geffry's then Mayor, said that Ferguson applyed them to James the II, and himself applyed them to the D. of M.* [This note refers to Robert Wensley, who was vicar of Cheshunt in Hertfordshire from 1672 to his death in August 1689: *Clergy of the Church of England Database* (http://theclergydatabase.org.uk/ accessed 29 December 2015). The "D. of M." refers to the Duke of Monmouth, who led a rebellion against James II in the first year of his reign. 'Ferguson' is Robert Ferguson, the Scottish Presbyterian minister who was one of the leaders of Monmouth's Rebellion: Robert Wensley, *Ferguson's Text Explain'd and Apply'd, in a Sermon Before the Right Honourable Sir Robert Geffery, Kt. Lord Mayor of London; ... December the 6th. Anno Dom. 1685* (London, 1686), 9.]

35   Jacob contradicts the generally accepted Protestant interpretation of the Antichrist being embodied in the papacy and Roman Catholicism, instead arguing that this imagery represents all false religious authorities and doctrines.

36   *Nodo junguntur in uno.*

37   "congluvies" means a company or group: *Dictionary of Medieval Latin from British Sources*, online (http://www.dmlbs.ox.ac.uk/publications/online, accessed 16 February 2018).

38   2 *Thess.* 2. 3, 8. ο ανθρωπος της αμαρτιας ο νιος της αρωλειας. ο ανομος.

only the Pope, or Turk, or any ONE Limb of Antichrist, as many falsly and foolishly have said, Laying this ruful character at doors (as they have thought) far enough from their own; but hereby he means (as he afterward says) the whole mystery of Iniquity,[39] however Hid and Cloakt; So the Apocalyptical Apostle John in the same breath says there are many Antichrists,[40] and yet they are all but ONE Antichrist, as being tho' Multitudes, yet but as ONE in wickedness:

At Antichrist then, in whatsoever Post or Profession, of what soever Region or Religion, is this prophecy Level'd, and herein an utter overthrow of his power is threatn'd, in order to the setting up of the Kingdom of Christ!

[...]

God hath begun overturning work in the World,[41] and made no small Speed with it in our day, and particularly, I must say, he hath done such great things by an ENGLISH General,[42] as no Foreigners have room to boast of, for some of which Successes we are this Day met together to bless the Name of the Lord of Hosts; and haply had all Allies been alike minded, our Thanksgiving for the overturning of the Enemy had swell'd much higher, God having endow'd the Gallant ENGLISH General with an extraordinary Spirit, such as the last Age has scarce produc'd the like, for Conduct and Courage, Fidelity and Ability for his Work, which pity it is should not be encouraged to the utmost! However, be the Overturnings now on foot, more or less slow, they are sure, and like to have their continuance in the world untill this my Text is fulfill'd; of which I shall now proceed to speak more distinctly having thus fully and clearly opened my way to it: [...]

1st. Let us with humble reverence inquire after the Author of all the Desolations here threatn'd: Him we find here exprest by this I, I will overturn, &c.[43] He whose Name alone is JEHOVAH, the Great I AM; this is his Name, and this is his Memorial to all Generations: He it is that is here to be understood as the Author of all these Convulsions and Revolutions.

It is the Lord of all who brings about all the Overturnings in the World. This Remark has Scripture Proof enough [...]

2dly. See we the Certainty of these Judgments being executed: They WILL certainly come, for God hath said the Word, I WILL overturn, &c. And if he

---

39   *ver. 7.*
40   *1Joh. 2. 18.* Αντιχριϛοι πολλοι. ο Αντιχριϛιος.
41   Jacob makes no specific assertions about when this overturning began, but, as the subsequent lines show, he certainly believes it is occurring in his time, in part through the victories of England and its allies over the French.
42   The Duke of Marlborough.
43   *Psa. 83. Last* [verse 18]. *Exo.3. 14. 15.*

WILL, who hath at any time resisted his WILL? We are ready to say in our Unbelief, can the Earth be overturn'd? Surely it will not be, by whom can it be? But all such ungodly Reasoning are here answer'd: The Lord WILL do it, and he is able to do all things after the Counsel of his own WILL. Let us then receive this Truth,

The Lord WILL certainly bring great Overturnings in the World; he hath said it, and he will do it. He is of one Mind in this matter, and none can turn him from it; tho' Noah and Moses and Samuel were here, they could not divert those Overturnings, which God WILL bring on the Earth. It was a great Acknowledgment the Lord extorted out of the Mouth of a haughty Monarch, All the Inhabitants of the Earth (saith he) are reputed as nothing to the Most High, and he doth according to his own WILL in the Army of Heaven, and Among the Inhabitants of the Earth, and none can stay his Hand, or say unto him, What dost thou?[44] [...]

3dly. Let us take a view of the Nature of those Desolations God has threatn'd to the World, and the Dominion thereof: I will overturn, overturn, overturn it, saith the Lord This is the kind of Judgment God will bring on the Earth, and upon all therein that opposes his Will, Overturning, He will turn it over, or overset it. He hath often shook the world, and made it, and the Inhabitants thereof, to reel as a drunken Man, or as a Vessel in a Storm; but hitherto he hath not overset, or turn'd quite over the whole Earth, and the Dominion thereof, as here he hath threatn'd to do; and will so accomplish, as that it shall never be able to recover it self from these Overturnings, as it hath Often done from some lesser Shakings, and Overthrowings, which it hath now and then, here or there, been exercis'd with: But Thorough-work will God now make of it, He will turn all over, so that nothing shall stand to oppose him.

Overturning then is the word, Overturning is the Thing; it is nothing less than Overturning which God has here threatn'd to the world, and its present Evil Constitution ...

Thus we see the Nature of the Desolations denounc'd in the Text; to assure us of the thoroughout Accomplishment of which, it is three times repeated, I will overturn, overturn, overturn it. THRICE is the Word pronounc'd, because the thing is establisht by God, and God will shortly bring it to pass; unto which also other Places in Holy Writ give witness, many of which I shall name to you in the Explication of these Words: At present suffice it to mention that remarkable parallel Prediction in Haggai, where we read, I will overthrow the Throne of Kingdoms, saith the Lord, and I will destroy the Strength of the Kingdoms

---

44 Dan. 4. 35. [The monarch referred to here is Nebuchadnezzar.]

of the Heathen, and I will overthrow the Chariots, and those that ride in them, and the Horses and the Riders shall come down, every one by the Sword of his Brother.[45] Here is a threefold Overthrowing threatn'd to the World, answerable to this in my Text, after which, Zerubbabel, that is, Jesus Christ, the true Destroyer of Babel, shall be made as a Signet, Glorious and Renown'd in all the Earth;[46] unto which the holy Apostle alludes, when he tells us, the things here below shall be shaken, and not only shaken, but turn'd over, or remov'd out of their present posture, that room may be made for the Kingdom of Christ, which can never be mov'd.[47]

The Nature and Certainty of these Desolations being thus Explain'd and Evinc'd to us, let us further enquire what may be the Meaning of the threefold Repetition of them [...]

[...] That God three times says he will overturn, it is to discover to us a hidden part of His Mind herein, a wonderful Ternary of Action is here to be understood, which take in brief thus: Hereby we learn,

1st, A threefold Season when he will overturn.[48]

2dly, A threefold Subject which he will overturn.[49]

3dly, A threefold Scourge by which he will overturn.[50]

The Time when he will overturn, the Partys whom he will overturn, and the Means by which he will overturn: All these are here pointed out to us, we may learn this great Mystery by this threefold use of the word overturn, of all which I shall speak, by the help of God, in this order.

1st, Thrice mentioning the word Overturn does give us light into the treble Season God will take to overturn the World, and its Constitution in. God hath been all along contesting with the World for it's Corruptions, and great Desolations he hath made here and there at several Seasons, which having not reform'd it, or brought it to his will, towards the End thereof (for the World is not Eternal as some have Dreamt, but shall have an End, towards which) there will be three Periods, or set Stages of Time, in which God will Issue forth in such desolating Judgments as were never before known; all which he will make use of in order to overturn the Earth, and the Constitution thereof.

---

45   *Hag.* 2.22.
46   This is a reference to Hag. 2:23. Zerubbabel returned to Jerusalem with the Jews after their captivity in Babylon ended, and he helped with the rebuilding of the Temple (Ezra 3:1–2, 8), and Jacob sees him as a prefiguring of Christ.
47   *Heb.* 12. 27. 28.
48   *Quando.*
49   *Quos.*
50   *Quomodo.*

Now these three Seasons are so very remarkable, and so Exceeding all others for both Wickedness and Judgments, that in Comparison thereof the times that precede them, are counted as nothing as so seem as it were to be bury'd in Silence, while these are only mention'd with an Emphasis, as being the chief Stages, and Ages of Action, in which such overturnings will be felt, as shall at last put an End to a sinful State here below, after which shall Succeed one most Glorious and Holy.

Of these three famous Times to speak with the greatest advantage, I must briefly refresh your Memorys with the repetition of some things I have formerly hinted unto you more fully.

The seven Churches of Asia, unto which our Lord wrote by his Servant John, were (as you have often had Evinc'd to you by several great Testimonies) not only Historically but also Prophetically intended; they were not only descriptive of those particular Churches, but figurative also of a sevenfold Church state; seven Periods, Stages and Ages of the Church are here design'd, from the Ascension of our Lord, unto his second Coming; The various States, Conditions and Exercises of Christ's Church during that long interval, are here held forth, from whence we may gather what shall befall his People in all his absence from them: Thus,

1st. The Apostolick Church-State, or the State of the Church in the days of the Apostles,[51] is to be learnt out of the Epistle to the Church of Ephesus, which word signifys desirable, as figuring out that desireableness there was in that Church-State!

2dly. The suffering state of the Church during the ten Persecutions,[52] is to be seen in the Epistle to the Church of Smyrna, which signifys Myrrhe or bitter, a wholesom bitterness then attending suffering Saints.

3dly The Exaltation of the Church both in Wor[l]dly Honour, and Wickedness,[53] which began in Constantine's time, when that voice was said to be heard, *Hodie venenum Injectum est in Ecclesiam*: The Church is now poyson'd, which poyson after made a ruful progress; this is to be gather'd from the Epistle to the Church of Pergamus, which signifys height, the Church then being got to a great height of Pomp and Pollution, common Companions God knows!

4thly. The wretched Effeminacy and Fornication of the Church-State which Ensu'd, and Brought great sufferings on the Few faithful, for a long tract of time

---

51   *The Ephesian, or 1st. state of the Church in Rev. 2. 1. 7.*
52   *The Smyrnean or 2d. Rev. 2. 8. 11.* [This is a reference to the Roman persecutions of the early Christian church.]
53   *The Pergamean or 3d. Rev. 2. 12. 17.*

during the Apostacy, which chiefly from Rome spread it self in all the Earth,[54] this is obvious in the Epistle to the Church of Thyatira, alluding (as Dr More ingeniously remarks) either to θυγατερ (Daughter) by which the Female Saint worship of that Age, and their Shaveling[55] Petticoat-men, their Monks, &c. are pointed to:[56] or to θυητηρια (Altar) by which their Altar-incense and their sacrificing of Saints, as Victims on an Altar, is set out.

5thly. The partial Reformation which began near 200 years ago, from some Grosser Corruptions in the Church, while yet there was more Name than Life of Religion to be seen,[57] this is set out in the Epistle to the Church of Sardis alluding to the Sardius stone, which is of a flesh colour by which the Carnality of this Church state, under all its pretences to Spirituality, is visibly discover'd.

6thly. The Calling of the Jews in Conjunction with the Gentiles, to make up the promis'd Oneness in the Church of Christ,[58] is represented in the Epistle to the Church of Philadelphia, which points out to that Brotherly Love which shall then be visible among the Saints.

7thly. The decay of Religion and Lukewarmness which Ensues hereon, and preceeds next and immediately the Coming of Christ to judge the World,[59] this is set forth in the Epistle to the Church of Laodicea, by which is discover'd that Judgment of the People, which God will Execute in the Latter days, wherein the Kingdom of our Lord Christ shall be Exalted over all.

This is that Account of the State of the Church of Christ, from his Ascension to his second Coming, in seven several Journeyings, Ages, Stages or Periods, of which the word of God speaks; By which we are not to understand, as if Each were of a Like Duration, some being Longer, some Shorter; but of whatsoever extent they be, the intent of God as to his People is here to be Learnt, and will be fulfilled in one or other, and all together of these States, and Conditions of his Church, until he Comes to make the Place of his feet Glorious, and Jerusalem to be the praise of the Whole Earth.

---

54 *The Thyatirean, or 4th. Rev. 2. 18. to End* [verse 29].
55 "Shaveling" means tonsured. Jacob applies the common English Protestant anti-Catholic interpretation to this verse.
56 See Henry More, *An Exposition of the Seven Epistles to the Seven Churches* (London, 1669), 77–83.
57 *The Sardian or 5th. Rev. 3. 1. 6.*
58 *The Philadelphian, or 6th. Rev. 3. 7. 13.* [The idea that the Jews would be converted to Christianity as a precursor to, or result of, Christ's second coming was a common apocalyptic belief in seventeenth-century England. See Johnston, *Revelation Restored*, 10, 13, 26, 37, 51–53, 56, 57–58, 146–147, 195, 211, 225, 228].
59 *The Laodicean, or 7th. State or Age of the Church Rev. 3. 14 to End* [verse 22].

Now of these seven States, Progresses, or Epochaes of the Church it is to be noted, that four are already past, and three only remain to be fill'd up; Those three which bring up the Rear of Antichrist's Reign, and the Churches Sufferings; and consequently Those three which are to be fill'd with Judgments in order to the overturning of the Earth, and its Administrations, and to the setting up of the Throne of Christ over all.

These three Stages of the Church that are yet to be run through, are the Sardian, the Philadelphian, and Laodicean, or the 5th, 6th, and 7th Church States, of which there is a more distinct and more remarkable account held forth for Judgments, and Overturning, than of any of the rest.

Hence in these three Church-States, there are three Wo-Trumpets to be Sounded,[60] intimating more dreadful Woes to be Executed now, Woes more to be remarkt, and that will make greater Work on the Earth, and it's Inhabitants, than all the Woes brought on the World from the beginning of the Creation unto these times.

It is in the first of these Church-States, the fifth in order of the seven, viz. The Sardian, that our Lot is Cast,[61] which we hope wants not much of being fill'd up, when the first of these Woes shall be pour'd on the Earth to overturn the Kingdom of Antichrist, and this is the first overturn in my Text spoken of; after which follows the second overturning in the Philadelphian or sixth Church-State, which is the second Woe; and this is brought up by the third overturning in the Laodicean or seventh Church-State, which is the third Woe;[62] upon which Woes being Executed the Kingdoms of this World become the Kingdoms of our Lord and of his Christ, who will then take to himself his Great Power and Rule and Reign over all; at what time will this Text be fulfill'd, that he shall Come whose right, the World and the Government of it is, and to him it shall be Given, Amen and Amen!

Thus is the word overturn Repeated thrice, to Point out this Treble time, in which the world and it's Constitution shall be overturn'd; Which times is represented in other Words, as we may see in sundry Places of holy Writ.

When Daniel was to be inform'd of the End of all the wonderful Revolutions in the World; by three several Periods of time, their Conclusion is Set out to him; all which have their Commencement at one and the same time, to wit, from the beginning of the Reign of the last and worst Antichrist, that second

---

60 *Rev. 8. 13. Ch. 9. 10. Ch. 11. 14. Call'd by Some Væ-Euge Tubæ, Wo-Joy-Trump. as Sounding Wo to Sinners, but Joy to Saints.*

61 Here Jacob demonstrates his belief that he lived in the Sardian period, when the first woe trumpet (i.e. the fifth) trumpet is sounded (Rev. 8:13).

62 *See Rev. 11. 14. to End* [verse 19].

Beast[63] that keeps under the true Church of Christ for so many hundreds of Years; in and at the End of each of which Seasons he shall receive an Overturning, which at Last shall make a total End of him.

The first of these Times is Set out by the prophetical term of Time, Times, and Half-Time,[64] which is the same with 3 Years and a 1/2, or 42 Months, or 1260 days,[65] each day for a Year, in which Antichrist prevails over the Church, which for it's paucity then is set out by two Witnesses,[66] and for it's imbecillity is represented by a Woman;[67] when these 1260 Years of Antichrist's Usurpations and Tyranny are over, he will then receive his first overturn, which will be in the Sardian, or 5th Church-State, call'd the first Woe; But this only Stunning, not making a full End of him,

There is a second Time set down in Daniel, wherein Antichrist shall receive a second overturn, at the End of 1290 Years,[68] that is thirty Years after the former, in the Philadelphian, or 6th Church-State, which will be his 2d. Woe; after which he will yet make some head, and therefore,

He shall have a third overturn, which will do his Business (as we say) forty five Years after the last blow, or 1335 Years[69] after his Usurpations over the Church of Christ, which will be given in the Laodicean or 7th Church-State, and will be the 3d. or Consuming Woe; and now will be Finisht or Compleated that Great round number of 2300 Years,[70] which Daniel heard in his days, to be the Time Limited for Antichrist's Dominion in all the four Monarchys; which Ends at the same time with the 1335 Years Reign of the last and worst Limb of Antichrist, unto which Time Whosoever comes, Blessed and Happy will he be,[71] for the Things which he shall then behold with his Eyes.

These are the three times in which Antichrist's Kingdom shall receive such terrible overturnings, as are set forth here by a treble repetition of the word overturn; God will overturn it at the End of 1260 years of its Exaltation, he will overturn it at the End of 1290 years, and again he will overturn it at the End of 1335 years of its Tyranny, after which it shall never rise again to the prejudice of the Saints.

---

63 Rev. 13:11–18.
64 *Dan. 12 ch. v. 7.* [Here and in subsequent references to the book of Daniel in this passage, Jacob is synchronizing prophetic timelines from Daniel with those in Revelation.]
65 *Rev. 11. 2. 3. Rev. 12. 6. 14.*
66 Rev. 11:3–13.
67 Rev. 12:1–6, 13–17.
68 [Daniel 12:] *v. 11.*
69 *v. 12.*
70 *Daniel 8. v. 13, 14.*
71 *Dan. 12. 12.*

If any shall say they understand not these Things, I shall not wonder thereat, since Daniel himself at first understood them not,[72] nor were they to be reveal'd till about the Times when they were to be accomplisht,[73] and even then, none of the wicked should understand them,[74] the Knowledge of these Things is Conceal'd from the Wise-Men of Babylon, while it is reveal'd to such as are Weak and Foolish ones in the Worlds Account? who yet (by Grace) are made Wise to Salvation thro' the Scriptures of Truth, by which God makes known unto those that fear him, and keep his Covenant, those things which he is about to do, and if any Man will do his will, he shall know of this Doctrine that it is of God!

Yet shall not I pretend to be wise above what i[s] Written, as such have been, who have attempted to fix set Times for the Commencements of these several Periods, which to do is an Insuperable difficulty, of which we may truly cry out, *Hic Labor Hoc opus est!* This is a Task that has foild all Mortals who have undertook it.[75]

The Continuance indeed of Antichrist's Reign is told us, and Carry'd down in the Close of it to three several Stages, in Each of which he shall have an overturn, but the Commencement of these Times is hid from all Flesh, no Man ever did or shall Successfully enquire into it; all that have offer'd at it have been found Lyars, and in the greatness of their Error have both Gone and Led astray; That the times of the End may not be certainly known, God hath hid from all Mortals the times of the Beginning; and this he hath done in Wisdom, to make us always upon our Watch; wherefore, tho' I dare affix (because the Scripture has done it to my hand) the several Stages of Antichrist, how long he shall Reign, after which times he shall be overthrown, yet shall I not presume to say at what precise Years he shall be overturn'd, and come to his End, because it is not possible for me to know from what Year these Stages take their Date, and since

---

72   *Daniel* 12. 8.
73   *v. 9*.
74   *v. 10*.
75   This statement, as well as the assertion in the following paragraph about other interpreters having "been found Lyars", demonstrate Jacob's criticism of the tendency of expositors to try to attach specific dates and timeframes to the fulfillment of apocalyptic prophecies. Jacob might have had in mind the recent case of Thomas Beverley, who published dozens of pamphlets in the 1690s predicting the destruction of the beast in 1697. After this and several modified dates passed, Beverley disappeared from public notice in 1701. See Warren Johnston, "Thomas Beverley and the 'Late Great Revolution': English Apocalyptic Expectation in the Late Seventeenth Century", in *Scripture and Scholarship in Early Modern England*, ed. Ariel Hessayon and Nicholas Keene (Aldershot: 2006), 158–175.

the Year cannot be known when these Times Began, neither can it be precisely determin'd when they shall End; However an End he shall have, and that at these three Seasons which we would hope are at hand, wherein God will give this treble overthrow to all Antichrist's Interest in all the World:

Which Isaiah also describes by three Words,[76] exactly answering to these three Times; the first is called Fear, a name suiting with that Spirit of fear which in the first overturning of Antichrist will possess the whole World, and under the power of which at this time most are, paleness gathering into their Faces, and fear making their Hearts fail them, with looking for the things that are coming upon them in their Citys, Courts, Camps and Churches: The second time is set forth by the Pit, because then such Pits in the second overturning shall be dug for the Wicked, as were never before seen in the World. The third Time is term'd a Snare, because the third overturning will come as a Snare on the Earth, which few looking for, will of Course take the most, these Things are elsewhere predicted, of which on the last Head I may speak more distinctly.

The same Prophet alludes to these three Seasons of overturning, in another place,[77] where speaking of the Coming of Christ to execute Vengeance on his Enemys, and to make his rejected Saints Glorious, He Intimates that then there shall be a Voice of noise from the City, by which the first time of overturnings is intended; which is followed by a voice from the Temple, which is the time of the second overturning; and then comes a Voice of the Lord that rendereth Recompence to his Adversarys, in the third and Last overturning of all who oppose his Interest.

Parallel unto which is that threefold Harvest, seen in a Vision by the beloved Disciple;[78] This I have not time fully to Explain but it seems to point out to a treble Season God will take to reap down, and turn over the World, and its Wicked Inhabitants.

And NOW, to put an End unto this first Interpretation of this threefold use of the word overturn, as it intends a threefold Time of Overturning, I will only allude unto that remarkable Providence which attended the Prophet Elijah in the Wilderness, when persecuted by Jezabel, as the true Church of a long Time has been by Antichrist; There the Prophet being call'd out by God, did both See and hear what may serve to illustrate this matter.

At three several times, in three several ways, by three several Overturnings, God shew'd him what he would do in the last Days: and yet it is said, the Lord

---

76   *Isaiah 24. 17. to 20*. [See the table and note 80 below.]
77   *Isaiah 66. v. 5, 6*. [See the table and note 80 below.]
78   *Rev. 14. v. 15, 17, 18*. [See also the table and note 80 below.]

was in none of these dispensations, that is, he was not seen in, nor came to the Prophet by any of them, till all of them were over, and then in a Small still Voice he made himself known to him.[79]

Answerably whereunto I may say, that before the Great and Notable day of the Lord, when Elijah shall be sent as a Messenger to make way for his coming, there shall be three several Overturnings, at three several Seasons or Stages of Time, which shall come three several Ways, and yet the Lord Jesus will not be seen by the most in any of them, until after they are all over, his Voice shall be heard, and his Face shall be seen by his Saints, who Exulting shall Cry out, this is he that we looked for, behold he is come and his Reward is with him; Amen! Even so come Lord Jesus.

And thus I have gone through with this first Explanation of the threefold use of the Term overturn, God hereby teaches us, that he will overturn the Kingdom of Antichrist in three several Seasons, Stages, or Periods of Time, which that they may be more distinctly understood by us, I shall draw up in this diagram, or Figure-Table.

A Prospect of the three several Seasons wherein God will overturn the Kingdom and powers of Antichrist.[80]

Overturn		Ch. state	Woe	Year of Antichrist		Voice	Harvest	Hearing of Elijah
1	Sardian	5	1	1260	Fear 1	1	1	1
2	Philadelph	6	2	1290	Pit 2	2	2	2
3	Laocidean	7	3	1335	Snare 3	3	3	3

This is the Sum of what we first gather from this threefold Threatning, that at these three several Seasons, that is throughout each of them, God will give singular Overturnings to the Interest of Antichrist, until at last it is totally overturn'd.

---

79 1 *Kings* 19. v. 11. 12.
80 In this table, Jacob synchronizes and connects apocalyptic prophecies with Old Testament prophecies that prefigure them. He begins with his main theme and text, the overturnings from Ezekiel 21:27, linking this to the prophecies of the fifth, sixth, and seventh church characteristics from Revelation 3, which he also synchronizes with the fifth, sixth, and seventh trumpets, the "woe" trumpets from Revelation 8:13–9:21 and 11:15–19. These, in turn, are synchronized with the 1260-year periods from Revelation 11:3 and 12:6 and the 1290 and 1335 years from Daniel 12:11–12. Jacob then associates these periods with visions and prophecies from Isaiah 24:17–18 (fear, pit, snare), and 66:6 (voices), Revelation 14:14–20 (harvests), and 1 Kings 19:11–13 (Elijah in the wilderness standing on the mount through wind, earthquake, and fire, then hearing God in a "still small voice"). As discussed previously, Jacob does not attach these precisely to specific dates or historical events.

2dly. I come now in the next Place to shew that this treble mention of the word overturn, doth also point out to the threefold Subject to be Overturn'd; Three there are, which in Congress or Confederacy do Constitute the power of Antichrist, and these three are here threatn'd to be overturn'd, whence it is said, I will overturn, overturn, overturn it, that is, the whole Posse of Antichrist, tho it be lodg'd in the hands of three that in conjunction seek to maintain it, I will overturn one, and another, and all, that Contribute unto its Support; all the Constituent parts of it shall be overturn'd.

The grand denomination of the three who together make up Antichrist, is given by the Holy Spirit under the Terms of the Dragon, the Beast, and the False Prophet,[81] these three in Conjunction constitute Antichrist; all the unclean Spirits in the World, owe their rise unto these three; whosoever is Unholy, Unjust and Abominable is so, as he is under the influence of one, or more, or all of these; [...]

1st. For the Dragon, who is not a Roman Emperor as some Dream but that old Serpent the Devil and Satan,[82] as holy Writ infallibly assures us; Is not he stil'd in so many Words, the GOD of this World? and do's he not preside in the hearts of most as God, blinding their Eyes, hind'ring them from seeing the Light of the Glorious Gospel of Christ,[83] Leading them Captive at his pleasure?[84] Is he not more obey'd and reverenc'd than the true God, hath he not more who follow his insinuations, and act according to his will, than do obey God himself, or walk up to his word? Surely, tho there are but few comparatively that do explicitly swear Allegiance to the Dragon, yet where will it be found, but more walk after him, and do his Works, than pay Homage to the God of Heaven? [...] This is the Dragon, the Devil and all his Angels, the God this World worships, and who therefore must have an overturn, whence it is said Once, I will overturn, that is, I will overturn the Dragon.

2dly. The Beast is another of the Heads of Antichrist, by which term we are to understand all those Powers, commonly call'd Civil, or Secular, which oppose the Interest of Christ; Those, I say, with all their Adherents, high or low, rich or poor, mighty or mob, whether heathen, or people of the Jews, who rage, and imagine vain Things; Those Kings of the Earth who set themselves, and those Rulers who take counsel against the Lord, and his Anointed, saying, Let us break their Bands asunder, and cast away their Cords from us;[85] These, and such

---

81 *Rev. 16. 13.*
82 *Rev. 20. 2.*
83 *2 Cor. 4. 4.*
84 *2 Tim. 2.* [verse 26].
85 *Psal. 2. 1, 2, 3.*

like, are called Beasts in Scripture, and well may they be so term'd, for in truth, they behave themselves like Beasts, not looking up to him that made them, but setting themselves against him, tho' he gives all Good Things unto them; [...] Now all those Powers commonly call'd Civil, or Secular, with all their Adherents, who corrupt themselves in what they do know, and oppose that which is Good which they know not,[86] who are yet in a Natural State, and never brought home unto God, all these come under the denomination of Brute Beasts; all which being opposite unto the Interest of Christ, shall be overturn'd, whence it is again said in my Text, I will overturn, that is, I will overturn the Beast.

3dly. There yet rests to be shown the other head of Antichrist, and that is the false Prophet; a Head he is, but yet so abject, dirty and mean, that he is elsewhere call'd a Tail, the Prophet that speaks lies (that is, the false Prophet) he is the Tail,[87] he lags and drags after his Masters, the Dragon and the Beast, and altho' he is advanc'd to be Head, and sometimes lords it as much as either of them, and often over the Beast, yet so base and servile is he, that hee'l be a Tail, or any thing, to advance his own Ends! This false Prophet is not a Name of any particular Man, as the Pope, Mahomet, or any other, tho' they be false Prophets with a Vengeance; But it is a General Term for corrupt Ecclesiastical, commonly call'd religious, or spiritual Powers, with all that adhere to them; Hereby we are to understand, all false Churches, Church-Officers, and Church-Members, under what Form or Profession soever; Let them be dignify'd or distinguish't never so, if they are not according to the Word of God they are false; all Pretenders then to Religion who are not truly religious, especially their Superintendents, Leaders and Guides, These are to be apprehended for, these are intended by the false Prophet; Against these we are caution'd very much in Holy Writ, for these are foretold that they shall abound in the Latter Day, as we see they do, insomuch that they are Accounted as GODS by their Followers;[88] What One Micah said of his Priest, Multitudes, Multitudes are now ready to say, if their false Prophets are like to be remov'd, Ye have taken away the Gods which I made, and the Priest, And what have I more? and do ye say what aileth thee?[89] How many, alas! do make Gods of their Priests, and obey their Voice more than his who is the True God, and hence this false Prophet is said to set in the Temple of God, as God, yea to exalt himself above, and against God,[90] and so is honour'd by the most, who make the false Prophets that deceive them, too

---

86   2 *Pet.* 2. 12.
87   *Isaiah* 9. 15.
88   *Matt.* 24. 2 *Pet.* 2.
89   *Judges* 18. 24.
90   2 *Thess.* 2 [verse 4].

much their hope, a poor Hope God knows, as will be seen when the World shall be rid of this false Prophet, who is to receive an overthrow, and hence it is said the third time, I will overturn, that is, I will overturn the false Prophet

Thus I have briefly shown to you those three who making up the Mass of Antichrist, are therefore to be overturn'd; [...]

These three are the main Props, supports and Pillars of that Interest which is opposit to God and his Christ in all the World; wherefore these three must be overturn'd, and because each of these Powers shall receive a special overturn, therefore doth he say Thrice, I will overturn, overturn, overturn it, that is, the Power of Antichrist as it is supported by this Dragon, Beast and False Prophet.

Hence in Scripture we read of a distinct overturning each of these shall receive,

1. The Beast shall be overturn'd and cast alive into a Lake of Fire burning with Brimstone:[91] Into which

2. The False Prophet also that deceiv'd the World with a shew of Religion, after his overturn, shall be cast:

3. And here the Dragon, even the Devil, that old Deceiver, being overturn'd shall be Confin'd with them; and all together shall be tormented night and day forever.[92]

Thus all these three Powers, Partys, Interests, or what else you can call them, whatsoever and whosoever is Diabolical, Beastial, or Hypocritical, all this, all these, shall be overturn'd, and tho' these shall receive their overturns gradually, in each of the three last Woes, yet it will be so compleat in the end, that none of these shall be left to molest Mankind, but the Dragon, the Beast, and the False Prophet, and what and whosoever is Diabolical, Beastial, or Hypocritical, shall all be overturn'd when this Word is fulfill'd, I will overturn, overturn, overturn it.

And thus have I given you a second Reason why the Word Overturn is thrice us'd, to figure out the overturning of each of the three Pillars that support the Kingdom of Antichrist which three are describ'd by other Names in Holy Writ; some of which I shall now rehearse unto you.

We read of three places in which the Bodys of the slain Witnesses of Jesus Christ are to lie expos'd to Shame, that is, the faithful Confessors of his Name are to be malign'd, persecuted and ridicul'd by three sorts, whose Names are Egypt, and Sodom,[93] and where our Lord also was Crucify'd, that is Jerusalem: Now these three Names of Places (as the Text tells us) are to be spiritually understood, and how? But of the Dragons power which is call'd Egypt, as that place

---

91   *Rev. 19. 20.* [Also applies to the false prophet below.]
92   *Rev. 20. 10.*
93   *Rev. 11. 8.*

was a Dragon to devour the Church; Sodom is set for the Beasts Authority as that was a most beastial place; and Jerusalem (the City where our Lord was Crucify'd) points out to the False Prophet, it haveing been a Nest for that sort of Creatures, than whom the faithful Witnesses of Christ have no more malignant Enemys; so that, the opposition Christ's Servants shall receive from this threefold power, the Diabolical, Beastial, and Hypocritical, is here set out by the names of those three places which were always so Inveterate against Christ, and his Servants, Egypt, Sodom, and Jerusalem, which spiritually shall be as surely overturn'd, as ever they were literally.

The same thing is also intended by those three Greek Letters (χ, ξ, ς) by which the Holy Spirit sets forth the Number of the Beast,[94] or the Quantity and Quality of those Powers which support the Antichristian Interest, by a suppression of the faithful Servants of Christ; they are not (as I conceive) to be taken Arithmetically as by most they are understood,[95] but Hierogliphically as it were, there being a mystical or hidden meaning couch under those three Letters, each of them being set for a whole Word, of which they are the Initial Letters; so ς stands for ςατανας, Satan or the Dragon; ξ stands for ξενος, a Stranger or Alien to God, by which the Beast is set out; and χ stands for χριςτιανος, by which is meant a counterfeit Christian, or the False Prophet. All which Diabolical, Beastly, and Hypocritical Powers work thro' Men, or are to be found among Men, whence they are said to be the Number of a Man; that is, they are all to be numbred, or found among Men; and this I conceive to be the true way of finding out the Wisdom couch in that mysterious Account of Antichrist, to which I shall but add, if this be not the only meaning of the place, I am sure its a true Interpretation; for put all Antichrist together, and these three Greek Letters (χ, ξ, ς) are the Initials of his Name: There is no Antichrist but what is Satanical, Beastial, and Hypocritical, each of which is here to be spelt out, and shall meet with a final Overturn.

Parallel unto these, is that other place in the Revelations, where the whole World is set out as one great City, and this is said to be divided into three parts,[96] which informs us, that all the Interest of Antichrist in all the Earth, is Supported by these three Parts of Partys, the Diabolical, Beastial, and Hypocritical; these

---

94 *Rev. 13. 18.*

95 The number of the beast was written out in these letters in the Greek *New Testament*. It was commonly understood that the number was found in the numeric values assigned to Greek letters: χ=600, ξ=60, and ς=6, which totaled 666. See David Brady, *The Contribution of British Writers between 1560 and 1830 to the Interpretation of Revelation 13.16–18: (The Number of the Beast) A Study in the History of Exegesis* (Tübingen: 1983), 303.

96 *Rev. 16. 19.*

three make up that Great City, call'd Babylon or Confusion, which comprehends all the Citys of the Earth, and is the name of the whole Antichristian Interest that is to be destroy'd, by this threefold Overturning.

Agreeably whereto, the Apostle describing the great Antichrist of these last days, gives him (as I before hinted) three denominations; He calls him ο Ανομος, That wicked One[97] by which term we may well understand the Dragon, whose common Title that is in Gods word; ο Ανθρωπος της αμαρτιας That Man of Sin[98] a Name most proper for the Beast; and ο νιος της αρωλειας That Son of Perdition[99] a Title well Suiting the False-Prophet, or Apostatis'd Professors, such as were Judas, Demas,[100] &c. these three in Congress make up the whole mystery of Iniquity,[101] and all Antichrist's Interest, which as we there read, is to be overturn'd.

Nor is it improper to conceive, that the Apostle has some respect unto these three, when speaking of the Warfare Christians are ingag'd in, he says, that we wrestle not against Flesh and Blood,[102] that is, we ingage not with Hosts and Armys of meer Men, but against Principalitys (by which we may understand those high Princely Powers, that fell from their first standing, the Dragon and his Angels' and against Powers) which may intend those who have Power over the Bodys of the Saints in this World, call'd the Beast and his Admirers; and against the Rulers of the darkness of this World and who keeps the World in darkness, like the False Prophet? Such as call themselves Spiritual Persons, but are indeed Earthly, whom the Apostle further describes, as noted for Spiritual wickedness in high or Heavenly Places, that is, they are such as pretend to be Spiritual, and to have High and Heavenly Places in the Church, but they are guilty of Wickedness, especially in keeping the World in darkness: These are the three against whom Christians now war, and which Christ will hereafter overturn.

[...]

When the Apostle John would set down the Worlds Cargoe, all that it could boast of, he says it Consisted of three particulars, the Lust of the Flesh, and the Lust of the Eyes, and the Pride of Life;[103] which three have their rise from these three Powers of Antichrist, and these are their off-spring, which they propagate

---

97   *2 Thess. 2. v. 8.*
98   *v. 3.*
99   *v. 3.*
100   *2 Tim. 4:10.*
101   *v. 7.*
102   *Eph. 6. 12.*
103   *1 John 2. 16.*

in all the Earth: Unto these three heads of Sin, may all the Corruptions stirring in the hearts of all Flesh be reduc'd; and these three seem to be thus under the conduct of Antichrist; unto the Dragon may the Pride of Life be well ascrib'd, Pride being the Cause of his Condemnation; The Beasts part is the Lust of the Flesh, and all that indulge this, shew under whose Banner they Fight; and the Lust of the Eyes is that which of looking into what God hath hid, than those who under a form of Godliness deny the power thereof; so that we see even in these most prevailing Vices (by which the first Adam being tempted in Paradise fell, but the second Adam tempted in a Wilderness overcame;[104] we see here) the threefold power of Antichrist, discovering its Self, which must therefore be overturn'd, that such hurtful Evils which Sum up all the sin of all Mankind, may no more be found in the World.

[...]

I shall conclude this Head, and shut up these Descriptions, and Illustrations of these Antichristian Enemys that are to be overturn'd, by alluding only to that threefold Composition of Antichrist of which we speak in our Catechism, Money, Power, and Policy; These three may well be said to take in all those Persons and Things which stand in the way of Christs Kingdom, and which therefore must be overturn'd; and these three are nearly ally'd unto those three we nam'd at first as Heads of Antichrist.

Money is a chief Ingredient in the Composition of the Antichristian Interest; it is by this, they who oppose Christ and his Saints do their Feats, This therefore is call'd (as a Man would call the Devil himself) the Root of all Evil, and in many respects it might be made out so to be; This comes under the Cognizance of the Dragon, or the Devil, and no wonder, since he causes this to be so much us'd against the Servants of Christ; of the pernicious Consequence of this, the very Heathens were so sensible, that they made Pluto stand both for the God of Riches, and of hell, intimating by having but one God for both, the near Cognation between these; and our Lord says as much, when he calls Riches by the Name of Mammon, saying, we cannot serve both God and Mammon.

Power is a Great Support of the Antichristian Interest, and this is much vested in the Beast, God himself having suffer'd him, for such a time, to have Power over the Bodies and Estates of his Servants to a great degree.

Policy is another Prop of the Antichristian Cause, unto which the false Prophet, or Corrupt Ecclesiasticks have Exceedingly Contributed; Upon this three-legg'd Stool (if I may use a homely Comparison) does the whole of the

---

104 The term "second Adam" is a reference to Christ, in which Adam is seen as a type for, and prefiguring of, Christ. Unlike Adam, Christ did not succumb to Satan's temptations: Matt. 4:1–11; Mark 1:12–13; Luke 4:1–13.

Antichristian Interest sit, which when God shall strike down, and turn over, as shortly he will do, when he has accomplish'd this threefold overturning threatn'd in the Text, then shall there be way made for that Kingdom of Christ, and his Saints, of which there is so much said, both in the Old Testament, and in the New.

Thus have I, in many Particulars, explain'd to you the second meaning of the treble Repetition of the Word overturn: It is to make known to us that threefold Subject God will overturn; there are three that Constitute Antichrist, each of which he will overturn, and therefore he says, I will overturn, overturn, overturn it, that is, All the Antichristian Interest.

[...]

A List of the Antichristian Forces which are to be overthrown.[105]

1	Overturn	Dragon	Egypt	ς	1	pt. of City	Wicked one	Principalities
2		Beast	Sodom	ξ	2		Man of Sin	Powers
3		False Proph^t	Jerusal^m	χ	3		Son of Perditⁿ	Rul^{rs} darkn^{ss}

Herod	Devilish	Pride Life	Highway	Ground	Money
Pilate	Sensual	Lust Flesh	Stony		Power
Jews	Earthly	Lust Eye	Thorny		Policy

[...]

3dly. I should now have explain'd the third meaning of this treble threatning, I will overturn, overturn, overturn it, and have shown, how it hath a respect to the threefold Scourge by which God will overturn.

---

105 Jacob again captures his preceding discussion in the form of tables, joining Old and New Testament prophecies that prefigure apocalyptic ones. The "overturning" of Antichristian forces are connected to the apocalyptic prophecies of the overthrow of the Dragon (Rev. 12:9, 20:2), the beast, and the false prophet (Rev. 19:20), as well as the number of the beast (in its Greek form, Rev. 13:18). The three parts of the city are a reference to the dividing of the city when the seventh vial is poured (Rev. 16:19). Jacob also connects apocalyptic events with the prophecy of the two witnesses lying dead in spiritual Egypt, Sodom, and Jerusalem (Rev. 11:8). He then links the three descriptors of the Antichrist from 2 Thess. 2:3, 8 with the destruction of worldly authorities listed in Eph. 6:12. The vices and attributes listed are connected with prominent opponents of Christ that endorsed his crucifixion in the New Testament account, and also with the places where unproductive seed fell in the parable of the sower in Matt. 13:4–7 and Mark 4:4–7. Finally, money, power, and policy are the three prominent supports of Antichristian interests according to Jacob.

As he will overturn at three Seasons, that is, in those several Period or Set-Stages of Time of which we have heard,

And as he will overturn those three Subjects, or grand Constituent Parts of Antichrist which have been nam'd to us,

So will he overturn by three Scourges, or ways and means which he hath prepar'd for this very End and Purpose:

By which we are not to understand, as if he would use one Scourge only at one of those Seasons, or against one of those Subjects; no, he will use them all in Every Season, and against Each Subject or Constituent part of Antichrist, tho' some may be more seen at some times, or more directed against some parts of Antichrist, than others.

What these three Scourges are, the Names and Nature of them, together with their use, I have not time Now to discover to you; least of all to explain the remaining part of the Text, and therefore I shall here abruptly (that I detain you not too long,[106] and so make a Fast of a Thanksgiving Day,[107] I say I shall here abruptly) break off, Referring what rests to be said, to another Season, when I hope to discourse these Things unto our Information and Edification, At present I shall only make a brief Application of what has been said, and Conclude.

We have heard what God is doing, and yet further about to do; He hath begun, and he will not altogether withdraw his Hand till he hath made an End of All the Power of Antichrist, He will not cease until he hath overturn'd, overturn'd, overturn'd it; What then rests on our part to be done, but to be prepar'd to meet him[108] in the way of those Judgments he is bringing on all the Earth, and upon what and whosoever therein resists his Will, and refuses Obedience to his Word; How we shall be thus getting ready, I shall, God willing, in the close of this Subject, set out to you as I am able; at this time let is suffice that I mention that use which is most suitable to this Day, and the Occasion of our present Assembling.

God hath been pleased to cause us to see some, and hear more of the Overturnings which are now in the World, what then is our present Duty? But to give thanks to his Great Name, for any such appearances as seem to forebode

---

106 As noted in the "Introduction", printed sermons sometimes contained elements like this that were retained from, or at least give the reader an impression mimicking, the sermon when it was delivered from the pulpit. Arnold Hunt has described this as "scripted extemporisation": Hunt, *Art of Hearing*, 159–160.

107 Jacob is making a humourous contrast between the celebratory mood of public thanksgivings and the more sombre tone of public fasts.

108 *Amos 4. 12.*

the destruction of Antichrist, and the Exaltation of the Kingdom of Christ; Let us rejoyce in all the overturnings, Greater or Lesser, which God gives to his Enemys; When He makes his Arrows drunk with Blood, (and his Sword devours Flesh) with the Blood of the Slain, and of the Captives, even from the Beginning of Revenges upon the Enemy[109] (when they are but begun.)

Then, says God, Rejoyce O ye Nations with his People, for that is a Time of Joy to the People of God, in whose Joy the Nations also should Rejoyce, because God will avenge the Blood of his Servants, and will render Vengance to his Adversarys, and will be Merciful unto his Land, and to his People.[110]

The overturning of the Enemys of Godliness is matter of Joy to the Saints; The Righteous shall rejoyce (says the Psalmist) when he sees Vengance Executed upon them;[111] It is on this account, the Land is this day Expressing their Joy; The whole Nation is now appointed to give Thanks unto God for the Overthrow lately given by the Forces of this Nation, under the Conduct of their Heroick General, unto those Inveterate Enemys of our Country and Religion, The French.[112] And surely if Joy is felt in us, and Praise is sung to God for this Defeat on one part or Joynt of the Antichristian Force, what Gladness will be conceived, what Gratitude will be exprest, when there shall be an overturning of All the Antichristian powers in the World? Then will that Command be put in Practice, Rejoyce over her, thou Heaven, and ye Holy Apostles and Prophets, for God hath Avenged you on Her;[113] and then will that Επινιϰιον or Song of Praise be Sung, Allelujah, Salvation and Glory, and Honour be unto the Lord our God, for True and Righteous are his Judgments, for he hath Judged the great Whore, which did Corrupt the Earth with her Fornication, and hath avenged the Blood of his Servants at her hand, and again they said Allelujah![114] which Glorious Things and Joyful Days the Lord hasten in his due Time, Amen, and Amen.

---

109   D[e]ut. 32. 42.
110   v. 43.
111   Psal. 58. 10.
112   Jacob is reminds his audience of the occasion of the thanksgiving, a military victory over the French. Anti-French sentiment is a common theme in British thanksgiving sermons throughout the eighteenth century, so many of which marked events during wars with France.
113   Rev. 18. 22 [sic]. [vere, Revelation 18:20. See also Rev. 17:1–2 and 18:2].
114   Ch. 19. 1, 2, 3.

A REMARKABLE
ACCOMPLISHMENT
OF A NOTED
SCRIPTURE PROPHECY,
AS APPLIED TO THE
HISTORY OF ENGLAND
DURING THE
LAST and PRESENT CENTURIES,
IN A
THANKSGIVING SERMON
PREACHED
By the Rev. RICHARD DOBBS, D.D.
OF
LISBURN, in the NORTH of IRELAND,
NOVEMBER 29th, 1759.
LONDON:
Printed for THOMAS WILCOX, at VIRGIL'S HEAD
opposite the NEW CHURCH in the STRAND,
M.DCC.LXII.

A Prefatory Advertisement.

The Apocalypse of St. John, Apostle and Evangelist, is a prophetic Book, and admits of a threefold Meaning. The first is the usual Application to civil Empires, such as are signified by the four Beasts in Daniel, according to the received Interpretation; which I meddle not with, having been well explained by Mede, More, Peganius,[115] &c. as to Times past. The second is applied to the Kingdom or Church of God external and political: and the third to the same Kingdom internal in the Mind of each true Christian: both which are considered by due Analogy in the following Discourse as to Times past in the reformed Church of England; and in an Exposition of the whole Apocalypse by paraphrastic[116] Notes in another Manuscript, consistently with that here given.
[...]

---

115 As discussed on pp. 208–209 above, Joseph Mede and Henry More were two prominent English expositors of apocalyptic prophecy in the seventeenth century. "Peganius" was the pseudonym of the German mystic and scriptural interpreter Christian Knorr von Rosenroth, who published *A Genuine Explication of the Visions of the Book of Revelation* (London: n.d.) in the later seventeenth century: Johnston, *Revelation Restored*, 27 note 10. Von Rosenroth and Henry More were acquainted with each other's work and corresponded: Marjorie Hope Nicolson (ed.) and Sarah Hutton (rev. ed.), *The Conway Letters: the Correspondence of Anne, Viscountess Conway, Henry More, and Their Friends 1642–1684* (Oxford: 1992), 318 note 18, 323 note 5.
116 I.e., in the form of a paraphrase.

Rev. vi. 2.

And I saw, and behold, a white Horse; and he that sat on him had a Bow, and a Crown was given unto him; and he went forth conquering, and to conquer.

This is the Vision seen by St. John, at opening the first of the seven Seals of the prophetic holy Scriptures by Christ the Lamb of God. To explain this prophetic Text rightly, it will be needful to give a concise View of the seven prophetic monitory[117] Letters in the second and third Chapters of this Book, with their Accomplishment particularly applicable to the national Church of England, and suited to the present Occasion.

[...] The seven Churches in Asia represent prophetically seven successive Periods of a national christian Church, during the gradual Formation of the civil Constitution out of the Ruins of a former well regulated Polity; similar to the Creation of this visible World in six Days out of a State of Disorder and Confusion, produced by the Fall of the Angels. For, as we are told by Moses, the divinely inspired Author of the Book of Genesis, In the Beginning, in a State of Perfection and Freedom, as the Original signifies, God three-one created the Heavens and the Earth [...] Then follows the historical Summary of the six Days Work, so contrived and executed by divine Wisdom, as analogically at one to describe the gradual Formation of this visible World, the Earth and its atmospheric Heavens, out of the abyssal turbulent Deep, and heavenly supernal Waters; and also of the new or regenerate Creation spiritual, out of the Ruins of the fallen World, and recoverable Faculties of penitent fallen man. Let us compare the seven Periods, each of twenty Years, in the Growth of the present happy British Constitution, with the Works and Sabbatism of the corresponding Days in the History of the Creation; to manifest that the same divine Wisdom guided and directed all in both Instances.

I. From A.D. 1620 to 1640 was the Foundation laid of regenerating the present happy British Constitution, in habitual Loyalty to it; by adhering firmly to legal Rights well understood, and exact Obedience to the Laws. For K. James 1st. had gradually subverted the happy Union of the three Estates in frequent Sessions of Parliament, that had always subsisted during the excellent Reign of Q. Elizabeth: and in 1621 sprang up that Light in Parliament of the necessary Distinction between the Promoters of absolute Power, and the Godlike Rule of a free Monarchy over free Subjects.[118] This Light was constitutionally formed by the Petition of Right in 1628 from both Houses of Parliament, obtaining the

---

117 "monitory" means warning.
118 This refers to the disputes that erupted during the meeting of the English Parliament in

Royal Assent of K. Charles 1st.[119] This Period ends with calling the Parliament of 1640, at the Desire of the People, and by Advice of the Lords.

2. In the next twenty Years to 1660, the Constitution was entirely dissolved during the civil War, and a new Firmament or Constitution framed under Cromwell's Usurpation: wherefore God did not approve of this second Day's Work as good, until, in the first Part of the third Day, the Executive was legitimately constituted by the Restoration in 1660, as formerly.[120]

3. The third Day's Work and Period of twenty years began with the Restoration of the executive Power in the Hands of Officers legally qualified and constituted by parliamentary Sanction of the three Estates flowing with united Affections to one Place, not many, as in the Times of the late civil Broils; so that the dry Land of a firm Establishment began to appear, with God's Approbation as good; which, at the divine Command conveyed by God's Vicegerent in the Charter of the Royal Society,[121] was soon clothed with the flourishing and useful Verdure of Arts and Sciences producing seed-full Systems of Practice, durable as Trees, whose Seed is in itself; i.e. producing its Like in those that serve an Apprenticeship to it. This also said to please God.

4. The two great Receptacles of Lights of the fourth Day's Work and twenty Years Period are the Bill of Rights, and that of the Protestant Succession,[122]

1621 over the rights of the House of Commons to free speech in its debates and in its advisory role to the monarch. There was an increasingly heated exchange of correspondence between James I and the House of Commons over this issue, instigated by the Commons' concern over the king's foreign policy. James eventually dissolved Parliament over this issue in December 1621, and this was an initial event in the souring of relations between Parliament and the monarchy in the 1620s.

119   In 1628 Charles I agreed to accept *The Petition of Right* in return for the promise of parliamentary subsidies to alleviate the king's worsening financial circumstances. The document listed Parliament's growing concerns over the government's imposition of non-parliamentary authority over the kingdom. In 1629 Charles I dissolved the English Parliament and ruled eleven years without calling another. The calling of Parliament in 1640 led to a further political breakdown over the next two years.

120   This paragraph mentions the outbreak of civil war in England (and Scotland and Ireland) in 1642. This eventually resulted in the execution of Charles I in 1649 and periods of republican government, the Lord Protectorship of Oliver Cromwell, and military rule. The monarchy was restored in England, Scotland, Ireland in 1660 with the return of Charles II to the throne.

121   The Royal Society of London was given its charter by Charles II in 1662, with the purpose of advancing knowledge in natural philosophy. Its early members included scientists like Robert Boyle and Isaac Newton.

122   The *Bill of Rights* was passed by the English Parliament in 1689 as part of the settlement that saw William III & Mary II take the throne in place of James II. It acknowledged the necessary role of Parliament in the government of England, and also included restrictions

absolving the People from Allegiance to all Popish Princes in the Line of Succession to the Crown; thereby securing to the Laity the free Use of the Bible in the vulgar Tongue, and Statute Laws parliamentary, &c. as two great Lights for both the divine Life and the civil: by which is given the clear Knowledge of what true Loyalty is; both in the Day of a legal Administration of public Affairs, subject to parliamentary Inquiry, and in the Night of an illegal disorderly one. And with an Act of Parliament confirming the Succession of the present Royal Family to the Crown, being Protestants, did this fourth Day's Work conclude in 1701, about nine Months before the Death of K. William, who under God procured these great Blessings for us by the Revolution of 1688, and its happy Consequences. This also said to be good.

5. In the fifth Day's Work, or Period of twenty Years, ending in 1720, was Loyalty to the Constitution combined with the Executive duly constituted, by legal Qualification of Officers according to Laws then framed for that Purpose. But a short four Years Administration, at the Close of a hitherto glorious Reign, would have endangered our whole Constitution, had not the good Providence of God again interposed, and fixed his late Majesty K. George 1st peaceably in the Throne; thus admirably disposing the Lights and Shades of this historical Creation-Piece, to give the more exquisite Delight, and manifest more sensibly the divine Author of this Work. And accordingly there is but one other Passage in the whole Bible where Days are termed Evening-Mornings; and that is in Daniel's Prophecy, (viii. 14.) of cleansing the Sanctuary after the Evening-Morning of 2300 prophetic Days, i.e. Years, which terminate in the Midst of the present sabbatic twenty Year Period. Upon some other Occasion this may be shewn strongly to confirm the present Application of the Mosaic History of the Creation. This God approved of as good.

6. The sixth Day's Work, from 1720 to 1740, which also had God's Approbation as good, united the executive Administration of Government with the legislative Authority of Parliament;[123] so as to begin and end with parliamentary Approbation of all public Measures in a remarkable Manner. The Earth God's Foot-stool, (Mat. v. 35.) i.e. those subject to Government produces after its Kind, by having the Proceedings of all Law Courts in the vulgar Tongue, according to an Act of Parliament made in this Period; the Cattle, i.e. judicial Proceedings

---

    against a Catholic monarch succeeding to the throne. The *Act of Settlement* (1701) ensured that the line of succession to the English throne would pass through the Protestant Hanoverian line after the reign of Anne.

123 This is a reference to Robert Walpole's long period as prime minister. Walpole's Whig ministry was in power throughout the 1720s and 30s, and saw extensive cooperation with George I and George II, seeing a unity of parliamentary with monarchical government.

by Statue Law, domestic Forms; the creeping Thing, i.e. judicial Proceedings by Common Law, gaining Authority by slow Progress of Custom; and Beasts of the Earth, i.e. judicial Proceedings by Civil Law and Equity, or Law of Nature and Nations, agrestic Forms. The God like Adam political is the Union of legislative and executive Perfection, with wise and powerful Loyalty to the Constitution, and abhorrent Opposition to Corruption. This created last for divine Communion in the perpetual Sabbatism of the seventh and all following Periods for ever.

The prophetic monitory Epistles of Christ to the seven Churches in Asia are fully and respectively applicable to the seven Periods of the political Creation of the British Constitution, with Regard to the State of the Church in those Periods. For in this Application the seven Churches are seven successive States of the Church fully reformed under Q. Elizabeth, and preserving her Constitution unaltered, during the Lapse of the Earth or civil Constitution under K. James Ist. and the Regeneration of it in the following Periods;[124] but in various Situations, on Account of the progressive Alterations of the civil System in Union with it. Wherefore the Letters are directed to the Angels, i.e. the divine Messengers, or Bishops and Pastors; and relate chiefly to the Execution of the pastoral Office, not at all to any Alteration of the Constitution of the Church, which is fully approved of in the Type of golden Candlesticks, under the immediate Government of Christ dressing the Lights.

The actual Accomplishment of these prophetic Epistles will fully appear from the following paraphrastic Application of them; which will at the same Time furnish ample Materials for joyful Meditation and grateful Thanksgiving, suited to this festival Day, in which we are to praise God and Christ our Saviour for the signal Success of his Majesty's Arms. This Success is clearly foretold in the Text by the crowned white Horse Rider going forth conquering, and to conquer; namely, in the Cause of God and Christ: Both literally, as the white Horse is the Ensign Armorial of the House of Brunswick, as Dukes of ancient Saxony, from whence is derived the Anglo-Saxon Empire in Britain, now ruled by the Electoral House of Brunswick:[125] And spiritually, as signifying a making war victoriously, mounted on righteous Impulse or Motives, through Christ, the Lamb

---

124 As with his comments on the constitution, Dobbs now implies that the Church of England had been perfectly reformed in Elizabeth's reign, but began to regress during the reigns of James I and Charles I in the early to mid seventeenth century.

125 Dobbs connects his main text, Rev. 6:2 with the current thanksgiving, giving it apocalyptic significance through the armorial symbolism of the Dukes of Brunswick and, through that, to the Hanoverian kings of Britain in the eighteenth century. See also notes 185 and 186 below.

of God that taketh away the Sins of the World, opening the Seal of Restraint by the Sacrifice of himself once offered, the Just for the Unjust. The Lion, the first of the four animal Forms of Christ-like Life seen in and around the Throne of God, as exhibited by the four Evangelists, four evangelic Prophets, and four first Books of Moses respectively, proclaims the War of the faithful Followers of Christ against his spiritual Enemies:[126] Accordingly Christ's Sermon on the Mount, related only by St Matthew,[127] declares the whole Plan of the christian Warfare. The literal Accomplishment fitly belongs to the Emblem sealed up, which connects the last of the seven monitory Letters, as co-existing with its Conclusion, to the spiritual Accomplishment exhibited by opening the first Seal. Let us proceed then to the paraphrastic Application of these Letters in Rev. second and third Chapters.

CHAP. II[128]

1. UNTO the Angel of the Church of Ephesus, i.e. the pastoral Administration of the Ephesine Period of twenty Years, zealous in the christian Life, write; for a lasting Instruction to the Pastors: These Things saith he that holdeth the seven Stars in his right Hand, i.e. Christ that supports, comforts and guides with divine enlightening Grace all the pastoral Negotiations in the Regeneration Process; who walketh in the Midst of the seven golden Candlesticks, animating the whole Regeneration Process with Christ-like Life progressive;

2. I know thy Works, among Converts from Popery in the zealous Ephesine Period of the reformed Church of England, from A.D. 1620 to 1640, and thy Labour, among the faithful christian Warriors against the spiritual Enemies of Christ and his Church, and thy Patience, or perfective Toleration of Adversaries treating thee injuriously for my Sake; and how thou canst not bear them which are evil, in thy Communion; but usest wholesom Discipline towards them: And thou hast tried them which say they are Apostles, i.e. deriving their Mission immediately from Christ; namely, the Sectarian, Puritan Teachers that reject the Need of regular Ordination according to ecclesiastic Succession, and Usage derived from Christ's original Institution;[129] and are not, what they pre-

---

126 Revelation 4:6–9.
127 Matt. 5–7.
128 This refers to chapter 2 of Revelation. What follows is Dobbs's extensive paraphrase and detailed, verse-by-verse interpretation of chapters 2 and 3 of Rev.
129 This identifies and condemns those who criticized the Church of England in the period leading up to the Civil Wars, singling out their challenges to its rules for ordination and to its claims of apostolic endorsement for its episcopal structure.

tend; and hast found them Liars, i.e. Impostors, by a fair Examination and full Confutation of their pretended Titles:

3. And hast borne repeated Injuries from false Brethren and concealed Popish Incendiaries, promoting Schisms and heretical Sects; and hast Patience, in Hopes of reclaiming the Weak and Deluded, and for my Name's Sake, i.e. through my divine Nature assisting, and after my Example, hast laboured in promoting my Church and Kingdom, against both Popish and Fanatical Antichristianism,[130] i.e. outward and inward, or public and private; and hast not fainted, or forsaken the Work.

4. Nevertheless I have somewhat against thee, because thou hast left thy first Love, i.e. abated of its Fervour, so conspicuous in the reformed Church of England, at its full Establishment in Union with the civil Power, under parliamentary Sanction, in the Reign of Queen Elizabeth; and even under the Fall of civil Liberty in James 1st's Reign. But in the Reign of King Charles 1st, Lord Clarendon[131] confesses, and the learned Mr. Mede[132] complains of, the Boldness and open Growth of Popery in this Period, which was much owing to a Popish Queen.[133]

5. Remember therefore from whence thou art fallen, and repent of thy Remissness against Popish Regulars, and Seducers of my People; and do the first Works of constant Watchfulness against Popish Intrigues and Labours to pervert my People, and of zealous Opposition to them; or else I will come unto thee in Judgment quickly, i.e. in the next twenty Years Period from 1640 to 1660, named of Smyrna, signifying Bitterness, namely, of Persecution; and will remove thy Candlestick, i.e. Church Establishment, out of his Place, i.e. of Union with the civil Establishment, and Protection by it:[134] For the Church Polity shall be violently shaken, and driven by a Tempest of Persecution,[135] dur-

---

130   This asserts that opponents to the Church of England ranged from Catholics to radical Protestants.
131   Edward Hyde (1609–1674), was a royalist supporter of Charles I, a government minister in the first half of Charles II's reign, and the author of a history of the civil war period, published posthumously as *The History of the Rebellion and Civil Wars in England, begun in the Year 1641*, 3 volumes (1702–1704).
132   Joseph Mede, the apocalyptic interpreter and author of *Clavis apocalyptica* (1627, 1632).
133   Here Dobbs suggests that the Church of England was backsliding towards Catholicism during Charles I's reign, in part based on the undue influence of the queen, the French princess Henrietta Maria.
134   In the period of civil war and the Interregnum in the 1640s and 50s, the episcopalian structure of the Church of England was dismantled and its form of service (*The Book of Common Prayer*) proscribed.
135   Persecution in the form of many Church of England clergy being removed from their livings in that period.

ing the confused Agitations of a dissolved Constitution, and civil Anarchy succeeded by various short-lived Forms of Government; except thou repent, and be zealous against Popish Emissaries and Counsels, both open and disguised; i.e. in Form of Sectaries and pretended Preachers of Reformation, as well as open Supporters of arbitrary Power and Popish Tyranny over Conscience and civil Liberty.

6. But this thou hast, that thou hatest the Deeds of the Nicolaitans, i.e. rebellious Carnalists, or Promoters of popular Reformation with unconstitutional Violence and unruly Mobs; which I also hate. John xviii. 11.[136]

7. He that hath an Ear, i.e. is disposed to listen to the Admonitions of Christ's Holy Spirit in the spiritual Meaning of these pastoral counsels, and be bettered by them, let him hear, and spiritually understand, what the Spirit saith unto the Churches in the following Part of these prophetic Parables; what goes before being directed to the Clergy alone. To him that overcometh the antichristian Powers public and private in this spiritual Warfare, will I give to eat spiritually of the Tree, i.e. fruit-bearing Counsel, of Life God-like, free, blissful and perpetual, which is in the Midst of the Paradise of God; i.e. central to divine Communion, whether social and public in the Church, or private in inward in the christian Heart. This was verified at the Restoration in 1660 to the faithful Sons of the Church of England, then endowed with Perpetuity.[137]

8. And unto the angel, i.e. pastoral Administration, of the Church in Smyrna, i.e. in State of bitter Persecution from A.D.1640 to 1660, write, for a standing Instruction to my Embassadors in such States: These Things saith the first and the last, i.e. the original and great Exemplar of the first and regenerated States of human Nature in Glory; which was dead, in the suffering State of Christ's human Nature, fitly termed last and lowest during incarnate Humiliation, and is alive now and for ever, by his Resurrection into his first or exalted State of supreme Dominion over the whole Creation, both literally in himself, and mystically in that of his Church and faithful Followers Christ-like; a

---

136 The term Nicolaitans is from the original verse (Rev. 2:6) and refers to a dispute in the early Christian Church. However, in the eighteenth century, the term was associated with antinomianism, a belief that grace freed believers from having to obey the law. See, for example, John Fletcher, *Logica Genevensis Continued. Or the First Part of the Fifth Check to Antinomianism* (London: 1774), 35. It is used here by Dobbs to criticize Calvinist calls for church reform in the 1640s. The citation of John is likely intended to be 18:3 (not 2), in reference to the band of men that accompanied Judas to arrest Jesus.

137 The restoration of the monarchy in 1660 was also accompanied by the initial reinstitution of Church of England clergy, structures, and services; this was officially confirmed in the 1662 *Act of Uniformity*.

sure Earnest to thee of the Resurrection of the national Church of England at the Close of this Period in 1660.

9. I know thy Works, watchful Labours now in the Time of Persecution, when none but faithful Pastors will accept of, or abide by, the Office; and Tribulation, under the Persecution; and Poverty of Spirit, in Meekness and Patience; (but thou art rich in heavenly Treasures of Faith and good Works) and I know the Blasphemy, in belying my Name or divine Nature they pretend to imitate, of them, the Puritanic Sectaries, and hypocritic Romish Emissaries personating them in Disguise,[138] which say they are Jews, my true Worshipers in Spirit and in Truth, taking judicial Vengeance of my Enemies; and are not, being fanatical Fifth-monarchy Men[139] and other Sectaries; but are the Synagogue, as having an outward Church Polity, of Satan the Tempter, by Romish Emissaries in Disguise labouring to divide and seduce; the Accuser, by informing against pretended Malignants, and the Persecutor of the Brethren that stood firm in the Faith and Practice of genuine Christianity.

10. Fear none of those Things which thou, the persecuted, true, pastoral Administration, shalt suffer: Behold, the Devil, or satanic Rulers, shall cast some of you, of the Clergy, into Prison, both outward in bodily Restraint, and inward in prohibiting and superseding You in the Exercise of your Office; that you may be tried, as to your Constancy of Loyalty to me; and ye shall have Tribulation ten Days: And so many Years, according to the prophetic Meaning of Days in this Book and Daniel, did the Sufferings continue of such as adhered to the Constitution of the Church of England, as established at the Reformation under Queen Elizabeth's Guardianship by divine Appointment; counting from the Murder of Charles I, who was its civil Head under God, and died a Martyr to it, to the Death of Cromwell; or from Charles II, taking the solemn League and covenant, to his Restoration.[140] Be thou faithful unto Death, of thy national Establishment, and I will give thee, truly reformed Church of England, a Crown of Life, perpetual as the Circle of the Crown or Diadem binding thy civil, national Head, by parliamentary Establishment at the Restoration A.D.1660.

---

138 It was commonly asserted that many of the radical Protestant sectarians in the 1640s and 1650s were actually Catholics in disguise, intent upon destabilizing the English church and state.

139 The Fifth Monarchy Men were a group of radical millenarians in mid-seventeenth-century England who believed that the advent of Christ's second coming and the Millennium would be initiated by the overthrow of worldly powers.

140 The "ten days" in this verse are interpreted as years, and Dobbs sees these lasting roughly from 1649 to 1660, from the death of Charles I and his son taking the Presbyterian Solemn League and Covenant to get the support of the Scots, to the fall of the Cromwellian protectorship and the restoration of the monarchy.

11. He that hath an Ear, Disposition to attend to spiritual Advices and Communications, let him hear, i.e. have by my creative or regenerative Power a spiritual Faculty of understanding and obediently listening to, what the Spirit, inward Meaning of the literal Prophecy, saith, in the following consolatory Promise, unto the Churches, during this regenerative Process of the fallen civil British Constitution. He that overcometh, in standing the Shocks of these Trials firmly, and preserving his Loyalty to me by adhering to my true Church, shall not be hurt of the second Death, by Dissociation political, at the final Destruction of these antichristian, persecuting Forms of Government.

12. And to the Angel, pastoral Administration, of the Church in Pergamus, third twenty Year Period of Exaltation and Safety by parliamentary Establishment at the Restoration A.D. 1660; for Pergamus signifies a strong Tower; write: These Things saith he which hath the sharp Sword with two Edges, literal and spiritual Execution of the Law, with civil and ecclesiastic Authority exercised by Christ's Vicegerent on the British Throne:

13. I know thy Works, of Zeal and diligent constancy; and where thou dwellest, in thy Pergamenian State of apparent Court Favour, seemingly countenanced; even where Satan's Seat is, the antichristian Tempter and Accuser of the Brethren; namely, a lurking Popish Faction and Interest at Court, concealed in the King, but avowed by the Duke of York, which designed to overturn the constitution by introducing Popery and absolute Power without Parliaments:[141] And thou, the Clergy, holdest fast my Name, against all false Worship through false Mediators; and hast not denied my Faith, in Favour of Antichristianism, even in those Days, the ten Years Persecution in the last vicennial Period, termed ten Days of Tribulation, wherein Antipas was my faithful Martyr, evidently meaning the Martyrdom of the Church of England, and its civil Head under Christ King Charles I; for Antipas, a Name truly characteristic of the Church of England in that Period, literally signifies Opposition to all; namely, the numerous Sects spawned by Antichristianism at that Time; and History records no such Person as Antipas in the literal Church of Smyrna; who was slain,[142] by dividing and seducing Protestants as well as literally, among you, Papists and popishly affected, whether open or disguised; by personating the

---

141 This suggests that Charles II had secret Catholic inclinations, as well as referring to the overt Catholicism of his brother and heir James, Duke of York. The issue of James's place in succession to the throne led to a political crisis between Charles II and Parliament in the late 1670s and early 1680s.

142 Antipas was an early Christian martyr in Pergamum: Shailer Mathews, "Antipas", in *Dictionary of the Bible*, ed. James Hastings et al (New York: 1909), 39. Dobbs interprets this as a reference to the martyrdom of Charles I.

Sectaries of several Denominations, according to your several Talents; where Satan, Accuser of the Brethren and Promoter of despotic Government usually the Successor of Anarchy, dwelleth; i.e. has got a King of Settlement at Court in this Pergamenian or third vicennial Period, by Means of a King popishly affected in his private Judgment, and an avowed Papist being presumptive Heir to the Crown.

14. But I have a few Things against thee, the pastoral Administration of this Period; because thou hast there them, some among you, that hold the Doctrine of Balaam, Enslaver of the People, who taught Balak, i.e. Exhauster of the People, namely, of God, to cast a stumbling Block before the Children of Israel, serious inward Christians, to eat Things sacrificed to Idols, to temporize with the Popish Faction for court Favour, acting against Conscience; and to commit Fornication, by holding Communion with an idolatrous Church.[143]

15. So hast thou also them that hold the Doctrine of the Nicolaitans, joining to Purity of christian Profession in the outward Form of Faith and Devotion the sensual Life of a Voluptuary, and licentious, disorderly Factiousness, under Pretence of Reformation; thus promoting Anarchy, and not true Liberty; which Thing I hate.

16. Repent; or else I will come unto thee quickly in the very next twenty Year Period, giving thee a Popish King[144] to humble thee and purge away thy Dross, by the Removal of Court Favour; and will fight against them of Satan's Seat, the antichristian Party, Balaamites, Nicolaitans, &C. with the Sword of my Mouth, God's Word judicially severing between the clean and unclean, in the zealous christian Spirit almost universally raised in Support of civil and religious Liberties, by the London Cafes written and preached against Popish and other Dissenters; and so producing the Revolution in 1688, which in some Time purged the Church of all her Clergy that were Friends to Tyranny or Anarchy in Church or State.[145]

17. He that hath an Ear spiritual, let him hear what the Spirit spiritual Meaning of these Letters, saith unto the Churches, both Clergy and Laity: To him that overcometh the Dangers he is exposed to in this third Period, from the fore-mentioned Blemishes of the Court and some of the Clergy, leading him to

---

143 The biblical reference is to the story of Balaam, who served as a soothsayer for Balak, king of the Moabites, in Numbers 22–24. Balaam was believed to have enticed the Israelites to worship Baal and to have sex with the Moabite women (Num. 25:1–3, 31:16). This reference is used as an analogy for the presence of Catholicism in and around Charles II's court.
144 I.e., James II.
145 I.e., the supporters of James II who favoured absolute rule and supported the king's Catholic beliefs.

violate his Conscience and inward Peace of Mind, will I give to eat spiritually of the hidden Manna, that heavenly instruction given inwardly to the Heart by the Holy Spirit, who delights to dwell in a pure Conscience, and fills the inward Life with Light and Joy inconceivable by all that fell it not within themselves; and will give him a white Stone of Justification firm and righteous, or of Acquittal at the judicial Bar of Conscience; and in the Stone of Acquittal or Salvation a new Name, i.e. regenerate Nature, written in a confirmed Habit, which no Man knoweth, saving he that receiveth it, as being wholly inward in the Heart.

18. And unto the Angel, i.e. pastoral Administration of the Bishops and Pastors, of the Church in Thyatira, the fourth Vicennium or twenty Year Period ending in 1700, taking its Name from the Sacrifice of the Mass openly tolerated, and Popery, of a persecuting Spirit, being rampant at Court; when a tyrannic antichristian Prince[146] trampled on the established Religion and Liberties of his Subjects, until his Abdication, and then promoted Plots and War to overturn the Constitution; write: These Things saith the Son of God, Redeemer of his People from Tyranny of Rulers and Slavery of Subjects religious and civil; regenerating them into perfect Freedom; who hath his Eyes like unto a Flame of Fire, consuming all Opposition from his and the Nation's antichristian Enemies, by a luminous flaming Zeal almost universal, to complete the Security of civil and religious Rights clearly defined for the Time to come by the two great Lights of this fourth Day's Work of political Regeneration: For the Revolution of 1688, by the Sanction of religious Tests and Oaths,[147] has placed in the constitutional Heavens of Religion the two great Lights of religious and civil Rights and Liberties of a free People, namely, the Laws of God in the Bible and Liturgy, the Laws of the civil Life in the Statute Book and Common Law, as declared in the Bill of Rights, and confirmed by the Coronation Oath;[148] and his Feet, i.e. Pillars of this happy Establishment, and Instruments of spiritual Progress, are like fine Brass, which in the prophetic Language signifies Wisdom of Incense or christian Devotion to Christ and God's Laws, and Loyalty to the State and national Laws.

---

146 James II, who succeeded to the throne on the death of Charles II in 1685.
147 The Revolution of 1688–1689 saw the re-imposition of the Test Act and its oaths to prevent Catholics from serving in positions of influence and political power. Similarly, the *Bill of Rights* (1689) imposed the necessity of communion in the Church of England to prevent Protestant dissenters from serving in positions of political power. An oath of allegiance to William and Mary was also imposed, causing some Anglican clergymen (nonjurors) to give up their livings.
148 In their coronation oath, William and Mary swore to abide by and govern based on the laws of England as established by Parliament.

19. I know thy Works, first Labours of this Period in outward Life and Discipline; and Charity, in striving to rescue the Souls of Men from Popish Slavery; and Service, in the Ministry, watching over Thy Flocks; and Faith, Trust in God through Christ; and thy Patience, bearing all with christian Fortitude, even the sending the seven Bishops to the Tower;[149] waiting for and expecting my Appearance in your Deliverance; and thy Works, in the inward Life consequential to Persecution, which discovers all false Brethren, and separates the Chaff from the Wheat; concluding these six Steps of thy good Behaviour with voluntary Associations for Reformation of Manners among the Laity;[150] and the last, i.e. thy inward Works, to be more, in Labour and Importance, than the first, i.e. thy outward Works, whose Value is estimated by Subserviency to inward Works: and thus thou hast improved the Talents committed to thy Trust.

20. Notwithstanding, I have a few Things against thee, because thou sufferest, by open Toleration, that Woman, Emblem of a Church Polity, Jezabel, which signifies Habitation of Curses, the true Character of the Popish Church, which calleth herself a Prophetess, i.e. an infallible Interpreter of God's Word or Laws, having no Voucher for it but her own Testimony, such is Popish Infallibility;[151] to teach, (note, this is directed to both Civil and Ecclesiastical Rulers of that Period, as not putting the Laws in force against Popish Friars and itinerant Preachers and Missionaries) and to seduce my Servants to commit Fornication, by Communion with that idolatrous Church; and to eat Things sacrificed unto Idols, in swallowing and feeding on their pernicious Doctrines of Merits, Indulgences, and Saint Mediators, &c.

21. And I gave her (Popish Jezabel) Space to repent of her Fornication, i.e. Idolatry, ever since the Reformation under Queen Elizabeth; and more particularly since my appearing against her in so extraordinary and miraculous

---

149   This refers to William Sancroft, (Canterbury), William Lloyd (St Asaph), Thomas Ken (Bath and Wells), Jonathan Trelawny (Bristol), John Lake (Chichester), Francis Turner (Ely), and Thomas White (Peterborough), who petitioned to James to resist his 1688 *Declaration of Indulgence* being read from Church of England pulpits. James had the bishops charged with seditious libel but they were acquitted in late June 1688. See Warren Johnston, "Revelation and the Revolution of 1688–1689", *The Historical Journal* 48/2 (2005), 362–363 and note 38.

150   This refers to the establishment of the Society for the Reformation of Manners in the early 1690s, with the intent of curbing immoral activity in England.

151   This is another attack on Catholic beliefs, with Jezebel symbolizing the promotion of false worship. The biblical reference is to Jezebel, the wife of the Israelite King Ahab. Jezebel caused Ahab to set up the worship of Baal (1 Kings 16:31–33) and she attacked the prophets of God (1 Kings 18, 19, and 21).

a Manner at the Restoration; and she repented not, but repeated her Sorceries under King James IId, who as another Ahab or Lover (for so the Name signifies) had drank her Philtres (Love Potions) and wedded her.

22. Behold I will cast her into a Bed of Languishing or Feebleness, as not able to stand before her Enemies, or walk erect; and them that commit Adultery with her, in forsaking Christ and his pure Worship in the established Church of England, to cohabit (even by occasional Communion[152]) with this antichristian idolatrous Religion of Rome Papal; into great Tribulation, by the Revolution under King William IIId. and Queen Mary; which put a final Period to Popish Government in Britain, and took away all Power from the Popishly affected, or even suspected to be so; except they repent of their Deeds, and truly and publicly forsake her, to return to true Christianity by abjuring openly her Errors in the Face of the Church.

23. And I will kill her Children, antichristian Separatists begotten of her, in the Sectaries sprung up in the preceding Period, and tolerated by K. James IId. using an illegal dispensing Power, for which they and the Papists gave him Addresses of Thanks; with Death, political by taking away that Toleration Establishment at the Revolution: and all the Churches, in future Regeneration Processes in other Nations, shall know, by this notorious and exemplary Instance of my judicial Advent to Britain; that I am he which searcheth the Reins, purging the Superfluities and Enormities of the civil Life; and Hearts, out of which proceed the Issues of the divine Life in the Church of God, or Sing and spiritual Death: and I will given, in this judicial Advent, unto every one of you, tolerated congregations, according to your Works; so narrowly will you be watched by the civil Power, that may indulge truly tender Consciences, but neither give universal Toleration, as in Holland, nor abrogate penal Laws.[153]

24. But unto you, the ruling Church Powers, I say, and unto the rest, namely, the reformed Laity, in Thyatira, this 4th Period sacrificial; As many as have not known this doctrine, of tolerating, under Sanction of an usurped Power

---

152 Like Joseph Jacob (see p. 209 and note 6 above), Dobbs also criticizes occasional conformity in the Church of England, which allowed those participants to then serve in public office. However, unlike Jacob's concern over maintaining the purity of Protestant dissent, Dobbs is criticizing Catholics for their occasional observance.

153 In this paragraph, Dobbs continues demonstrating his pro-Anglican stance, though now directed at Protestant dissent. He condemns Protestant dissenters for thanking (like Catholics did) James II for his arbitrary dispensation of penal laws against them. Dobbs distinguishes the *Toleration Act* (1689) under William and Mary from James's *Indulgence* in 1687 and 1688 by saying that the 1689 legislation continued to defend the purity of the church and constitution of Britain (though he seems to forget the Scottish Presbyterian Kirk here) by keeping dissenters from serving in political office.

dispensing with Law, this adulterous Jezabel to seduce my Servants to Idolatry, which is high Treason against me, at the Time Treason against the State in civil matters is so severely punished, and that justly; and which have not known the Depths of Satan, the murderous private Assassinations, open Massacres, inquisitorial Tortures, and persecuting Spirit of this sensual idolatrous Romish Church, literally practised, and openly defended when she has Power; but where she wants it, darkly and in secret, serpentine, poisonous Insinuations, sowing Divisions and exciting a persecuting Spirit, wherever she can, amongst those that have forsaken her Communion; as they proverbially speak, in this Revolution Period, when Abundance of learned and judicious controversial Writings made these Things manifest to all, and in every Mouth:[154] and at this Time was this Spirit of Persecution and Assassination supported by a whole Party struggling for the Establishment of tyrannic Dominion over Conscience, even by Assassination Plots against K. William IIId,[155] as formerly against Q. Elizabeth: I will put upon you, thus qualified, none other burden, or Talk, save what follows in the next Verse; whilst the persecuting, nonjuring, schismatical Supporters of Tyranny[156] will themselves become obnoxious to the Laws, and Slaves to a Constitution they had Hopes of destroying, and obstinately continued to struggle against and undermine.

25. But that which ye have already, religious and civil Liberties, and Freedom to support them by your exemplary Lives and strong argumentative Reasonings, both in public Discourses and private Conversations; hold fast, in using properly these Blessings, till I come, in opening the seven Seals at the Beginning of seven twenty Year Periods or Vicenniums, one for each; to establish you for ever, both in this World and the next, in the Possession of these inestimable Blessings of outward good Government wise and powerful, by quickening and consummating the inward Life suitably to the great Perfection of the outward Constitution completed during the 140 Years ending at A.D. 1760.

26. And he that overcometh the Subtilties of the Adversary in this Struggle for Liberty, and keepeth, by his watchful Cooperation, my Works, and Labours

---

154 Dobbs again turns his attention to attacking Catholicism and the papacy, accusing that church and its government of policies of persecution and violence against Protestant believers and governments. Dobbs also suggests that these activities were occurring during the 1680s in England, but only exposed in 1689 and after.
155 An assassination plot against William III was discovered and prevented in 1696.
156 Nonjurors were those who would not take an oath of allegiance to William and Mary because it would violate their previous oath of loyalty to James II (see also note 147 above). Dobbs is accusing them of betraying the church and the constitution in their stance.

of Love, in restoring this true christian Liberty to the Church at the Revolution, which was peculiarly one of my Redemption Works, as the Restoration was another, and the original Reformation in the sixteenth Century a third, and the Ground-work of both the Restoration and Revolution; unto the End, of these seven Regeneration Periods of the outward Constitution at 1760; to him will I give Power over the Nations, i.e. idolatrous uncovenanted Gentiles, or random Livers, both in public and private Life; ruling them by penal Laws, and pouring out my seven Vials penitential over them.[157]

27. (And he shall rule them with a Rod of Iron, or inflexible Chastisement; as the Vessels of a potter, very brittle through the natural Fearfulness and effeminate Inconstancy of Voluptuaries, and irregular, licentious Livers; shall they be broken to Shivers, and have their factious Combinations frustrated) even as I received of my Father, in the Destruction of the rebel Jews, hardened in Impenitence, by Titus A.D. 70, and by Adrian A.D. 135.[158]

28. And I will give him the Morning Star, the Light of experimental and civil Philosophy planned and published A.D. 1620 by Bacon Lord Verulam,[159] under the almost prophetic Title of Instauratio Magna, i.e. the great Restoration, namely, of the true Knowledge of Nature lost by the Fall of Man; so well does it fit the History of this British Regeneration, which began in that very Year, and was executed in Britain chiefly till A.D. 1760, when it becomes the Morning Star by Application to the Interpretation of Scripture Prophecies; which, when fully opened in the last of the seven Seals disclosed, will constitute the Day Star of clear prophetic Light of Scripture, to the Confusion of Infidels and all the Powers of antichristian Darkness.

29. He that hath an Ear, let him hear what the Spirit, or spiritual Meaning of these Letters, saith unto the Churches.

---

157 This suggests Dobbs's belief that the seven vials (Rev. 16) would be poured out against all those who are not Anglican believers.

158 Titus Flavius Vespasianus was a son of the Emperor Vespasian, and later became Roman emperor from 79 to 81 A.D. Titus was a commander in the war against the Jewish revolt, and he captured Jerusalem and destroyed the Second Temple in 70 A.D. "Adrian" refers to the Roman emperor Hadrian (r.117–138 A.D.). Hadrian allowed a shrine to Jupiter to be built on the site of the Temple in Jerusalem, which caused a Jewish revolt in 132 A.D. that was put down in 135 and saw the renaming of the province and the end of the nation of Judea: Guy Edward Farquhar Chilver, "Titus", and Eric Herbert Warmington, "Hadrian", in *The Oxford Classical Dictionary*, ed. N.G.L. Hammond and H.H. Scullard, 2nd ed. (Oxford: 1970), 1080, 485.

159 Francis Bacon (1561–1626), whose work *Instauratio magna* (*The Great Instauration*) called for the advancement of natural philosophy through the development of empirical methodology.

CHAP. III.

1. And unto the Angel, pastoral Administration, of the Church in Sardis, i.e. Joy triumphal, namely, for Victory over her Enemies, and those of the reformed Church in Q. Ann's Reign, and peaceful Accession of K. George 1st. to the British Throne, and Establishment of the Succession in the Protestant Line, by extinguishing the Rebellion of 1715,[160] during this fifth vicennial Period of the British Regeneration, write: These Things saith he that hath the seven Spirits, i.e. spiritual regenerative Operations, of God, who is the Fountain of Dominion and of the divine Life; and the seven Stars, seven Angels, as interpreted by Christ himself (1. 20.[161]) i.e. pastoral Administrations in the Churches, and their seven successive States; all under the Government of Christ in his sacerdotal Office dressing their Lights: I know thy Works, repeated in all the Epistles, to denote that each Regeneration Day has its own proper Works characteristic of it, and distinguishing it from the rest; that thou hast a Name, that of the reformed Church of England outwardly professed and supported; that thou livest, in outward Shew, and art dead, as to suitable Practice in the inward Life.

2. Be watchful, and strengthen the Things which remain, that are ready to die; the Doctrine of the holy Trinity, and Regard for revealed Religion and the holy Scriptures, attacked and defended strenuously in the Trinitarian, Socinian, and other Controversies during this fifth Period:[162] for I have not found thy Works of Superintendence over the English Church, or this Period itself, perfect before God, i.e. fully accomplished in his all-discerning Sight.

3. Remember therefore how thou hast received, from the foregoing Periods the divine Blessings thou art possessed of, and the Form of sound Words, i.e. healing Laws (2. Tim. 1. 13.) contained in the holy Scriptures and three scriptural Creeds thou art entrusted with; and heard of the noble Stand made in those Periods in Defence of the Truth; and how blest with Success and most signal providential Deliverances in Times of greatest Distress; and hold fast what thou hast received; and repent of thy inactive Sloth. If therefore thou shalt not watch, and use properly those inestimable Talents committed to thy Trust; I will come

---

160 The first Jacobite rebellion, in response to the succession of George I, the first Hanoverian claimant to the British throne, began in 1715. It was led by supporters of James Francis Edward Stuart, the son of James II and claimant from the displaced Stuart royal line. The rebellion was put down by the end of the year.
161 I.e., Rev. 1:20.
162 This is a reference to the disputes over anti-Trinitarian beliefs in England during the early eighteenth century.

on thee, with a judicial Appearance, taking from thee those Talents of spiritually opening to the christian Laity the sacred Depositum of the holy Scriptures, and so leave thee to the feeble ineffectual Defence made by human Reason against the deistic Assaults of the Adversary,[163] turning the holy Scriptures to Ridicule, through want of a clear Interpretation of the many Obscurities still remaining to be removed by the united Labours of Divines; as a Thief will I come, by gradual unobserved Steps of divine Providence, giving free Leave to the Assailants to keep thee fully employed in managing thy carnal Weapons of human Reason applied in this spiritual Combat, according to thine own Choice; and thou shalt not know what Hour I will come upon thee, so leisurely wilt thou lose the full, true, inward Meaning of the prophetic Part of God's holy Word, by neglecting to use it in thy Disputes with Infidels, which I have suffered to come upon thee, that thou mightest be awakened from thy Stupor as to the further Opening of the Scriptures, now become absolutely necessary for thy Health and very Existence itself; so mightily has Infidelity prevailed against the Argumentations of mere Reason void of divine Authority, which is only to be found in the holy Scriptures: for my luminous Advent, with Millennium sabbatic noonday Light Perfective of my faithful Followers, is now approaching,[164] when the Wisdom of divine Providence will be laid open in the full and clear Interpretation of the holy Scriptures, by which Sword of my Mouth[165] I will confound all the united Forces of the Powers of Darkness in the Midst of their exulting Triumphs over the Reasonings of Men, that have not been sufficient to extirpate any one habitual Vice, when unsupported by the Authority of Government and the Laws.

4. Thou hast a few Names, i.e. Characters, even in Sardis, this trying Period, when almost all have forsaken the right Use of the Scriptures, and betaken themselves to it's literal Sense only, and to the carnal Weapons of mere human Reason; which have not defiled their Garments, i.e. spiritual Armature for habitual Defence; and they shall walk with me, for their Guide in their spiritual Progress in Regeneration both of themselves, being Pastors and Rulers, and their Flocks, more especially; these Admonitions regarding their Office in opening the Scriptures and teaching how to be Followers of Christ in the Regeneration; in white, i.e. habitual, moral Righteousness, in Exercise of Power guided by Wisdom and rooted in Goodness; being the Justification of the Saints,

---

163 "Depositum" means a store. This passage also refers to the concerns over deistic beliefs in the early eighteenth century.
164 Dobbs is here talking about the advent of an earthly establishment of Christ's Millennial kingdom in the future.
165 Rev. 19:15, 21.

as interpreted in xix.8. of this Book:¹⁶⁶ for they are worthy, having fulfilled the Works required of this Period in their Adm[i]nistration.

5. He, of the yet unenlightened, that overcometh the Dangers of turning Infidel or Heretic in this Period, the same shall be clothed in white Raiment, be habitually enlightened and furnished with the graces of the Holy Spirit in the next or Philadelphian Period of Illumination and opening the Scriptures, or furnishing the Key of David for it; and I will not blot out his Name, i.e. characteristic Nature or Form of Life, out of the Book of Life, eternal or perpetual, established in the Close of the sixth and in the whole seventh Period with divine sabbatic Communion; but I will confess his Name, retain his Form of Life, as consistent with Christianity, in my Kingdom; before my Father, in the divine sabbatic Communications of the seventh Period; and before his Angels, the pastoral Administrations regenerative of other national Churches.

6. He that hath an Ear, let him hear what the Spirit, i.e. spiritual Meaning, saith unto the Churches.

7. And to the Angel, pastoral Administration, of the Church in Philadelphia, i.e. Period of brotherly Love, being the sixth from A.D.1720 to 1740; a twenty Years Administration uniting the legislative and executive Powers in such constant Harmony, that all ministerial Measures were subjected to parliamentary Inquiry, and approved of by it. This Harmony expired with that peaceful Period, which occasioned the Resignation of that Minister in 1741;¹⁶⁷ a Period justly named peaceful, as it was a negotiating Period, and the Minister of a highly benevolent Character in private Life, and remarkably pacific in his public Administration. No other Administration before this could boast of so long a Continuance as twenty Years in the same Person, being exactly synchronal or commensurate to the sixth vicennial Period consummative of this Regeneration Week of Vicenniums, to be habitually confirmed during the sabbatic Noon of the seventh in State Laodicean, and perpetuated through all succeeding Times; write. These Things saith he that is holy, and will no longer bear with them that profane his Name and his Word; but with the Brightness of his Coming will destroy their Works that tend to darken his Glory; he that is true to his Promises given formerly to his faithful Servants the Prophets, and through them to his faithful Servants the Prophets, and through them to his faithful People in all Ages of the Church; he that hath the Key of David, a prophetic Name of Christ in militant State, signifying the Beloved; and accordingly a Voice from Heaven after his Baptism (Matt. iii. 17.) declares him God's beloved

---

166   I.e., Rev. 19:8.
167   This refers to the resignation of Robert Walpole. Walpole's two decades in power was also marked by a prolonged period of peace in Britain.

Son; he that openeth the holy Scriptures to furnish Instructions for the Government of Life and Attainment of Happiness, by the Assistance, or illuminating Grace, of the Holy Spirit given by Christ where and when and to whom and in what Measure seems fitting to Christ's divine Wisdom in his Dispensations to his Church; and no Man shutteth, i.e. can hinder his divine Gifts from taking Place; and shutteth to unqualified Times and Persons the inward spiritual Meaning of the holy Scriptures; i.e. to such as either desire not to find a spiritual Meaning there, or will abuse it, or live in Times not ripe for such Communications; and no Man openeth, i.e. can interpret the holy Scriptures fully and truly without the Spirit of Christ:

8. I know thy Works of healing Benignity and christian Charity truly Philadelphian, the Badge of Christianity: Behold, I have set before thee an open Door, (vi. 1.[168]) and no Man can shut it, i.e. hinder thee to understand the Scriptures, if thou wilt use the Key of David; namely, purify thy Heart by Faith and Repentance, as David did: for thou hast little Strength, and yet fainted not, nor gave back from the Combat in defence of my Honour against Arians, Socinians, Deists, &c. and hast kept my Word, not joining my Adversaries in the Profanation of it, or exposing it to their Buffoonery and ridiculous Test of Ridicule among ignorant, ridiculous, or abominable Judges; and hast not denied my Name, i.e. mediatorial Character, as Socinians do my Satisfaction of divine Justice in fallen Man's Stead; nor Union of divine and human Natures, as both Arians and Socinians do;[169] nor my Love signally manifested in the Redemption of Man through my own Blood, and required in my Followers, as the Badge of their holy Profession, signified in the Name of your Church in this Period.

9. Behold, I will make them of the Synagogue of Satan, i.e. of a persecuting Church, of a Spirit slavish to tyrannic Governments, and disloyal to a free God-like Government of a free People; (which say they are Jews, i.e. Worshipers of the true God in Spirit and in Truth, and the only true christian Church in Britain, despising Court Favour and temporal Prosperity; and are not, being Non-jurors to a lawful rightful Government, one of divine Appointment and God-like Constitution in it's now regenerate State; and schismatical Separatists from a true, sound, christian Church; but do lie, in idolatrous Adherence to a Phantom of true christian Fortitude; i.e. in Reality, blind Obstinacy and inveterate, malignant Opposition to divine Providence and christian Liberty lawfully established:[170]) Behold, I will make them to come and worship before thy Feet; i.e. do Honour to thy Goings, Pillars of Government, and Course of Life;

---

168 I.e., Rev. 6:1.
169 Here is another criticism of anti-Trinitarian beliefs and the denial of Christ's divine nature.
170 Again, Dobbs criticizes all those who are outside of the Anglican Church.

and sue for Pardon of their own fruitless Disloyalty; and to know that I have loved thee, by the great Light of my glorious Appearance, first in thy Favour, and then in the following Periods of opening the seven Seals, and founding the seven Trumpets against my Adversaries and those of my true Church all over the World.

10. Because thou hast kept the Word of my Patience, in keeping the Expectation alive of my coming to Judgment, against the Scoffers who say, Where is the Promise of his coming? I also will keep thee, this Philadelphian Period of the British Regeneration of Church and State united; from the Hour, i.e. Time or Season, of Temptation, i.e. Trial, which shall come upon all the World, in those Revolutions that must come to pass in other Countries, before my Empire of a free Monarchy with parliamentary Legislation to a free People fully possessed of their rightful Liberties religious and civil, exemplified in the British Constitution, can every where take place, and be fully enjoyed with universal Peace and Righteousness;[171] to try, make white and purify (Dan. xii. 10) them that dwell upon the Earth, i.e. civil Governments; the Church being named the Kingdom of Heaven.

11. Behold, I come quickly; beginning these Trials in the very next Vicennium, i.e. Period of twenty Years from A.D. 1740 to 1760: hold that, parliamentary Constitution, fast which thou hast; that no Man, by subjecting thee to foreign Dominion or Servitude, take thy Crown of Perpetuity.

12. Him that overcometh, in continuing to preserve this parliamentary Constitution conservative of religious and civil Liberties; will I make a Pillar in the Temple of my God; i.e. a stable and durable Polity supporting the universal Empire of Christ, composed of all the Governments upon Earth regenerated after the British Model; whence his Title of King of Kings and Lord of Lords: and he, that Pillar Polity, shall go no more out; i.e. not lose his Dominion or Rank among his Fellow Polities: and I will write upon him, in confirmed Habit through the Operation of my Holy Spirit, the Name of my God, the divine Image lost by Man's Fall, and the Name of the City of my God, the divine Likeness animating that Image, or outward God-like Constitution with inward God-like Life loyal to God and Christ; which is new Jerusalem,[172] signifying the Revival of the peaceful beatific Vision, lost by the Fall of Man, which cometh down out of Heaven from my God, as his free Gift to his redeemed Creation restored to his Favour through Christ: and I will also write upon him my new Name,

---

171 Dobbs here proclaims a kind of constitutional evangelicalism and millenarianism, asserting that Christ's kingdom will not come to earth until English ecclesiastical and British constitutional structures and principals are spread throughout the world.
172 Rev. 21:2.

derived from my Kingly Office, illuminating all my subordinate Governments with legislative and executive Wisdom revealed in the Scriptures, then clearly interpreted.

13. He that hath an Ear, let him hear what the Spirit, i.e. inward Meaning, saith unto the Churches.

14. And unto the Angel, pastoral Administration, of the Church of the Laodiceans, signifying righteous political Constitution of the people; where Loyalty to the Constitution is happily united with free parliamentary Legislation by Kings, Lords, and Commons; and both with a Patriot Administration of Government by lawful, constitutional, executive Powers in a truly Patriot King and his Ministers; write: These Things saith the Amen, i.e. the faithful and true Witness, Christ, (John xiv. 6.) who has sealed it with his Blood; that he will take Vengeance on his Enemies, the Oppressors of his People, in a future Judgment at his last Advent; and one, even in this World, at every other Advent; as in this Laodicean Period, by extinguishing the Rebellion in Britain against the best of Constitutions and a truly paternal Administration; and punishing it's Abettors. It was excited by Sensuality, Lust of absolute Power, and Popish Emissaries, in Favour of tyrannic dominion and a persecuting Church.[173] He has also promised that the Gates of Hell shall not prevail against his Church; the Beginning, or supreme Ruler in this mediatorial Dispensation, of the Creation of God, both literally, and in the Regeneration Process.

15. I know thy Works; let the Pastors be ever mindful that Christ inspects their Behaviour and superintends all Things; that thou art neither cold nor hot; but luke-warm under the abused Name of Moderation, as to the spiritual Health of my People and Interests of my Church;[174] I would thou wert either cold, in quite relinquishing the Charge thou hast undertaken, that thy Flock might not be deceived in trusting to spurious Moderation and Meekness, in forbearing to admonish and speak freely and zealously in my Name, when open Sin and Profaneness call for suitable Rebukes and Admonitions; or hot, i.e. zealous in my Cause, with Prudence and Wisdom.

---

173   This is a reference to the second Jacobite rebellion, which began in 1745. It was led by Charles Edward Stuart, the grandson of James II. This last attempt to put a Stuart claimant on the throne saw Jacobite supporters take control of Edinburgh in the late summer and then invade England in the fall. Though Jacobite forces reached as far as Derby in Derbyshire, they retreated back into Scotland in December, and were ultimately defeated at the Battle of Culloden on 16 April 1746 (O.S.). Dobbs associates Stuart rule with absolute monarchy and with Roman Catholicism, which he describes as tyrannical and persecuting.

174   Here Dobbs seems to criticize low church Anglican moderation, which he equates with the "lukewarm" nature of the Laodicean church (Rev. 3:16).

16. So then, because thou art luke-warm, and neither cold nor hot, I will spue thee out of my Mouth, i.e. reject thee from using spiritually the Sword of my Mouth, my Word or the spiritual meaning of the Scriptures; which I will take from thee, and bestow upon the seven following vicennial Periods of the seven Seals, that will hunger after what thou dost nauseate and reject.

17. Because thou sayest, I am rich in spiritual Gifts, and increased with Goods, or have enriched my Flock by my excellent Labours and many learned Writings in Defence of Religion and a virtuous Life; and have Need of Nothing more for that Purpose; and knowest not that thou art wretched in suffering Obduracy, Insensibility and Blindness in religious Matters to increase; and miserable, to be pitied for thy helpless State or successless Labours, through Want of that farther Knowledge of the Scriptures which is now offered to thy Acceptance in the Key of David; and poor, in making few Converts from Infidelity and Heresy; and blind, in needing and refusing to use the Key of David, to obtain that farther Understanding of God's Word so necessary for thee; and naked, for Want of that spiritual Armature, the full Knowledge of the Scriptures void of all Obscurity in their Meaning, which you ought to be clothed in against Deists and Infidels and Heretics, rather than in scriptureless Argumentation. xii. 1.[175]

18. I counsel thee to buy of me, by giving up in Exchange thy Confidence in mere human Reasoning scriptureless and void of Authority; Gold, solid, meek Goodness and Loyalty; tried in the Fire, purged of all Dross, by patient bearing of Injuries and Reproach, in thy contending for the Faith and the Word of God delivered to thy Keeping; that thou mayest be rich in spiritual Gifts growing out of that rooted Goodness; and white Raiment, habitual justifying Righteousness, through Illumination of God's Holy Spirit, in understanding the Scriptures; that thou mayest be clothed with defensive Armour, in thy Disputes against my Adversaries and thine; and that the Shame of thy Nakedness do not appear, in being obliged to use cunning Evasions and subtile unintelligible Distinction, in Disputation with the Enemies of true Religion, whose deistical Principles regard only temporal Welfare and the Good of civil Society in this present World, without acknowledging Faith in the holy Trinity, i.e. in the true God, as the great primary Fundamental of true Religion; a Doctrine fully established in the holy Scriptures, but intelligible only to the pure in Heart (Mat. v. 8, 3.) and the humble Christian; and anoint thine Eyes spiritual with Eye-salve, a spiritual Oil stopping animal Rheum, turning the Attention from worldly Things to spiritual; that thou mayest see clearly in spiritual Matters.

---

175 I.e., Rev. 12:1.

19. As many as I love, I rebuke and chasten; therefore this severe Admonition and Dispensation of thy successless Struggles with Deists and Infidels, still growing in Number, are Marks of my Love, intended to lead thee to greater Perfection and Happiness in a more full Understanding of the Scriptures, and, through them, of my Works of Creation and Providence: be zealous therefore and repent of thy Luke-warmness and Want of scripture Knowledge, or Neglect of improving it.

20. Behold, I stand at the Door of the Heart in private Life of Christians, of the Seat of Government in public Societies; (iv. 1, &c.[176]) and knock for Admittance to open the Scriptures to you, as formerly I did to the two Disciples in the Way to Emmaus:[177] if any man, or christian Society, hear my Voice, i.e. be obedient to my Calls in the inward Impulses of my Holy Spirit, and open the Door freely and with Desire; I will come in to him, and will sup with him, in taking Delight to instruct him, i.e. feed him with Angel's Food, fitted for conducting the social Life during the Night of civil Administration in the Christ-like Discharge of social Duties, as well as in the Duties of religious Devotion, during the Day of the divine Life; and he with me, in feeding delightfully on these heavenly viands of spiritual Instruction in divine Truths.

21. To him that overcometh the Luke-warmness and conceited Self-sufficiency, the epidemic Distempers, of this Laodicean Period, which expires with A.D.1760; will I grant to sit with me in my Throne, enlightened and established in the christian Life; (v. 5, 7.[178]) even as I also overcame, during my incarnate Humiliation and Ministry before my Ascension; and am set down, established, with my Father, supreme Creator and Ruler of all other Beings, in his Throne of eternal Dominion in the divine Life: (iv. 3. v. 6.[179]) Thus blessing every faithful Disciple at last, both in his private and social Capacity, with God-like Liberty and divine Communion through my human Nature, the Leader and Captain of his Salvation consummated in this sabbatic Establishment.

22. He that hath and Ear for spiritual Truths, let him hear what the Spirit, inward Meaning, saith unto the Churches, i.e. the seven Ages regenerative of the divine Life lost in the Fall.

---

176   I.e., Rev. 4:1.
177   Luke 24:13–27. This is the account of Christ presenting himself to two of his disciples after the Crucifixion.
178   Rev. 5:5, 7 [sic], [vere, Rev. 4:5, 7].
179   I.e., Rev. 4:3 and 5:6.

The next Vision introductory to the Opening of the seven Seals[180] well described by prophetic Emblems the Exterior of our present excellent Constitution, which is to be completed in it's interior Life by opening the seven Seals, during six Vicenniums, i.e. twenties of Years. Under the seventh Seal Period are seven War Trumpets to be sounded,[181] during six twenties more, against Antichristianism in all foreign States. The seventh Seal is opened A.D. 1881; its Period contains the seven Trumpets. The seventh Trumpet is to begin to sound A.D. 2000[182] ending, and 2001 beginning; when the Kingdoms of the World (του κοσμου) are declared, by the supreme Power in every State, to be the Kingdoms of our Lord and of his Christ; and he shall reign for ever and ever i.e. for Regeneration Ages political, composed of Regeneration Ages of Individuals (εις του αιωνας των αιωνων) in endless Succession of spiritual Generations infinitely multiplied during Christ's millennial Reign (when Satan and satanic Powers on this Earth are to be chained up[183]) until the last Judgment of the Apostate Nations seduced by Satan set at Liberty;[184] and then also during Christ's eternal Kingdom, as Assessor with the Father; (John xvii. 5, where κοσμον is mediatorial World, this visible incarnate System, to which even Christ's human Nature was pre-existent; Rev. xxi 1, 3, 5, 9, 22; xxii. 1, 3, 5, 13, 21; 2 Pet. i. 11; 1 Cor. xv. 22, 24, 26, 28.) after putting all Enemies under his Feet, and Christ's surrendering his mediatorial Kingdom to the father; that Christ's eternal Kingdom may take Place and god be all in all for ever.

This Chain of prophetic Times is fully confirmed by other Prophecies in the Bible. The Opening of the first Seal exactly corresponds to the present State of Things. The white Horse Rider having a Bow, (significant of righteous Aim and Impulse, true christian motives for making War; as (Rev. xix. 11.) Christ seated on a white Horse is faithful and true, and in Righteousness doth he judge and make War,) and having a Crown triumphal; for he goes forth conquering, and to conquer the Enemies of Christ and his Church; are very applicable to our righteous King,[185] and his great Ally the King of Prussia, who by his Mother is

---

180   Rev. 6–8:5.
181   Rev. 8:6–9:20, 11:15–19.
182   Dobbs predicts that the opening of the seven seals will follow the period of the prophecies of the seven churches, which he has just meticulously described, that will end in the year 1760. The first six seals extend in twenty-year intervals from 1760–1880; the seventh seal contains the seven trumpets, which again encompass periods of twenty years: thus, the seventh trumpet will sound in the year 2000, and this will initiate the Millennial reign of Christ on earth, which Dobbs describes in the passage that follows.
183   Rev. 20:2–3.
184   Rev. 20:7–15.
185   Dobbs anchors his apocalyptic exegesis in the events and figures of his day. Here he asserts

also of the House of Brunswick, whose signal Success, in the Cause of Christ and his regenerate Church and British Constitution, against a most powerful antichristian Confederacy, manifestly declares the British Constitution to be God's favourite Work, and it's Preservation the continual Object of his Providence.

The glorious Victory at Minden, at a most critical Time, was gained by a Prince of Brunswick, having therefore a white Horse in his Coat of Arms also:[186] so literally is this Prophecy in Part accomplished; what remains being in the Womb of future Times. But the spiritual Accomplishment, in filling all offices of Church and State with Men of Integrity and serious Christians, in all Respects duly qualified by proper Education for their respective Offices, aimed at under the first Seal, and fully obtained under the seventh, is still more important; of which we have an Earnest in the zealous Efforts against Bribery and Corruption, and the present uncorrupt Administration under a righteous King, truly the Father of his People.

The Blessings of Plenty and Peace at Home, and the remarkable plentiful harvest we have had, without which we could not victual our Fleets and Armies, or repel the Invasion intended by a cruel Enemy reduced to Despair; whilst some neighbouring Countries have felt the Ravages of War, and the insolent Cruelties of a rapacious Enemy, whose discovered Intention was to lay whole Provinces waste; are Gifts from the good and merciful Providence of God ever to be had in thankful Remembrance.

It is very manifest from the Words of my Text, and the Exposition upon this Occasion given of the prophetic Letters of Admonition to the seven Churches in Asia, as applicable to the State of our excellent and well constituted Church and the British civil Constitution, during it's Growth to its present Perfection; that all has been conducted by the good Providence of God, under the Administration of Christ in his mediatorial Kingdom; and that the great Success of his

---

that the opening of the first seal, initiated by a rider on a white horse going out to conquer (Rev. 6:2), signifies George II (r.1727–1760), whose royal coat of arms, like those of his father and grandson, contained a white horse on a red background. See for example "Accession of George I", *College of Arms* (http://www.college-of-arms.gov.uk/news-grants/news/item/105-accession-of-george-i, accessed 24 February 2018). Dobbs also links this to the white horse and rider in Rev. 19:11. This passage also refers to Frederick II (the Great), king of Prussia (1740–1786), who was Britain's ally in the Seven Years' War. See also note 125 above.

186   Dobbs further argues that the victory at Minden on 1 August 1759 (N.S.) in Prussia during the Seven Years' War, which is one of the victories being celebrated during this thanksgiving day, was directly connected to the opening of the first seal. This is through Prince Ferdinand of Brunswick, one of the victorious commanders, whose coat of arms also included a white horse.

Majesty's Arms in this just and necessary War is by the same divine Appointment, and foretold above sixteen Centuries and an Half ago; as also the noble Stand made by his great and good Ally the King of Prussia against a most powerful Combination to oppress him, as being under God and Christ the chief Support, in union with our King, of the Protestant Church on the Continent; upon which Account the Head of the antichristian Romish Church has given to the Empress Queen the Title of Apostolic, and to her chief General a consecrated Sword.[187]

Let us therefore, in our several Stations, strengthen the Hands of our good King in Prosecution of this War under the Banners of Christ, in Order to a good and lasting Peace: and with grateful hearts let us pour out our Souls unto God and Christ in Prayers of Thanksgiving and spiritual Songs, for the great and signal Victories already obtained, and the happy Prospect before us; always mindful to be earnest in our Endeavours to live suitably to the excellent Blessings we enjoy, and to our holy Religion, as the most acceptable Sacrifice through Christ.

Now to God the Father, God the Son, and God the Holy Ghost be ascribed, as is most due, in all the Churches of the Saints, the Kingdom, the Power and the Glory, for ever and ever. Amen.

---

187 Again, Dobbs connects the events of the Seven Years' War to the fulfillment of apocalyptic prophecy, favourably reiterating the alliance between George II and Frederick the Great. He then goes on to note that Maria Theresa, the Habsburg empress of Austria (r.1740–1780) and her forces, who fought against Britain and Prussia in the Seven Years War, were being endorsed by the Roman Catholic Church.

Bibliography

Manuscripts

Aberdeen, Aberdeen University Library (AUL), Sir Duncan Rice Library, MS 3320/6, partial translation of Pierre Poiret, *L'Économie divine, ou système universel et démontré des œuvres et des desseins de Dieu envers les hommes* (Amsterdam: 1687), containing correspondence between George Garden and James Cunningham.

Aberdeen, Aberdeen University Library (AUL), Sir Duncan Rice Library, MS 512, Antoinette Bourignon, "Antichrist Discovered", manuscript translation of *L'Antechrist Decouvert* (Amsterdam: 1681).

Aberystwyth, National Library of Wales (NLW), MS 584, Personal memorandum-book, Philipps family mss.

Berlin, Staatsbibliothek, Nachlaß A.H. Francke, Kapsel 30—England betreffend.

Cambridge, Gonville and Caius College (G & C), MS 725/752, [Thomas Haywood], "An Essay towards the Life or rather some account of the late Learned and pious Francis Lee, M.D." (1722).

Dundee, Dundee University Archives, BrMS 2/5/2, Katherine Pringle, Lady Abden, "The Last Revelation that shall be putt in print to the sons and children of men".

Dundee, Dundee University Archives, BrMS 2/5/3, warnings delivered under divine inspiration by James Cunningham, Thomas Dutton, Margaret Irvine, Guy Nutt and John Potter.

Dundee, Dundee University Archives, BrMS 4/6/2/1, Brechin Diocesan Library, record of donations, 1856–1888.

Edinburgh, Edinburgh University Library (EUL), La.III.708, verses delivered by the eternal spirit under divine inspiration.

Edinburgh, Edinburgh University Library (EUL), La.III.709, warnings of the eternal spirit delivered under divine inspiration.

Edinburgh, Edinburgh University Library (EUL), MS 2097.8, letters to Colin Campbell

Edinburgh, National Library of Scotland (NLS), Acc. 4796/104/2, packet of miscellaneous items, including [Alexander, 4th Lord Forbes of Pitsligo], "Of the Simplicity of the Interiour & the Conformity to the holy Scripture".

Edinburgh, National Library of Scotland (NLS), Acc. 4796/104/B, letters to Andrew Michael Ramsay.

Edinburgh, National Library of Scotland (NLS), Acc. 8592, warnings delivered under divine inspiration.

Edinburgh, National Library of Scotland (NLS), Adv. 25.5.53, "Catalogue de plusiers auteurs qui on ecrit de matieres Mystiques et qui les ont eclairies".

Edinburgh, National Library of Scotland (NLS), MS 2686, warnings and songs delivered under divine inspiration.

Edinburgh, National Library of Scotland (NLS), MS 3859, Girolamo Savonarola, "The Simplicity of the Xtian Life", translated by Alexander Falconer of Delgaty.

Edinburgh, National Library of Scotland (NLS), MS 5166, warnings delivered under divine inspiration by James Cunningham.

Edinburgh, National Library of Scotland (NLS), MS 9847, Correspondence of the Lundie family.

Edinburgh, National Records of Scotland (NRS), CC20/4/16, testament of John Wardlaw.

Edinburgh, National Records of Scotland (NRS), CC20/4/18, testament of Christian Wardlaw.

Edinburgh, National Records of Scotland (NRS), CH1/2/28/3, papers of the General Assembly of the Church of Scotland, main series, 1709.

Edinburgh, National Records of Scotland (NRS), CH12/12/210, Mr Graham of Dunfermline His Account of Presbyterian Principles & Doctrine.

Edinburgh, National Records of Scotland (NRS), CH12/12/669, Latin letter from Pierre Poiret concerning the prophets in Britain.

Edinburgh, National Records of Scotland (NRS), CH12/20/11, volume of religious works collected for Mary Baird.

Edinburgh, National Records of Scotland (NRS), GD1/53/721, list of prisoners at Preston.

Edinburgh, National Records of Scotland (NRS), GD124/15/1081, letters to Lord Grange from Jean Forbes.

Edinburgh, National Records of Scotland (NRS), GD95/1/1, charter of the Society in Scotland for Propagating Religious Knowledge.

Geneva, Bibliothèque de Genève, Ms. fr. 605, "Documents concernant les inspirés, par Nicolas Fatio".

Glasgow, Mitchell Library (GCA), MS 562590, Letters from James Cunningham, John Forbes of Monymusk and Thomas Dutton concerning the prophets' mission to Scotland.

Glasgow, Mitchell Library (GCA), MS 562588, Gianfrancesco Pico della Mirandola, "Life of the Reverend Hieronmus Savonarola of Ferrara written by the most Illustrious Prince John Francis Picus Lord of Mirandula and Count of Concordia", translated by Alexander Falconer of Delgaty.

Gloucester, Gloucestershire Archives, D3549/6/2/2, memorial of James Greenshields.

Halle, Archiv der Franckeschen Stiftungen (AFSt), H D 60.

London, Dr Williams's Library (DWL), MS 186.18 (1).

London, Dr Williams's Library (DWL), MS 186.18 (2), a, b.

London, Henry Hoare and Co., HB/8/T/15, Letters etc to Henry Hoare (Good) re division of Rebekah Hussey's estate and administration of her codicil.

London, Lambeth Palace Library (LPL), MS 1048a.
London, Lambeth Palace Library (LPL), MS 1559.
London, Lambeth Palace Library (LPL), MS 942, no. 141.
London, National Archives, Prob/11/546/79, will of Rebekah Hussey.
London, National Archives, Prob/11/612/108, will of James Keith.
London, The Swedenborg Society, MS A/25.
Manchester, Chetham's Library, 3.F.3.46 (a).
Oxford, Bodleian Library (Bodl.), MS Rawlinson A354, [John Pordage], "A tract of Christ's birth and incarnation". Manuscript in James Keith's library.
Oxford, Bodleian Library (Bodl.), MS Rawlinson A404, transcript of a treatise intended to serve as preliminary to a mystical work by Dr. John Pordage; manuscript in James Keith's library.
Oxford, Bodleian Library (Bodl.), MS Rawlinson A405, transcript of a treatise intended to serve as preliminary to a mystical work by Dr. John Pordage; manuscript in James Keith's library.
Oxford, Bodleian Library (Bodl.), MS Rawlinson C602, Francis de la Combe, "A short letter of instruction shewing the surest way to Christian perfection"; manuscript in James Keith's library.
Oxford, Bodleian Library (Bodl.), MS Rawlinson C858, "An introduction to divine wisdome, comprised in divers spirituall treatises which containe the secrets of mystick theology", translation of Maur de l'Enfant-Jésus, "L'entrée de la divine sagesse"; manuscript in James Keith's library.
Oxford, Bodleian Library (Bodl.), MS Rawlinson D832, diary of Richard Roach.
Oxford, Bodleian Library (Bodl.), MS Rawlinson D833, diary of Richard Roach.
Oxford, Bodleian Library (Bodl.), MS Rawlinson D1262, Ann Bathurst's visions; manuscript in James Keith's library.
Oxford, Bodleian Library (Bodl.), MS Rawlinson D1263, Ann Bathurst's visions; manuscript in James Keith's library.
Oxford, Bodleian Library (Bodl.), MS Rawlinson D1338, Ann Bathurst's visions; manuscript in James Keith's library.
Oxford, Bodleian Library (Bodl.), MS Rawlinson D42, Preliminary treatise on the right method of finding out truth, translated by Rev. Young; manuscript in James Keith's library.
Oxford, Bodleian Library (Bodl.), MS Rawlinson D43, Thomas Heywood's translation of Pierre Poiret, "De eruditione triplici solida, superficiaria et falsa"; manuscript in James Keith's library.
Oxford, Bodleian Library (Bodl.), MS Rawlinson D44, George Anderson's translation of Pierre Poiret, "De eruditione triplici solida, superficiaria et falsa"; manuscript in James Keith's library.
Oxford, Bodleian Library (Bodl.), MS Rawlinson H74, Antoinette Bourignon, "Sound

Advices and Instructions", translation of *Avis et instructions salutaires* (Amsterdam: 1684); manuscript in James Keith's library.

St. Andrews, St. Andrews University Library, MS 1012, warnings of the Holy Spirit delivered under divine inspiration.

Printed Primary Sources

Anon., *A Form of Prayer, and Thanksgiving to Almighty God: To be Used on Thursday the Twenty Third of August next ... For the Late Glorious Success for Forcing the Enemy Lines in the Spanish Netherlands, by the Arms of her Majesty and Her Allies ...* (London: 1705).

Anon., *La Theologie réelle vulgairement ditte la theologie germanique. Avec quelques autres traités de même nature* (Amsterdam: 1700).

Anon., *La Vie de Sainte Elisabeth, fille du Roy de Hongrie, Duchesse de Turinge, et premiere religieuse Du troisiéme Ordre de Saint François* (Paris: 1702).

Anon., *Propositions Extracted From the Reasons for the Foundation and Promotion of a Philadelphian Society* (London: 1697).

Anon., *Reasons for the Foundation and Promotion of a Philadelphian Society* ([London: 1697]).

Anon., *The Declaration of the Philadelphian Society of England, Easter-Day, 1699* (1699).

Anon., *The Holy Life of Mon'. De Renty, a Late Nobleman of France ... Written in French by John Baptist S. Jure. And Faithfully Translated into English, by E.S. Gent* (London: 1658).

Anon., *Warnings of the Eternal Spirit, Pronounced at Edinburgh, Out of the Mouths of 1. Anna Maria King. 2. John Moult. 3. Mary Turner. 4. Ann Topham* (Edinburgh: 1709).

Anon., *Warnings of the Eternal Spirit, Pronounced at Edinburgh, Out of the Mouths of Margaret Mackenzie and James Cunningham* (London: 1710).

Benson, J., *Four sermons on the second coming of Christ and the future misery of the wicked* (London: 1781).

Besse, Joseph (ed.), *The Life and Posthumous Works of Richard Claridge*, 3rd ed. (London: 1836).

Beverley, Thomas, *An Exposition of the Divinely Prophetick Song of Songs* (1687).

Beverley, Thomas, *The Prophetical history of the Reformation* (1689).

Boehme, Jacob, XL. *Qvestions Concerning the Soule*, trans. J[ohn] S[parrow] (London: 1647).

Bourignon, Antoinette, *Le Nouveau Ciel et la Nouvelle Terre* (Amsterdam: 1679).

Bourignon, Antoinette, *The Academy of Learned Divines*, trans. George Garden and James Keith (London: 1708).

Bourignon, Antoinette, *The Confusion of the Builders of Babel* (London: 1708).

Bourignon, Antoinette, *The Light of the World* (London: 1696).
Brothers, Richard, *A Revealed Knowledge of the Prophecies and Times, Book the First, wrote [sic] under the direction of the Lord God and published by His Sacred Command, it being the first sign of Warning for the benefit of All Nations;* ... (London: 1794).
Bulkeley, Richard, *An Impartial Account of the Prophets: in a Letter to a Friend* (London: 1707).
Burnet, Gilbert, *Three Letters Concerning the Present State of Italy* (London: 1688).
Cavalier, Jean, *Memoirs of the Wars of the Cevennes* (Dublin: 1726).
Dobbs, Richard, *A Remarkable Accomplishment of a Noted Scripture Prophecy, as Applied to the History of England During the Last and Present Centuries, in a Thanksgiving Sermon* (London: 1762).
Fletcher, John, *Logica Genevensis Continued. Or the First Part of the Fifth Check to Antinomianism* (London: 1774).
Forbes, John, *The Jacobite Cess Roll for the County of Aberdeen*, ed. Alistair and Henrietta Tayler (Aberdeen: 1932).
Garden, George, *An Apology for M. Antonia Bourignon in Four Parts*, trans. James Keith (London: 1699).
Guyon, Jeanne, *A Short and Easie Method of Prayer* (London: 1703).
Harvey, John (ed.), *The Appearance of Evil, Apparitions of Spirits in Wales by Edmund Jones*, (Cardiff: 2003).
Henderson, G.D. (ed.), *Mystics of the North East* (Aberdeen: 1934).
Hoadly, Benjamin, *A Brief Vindication of the Antient Prophets* (London: 1709).
Hurd, R., *An Introduction to the Study of the Prophecies concerning the Christian Church* ... (London: 1772).
Jacob, Joseph, *Desolations Decypher'd and the Kingdom of Christ Discover'd. In a Sermon Preacht the 23d of the 6th Month, 1705. Being the Day of Thanksgiving For the Late Success of the Army, Under the Conduct of John Duke of Marlborough* (London: 1705).
Jaeger, Johann Wolfgang, *Dissertatio historico-theologica, de Johannæ Leadææ Anglo-Britan. Vita* (Tübingen: 1712).
Jaeger, Johann Wolfgang, *Historia Ecclesiastica, cum parallelismo profanæ, in qua Conclavia Pontificum Romanorum fideliter aperiuntur et sectæ omnes recensentur*, vol. 2 (Hamburg: 1717), part ii.
Knorr von Rosenroth, Christian, *A Genuine Explication of the Visions of the Book of Revelation* (London: n.d.).
Lead, Jane, "Lebenslauff der Autorin", in *Sechs Unschätzbare Durch Göttliche Offenbarung und Befehl ans Liecht gebrachte Mystische Tractätlein* (Amsterdam: 1696), 413–423.
Lead, Jane, *A Fountain of Gardens*, 3 vols (London: 1697–1701).
Lead, Jane, *A Living Funeral Testimony* (London: 1702).
Lead, Jane, *A Message to the Philadelphian Society* (London: 1696).

Lead, Jane, *A Revelation of the Everlasting Gospel-Message* (London: 1697).
Lead, Jane, *The Ark of Faith: or A Supplement to the Tree of Faith, &c.* (London: 1696).
Lead, Jane, *The Enochian Walks with God* (London: 1694).
Lead, Jane, *The Heavenly Cloud Now Breaking* (1681; 2nd ed., London: 1701).
Lead, Jane, *The Messenger of an Universal Peace: or a Third Message to the Philadelphian Society* (London: 1698).
Lead, Jane, *The Revelation of Revelations* (1683; 2nd ed., London: 1701).
Lead, Jane, *The Tree of Faith: or, The Tree of Life* (London: 1696).
Lead, Jane, *The Wars of David and the Peaceable Reign of Solomon ... Containing I. An alarm to the holy warriours to fight the battels of the Lamb. II. The glory of Sharon* (London: 1700).
[Lee, Francis & Roach, Richard (eds)], *Theosophical Transactions by the Philadelphian Society, Consisting of Memoirs, Conferences, Letters, Dissertations, Inquiries, &c.* (London: 1697).
[Lee, Francis], *Der Seelig und aber Seeligen Jane Leade Letztere Lebens-Stunden*, trans. Loth Fischer (Amsterdam: 1705).
[Lee, Francis], *The State of the Philadelphian Society* (1697).
Mede, Joseph, *Clavis Apocalyptica, or, A prophetical key by which the great mysteries in the revelation of St. John and the prophet Daniel are opened ...* (London: 1651).
Mede, Joseph, *The Key of the Revelation, searched and demonstrated out of the naturall and proper charecters of the visions* (London: 1643).
Mission, François-Maximilien, *A Cry from the Desert*, 2nd ed. (London: 1707).
More, Henry, *An Exposition of the Seven Epistles to the Seven Churches* (London: 1669).
Nichols, John (ed.), *Illustrations of the Literary History of the Eighteenth Century*, vol. 4 (London: 1822).
Poiret, Pierre (ed.), *Bibliothecca Mysticorum Selecta* (Amsterdam: 1708).
Poiret, Pierre, *L'Ecole du pur amour de Dieu ouverte aux Savans & aux Ignorans dans la vie merveilleuse d'une pauvre fille idiote, païsanne de naissance & servante de condition, Armelle Nicolas* (Cologne: 1704).
Poiret, Pierre, *Le Saint refugié, ou la vie & la mort edifiantes de Wernerus ... mort à **L'an 1699* (Amsterdam: 1701).
Poiret, Pierre, *The Divine Œconomy*, vol. 6 (London: 1713).
Roach, Richard, "Solomon's Porch: or the Beautiful Gate of Wisdom's Temple. A Poem; Introductory to the Philadelphian Age", in Lead, Jane, *A Fountain of Gardens*, vol. 1 (London: 1697).
Roach, Richard, *The Great Crisis: or, the Mystery of the Times and Seasons Unfolded* (London: 1725).
Roach, Richard, *The Imperial Standard of Messiah Triumphant* (London: 1727).
Stirredge, Elizabeth, *A Faithful Warning to the Inhabitants of England, and Elsewhere, With An Invitation Of Love Unto All People, To Call Them To Repentance, And Amend-*

ment Of Life; For By So Doing, Many Have Escaped The Judgments That Have Been To Be Poured Down Upon Their Heads* (London: 1689).

Storey, Matthew (ed.), *Two East Anglian Diaries, 1641–1729*, Suffolk Records Society, vol. XXXVI (1994).

The Post Boy (22–24 September 1709).

Tillotson, John, *A Sermon Preached before the King and Queen at White-Hall, the 27th of October, Being the Day Appointed for a Publick Thanksgiving to Almighty God, for the Signal Victory at Sea: for the Preservation of His Majesty's Sacred Person, and for his Safe Return to His People* (London: 1692).

Waple, Edward, *The Book of the Revelation Paraphrased; With Annotations on Each Chapter* (London: 1693).

Wensley, Robert, *Ferguson's Text Explain'd and Apply'd, in a Sermon Before the Right Honourable Sir Robert Geffery, Kt. Lord Mayor of London; ... December the 6th. Anno Dom. 1685* (London: 1686).

Whiston, William, *An Essay on the Revelation of Saint John, so far as concerns the past and present times* (London: 1706).

Secondary Sources

Aaron, David H., "Shedding light on God's body in Rabbinic midrashim: reflections on the theory of the luminous Adam", *Harvard Theological Review* 90 (1997), 299–314.

Apetrei, Sarah, "'Between the Rational and the Mystical': The Inner Life and the Early English Enlightenment", in *Mysticism and Reform, 1400–1750*, ed. Sara. S. Poor and Nigel Smith (Notre Dame, IN.: 2015), 198–219.

Apetrei, Sarah, *Women, Feminism and Religion in Early Enlightenment England* (Cambridge: 2010).

Arms, College of, "Accession of George I", *College of Arms*, online (http://www.college-of-arms.gov.uk/news-grants/news/item/105-accession-of-george-i, accessed 24 February 2018).

Aston, Nigel, "Rationalism, The Enlightenment and Sermons", in *The Oxford Handbook to the British Sermon 1688–1901*, ed. Keith Francis and William Gibson (Oxford: 2012).

Bahlman, Dudley W.R., *The Moral Revolution of 1688* (New Haven: 1957).

Barker, J.R., "Lord Gardenstone's library at Laurencekirk", *The Bibliothek* 6 (1971), 41–52.

Berman, Ric, *Espionage, Diplomacy & the Lodge: Charles Delafaye and The Secret Department of the Post Office* (Old Goring: 2017).

Bowerbank, Sylvia, *Speaking for Nature: Women and Ecologies of Early Modern England* (Baltimore, MD: 2004).

Brady, David, *The Contribution of British Writers between 1560 and 1830 to the Interpretation of Revelation 13.16–18: (The Number of the Beast) A Study in the History of Exegesis* (Tübingen: 1983).

Brown, Kenneth O., "John Wesley, Post or Premillennialist?", in *Methodist History* 28 (1989), 33–41.

Brown, Stewart J. and Tackett, Timothy (eds), *The Cambridge History of Christianity vol VII: Enlightenment, Reawakenings and Revolution, 1660–1815* (Cambridge: 2006).

Bulman, William J., *Anglican Enlightenment, Orientalism, Religion and Politics in England and its Empire, 1648–1715* (Cambridge: 2015).

Burns, William E., "London's Barber-Elijah: Thomas Moor and universal salvation in the 1690s", *Harvard Theological Review*, 95 (2002), 277–290.

Byrd, James P., *Sacred Scripture, Sacred War, The Bible and the American Revolution* (Oxford: 2013).

Carlson, Eric Josef, "The Boring of the Ear: Shaping the Pastoral Vision of Preaching in England, 1540–1640", in *Preachers and People in the Reformations and Early Modern Period*, ed. Larissa Taylor (Leiden: 2001), 249–296.

Carmody, W.P., *Lisburn Cathedral and Its Past Rectors, with an Appendix* (Belfast: 1926), online (www.lisburn.com/books/lisburn_cathedral/cathedral-2.htm, accessed 30 December 2015).

Chandler, David and Beckett, Ian (eds), *The Oxford History of the British Army* (Oxford: 1994).

Chilver, Guy Edward Farquhar, "Titus", in *The Oxford Classical Dictionary*, N.G.L. Hammond and H.H. Scullard, 2nd ed. (Oxford: 1970), 1080.

Claydon, Tony, "Latitudinarianism and Apocalyptic History in The Worldview Of Gilbert Burnet, 1643–1715", *The Historical Journal* 51/3 (2008), 577–597.

Claydon, Tony, "Protestantism, universal monarchy and Christendom in the ideology of William's war, 1689–1697", in *Redefining William III: The Impact of the King-Stadholder in International Context*, ed. Esther Mijers and David Onnekink (Aldershot: 2007), 125–142.

Claydon, Tony, *Europe and the making of England, 1660–1760* (Cambridge: 2007).

Clergy of the Church of England Database (http://theclergydatabase.org.uk, accessed 29 December 2015).

Cody, Lisa, "'The Doctor's in Labour'; or a New Whim Wham from Guildford", in *Gender and History* 4 (1992), 175–196.

Cosmos, Georgia, *Huguenot Prophecy and Clandestine Worship in the Eighteenth Century: "The Sacred Theatre of the Cévennes"* (Aldershot: 2005).

Crome, Andrew, "The 1753 'Jew Bill' Controversy: Jewish Restoration to Palestine, Biblical Prophecy, and English National Identity", in *English Historical Review*, 130/547 (2015), 1449–1478.

Deconinck-Brossard, Françoise, "Eighteenth-Century Sermons and the Age", in *Crown and Mitre: Religion and Society in Northern Europe Since the Reformation*, ed. W.M. Jacob and Nigel Yates (Woodbridge: 1993), 105–121.

Dictionary of Medieval Latin from British Sources (http://www.dmlbs.ox.ac.uk/publications/online, accessed 16 February 2018).

Ditchfield, G.M., "Sermons in the Age of the French and American Revolutions", in *Oxford Handbook of the British Sermon 1688–1901*, ed. Keith Francis and William Gibson (Oxford: 2012), 275–288.

Eijnatten, Joris van, *Preaching, Sermon and Cultural Change in the Long Eighteenth Century* (Leiden: 2009).

Falkner, James, *The War of the Spanish Succession 1701–1714* (Barnsley: 2015).

Farooq, Jenifer, *Preaching in Eighteenth-Century London* (Woodbridge: 2013).

Force, James E. and Popkin, Richard H. (eds), *Millenarianism and Messianism in Early Modern European Culture: Volume III: The Millenarian Turn: Millenarian Contexts of Science, Politics and Everyday Life in Anglo-American Life in the Seventeenth and Eighteenth Centuries* (Dordrecht: 2001).

Francis, Keith and Surridge, Robert, "Sermons for the End Times: Evangelicalism, Romanticism and the Apocalypse in Britain", in *The Oxford Handbook to the British Sermon*, ed. Keith Francis and William Gibson (Oxford: 2012), 374–389.

Froom, Leroy Edwin, *The Prophetic Faith of Our Fathers, The Historical Development of Prophetic Interpretation*, 4 vols (Washington D.C.: 1946–1954).

Garrett, Clarke, "Joseph Priestley, the Millennium and the French Revolution", *The Journal of the History of Ideas* 34 (1973), 56–61.

Garrett, Clarke, *Respectable Folly: Millenarians and the French Revolution in France and England* (Baltimore: 1975).

Garrett, Clarke, "Swedenborg and the Mystical Enlightenment in Late Eighteenth-century England", *The Journal of the History of Ideas* 45 (1984), 67–81

Gibbons, Brian J., "Roach, Richard [*name in religion* Onesimus] (1662–1730)", ODNB, online (http://www.oxforddnb.com/view/article/23704, accessed 4 November 2019).

Gibson, William and Begiato, Joanne, *Sex and the Church in the Long Eighteenth Century* (London: 2017).

Gibson, William, "English Provincial Engagements in Religious Debates: The Salisbury Quarrel 1705–15", in *The Huntington Library Quarterly* 80/1 (2017), 21–45.

Gibson, William, "Strenae Natalitia: Ambivalence and Equivocation in Oxford in 1688", in *History of Universities*, vol. XXXI/1 (2018), 123–142.

Gibson, William, *Enlightenment Prelate: Benjamin Hoadly 1676–1761* (Cambridge: 2004).

Glasson, Travis, *Mastering Christianity Missionary Anglicanism and Slavery in the Atlantic World* (Oxford: 2011).

Gordon, Alexander, revised by Mercer, M.J., "Jacob, Joseph (*c.*1667–1722)", *Oxford Dictionary of National Biography* (ODNB), online (http://www.oxforddnb.com/view/article/14572, accessed 30 December 2015).

Green, Ian, "Orality, Script and Print: the Case of the English Sermon c.1530–1700", in *Cultural Exchange in Early Modern Europe, Volume I: Religion and Cultural Exchange in Europe, 1400–1700*, ed. Heinz Schilling and István György Tóth (Cambridge: 2006), 236–255.

Greig, Martin, "Elijah in Dorset: William Freke and Enthusiasm in England and the Atlantic World at the Turn of the Eighteenth Century", *Church History* 87/2 (2018), 424–451.

Gribben, Crawford, *Evangelical Millennialism in the Trans-Atlantic World, 1500–2000* (Basingstoke: 2011).

Hamilton, Alastair, *The Apocryphal Apocalypse: The Reception of the Second Book of Esdras (4 Ezra) from the Renaissance to the Enlightenment* (Oxford: 1999).

Harrison, J.F.C., *The Second Coming and Popular Millenarianism, 1780–1850* (London: 1993).

Hart, Arthur Tindal, *William Lloyd 1627–1717* (London: 1952).

Harvey, Karen, *The Imposteress Rabbit Breeder, Mary Tofts and Eighteenth-Century England* (Oxford: 2020).

Hempton, David, "Evangelicalism and Eschatology", *Journal of Ecclesiastical History* 31/2 (1980), 179–194.

Hessayon, Ariel, *"Gold Tried in the Fire": The Prophet Theaurau John Tany and the English Revolution* (Aldershot: 2007).

Hessayon, Ariel (ed.), *Jane Lead and her Transnational Legacy* (London: 2016).

Hirst, Julie, *Jane Leade: Biography of a Seventeenth-Century Mystic* (Aldershot: 2005).

Hochhuth, C.W.H., "Geschichte und Entwicklung der philadelphischen Gemeinden, I: Jane Leade und die philadelphische Gemeinde in England", *Zeitschrift für die historische Theologie* 35 (1865), 171–290.

Hunt, Arnold, *The Art of Hearing: English Preachers and Their Audiences, 1590–1640* (Cambridge: 2010).

Hutin, Serge, *Les Disciples Anglais de Jacob Boehme aux XVIIe et XVIIIe siècles* (Paris: 1960).

Illife, Rob, *Priest of Nature, The Religious Worlds of Isaac Newton* (Oxford: 2017).

Ingram, Robert G., *Reformation without End: Religion, Politics and the Past in Post-Revolutionary England* (Manchester: 2018).

Jacob, James R. and Jacob, Margaret C., "The Anglican Origins of Modern Science: the Metaphysical Foundations of the Whig Constitution", *Isis* 71 (1980), 251–267.

Jacob, Margaret C., *The Newtonians and the English Revolution* (Ithaca, N.Y.: 1976).

[Jenkins, R.C.], "Miracles, Visions, and Revelations, Mediaeval and Modern", *The British Quarterly Review* 58 (1873), 168–188.

Johnston, Warren, *Revelation Restored: The Apocalypse in Later Seventeenth-Century England* (Woodbridge: 2011).

Johnston, Warren, "Revelation and the Revolution of 1688–1689", *The Historical Journal* 48/2 (2005), 351–389.

Johnston, Warren, "Thomas Beverley and the 'Late Great Revolution': English Apocalyptic Expectation in the Late Seventeenth century", in *Scripture and Scholarship in Early Modern England*, ed. Ariel Hessayon and Nicholas Keene (Aldershot: 2006), 158–175.

Jones, J.R., *Marlborough* (Cambridge: 1993).

Jue, Jeffrey K., *Heaven Upon Earth: Joseph Mede (1586–1638) and the Legacy of Millenarianism* (Berlin: 2006).

Korshin, Paul, "Queuing and Waiting: The Apocalypse in England, 1660–1750", in *The Apocalypse in English Renaissance Thought and Literature*, ed. C.A. Patrides and Joseph Wittreich (Manchester: 1984).

Laborie, Lionel, *Enlightening Enthusiasm, Prophecy and Religious Experience in Early Eighteenth Century England* (Manchester: 2015).

Lamont, William M., *Richard Baxter and the Millennium: Protestant Imperialism and the English Revolution* (London: 1979).

Mack, Phyllis, "Dreaming and Emotion in Early Evangelical Religion", in *Heart Religion: Evangelical Piety in England and Ireland, 1690–1850*, ed. John Coffey (Oxford: 2016), 157–180.

MacPherson, F.M., "Philosophy and religion", in *Mitchell Library, Glasgow: 1877–1977*, ed. D. Crawford Soutter (Glasgow: 1977), 43–45.

Mandelbrote, Scott, "Becoming Heterodox in Seventeenth-Century Cambridge: The Case of Isaac Newton", in *Erudition and Confessionalisation in Early Modern Europe*, ed. D. Levitin and N. Hardy (Oxford: 2019), 300–394.

Mandelbrote, Scott, "Newton and Eighteenth-Century Christianity", in *The Cambridge Companion to Newton*, ed. R. Iliffe and G. Smith (Cambridge: 2016), 554–585.

Mandelbrote, Scott and Pulte, Helmut (eds), *The Reception of Isaac Newton in Europe* (London: 2019), 3 vols.

Manuel, Frank E., *The Religion of Isaac Newton* (Oxford: 1974).

Mather, F.C., *High Church Prophet, Bishop Samuel Horsley (1733–1806) and the Caroline Tradition in the Later Georgian Church* (Oxford: 1992).

Mathews, Shailer, "Antipas", in *Dictionary of the Bible*, ed. James Hastings et al (New York: 1909), 39.

McDowell, Paula, "Enlightenment Enthusiasms and the Spectacular Failure of the Philadelphian Society", *Eighteenth-Century Studies* 35 (2002), 515–533.

Newport, Kenneth, "Methodists and the Millennium: Eschatological Expectation and the Interpretation of Biblical Prophecy in Early Methodism", in *Bulletin of the John Rylands Library* 78/1 (1996), 103–122.

Nichols, John, *Illustrations of the Literary History of the Eighteenth Century*, vol. 4 (London: 1822).

Nicolson, Marjorie Hope (ed.), and Hutton, Sarah (rev. ed.), *The Conway Letters: the Correspondence of Anne, Viscountess Conway, Henry More, and Their Friends 1642–1684* (Oxford: 1992).

O'Garda, Cormac, *Famine: A Short History* (Princeton, N.J.: 2009).
Oddy, John Arthur, "Eschatological Prophecy in the English Theological Tradition, c.1700-c.1840", PhD thesis (London University: 1982).
Orchard, S.C., "English Evangelical Eschatology, 1790–1850", PhD thesis (Cambridge University: 1969).
Powicke, Frederick, *The Reverend Richard Baxter, Under the Cross (1662–1691)* (London: 1927).
Redwood, John, *Reason, Ridicule and Religion, The Age of Enlightenment in England 1660–1750* (London: 1976).
Riordan, Michael B., "Discerning Spirits in the Early Enlightenment: The case of the French Prophets", in *Knowing Spirits, Knowing Demons in the Early Modern Period*, ed. Michelle D. Brock, Richard Raiswell and David R. Winter (New York: 2018), 265–290.
Riordan, Michael B., "Mysticism and Prophecy in Scotland in the Long Eighteenth Century", PhD thesis (University of Cambridge: 2015).
Riordan, Michael B., "The Episcopalians and the Promotion of Mysticism in North-East Scotland", *Records of the Scottish Church History Society* 47 (2018), 31–56.
Riordan, Michael B., "Mysticism and Prophecy in Early Eighteenth-Century Scotland", *Scottish Historical Review*, vol. 98, supplement (October 2019), pp. 333–360.
Rowell, Geoffrey, "Scotland and the 'mystical matrix' of the late seventeenth and early eighteenth centuries: an exploration of religious cross-currents", *International Journal for the Study of the Christian Church* 14 (2014), 129–144.
Ryan, Linda A., *John Wesley and the Education of Children: Gender, Class and Piety* (London: 2017).
Schwartz, Hillel, *The French Prophets: The History of a Millenarian Group in Eighteenth-Century England* (Berkeley, CA: 1980).
Scott, Hew, *Fasti Ecclesiae Scoticanae: The Succession of Ministers in the Church of Scotland from the Reformation*, vol. 1 (Edinburgh: 1905).
Shaw, Jane, "Mary Toft, Religion and National Memory in Eighteenth-Century England", *Journal for Eighteenth-Century Studies* 32/3 (2009), 321–338.
Shaw, Jane, *Miracles in Enlightenment England* (London; New Haven: 2006).
Smith, Robert A.L., *History of the Clan Lundy, Lundie, Lundin* (Glasgow: 2005).
Snobelin, Stephen, "'A Time and Times and the Dividing of Time': Isaac Newton, the Apocalypse, and 2060 A.D.", *Canadian Journal of History* 38/3 (2003), 537–551.
Sperle, Joanne, "God's healing angel: A biography of Jane Ward Lead", PhD thesis (Kent State University: 1985)
Stalcup, E., "Sensing Salvation: Spiritual Experience in Early British Methodism, 1735–65", PhD thesis (Boston University: 2016).
Stievermann, Jan, *Prophecy, Piety, and the Problem of Historicity. Interpreting the Hebrew Scriptures in Cotton Mather's Biblia Americana* (Tübingen: 2016).

Strong, Rowan, "Eighteenth Century Mission Sermons", in *The Oxford Handbook to the British Sermon*, ed. Keith Francis and William Gibson (Oxford: 2012), 497–512.

Temple, Liam P., *Mysticism in Early Modern England* (Martlesham: 2019).

Thomas, Keith, *Religion and the Decline of Magic, Studies in Popular Beliefs in Sixteenth and Seventeenth Century England* (Oxford: 1971).

Toomer, G.J., "Edward Pococke, (1604–1691)", *ODNB*, online (www.oxforddnb.com/view/article/22430, accessed 7 April 2020).

Thune, Nils, *The Behmenists and the Philadelphians: A Contribution to the Study of English Mysticism in the 17th and 18th Centuries*, trans. G.E. Björk (Uppsala: 1948).

Valenze, Deborah, "Prophecy and Popular Literature in Eighteenth Century England", *Journal of Ecclesiastical History* 29/1 (1978), 75–92.

Van Hyning, Victoria, and Dutton, Elizabeth, "Augustine Baker and the mystical canon", in *Dom Augustine Baker 1575–1641*, ed. Geoffrey Scott (Leominster: 2012), 85–110.

Walker, Daniel, *The Decline of Hell. Seventeenth-Century Discussions of Eternal Torment* (London: 1964).

Walton, Christopher, *Notes and Materials for an adequate Biography of the celebrated divine and theosopher, William Law* (London: 1854).

Warmington, Eric Herbert, "Hadrian", in *The Oxford Classical Dictionary*, ed. N.G.L. Hammond and H.H. Scullard, 2nd ed. (Oxford: 1970), 484–486.

Whitford, David M., *The Curse of Ham in the Early Modern Era: The Bible and the Justifications for Slavery* (Farnham: 2009).

Williamson, Arthur, *Apocalypse Then: Prophecy and the Making of the Modern World* (Westport, CT: 2008).

Websites

"Keith, James", in *Royal College of Physicians, Lives of the Fellows* [Munk's Roll], online (http://munksroll.rcplondon.ac.uk/Biography/Details/2519).

Index

Abbot, Theophilus [*pseud.*]   43, 48, 54, 57, 58, 59, 61n126, 61–62, 67
Abden, Katherine Pringle, Lady, *see* Pringle, Katherine, Lady Abden
Aberdeen   161, 162, 163, 166, 168, 191n117
Act of Succession (1701)   213, 244–245, 244–245n122, 258
Adam   164, 171–173, 173n77, 180, 184
adiaphora   174n80
Alderidge, Thomas   185n108
Anabaptists   6, 16
Anglicanism / Anglican (Church of England)   10, 12, 23n109, 25, 28, 157, 161, 207–208, 211, 211n9, 212–214, 219–220, 220n29, 246, 246n124, 247–266
  Anglican service, Episcopalian use of 161
Anne, Queen of England, Scotland, and Ireland; Queen of Great Britain   210, 210n7, 213, 218, 258
anti-Trinitarianism   3, 258, 258n162, 261n169, 264
Antichrist   1, 12, 187, 211, 220–222, 221n35, 227–240, 238n, 248, 251, 255, 267, 268
  Age of   163, 175n84, 176n85, 180n97
  man of sin   211, 221, 236, 238
anticlericalism   38, 179n96
Apocalypse   2, 3, 4, 5, 10, 18, 27, 34, 176n85
apocalyptic prophecy   207–268
apostolic age   11, 191
Archippus [*pseud.*]   107
Arianism   1, 13, 214, 261
Asseburg, Rosemunda Juliana von   60n122, 122
Augustus II the Strong, Elector of Saxony 44n54

Babylon, Fall of   160
Bacon, Francis   214, 257, 257n159
Bagot, Lewis   12
Baker, David "Augustine"   195n127
Ballantre, Ayrshire   191n117
baptism   179–180
Barach / Barak [*pseud.*]   49, 50, 51n89, 58
Barenz / Beerens, Catherina   45n62, 47–48n68, 50, 51, 64

Bathurst, Anne   36, 64n133, 111, 120, 131, 133, 138, 144, 153
Bathurst, John   33, 55n106, 59n119, 114–117
Bâville, Nicholas Lamoignon de   159
Baxter, Richard   13
Bayreuth   60n123
Behrens, Leffmann   47, 48
Bell, George   19
Bengel, Johannes Albrecht   18
Beverley, Thomas   39, 40, 149, 229n75
Bible, literal sense of   167, 179, 184, 192
Bible, spiritual sense of   167, 192
Bill of Rights (1689)   213, 244–245, 244–245n122, 253, 253n147
Birmingham, Warwickshire   160, 188, 188n112
Blagrave, Charles   114, 115
Blagrave, Daniel   114n235
Blagrave, Elizabeth   33, 114
blasphemy   172
Boehme, Jacob   22, 31, 34, 36, 97, 99n210, 115, 123, 124, 193, 193n124
Book of Common Prayer   161, 248n134
Bourignon, Antoinette   35n10, 95n187, 98, 100, 158, 163–165, 167, 173, 173n77, 173n78, 174n80, 174n81, 175n84, 176n85, 179n96, 180n97, 193, 193n124, 196, 205, 205n147
Boyle, Robert   244n121
Boyle Lectures   5
Bray, Thomas   8
Breckling, Friedrich   34, 50n86, 60n120&123
Brice, Edmund   143
Bridges, Charles   39
Bromley, Thomas   33, 60, 87, 116, 117, 134, 143, 147, 152, 157
Brothers, Richard   9
Brownists   6
Bulkeley, Richard   178n95
Burkersroda, Augustin von   43n44, 44, 48
Burkersroda, Lucie Ölgard von   43n44, 44–45
Burman, William   33
Burnet, Gilbert   21, 198n130
Burnet, Thomas   4

INDEX

Calthorpe, Barbara 85n170
Calthorpe, Mary 82n161
Calvinism 159, 165, 172n76
Cambridge University 208–209
Cameron, Isabel 168, 191, 191n117
  letter addressed to 193–197
Camisards 16, 41, 159, *see also* French Prophets
Campbell, Patrick, of Monzie 203n144
Campion, Abraham 21
Cavalier of Sauve, Jean 159–160
ceremonies 68, 179–180
cessationism 175n83
Cévennes / Cénevols 159
Chaila, Francois de Langdale du 159
chapbooks 15
Charles I, King of England, Scotland, and Ireland 97, 209, 244, 244n119, 244n120, 246n124, 248, 248n131, 248n133, 250, 250n140, 251
Charles II, King of England, Scotland, Ireland 24, 50, 97, 244n120, 244n121, 250, 250n140, 251, 251n141, 252, 252n143
Charles II, King of Spain 159
Cheyne, George 162
Church of England, *see* Anglicanism / Anglican
Church of Ireland 212
Church of Scotland 172n76, *see also* Presbyterians / Presbyterianism
Churchill, John, Duke of Marlborough 210, 210n7, 216, 218, 222, 240
Civil Wars, British 6, 33, 213, 244, 247n129, 248n134, 248–249
Claridge, Richard 36–37
Coe, William 14
Colchester, Essex 160
College of Justice (Scotland) 169
Comet, Halley's 4
consolation, son of 58
consolation, spiritual 192, 194, 198, 201, 204n145
Conyers, George 128n266
Coughen, John 34, 157
Craighall, Fife 25, 26, 163
Craighall, Sir Thomas Hope 6th Bart, *see* Hope, Thomas, 6th Bart of Craighall
Cressy, Serenus 167
Crisp, Tobias 84

Critchlow, Rebecca [Irena?] 121–122, 153
Cromwell, Oliver 131n273, 244, 244n120, 250, 250n140
Cunningham, James 24, 26, 163, 166–170, 177n88, 182n100, 191n117, 198n129, 191n131
  letters by 198–206
Cyrus [*pseud.*] 65

Dalrymple, David, Lord Hailes 160
Danckelmann, Eberhard von 62
Daniel, Book of 1, 3, 10, 12, 215, 242
  synchronisation with Revelation's prophecies 227–229, 231n80, 245
  time periods mentioned in 227–228
Davies, Howel 20
Deboray, Mrs 114
Deichmann, Heinrich Johann 37, 49, 50n85, 51, 53n100, 55, 57n110, 59, 64
Deism 214, 264, 265
Delgaty, Aberdeenshire 169
Denijs, Tanneke 34
Désert, le (Cévennes mountains) 159–160
Devil 55, 61, 158, 165, 175, 176n85, 180, 183, 185n107, 186n110, 189, 195, 202, 232, 234, 237
devotional literature 162
discernment, spiritual, Christian doctrine of 186, 186n110
dissenters 6, 7, 13, 16, 28, 161, 209, 211, 213, 216n, 219–220, 220n29, 247–248, 249, 250, 250n138, 251–252, 253n147, 255, 255n153, 257, 257n157, 261
  occasional conformity in Church of England 209, 209n6, 217, 217n17, 255, 255n153
Dobbs, Richard 27, 28, 29, 207, 208–209, 212–215, 240–268
Dodwell, Henry 96
Domitian, Roman Emperor 176n86
Dundee 161, 169
Dunfermline, Fife 172n76
Dutton, Thomas 24, 25, 26, 27, 160, 164, 166–167, 169–170, 187n111, 199, 199n132, 202–203
  letters by 185–197

East Barns, Fife, *see* Cunningham, James, of Barns

ecstasy 158, 164, 166
Edinburgh 25, 26, 27, 158, 160–161, 164, 166–167, 187, 187n111, 188–189, 193n123, 196–197, 200, 203n143, 263n173
Edward VI, King of England and Ireland 211n9
Elijah, biblical prophet 7, 13, 138, 230, 231
Elixheim, Battle of (1705) 210n8, 218n19
Elizabeth I, queen of England and Ireland 10, 75, 211n9, 243, 246, 246n124, 248, 250, 254, 256
Emes, Thomas 175n83, 188n112, 190, 200n134
Enfield, Middlesex 160
Engelbrecht, Hans 98, 102
Epaphras [*pseud.*] 52
Epenetus [*pseud.*] 53, 55, 128
Episcopalians, Episcopacy 25, 160–163, 172n76, 174n80, 203n144
Erroll, Aberdeenshire 170
Erroll, Margaret Hay, Countess of 170
Erskine, Col. Robert 183n102
Erskine, James, Lord Grange 168n64
Erskine, John, 22nd Earl of Mar 183n102
Eutychus [*pseud.*] 44, 48, 53, 57, 64
Evangelicalism 12, 17, 20, 262n171
Everard, John 143
Exclusion Crisis 27

Faber, Albert Otto 98n205
Faber, G.S. 12
Fage, Durand 160
Falconer, Alexander 168–170
Falconer, David 169
Fall, of Babylon 160
 of Man 164–165, 173
famine 177, 177n92
Fatio de Duillier, Nicolas 167, 185, 185n108, 199
Ferdinand of Brunswick 214, 246, 246n125, 267n186
Fifth Monarchy Men / Fifth Monarchists 6, 11, 250, 250n139
Fischer, Loth [Gideon] 34, 42, 43, 44, 45, 48, 49, 53, 57, 58, 64, 68, 82, 102, 104, 106, 107, 109, 111
FitzJames, Henry 50n87
Forbes, Alexander, 4th Lord of Pitsligo 163, 166, 168, 192n118

Forbes, James 16th Lord Forbes, 26, 189n114&115
Forbes, Jean 166, 168n44
Forbes, John, of Monymusk 166, 168–169
Fowler, Edward 16
Francke, August Hermann 39, 42n40, 43n44, 49n77, 157
Frederick II (the Great), King of Prussia 266, 266–267n185, 268, 268n187
Freher, Dionysius Andreas 49, 59, 64
Freke, William 13
French Prophets 5, 13, 16, 17, 18, 23, 24, 25, 27, 159–160
French Revolution 12, 18

Garden, Alexander 169
Garden, George 25, 163, 166, 168, 173n77, 174n80, 175n84, 176n85, 191n117, 199n131
Garden, James (senior) 191n117, 195n127, 199
Garden, James (junior) 164, 168, 191, 191n117
Gardenstone, Francis Garden, Lord 169
Garrett, Walter 7
George I, King of Great Britain and Ireland 245, 245n123, 258, 266–267n185
George II, King of Great Britain and Ireland 214, 245n123, 246, 246n125, 266–268, 266–267n185
Germ[ania?], Debora[h] [*pseud.*] 50, 51, 52, 58
Gichtel, Johann Georg 34, 44n57, 51n92, 59
Gilman, Caleb 36
Gilman, Dr 133
Glasgow 161, 170
Glorious Revolution, *see* Revolution of 1688–1689
Gordon, Katherine 165, 168
 letter addressed to 193–197
Gordon, Kenneth 168, 193, 193n123
Gordon, William 191n117
Grahame, James 172n76
Grange, James Erskine, Lord 168n64
Great Northern War 177n93
Greenshields, James 25, 161
Gurnall, William 83n163
Guttenberg 60n123
Guyon, Jeanne-Marie Bouvier 102, 163, 164, 204n145
Gyles, John 161, 187n111, 203, 203n143

INDEX

Hachenberg, Johann Caspar von   110n232
Hadrian, Emperor of Rome   257, 257n158
Halberts, Johanna   155–156
Halford, Stephen   188n112
Hallifax, Samuel   12
Harde, Geoffrey   115, 117
Harley, Edward   8
Harley, Robert, 1st Earl of Oxford   183n102
Hartley, Thomas   18
Hattenbach, Johann Salomon   51n93, 54, 66
Hay, Margaret, Countess of Erroll   170
Heaven   4, 9, 61n124, 80, 83, 90, 102, 171, 172n76, 174, 178, 182, 198, 199, 240, 262
Hebrew   182, 182n100
Henderson, G.D.   166
Henrietta Maria, Queen consort of England, Scotland, and Ireland   248, 248n133
Herbert, Philip   5th Earl of Pembroke 97, 143
Hill, Oliver   143
Hoadly, Benjamin   178n95
Hollgraffen / Hollgrave, Dr   55, 60
Hollis, Isaac   17
Hooker, Edward   33
Hope, Thomas, 6th Bt. of Craighall   25, 163
Horneck, Anthony   157
Horsley, Samuel   10, 12
Hotham, Charles   97n199
Hotham, Durand   97n199
Huguenots   16, 23n109, 159, 160
Hume, David   169
Hurd, Richard   12
Hussey, Rebecca   162
Hussey, Thomas   162
Hyde, Edward, Lord Clarendon   248, 248n131

Independents   2
Ireland   33, 38, 187n111
Irvine, Margaret, Lady Clava   165, 168, 169, 193n119, 194n125

Jacinct [*pseud.*]   55, 67
Jackson, Samuel   90
Jacob, Joseph   27, 28, 207, 208–212, 215, 216–240
Jacobite rebellions 1715 and 1745   29, 33, 38, 165, 168, 194n125, 258, 258n160, 263, 263n173

Jaeger, Johann Wolfgang   32, 155n291, 156n294
Jael [*pseud.*]   52, 58, 67, 128–129
James I & VI, King of England, Scotland, and Ireland   211n9, 243, 243–244n118, 246n124, 248
James II & VII, King of England, Scotland, and Ireland   4, 6, 7, 17, 24, 38, 50n87, 221n34, 244n122, 251, 251n141, 252, 252n143, 253–254, 254n149, 255, 255n153
Jerusalem   9, 13, 119, 129, 220, 226, 234, 235, 257n158
Jews   1, 5, 8–9, 13, 17, 35, 70, 72, 99, 120, 121, 142, 160, 177, 201n138, 219, 220, 226, 226n58
John the Divine, St.   177
Jones, Edmund   20
Jones, William   12

Keith, Gilbert   193n119
Keith, James   162, 163, 169, 189n114
Keith, Robert   191n117
Kelpius, Johann   50n85
Ken, Thomas   254, 254n149
King, Anna Maria   160n10, 187n111
King's College, Aberdeen   160–161
Knorr von Rosenroth, Christian   242, 242n115
Knyphausen, Dodo von   35, 44n52, 45n60, 52n96, 55n105&108, 62n128, 64, 67n148
Knyphausen, Franz Ferdinand von   44n52, 57n111, 127–128
Knyphausen, Friedrich Ernst von   44n52, 57n111, 127–128
Kortholt / Karthold   45, 46–48, 49, 50, 51, 55, 62–63, 64
Kortholt, Christian   45n61
Kortholt, Matthias   45n61
Kortholt, Sebastian   45n61
Kuhlmann, Quirinus   41, 55n106, 59, 116n240

La Hogue (naval battle)   208
Lake, John   254, 254n149
Languedoc   159–160
Lapthorne, Richard   22
Latitudinarianism   6, 13, 22
Laurencekirk, Aberdeenshire   169
Lawton, Mrs   117

Lead, Jane   22, 23, 24, 31–41, 42–53, 55–58, 59, 63, 64, 65–68, 70, 72, 82–89, 90–94, 95–96, 104–113, 121, 123–128, 132, 133, 136, 137, 144, 147–148, 150, 152–153, 155–156, 157
Lead, John   85n170, 86
Lead, William   85n169&170
Lee, Barbarie, née Walton, née Lead [Lydia]   37, 44, 46, 48, 49n77, 86n173, 120n249, 129
Lee, Deborah Jemima   120n249
Lee, Francis [Timotheus / Timothy]   31, 35, 36, 37, 39, 40, 42, 44, 45n58, 46n64, 48, 49n77, 52n96, 53n100, 59, 60n122, 65n142, 82, 86n173, 90, 95–103, 104–113, 120, 121, 127–128, 129, 132, 144, 147–148, 152, 156n294, 157
Lee, William   48n76
Leibniz, Gottfried Wilhelm   31, 45n61
Leiden, University of   157n297, 162
Linlithgow   164, 169
Lloyd, William, bishop of St Asaph   2, 4, 10–11, 16, 254, 254n149
Locher, Heinrich   68
Louis XIV, King of France   38, 159
Ludolf, Heinrich Wilhelm   42n40, 44n56
Lundie, Archibald   158n1, 160n13, 161n14, 162, 166, 170n74
Lundie, James   160n13, 161n14, 162, 170n74

M., A. (Charles II's illegitimate daughter?)   50n86
Mackenzie, Margaret   168n63
Maria Theresa, Empress of Austria   268, 268n187
Marion, Elie   160, 185, 185n108, 199
Mary II, Queen of England, Scotland, and Ireland   11, 24, 244n122, 253n147, 255, 255n153
Matthias [*pseud.*]   42, 52, 65, 123
Mazel, Abraham   159
Mede, Joseph   2, 5, 208–209, 211, 211n9, 242, 242n115, 248, 248n132
Meschmann, Christian   156
Methodism   4, 18, 19, 20
Middleton, George   160–161
Middleton, Helen   168, 193n119
Middleton, Margaret   160–161
Middleton, Patrick   203, 203n144

millenarianism   1–30, 207–208, 210, 214–215, 262n171
millennium   2, 5, 6, 9, 13, 18, 20, 21, 28, 29, 210, 215, 218, 224, 227, 240, 250n139, 259, 260, 262–263
Minden, Battle of (1759)   214, 214n15, 267, 267n186
miracles   11, 22, 38, 72, 74, 165, 175, 175n83, 205
Mirandola, Giovanni Pico della   170
Missions (Protestant)   21
Molinos, Miguel de   198, 198n130
Monumusk, John Forbes of, *see* Forbes, John, of Monymusk
Moor, Thomas   7
More, Henry   208–209, 211, 211n9, 226, 242, 242n115
Morrison, Susanna   168n65
Moult, John   187n111, 203n143
Muggletonians   6
Muhammad   233
Murray, Dr   133, 139
mystical theology   3, 12, 100, 157, 159, 161–168, 186, 189–193, 195

Napoleon   9, 10
Nassau d'Auverquerque family, female member of   48
Nelson, Mrs   116
Newton, Isaac   2, 3, 4, 12, 38, 185n108, 214
Newton, John   20
Newton, Thomas   11–12
Noble, Samuel   187n111
nonjurors   253n147, 256, 256n156

Orem, Katherine, *see* Gordon, Katherine
Orem, Thomas   165, 191n117, 193n119
Orange, Principality of   159
Overkirke, Lady, *see* female member of the Nassau d'Auverquerque family
Oxenbridge, Clement   116n242
Oxenbridge, Joanna   36, 116, 132, 138

Papacy   1, 6, 9, 11, 198n130, 209, 211, 211n9, 213, 221n35, 221–222, 233, 245, 247–249, 251–256, 263, 268
Parliament   28, 209n6, 213, 243–246, 262–263
Pauli, Oliger   99n208, 125

Peckitt, Henry   90
Pell, Sir Valentine   83n163, 85n170, 86n171
Perceval, Spencer   8, 10
Petersen, Johann Wilhelm   34, 42n40, 60n122
Petersen, Johanna   34
Petition of Right (1628)   213, 243
Petrucci, Pietro Matteo   93
Philadelphia (church of)   34, 39, 94, 101, 134, 135, 142, 151, 154, 213n13, 214, 226, 227, 228, 260, 261, 262
Philadelphians / Philadelphian Society   13, 16, 17, 23, 32, 33, 34–41, 42–69, 70–81, 94, 95–113, 134–155, 157, 162, 172n76, 177n91
Philip V, King of Spain   159
Philipps, Sir John   13
Pight, Helen   33
Pocock, Edward   7
Pocock, Mary   33, 117
Poiret, Pierre   95, 99nn207&211, 100n214, 102n217, 104, 162, 173n76, 190n116, 192n118, 195n127, 200, 200n136
Polonnus   123
Pope, *see* Papacy
Pordage, Francis   33
Pordage, John   33, 58, 60, 87, 88, 97, 123, 134, 143, 144, 147, 152, 153, 157
Pordage, Mary, *née* Freeman   134, 143, 144, 147
Pordage, Samuel   98
Potter, John   169, 188n112
predestination   34, 154, 165, 172, 172n76, 181
Presbyterians, Presbyterianism   17, 25, 37, 98, 127n263, 161–162, 172n76
Preston, Battle of (1715)   168
Pringle, Katherine, Lady Abden   158, 164–170, 185–187, 189, 191n117, 192–194, 202–203
   prophecies delivered by   171–184
Protestant dissent and nonconformity, *see* dissenters
Pulham, Norfolk   188, 188n112
purgatory   165
Puritans   8, 23, 213, 247, 250

Quakers   14, 16, 36, 40, 46n65, 135, 140, 143n282, 189n114, 196n128
Quietism   42, 158, 198n130

Ramsay, Andrew Michael   166, 189, 189n114, 198n129, 201
Rantzau, Christoph baron von   43n44
Reichenbach, Marie Sophie von   122
Reformed theology   172n76
Restoration of monarchy in England, Scotland, and Ireland (1660)   161, 207–208, 213, 244, 244n140, 249, 251–252, 257
Revelation, Book of   1, 3, 5, 7, 8, 9, 12, 18, 28–29, 34, 40, 71, 83, 150, 176n86, 177
   beasts   208, 211, 221, 227–228, 232–238, 238n
   dragon   98, 211, 232–238, 238n
   false prophet   211, 232–238, 238n
   new Jerusalem   58n112, 83, 140, 262
   number of the beast   153, 235, 235n95, 238, 238n
   seven churches prophecy   134, 208, 210, 213, 213n, 214, 225–228, 231n80, 243–265
   seven seals prophecy   211n9, 214–215, 243, 257, 262, 266n182, 266–267, 267n186
   seven trumpets prophecy   210, 211n9, 215, 227–228, 231n80, 262
   seven vials prophecy   177, 211n9, 238n, 257
   synchronisation of prophecies   209, 210, 227–228, 231n80, 238n, 242
   time periods mentioned in   227–230, 229n75, 231n80
   two witnesses prophecy   210, 228, 234–235, 238n
   white horse   29
   whore of Babylon   3, 8, 208, 236, 240
   woman in the wilderness   40, 59, 134, 210, 228
Revolution of 1688–1689   6, 7, 8, 27, 33, 38, 159, 209, 213, 244–245n122, 245, 252, 253, 253n147, 257
Ripendale, Mr   49, 63n131
Roach, Richard [Onesimus]   23, 34, 35, 36, 39, 40, 44, 46, 65, 70–81, 95–96, 120, 121, 126, 127, 128, 129, 131–155, 157
Rosehearty, Aberdeenshire   25, 163, 166, 205
Rowland, Daniel   20
Royal Society   36, 38, 143n282, 214, 244, 244n121

Sabberton, Joseph   33, 40, 87
Sancroft, William   4, 254, 254n149
Savonarola, Girolamo   169–170
Sayn-Wittgenstein-Berleburg, Hedwig Sophie von   104n220
Sayn-Wittgenstein-Hohenstein, Luise Philippine von   104n220
Scheller, Mr   53, 53n100, 65
Schmidberger, Isaac   57, 59–61, 64
Scott / Schott, William   50, 50n84, 55, 59n115
Scott, James, Duke of Monmouth   221n34
Scrope, John   160
Second Coming of Christ   1, 2, 5, 7, 10–11, 13, 15, 17, 18, 19, 20, 21, 22, 25, 27, 29, 41, 160, 163, 182, 225, 226, 231, 240, 250n139
sermons   8, 10, 11, 12, 20, 21, 22, 27–29, 84, 90, 91, 92, 143, 207–268
Seven Years' War (1756–1763)   207, 214, 214n15, 267, 267n186, 268
Sheppard, Nathaniel   188n112
Sherlock, Thomas   11, 12
Shipton, Mother   15
Silas [*pseud.*]   49, 52, 54, 55, 56, 58, 59, 61n126, 63, 68, 130
slavery   20, 21, 253
Society for the Promotion of Christian Knowledge   8, 26, 39
Society for the Propagation of the Gospel in Foreign Parts   20, 26, 39
Society for the Reformation of Manners   39, 254, 254n150
Society in Scotland for Propagating Christian Knowledge   25, 177n94
Socinianism   214, 258, 261
Southcott, Joanna   9–10, 22, 31
Spanish Succession, War of the (1701–1714)   5, 27, 177n91, 207, 210, 210n7&8, 218, 218n19
Spence, David   168
Sprögel, Johann Heinrich   125
Sterrell, Mary [Hephzibah?]   37, 46n65, 49n77, 127n264
Stirling   164, 169, 171–182, 184, 203n144
Stirling Castle   169, 183–184
Stirredge, Elizabeth   13–14
Stuart, Charles Edward   263n173
Stuart, James Francis Edward   258n160
Sutcliffe, Joseph   18

Swarzin / Swarsin   53
Swedenborg, Emanuel   9, 31

Tenison, Thomas   23, 42, 70
Test Acts (1673, 1678, 1689)   253, 253n147
thanksgiving days   207–268
Tillotson, John   21, 24, 208
Tindal, Matthew   2
Tisshenn / Thijssen, Madam   111
Titus Flavius Vespasianus, emperor of Rome   257, 257n158
Toft, Mary   15
tongues, gift of 194, *see also* miracles
Topham, Anne   160n10, 187n111
Tory party   213
Tovey, Joseph   189n114, 196n128
Trelawny, Jonathan   254, 254n149
Trinity, doctrine of   3, 96
Turks   221–222
Turner, Francis   254, 254n149
Turner, Mary   160n10

Vandeput, Mr   44
Vandeput, Peter   44n51
Villiers, George, second Duke of Buckingham   97

Walpole, Robert   214, 245n123
Walton, Mr   86n173
Walton, Christopher   31–32, 90
Waple, Edward   23, 39, 40, 42
Warburton, William   2, 12
Ward, Hamond the elder   32, 82
Ward, Hamond the younger   84n164
Ward, John ('Zion')   10
Ward, Mary, née Calthorpe   32, 82n161
Wardlaw, Christian   164
Wardlaw, John   164
Wastin, Mr   122
Weinich, Johann Jacob [Tychicus]   52, 52n96, 68, 109
Wemyss, David, Earl of Wemyss   189n114
Wensley, Robert   221n34
Wesley, Charles   15, 17, 18
Wesley, John   4, 15, 17–18, 19
Wesley, Samuel   17
Wetstein, Mr   99, 102
Wetstein, Gerhard   99n209
Wetstein, Hendrick   99n209

INDEX

Wetstein, Rudolph   99n209
Whig party   160, 213, 214, 245n123
Whiston, William   2, 5, 13, 15
White, Jeremiah   131, 153
White, Thomas   254, 254n149
William III, King of England, Scotland, and Ireland   33, 38, 159, 244n122, 245, 253n147, 255, 255n153, 256, 256n155

Williams, William   20
Withrow, Abraham   200, 200n134

Young, Elizabeth   193n119

Zoller, Johann Jacob   51, 52, 54